Province of Freedom

PROVINCE OF FREEDOM

A History of Sierra Leone

1787–1870

by

JOHN PETERSON

NORTHWESTERN UNIVERSITY PRESS

Evanston 1969

Published in the United States of America in 1969
by Northwestern University Press
under arrangement with Faber and Faber Ltd., London

Library of Congress Catalog Card Number: 76–86901

SBN 8101–0264–1

Printed in Great Britain

TO

MY MOTHER AND FATHER

Contents

9

Illustrations

Maps

Preface

This study is called *Province of Freedom* not from ignorance of the fact that Granville Sharp's original Province of Freedom lasted only four years, from 1787 to 1791, but because a succession of freed slaves were able to create their own province of freedom in Sierra Leone during the nineteenth century. The main theme of the study is that the British who came to rule Sierra Leone after 1791 were unable to do so with consistent and overall effectiveness, particularly in the areas of local government and the administration of justice. The resultant administrative and legal void was filled by the settlers and Liberated Africans who were able to establish effective control of the political, economic, and social dimensions of their society. *Province of Freedom* concentrates on the development of Liberated African society between 1807 and 1870. The contact between the Liberated Africans and the Europeans who came to administer, to trade, to convert, and to teach produced an Afro-European society by the second half of the nineteenth century. The cultural product of this contact is known as Creole society. The secondary theme of this study is that Creole society has a much wider cultural spectrum than is usually attributed to it; it is far more Afro-European than a mere 'Black Englishman' carbon copy of the culture of western Europe.

There were three groups of immigrants to Sierra Leone before 1807: the Original Settlers of 1787, the Nova Scotians of 1792, and the Maroons of 1800. I have called these three groups 'settlers' in this study. 'Liberated Africans' refers to the 60,000 to 70,000 Africans who were saved from the holds of the slave ships trading illegally after 1807 and settled in Sierra Leone. The children of the Liberated Africans are called 'Creoles' in

13

this study as they were originally. Their culture tended to be more European in its outward forms largely because its geographical focus was Freetown. But Creole society also embraced a wide variety of cultural forms which had their origins in the African past of its members. One can only call the Creole a Europeanized African if one remembers that his society encompassed such crucial institutions as the *asusu*, the *awujo*, and the *Agugu* society. His language, *Krio*, and his staple foods such as fufu were not European, but rather indices of the Afro-European cultural fusions which had taken place in the society itself. The Creole then is a second generation immigrant to Sierra Leone, descended from Liberated African parents, whose cultural pattern was Afro-European.

Province of Freedom is a revised form of the author's doctoral dissertation, done for the Department of History and the Program of African Studies at Northwestern University, Evanston, Illinois, U.S.A., in 1963. It is based on research in the United Kingdom and Sierra Leone between 1958 and 1960 which was made possible by a grant from the Ford Foundation; in Washington, D.C. and Salem, Massachusetts in 1963 on a research grant from Kalamazoo College; in Stanford, California in 1964 on a research fellowship from the Hoover Institution; and in the United Kingdom in 1965 on a grant from the Great Lakes Colleges Association. The Ford Foundation financed a period of writing in 1960 and 1961 as did also the Program of African Studies, Northwestern University during 1961. The author is much indebted to these institutions for their assistance.

The list of individuals to whom the author is indebted is long. The earliest research at Northwestern was assisted by the advice of Dr. Otto Koenigsberger, Mr. Thomas Hodgkin, and Professor K. O. Dike. Professors J. D. Hargreaves, George Shepperson, Michael Banton, and Kenneth Little were generous and helpful with advice and direction during this study's dissertation stage. Thomas Hodgkin kindly opened the papers of his great-uncle, Dr. Thomas Hodgkin, at Crab Mill for me to read. More recently, I have benefited from the help and advice of Michael Crowder. The author is appreciative of the assistance given by archivists, librarians, and the staffs of the Church Missionary Society, London; the Methodist Missionary Society, London; the Public Record Office and the British Museum, London; Friends House Library, London; Rhodes House Library of Oxford University; the Sierra Leone Government Archives and the Fourah Bay College Library, Freetown; the Deering Library, Northwestern University; the Kalamazoo College Library; the National Archives and the Library of Congress, Washington; the Peabody Museum, Salem; and the Stanford University Library and the Hoover Institution at Stanford. I wish to extend my deep gratitude to the many Freetonians and Sierra Leoneans who assisted me during the period of my research work in their country. The administration of Fourah Bay College of the University of Sierra Leone was particularly helpful. Professor Arthur T. Porter gave considerable assistance for which I am very grateful. The work in East Freetown would have been impossible without the help of Mr. Leslie Proudfoot, then Director of Extra-Mural Studies at Fourah Bay College, and Mr. Mohammed Koroma. Without the help of these men and innumerable others the research in Freetown would not have been so inclusive of the city's varied social and cultural character.

I wish to acknowledge the kind permission of the Public Record Office, London, to reproduce the map of the Sierra Leone Colony in 1853 (CO267/234) and the map of Freetown in 1883 (MP/H/650), of the British Museum to reproduce the map of Sierra Leone in 1870 (65640. 10), and of the Church Missionary Society to reproduce the photographs.

My thanks extend to Henry Wilson, George Brooks, LaRay Denzer, Lacey Baldwin Smith, Jan Vansina, John McLane, and Christopher Fyfe for their criticisms of the dissertation and their suggestions which helped in the preparation of the manuscript for publication. For nearly ten years Christopher Fyfe has been of continuing assistance to me in my study of Sierra Leone history. He has generously provided many sources from his own collection of books and manuscripts as well as being of help as a critical director of my research during its earliest period. This study has benefited greatly from our numerous and long discussions; Christopher Fyfe has given freely from his vast fund of knowledge and for this I am grateful. I thank my wife, Jeanne, for her untiring support and assistance in the preparation of the manuscript for publication.

Finally, I express my great debt to Professor Franklin D. Scott, Department of History, Northwestern University and to the late Professor Melville J. Herskovits, Director of the Program of African Studies. Professor Scott's patience and helpful criticisms of this study from the beginning have been of continual value. The late Professor Herskovits never ceased to be a source of stimulation and encouragement to me and for this I shall be forever grateful.

JOHN PETERSON
Department of History, Fourah Bay College,
University of Sierra Leone
Freetown, Sierra Leone
1 October 1968

I

The First Twenty Years, 1787–1807

For three years, between 1771 and 1774, Henry Smeathman traversed the creeks and rivers, the islands and sandy coastline around the Sierra Leone estuary on Africa's west coast. He lived on the Banana Islands, just off the mainland at the southern end of a mountainous peninsula twenty-five miles long and ten miles wide which jutted northward into the sea before ending at the wide mouth of the River Sierra Leone. Smeathman was an amateur botanist sent out to West Africa to collect specimens for Sir Joseph Banks at Kew Gardens. He collected his plants and enough additional information to present a paper on termites upon his return to England. Beyond this, Henry Smeathman devoted considerable thought to the future of West Africa. Europeans knew little about it, but wanted to know more. From his vantage point on the Banana Islands he could spend long hours looking across the water separating him from the mainland and see the toweringly splendid, verdant mountains of Sierra Leone. The vision of a lush paradise presented itself. The island upon which he lived was governed by the Caulkers, an Afro-European family descended from an English trader and the daughter of an African chief. The Caulkers controlled much of the land to the south along the coast, and Smeathman pondered the possibility of forming a domain not unlike that of his hosts. Back in England after his return via the West Indies and another period of work in France, the botanist's thoughts returned to the West African coast and he began to envisage a new type of settlement. Smeathman's ideas met

17

receptive ears by the 1780's, for by then there were others interested in the possibilities of Africa. With the Revolutionary War over in America, Britain was forced to rethink its future in the New World. Voices began to be raised against the slave trade, the basis of British trade with the Americas. Still others philosophized from their intense faith in natural order and natural rights about a perfect society, and dreamed of constructing somewhere a new utopia. In 1783 Smeathman presented a plan for such a settlement, based on agriculture. His idea was to begin a plantation culture in West Africa based on free labour which would replace the diminishing one based on slave labour in the West Indies. Its social ramifications were revolutionary for it was to be a free community of equal black and white citizens living in a society based on the principles of democratic liberalism.[1]

Smeathman found an audience for his scheme in the Black Poor, a group of free but destitute Negroes living in London in the 1780's, and in a group of English philanthropists which set about seeking a solution to the racial problem facing the British capital increasingly after the end of the American Revolution. But the hope of creating a commercially profitable plantation economy in West Africa was not the only economic factor in Smeathman's thinking. His own prospects had been lean following the three-year trip sponsored by Sir Joseph Banks. In the 1780's he spent much of his time unemployed and his request for a payment of £4 per settler no doubt affected his memories of the Banana Islands and the Sierra Leone estuary and his testimony when asked about it in 1786. Although he had advised the British government against forming a prison colony in West Africa in 1785 because it was unhealthy, a year later he spoke only of good soil, healthiness, and the promise of riches through trade.[2] The convincing word picture painted by the amateur botanist led an influential group of English philanthropists which had formed itself into a committee to relieve the plight of the destitute Black Poor to select Sierra Leone as the site for their colony. Henry Smeathman received the appointment to

18

take charge of the expedition planned to depart late in 1786. Unfortunately, Smeathman died before the voyage of settlement began. He had, however, focused the attention of the surviving planners on the tiny mountainous peninsula on the West African coast called, since the Portuguese first came upon it in the fifteenth century, Sierra Leone.

GRANVILLE SHARP AND THE ORIGINAL PROVINCE OF FREEDOM

When the Black Poor had first heard of Smeathman's ideas, they had gone to their friend and benefactor in London, Granville Sharp. The former government civil servant, who had long served the interests of the blacks living in London, had himself pondered a similar solution to the growing social problem of the Black Poor. Beginning in the mid-1760's, Sharp had been concerned with the pressing social issues of the day. Since 1767 slavery had been his special concern. He had found the institution of slavery unnatural in that it was unsanctioned by any form of universal law. Involved in the act of freeing slaves brought to England by their masters from the New World, Sharp had studied English law and found nothing in it which allowed for the institution in Britain itself. In 1772 he sponsored the action brought by the slave James Somerset against his master. In the decision, Lord Mansfield stated that it was not possible under English law for a master forcibly to remove his slave from England for the purpose of sending him back to the New World to be sold. In spite of the tradition which has grown up concerning the decision to the contrary, Lord Mansfield did not declare a complete prohibition of slavery under English law nor did he state that the moment a slave set foot in England he was free. Some judges before him had done so, but others, equally prominent, had declared in favour of slavery in England. The abolition propagandists were the ones who made something more of the decision than the Chief Justice had intended. They heralded the event as the abolition of slavery in England, and over the years it came to be so regarded.[3]

Sharp's role in the court case put him at the forefront of the abolitionists' cause in Britain and made him the adviser and confidant to the growing numbers of freed slaves in London. They called on him regularly and he offered them assistance in time of need. The larger numbers of free blacks in London resulted, however, not from the ramifications of the Mansfield Decision, but from the increased unemployment among London Negroes following the end of the American Revolutionary War. Many had worked aboard the ships sailing between Britain and America during the war and some, having begun the war as slaves on American plantations, had fled to the British side on the promise of freedom and land after the war, and now had come to England to seek employment. But most of them failed to find employment, and sensitive, concerned Englishmen like Sharp had begun to search their minds for a sensible solution to the growing social problem of the Black Poor. In addition to his active pursuit of the slavery problem, Granville Sharp had spent much time thinking about those two subjects which one associates with the enlightened outlook of the eighteenth century: natural rights and natural law. As with most who thought about such things, Sharp eventually constructed in his own mind a visionary utopia, a perfect society. Some time in 1783, he penned a memorandum on the subject which he published in a much expanded form in 1786 under the title, *A Short Sketch of Temporary Regulations (Until Better Shall be Proposed) for the Intended Settlement on the Grain Coast of Africa near Sierra Leone.* Thus Sharp was naturally in a receptive mood when the Black Poor approached him for advice on the proposed Smeathman plan for a colony in West Africa. If Smeathman's contribution was the site in West Africa, Sharp's was far more significant, for he gave the idea a radical, exciting governmental form and secured from the Treasury a large grant to finance the settlement in Sierra Leone. Sharp gave to the experiment in colonizing the name, Province of Freedom, which, although his first venture failed within four years, still served as a fitting summary title for the events of the colony's first century of existence.

The basis of Sharp's thinking on the subject of a perfect society in West Africa was that natural man could be civilized through reason alone. His scheme for the government of the Province of Freedom, therefore, was intended 'for a race of men *supposed* to be *uniformly open to the persuasions of reason*'.[4] The basis of his government for the colony was a system which he thought to be the ancient one of Israel and of England under King Alfred: that of frankpledge. Its reverence for the values of balance and reason, however, show it to be more the product of the fertile enlightened imagination of its eighteenth-century author rather than anything from the ages past. The community, which was to be entirely self-governing, was to be divided equally into tithings and hundreds. The tithings were groups of ten families each of which elected annually a leader, the tithingman. Every ten tithingmen elected annually an hundredor, and together the tithingmen and hundredors were to form the necessarily minimal government of the settlement. Their function was primarily to keep order, so in them was vested the judicial power of the province. Such a government was preferred by Sharp because its simplicity guaranteed that all men were capable of understanding and participating in it. It was government by equally proportioned groups, each of which was part of a more powerful body.

Sharp prohibited slavery in the Province of Freedom. The economic basis was to be free labour. To him, labour, not cash, was the standard of trade. In his *Short Sketch* he wrote, '*Human Labour* is more essential and valuable than any other article in new settlements, which chiefly depend on the cultivation and produce of the earth for their subsistence and commercial profit'.[5] The amount of labour needed to produce a commodity therefore determined its value. He thought in terms of the number of days of labour involved in production. A day's labour was to be one eight-hour day. Sharp believed that his system afforded 'an excellent substitute for money as a medium of traffic and exchange, whereon a *paper currency* may be established, which will always bear an *intrinsic value* . . . .'[6] Land in the Province of Freedom, like power, was to be equally divided among the settlers. Taxation was to be direct and consisted of sixty-two days' labour per year for the government. [7] Sharp had written in 1776 that the 'purpose of all good government is liberty, with protection from personal injuries, and the security of private property'. [8] His *Short Sketch*, the social contract for the Province of Freedom, provided for a government whose aims would fit his earlier pronouncement. His plan reflected the humanitarian interests of his age. It rested on the firm faith which eighteenth-century man had in rational planning and in his ability to construct a perfect society. Some thought he had gone too far, and certainly his gradual withdrawal from the scene after 1791 and the end of his Province of Freedom indicated that he 'regretted the demolition of that ideal fabric of happiness which he had wished to raise for an afflicted portion of mankind'. [9]

Smeathman's vision for the Sierra Leone venture was primarily economic and commercial; Sharp's was rational and humanitarian. A third force played its part in the general movement to establish a colony for freed slaves in West Africa: the desire to convert the heathen. Reports from India and Africa together with the recognition of social abuse at home aroused the conscience of the evangelical left wing of the Church of England. Involved by 1787 in the general reform movement, this small but militant group met regularly at Henry Thornton's estate at Battersea on the apron of Clapham Common. The group, Wilberforce, John Venn, Charles Grant, James Stephen, Zachary Macaulay, and Thornton himself—the Clapham Sect—successfully propagandized the cause of abolition, and, in organizational technique, established a standard for similar movements throughout the following century. [10] The Clapham evangelicals gave to the Sierra Leone venture its meaning as a tangible symbol in the fight for abolition. If to the enlightened mind the new settlement served as an escape hatch for a particular English social problem and a chance to construct the perfect society on earth, to the evangelical it was the fertile ground from which the growth of European civilization and Christianity would soon encompass the entire African continent. To civilize and Christianize the African thus became the popular call of the time.[11]

Plans to establish a colony for freed slaves and to resettle the Black Poor in Sierra Leone went ahead throughout 1786. The idea appealed to more than just the Black Poor, however, and among those who left Britain for Sierra Leone early in 1787 were some, white as well as black, who simply sought their fortunes overseas. Nearly 700 originally signed up for the colonizing expedition, but fear of being sent to a convict settlement had greatly reduced the numbers by the time of departure. Only 456 passengers were aboard the three transports when, together with the *Nautilus*, a naval sloop, they sailed from Portsmouth harbour in February 1787. Over 100 of these were white colonists. Early difficulties foretold the disaster which awaited most in Sierra Leone itself. The colonists selected headmen before they left and these leaders quickly ran foul of the official representatives of the London Committee which organized the expedition. Oladuah Equiano, himself a former West Indian slave, who was appointed Commissary for the trip and who would two years later publish his abolitionist autobiography, *Equiano's Travels*,[12] quarrelled with Joseph Irwin, the agent appointed in Smeathman's stead by the Committee. When a severe storm struck the convoy, separating the ships so that they were forced to regroup in Plymouth harbour, the Committee dismissed Equiano. Desertion added to the toll already exacted by death and dismissal. Nearly 100 colonists were lost before the expedition again put to sea in April. Some were replaced and a total of 411 finally left Britain.

The delay at Plymouth proved decisive. The expedition under Captain Thompson of the *Nautilus* finally arrived in May 1787. Thompson purchased land for the settlement, twenty miles square on the south bank of the Sierra Leone estuary, 8°N, 13°W, from the local Temne chief. The site was just below the northern extremity of the mountains on the bay used for

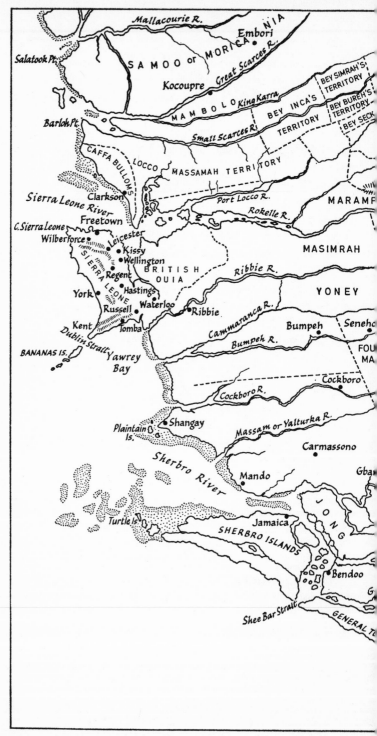

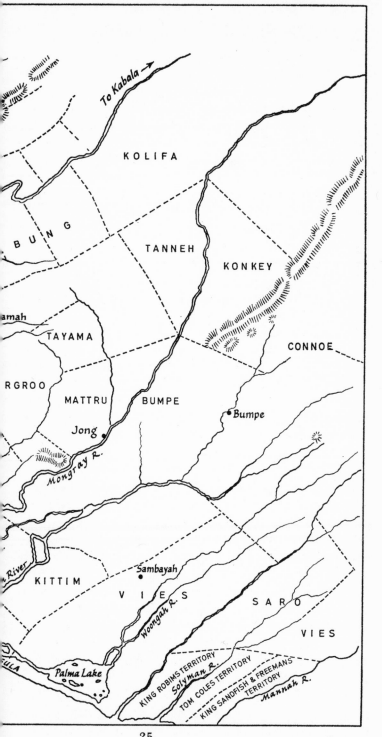

To Kabala →

KOLIFA

BUNG

TANNEH

KONKEY

amah

TAYAMA

CONNOE

RGROO

MATTRU   BUMPE

Jong   • Bumpe

Mongray R.

River

Sambayah

KITTIM

V I E S

SARO

Woongah R.

VIES

ULA

Palma Lake

KING ROBINS TERRITORY

Solyman R.

TOM COLES TERRITORY

KING SANDFISH & FREEMANS
TERRITORY

Mannah R.

centuries by slavers as a good watering place. There the Sierra Leone colonists settled, calling their village Granville Town after Sharp. But before they could build permanent housing, the annual rains had begun in June. Already weakened by the long voyage, the settlers now began to fall victims of disease and the climate. By September, 86 emigrants were dead, 15 had run off; only 276 of the 377 who landed in May remained in Granville Town. By early the following year the number diminished to 130, most of the rest having sought their fortunes in the surrounding country. A shipload of supplies sent by Sharp arrived in August 1788, and saved the little settlement from complete ruin.[13]

The tiny colony of settlers, the original Province of Freedom, made a serious attempt to follow Sharp's constitution. The community was organized as he prescribed, tithingmen and hundredors were elected and the government of the Province lay in their hands. But even the little news that reached the colony's humanitarian benefactor in Britain indicated that all was not well. He wrote in October, 1787, that he had 'had but melancholy accounts of my poor little ill-thriven swarthy daughter, the unfortunate colony of Sierra Leone'.[14] Still, he held tenaciously to his dream of freedom for the blacks. A year later the news that King Tom, a local Temne sub-chief, had sold two of the settlers into slavery moved Sharp to confess: 'This was the more mortifying to me, because I had hoped to secure not only the *privileges*, but the title also, of the *Province of Freedom* to the new settlement.'[15] In March 1789, he told John Jay, soon to be an official of the American government, that he wished that Sierra Leone could be a 'happy asylum' for freed slaves from America and the West Indies as well as from Britain.[16] In November he reminded the settlers at Granville Town that they must always protect 'the law of natural right and justice in the Province of Freedom'.[17] But a month later and long before his letter arrived, the first Granville Town lay in ashes, burned to the ground in December 1789, by King Jimmy, King Tom's successor, in retaliation for the earlier burning of one of his towns by sailors from a British warship.[18] Philosophical dreams

26

aside, the first settlement had become in reality the victim of climate, disease, poor soil, and the political vicissitudes of life constantly threatened on one hand by European ship captains and on the other by the local population.

The members of Sharp's Province of Freedom fled for their lives and for all purposes his dream of a self-governing colony also lay in the ashes of the destroyed Granville Town. The other English benefactors sought a more tightly organized form of association under which the colony might go forward. In 1790 they formed the St. George's Bay Association which, the following year, received its charter as the Sierra Leone Company. Although the charter reflected their faith in the original aims, the Directors elected the businessman Henry Thornton to the chairmanship, rather than Sharp. The Company continued to see its primary role in terms of suppressing the slave trade by introducing Christianity and civilization along the coast. It continued to forbid the slave trade in the colony; further, it promised to open schools for all the people of the area and it guaranteed government according to the laws of England.[19] The newly chartered Company lost no time in appointing an agent, Alexander Falconbridge, who arrived in Sierra Leone early in 1791. He collected together forty-eight of the former residents of Granville Town, and moved them two miles eastward along the estuary to a location near Fourah Bay where he founded a second settlement, a village of seventeen huts which was also called Granville Town. For six months he stayed in Sierra Leone, assisting in the planting of crops and visiting neighbouring African villages. Then, in mid-1791, he returned to report to the directors in London.[20]

THE NOVA SCOTIANS AND THE FOUNDING OF FREETOWN

Obviously the settlement needed more colonists than the forty-eight who comprised the second Granville Town. Earlier attempts to introduce new settlers had failed. Then a rare opportunity presented itself when a Nova Scotian Negro named

Thomas Peters risked the hazardous Atlantic passage to Britain in 1791. He represented freed slaves who, like many of the original Black Poor, had fought with the British during the Revolutionary War in exchange for their freedom and some land after the end of hostilities. The American victory had forced their exodus together with the white loyalists to the British settlement at Nova Scotia. There the former slaves had failed to secure land and were instead employed as farm labourers. Peters came to Britain to protest against the conditions of the freed slaves in Nova Scotia. He naturally contacted Sharp and was befriended by Henry Thornton who offered to settle the freed slaves from Nova Scotia in Sierra Leone. After the Company secured the promise of support from the British government, Peters returned with plans to organize the expedition to Sierra Leone. Lieutenant John Clarkson of the Royal Navy also went to Nova Scotia for the Company to oversee the arrangements for the voyage. In spite of the minimal cooperation of the Nova Scotian government, almost 1,200 free Negroes left Nova Scotia for Sierra Leone in January 1792.

Three months later the first ship sailed into the Sierra Leone estuary. The Nova Scotian settlers, as this second important group has been called in subsequent history, founded a new settlement at the site of the original Granville Town, and named it Freetown. Sickness and death again took an initial toll as the rainy season caught the new immigrants ill-prepared. Difficulties of a more political nature added further complications to the events of the first few months. Peters, as the one who had made the original voyage to Britain, sought power within the new settlement. But this attempt put him in conflict with Clarkson, whom the company had given overall responsibility as superintendent of the colony. A minor struggle for power ensued during which Peters was personally and politically discredited. Clarkson had won the respect of the immigrants long before their departure from Nova Scotia. His own religious sense made him a natural leader of a group which itself was intensely religious and whose own social sub-structure was based on dissenting chapels. This initial if minor struggle between Nova Scotian aspirations for control and the Company government ended with Peters's death in June of the first year.[21] The settlement under Clarkson struggled through the first few weeks successfully; by August the remainder of the original group of settlers at Granville Town joined the new community at Freetown.[22] By the end of the rains the new settlement began to show signs of its future development. The first huts were built along regular streets which Clarkson named for the twelve directors of the Sierra Leone Company.[23] Such accomplishments did not come without difficulty. Clarkson reported that confusion and mismanagement besieged him. Settlers seldom reported for work, the rains hampered building, mutual jealousies led to trouble among the women, and 'absurd notions of rank and consequence' produced open dissension among the men.

The minor political contest with Peters had reflected Clarkson's own tenuous hold on authority. The Company's charter called for government by a council of eight equals in which Clarkson had only the casting vote, but such a government proved unworkable. Clarkson protested that nothing was done in the colony because no agreement could be reached in the council. In July 1792, the Company came to the rescue by introducing a tested and proved form of colonial government: government by a Governor and council of two members. Clarkson was appointed the first Governor. The first two members of the council were also servants of the Company: William Dawes, a Marine lieutenant with experience at Botany Bay, and Zachary Macaulay, the by-then-ardent abolitionist who had been an estate manager in Jamaica.[24]

In spite of his new power, Governor Clarkson continued to rule by persuasion, preaching to the Nova Scotians, pushing them to action, pleading with them to end their hatred and distrust of the European, and thus hoping that their trust in him would be transferred more generally to the Company itself.

His policy did bear some fruit. By the end of 1792 Clarkson wrote that the colony gained strength daily. Poverty continued to be a problem, but the Nova Scotians were growing produce in their gardens, they were raising hogs, twelve fishing boats went out daily, and enterprising settlers went to Gambia and Bunce islands to trade for rum.[25] Soon after thus describing the colony's activity, Governor Clarkson left to return to Britain, his commitment to the Company fulfilled. William Dawes succeeded him as the settlement's Governor.

Just before he left, Clarkson had made an attempt to establish a more effective control of the settlers. Already the Nova Scotians had begun to grumble about the amount and quality of land available to them. Cheated once in Nova Scotia, they were particularly keen that the Company's promises to them should be kept. The fact that pledges were broken—promised 20 acres when in Nova Scotia, they received on the average only 5 in Sierra Leone[26]—was the one continually gnawing factor which subverted good relations between Company and settler for the remaining years of Company rule. Clarkson divided the settlement into tithings, districts of ten families, a system reminiscent of Sharp's earlier experiment, but now intended to give the Company more control. The system provided the settlers themselves with a means of organization by which they effectively protested against Company government in the following years.

Clarkson's common experience with the Nova Scotians guaranteed him a smooth sailing as their Governor. But from the outset they distrusted Dawes, his successor. Unwilling to challenge Clarkson directly on the matter of land, they were quick to confront Dawes with the charge of refusing to keep all of the promises made to them in Nova Scotia by the Company. He did little things which irritated them as well. Prices at the Company store were raised and he was found to be watering the rum. As time wore on, it became obvious that the era of good feeling which had characterized Clarkson's tenure was over. In 1793, the settlers drew up a petition against Dawes and sent it with two representatives to the Company in London. The Directors found their complaints unacceptable, and when the representatives returned empty-handed the dissatisfaction of the settlers increased. Further price rises at the store led them to threaten Dawes with the fate of Louis XVI.[27]

Distress and frustration continued to characterize relations between settler and Company throughout 1793 and 1794. The store ship for the colony was destroyed by fire, Dawes's ill health caused his return to Great Britain, and Macaulay who succeeded him as Governor proved no more agreeable to the settlers. Then complete disaster again struck at the tiny Sierra Leone venture. In September 1794, the town was entirely destroyed by the French. Two years earlier Governor Clarkson had written to his friend Lafayette in Paris asking him to see that Sierra Leone—an international task, he called it—should be spared in the event of a general war.[28] Nonetheless, late in September 1794, French ships sailed into the harbour and began to fire on the town. After the initial destruction, the ships landed their crews and the town was further pillaged and burned. The company building was destroyed, animals were slaughtered, the church was desecrated, and some settlers who fled to the surrounding countryside died of starvation. The French remained until the middle of October, when they finally sailed out to sea. They left 120 European sailors taken from previously captured ships, and £55,000 worth of damage to the town.[29]

The job of rebuilding what little there had been was now even more arduous. Dissension among the settlers grew loud again on the question of land. The Company, feeling the huge financial strain of trying to supply the colony during the Anglo-French wars with prohibitively high insurance charges and almost predictably larger losses, had introduced quit rents to secure greater revenue. At a rate of one shilling an acre, the Company's land tax was fifty times higher than that of New South Wales at the same time.[30] The settlers, already disappointed with the Company's failure to provide them with a more favourable situation, refused to pay, saying the land had been promised to them *'free of all expense'*.[31] They found the tax all the more oppressive since Clarkson had promised them they would never be subject to it.[32] To the earlier dispute over not receiving the promised amount of land was now added the matter of taxation. Governor Macaulay offered to pacify the settlers by giving them the promised twenty acres of land, but they refused since the quit rent was tied to the new offer.[33] Efforts to solve the tax difficulty succeeded in producing over the years only considerable discontent and insubordination on the part of the settlers. They never produced any revenue since a tacit compromise between settler and government permeated the whole dispute: the right of collecting the tax was never formally relinquished by the government, but it was never paid by the settlers.[34]

Amid continuing dissension the settlers rebuilt the town. Freetown became more comparable in plan to a European or American commercial town of the early nineteenth century. Houses were of a wood frame construction, the architectural design showing them similar to the houses of New England. They were built on regular lots, forty-eight by seventy-six feet, and set along streets which were intersected at right angles by cross streets so as to form rectangular blocks. Nine streets ran in a north-west–south-easterly direction from the harbour to the mountains which formed a protective shell behind the town. Crossing these were three longer, parallel ones which ran from the south-west to the north-east. This basic urban plan, set out finally after the French attack of 1794, continued the same throughout the history of the city. The three latter streets eventually received their present names: Water, Oxford, and Westmoreland streets. The rectangular blocks of central Freetown came to house the major commercial establishments of the colony and the homes of the more well-to-do citizens. As the city grew, however, new additions were far less regular, reflecting the lesser degree of planning and the differing needs and concepts of urban life among the later African immigrants as opposed to the earlier Nova Scotian group. Roads from the surrounding country fed into the basic rectangular block section and the newer sections of Freetown grew as separate communities located off these roads. Gradually the pressure of an expanding population merged the separate communities together.

By 1796 the town comprised between 300 and 400 houses. Although small, those of the Nova Scotians were always partitioned into rooms. Set on stone foundations, the houses stood two or three feet off the ground; floors were wood and the roofs were grass or shingled. The separate rooms offered privacy within the house and they were furnished so as to reflect specialization of function. Since the houses were wood, the preparation of food was done in the yard behind the house or in a separate cookhouse. This meant that much of the daily activity of the household was carried on outside.[35]

Rebellion, War, and Financial Disaster

Zachary Macaulay, who left the colony in 1795 and returned as Governor in 1796, retired finally in 1799. Thomas Ludlam, another English employee of the Company, succeeded Macaulay. Increasingly fearful of the threat of settler rebellion, the Directors of the Company felt the need for additional powers. Experience had shown, for example, that the governor and council lacked sufficient legal title to enforce their authority. The Company therefore petitioned the Crown for a new charter. The Directors cited as justification their growing responsibility, particularly in regard to the anticipated arrival of nearly 600 Maroon settlers from Jamaica.[36] The Crown replied with a new charter, granted in July 1799. The charter gave the needed legal sanction to the government of the Freetown colony. It recognized the Company's sole responsibility to appoint governor and council. It gave the council judicial as well as administrative powers. The governor and council appointed a court of civil jurisdiction under a mayor, and a Court of Requests for the recovery of small debts. The new charter gave all settlers the right of trial by jury in civil and criminal cases.[37] Finally, but

33

most importantly, the charter ended the days when the Nova Scotian settler was able to elect tithingmen and hundredors to influence the governor and council. The charter did not allow for the continuation of even a modified form of Sharp's constitution.

Still anxious about their position as governors of the colony, the Company requested, and the Crown dispatched, a detachment of the Royal Africa Corps to Freetown. But before either the charter or the troops arrived, the Nova Scotians rebelled. Charging that the Company had not kept its promises, particularly regarding land, the insurrectionists were able to rally many settlers behind their standard. The settler force outnumbered the Company troops; company government was apparently to crumble. At the critical moment, however, 550 Maroons accompanied by forty-five soldiers of His Majesty's 24th Regiment arrived and threw the balance to the Company side. The rebellion ended quickly. Of the thirty-five rebels taken prisoner, two were tried and executed while the remainder were expelled from the colony.[38]

Suppression of the 1800 settler rebellion did not end the difficulties. Some of the exiled rebels returned a year later leading, with King Tom, a local Temne chief, an attack on the town. In the initial thrust, the invaders drove through the streets to the Company fort, killing twelve and wounding several others, including Governor Dawes who had returned in January 1801, to succeed Ludlam. The wounded but bayonet-swinging Dawes regrouped his troops and drove the invaders into the fields surrounding Freetown. There they remained for nearly a month, posing a visible threat to the community. Periodically a force from the town drove them further into the bush, and eventually a truce was signed by which King Tom ceded to the Company his lands west of Freetown as far as the sea. The truce was short-lived. Less than five months later King Tom, again allied with some exiled settlers, returned with about 400 Temne and Susu warriors. The attack lasted only twenty minutes before being brutally repelled by the Company force.

The Temne chief lost nearly one-quarter of his contingent as the Company troops drove his men from Freetown.[39]

Six months of war or constant threat of attack exacted a heavy toll from the colony. Two years before the first Temne war the community, with 650 acres in cultivation, had had an agricultural production abundant for its needs.[40] But nothing was grown during the attacks of 1801 and 1802. Cultivators, mainly women and children, refused to go to the fields, fearing for their safety. It was not until late 1802 that farmers again ventured out of town into the fields.[41] Moreover, all the cattle in Freetown had been slaughtered during the wars in order to feed the population. Thus a supply of meat had to be secured from traders in the rivers north of Freetown, and the price of beef nearly doubled. Finally, the newly arrived Maroons, kept from harvesting their first crops by the wars, had to be supplied entirely from Company rations.[42]

The early settlers had been hampered in their agricultural work by the restricted fertility of the soil and the intermittent taxation quarrels with the Company. The added burden of the Temne wars accentuated the already prevalent trend among the Nova Scotians to leave the fields and seek their livelihood in trade and by their skills as craftsmen. This tendency proved to be the economic salvation of Nova Scotian society in Sierra Leone. It did not, however, bring even minimal prosperity to the Company, which had hoped for a bounty from agricultural exports. In fact, without agricultural produce to export, and because of the increased need for public works projects to keep the craftsmen employed, the colony became an increasing financial burden to the Company.[43]

In London the Company was already in serious financial difficulties of its own. The costs of supplying the settlement during the Anglo-French wars had been astronomical. Only one of six ships sent out to Sierra Leone during 1798 and 1799 reached Freetown. Four were captured and another was shipwrecked.[44] Even though the Company's interest had been fundamentally philanthropic, it was clear by 1800 that the venture would not only not produce even the small, anticipated return, but it would merely continue to drain away capital as fast as it was produced. Only a bare fraction of the original investment remained in the Company treasury when the Chairman, Thornton, appealed to Parliament for aid in 1800. Two years later a committee of the House of Commons recommended a parliamentary grant of £19,000, £4,000 directly to the colony plus £15,000 for defence. The Company's Directors felt the £4,000 grant insufficient, and eventually secured instead a £10,000 annual grant. Satisfactory as it was, the grant only helped to defray the mounting cost of the colony's government.

By 1802 it was clear that the Company could not succeed as a commercial venture. The Sierra Leone Company had denied itself the riches of the slave trade and in Sierra Leone no substitute was found. With the Crown continuing to assume a greater financial share of the cost of governing the colony, and the Company still losing money commercially, it became necessary finally for Thornton to request that Parliament assume the responsibility of governing Sierra Leone. In September 1806, on the recommendation of the Committee of the Privy Council, a bill to that effect was introduced in Parliament. The bill received the Royal Assent in August 1807 and, on 1 January 1808, Sierra Leone became a Crown Colony. The last of the Company governors, Thomas Ludlam, in reviewing the causes of the Company's failure, wrote that considering all the unforeseen difficulties—from French invasion to settler rebellion and Temne attack—'the wonder is that the Colony exists rather than it has not flourished'.[45]

NOVA SCOTIAN SOCIETY: CHURCHES, GOVERNMENT, TRADE

But Ludlam did not really have to wonder long about why the colony continued to exist in 1807. The explanation lay, as it was to lie throughout the nineteenth century, in the resilience of the population in the face of hardship. The Company had failed, but the colony did not. The major characteristic of the Nova Scotian settlers was their independence. Independence, which at times went so far as open defiance of the Company government, provided the settler with the minimal requirements for survival. It led him to defy the government on the question of the quit rents. It led him to put his primary trust before 1800 in his own institutions of government, the tithing-men and hundredors. It led him to continue worshiping in his own dissenting chapels rather than in the Established church of the Company and to use his chapel as the important political and social institution it had first become in the earlier days in Nova Scotia. It led him finally to seek his fortune in trade when agriculture failed to produce the fulfilment of his dreams of a promised land. The colony survived because the Nova Scotian settlers were able to make of the new opportunity provided for them by the Company in Sierra Leone something of their own province of freedom.

Sharp's original dream of a Province of Freedom had lasted only four years; then the Company had entered the picture and had established a government more on the principles of an enlightened despotism than on those of a self-governing province. But while the Company's fortunes were directed by Clarkson, Dawes, Macaulay, and Ludlam, those of the Nova Scotians themselves were in the hands of their preachers and their annually elected tithingmen and hundredors. The preachers had been central to the organization of the freed slaves in Nova Scotia. They had played a key role in the plans for the exodus to Sierra Leone. Governor Clarkson had spoken to the prospective settlers in their churches. The preachers had led their people ashore at the site of Freetown, and had continued to lead the new Sierra Leoneans once they were settled. The Nova Scotian chapel became the 'vital centre of public opinion and communal action, and the preachers to a large extent the key to government'.[46]

Three groups of religious dissenters were represented in the Nova Scotian population, Baptists, members of the Countess of Huntingdon's Connection, and Methodists. All were embraced by the settlers while they were in the New World. David George, born in the 1740's to slave parents and converted on a Georgia plantation, led the Nova Scotian Baptists. Arriving in Nova Scotia in 1782, having fought with the British in the Revolutionary War, he preached and founded several Baptist congregations. Together with most of his congregation, he accepted John Clarkson's offer to go to Sierra Leone in 1791. George formed a close attachment to Clarkson and took charge of the emigrants on his ship. The chapel he built in Freetown became a political as well as a religious institution; George was the leader of his people. His continuing devotion to Clarkson in Sierra Leone guaranteed the loyalty of most Baptists to the government. In the protests and rebellions against the government, the Baptists tended to remain loyal.[47]

The Countess of Huntingdon had led a group of Anglicans which split away from the Established Church during the eighteenth century in much the same fashion as had the Wesleyans. Her movement spread to the American colonies almost immediately and hence was to be found among the Nova Scotian settlers in the New World. John Marrant, a Negro born to free parents in Charleston, South Carolina, had introduced the Huntingdon Connection to Nova Scotia after the end of the Revolutionary War. When Marrant died in 1791, leadership of his congregation fell to Cato Perkins, who also had been born in Charleston. The leading preacher of the Connection after Marrant's death was William Ash. Both Perkins and Ash were headmen of groups of Nova Scotians during their passage to Sierra Leone. Perkins's leadership ability, based in the Huntingdonian chapel, extended well beyond his immediate religious group once the Nova Scotians settled in Sierra Leone. He became an important leader of settler opposition to the Company government. He was one of the two immigrants sent to London in 1793 with the petition of protest against Governor Dawes. With the petition unanswered and the oppression of the government mounting throughout the 1790's, Perkins and many of his religious followers supported the opposition to the government. Although Perkins himself refused to participate, many Huntingdonians took part in the 1800 settler rebellion. Perkins's death in 1805 followed that of Ash by drowning in 1801; leadership of the Connection fell to John Ellis, a Maroon, who led the religious group during its next period. The arrival of more freed slaves after 1808 opened up an important field of mission work for the Connection which in turn guaranteed the continuation of the little sect in Sierra Leone.[48]

The history of the 223 Sierra Leone members of the Methodist church in 1793 had been similar to that of the Countess of Huntingdon's Connection. In 1793 their chapel in Birch Town, Nova Scotia, had been the scene of one of Clarkson's most moving and emotional performances seeking settlers for Sierra Leone. There he had promised them free land. The Wesleyan leader of the Nova Scotians, already blind and lame, was Moses Wilkinson; his foremost preacher, Luke Jordan, took over the important political responsibilities of a Nova Scotian religious leader which Daddy Moses was unable to perform. Both had escaped from Virginia plantations and had found their way to Nova Scotia. Jordan became a 'captain' or headman of a group of immigrants during the voyage across the Atlantic. Once in Sierra Leone the group, under Jordan's leadership, became persistent critics of the Company government. Some became involved in a dispute with Macaulay over Company property found in their possession after the French attack of 1794. What appeared to the Governor as outright stealing was defended by the Nova Scotian Methodists as protecting Company property or even more simply taking that which they otherwise thought was theirs. In the quit rent dispute, Wilkinson's congregation threatened to expel members who paid the tax to the government. New regulations governing marriage and a subsequent irresponsible threat by the Company chaplain that the chapels would be closed so that all might worship in the Established church led to a bitter petition from 128 members of the Methodist church. Although none of the leaders of Wilkinson's

39

church participated in the 1800 rebellion, its challenge to the Company government clearly reflected the sympathies of many Nova Scotian Methodists who had long been effective critics of the European establishment.[49]

Religiously, Nova Scotian Christianity was characterized by its simplicity and its lack of intense denominational rivalry. Competitive sectarianism was only introduced by European chaplains who proved unsuccessful in their attempt to divide and rule. Andrew Walls has pointed out that the Nova Scotians arrived in Sierra Leone 'convinced and instructed Christians, with very firm, if not always very consistent beliefs'. They were revivalists only in the sense that their contact had been with religious movements which arose from the eighteenth century Evangelical revival. 'Christianity was for them dynamic and personal; no matter of doctrine could be indifferent; the personal experience of the individual and his sharing in fellowship with others—the sense of being the people of God—was a matter of profound importance'. The Nova Scotians remained dissenters. The subsequent history of their group showed them continuing to worship as Baptists, Huntingdonians, and Methodists. They consistently absented themselves from the Anglican churches. When they declined as a group so too did their chapels. Christianity was central to their early experience in Sierra Leone, and whatever 'excesses marked it, whatever pagan elements remained, whatever acts of uncharitableness or folly perverted it, the religion of this people, twice uprooted from their homes, and with bitter experiences of treachery as well as slavery, welded them together'.[50]

After Sharp's Province of Freedom had failed, the Sierra Leone Company allowed one of its most important manifestations to continue: the system of organizing the community on the basis of tithingmen and hundredors. What seemed to the Company to be an efficient system of organization, in reality emerged as the Nova Scotians' personal and effective mode of influencing the government. In many ways it was a government in its own right. From the already established religious communities among the Nova Scotians came those who were annually elected to political office. Ideally the tithingmen and hundredors were to be the means by which the governor and council maintained contact with, and control of, the population. Functionally these institutions developed more as a settler pressure group in what surely seemed to many to be their eternal struggle against the European's government. Re-instituted by Clarkson in 1792, the tithingmen and hundredors had the power to propose legislation to the governor and council. In 1794, the elected officials sent a strong protest to Governor Macaulay concerning the sacking of some Nova Scotian employees of the Company. In a riot which ensued the officials refused to exercise their responsibilities as peace officers until Macaulay himself had spoken to them about their larger grievances over the land allotments. A further attempt by the government later the same year to tax new allotments led to successful protests from the tithingmen and hundredors and a revocation of the already announced conditions. When the government asked for a flat payment for the new land, none took up the offer. Stern warnings from Macaulay followed in 1795. Gradually the annual election of the Nova Scotian representatives developed into a means by which the settlers voiced their displeasure with the Company. The hundredors and tithingmen became markedly anti-government. Macaulay realized as well that dissatisfaction concerning the sensitive area of land was also focused in the elected officials. He reminded them of their ultimate dependence on the government and held out the hope of their institution developing into a legislature of its own. The hundredors and tithingmen took up the promise and during 1795 and 1796 they reorganized themselves into a proto-legislative body and proposed a host of laws which the governor and council adopted. By 1796, Macaulay himself was consulting the Nova Scotian officials on his own proposals, obtaining their prior approval of future legislation. Such evidence of settler-Company cooperation, however, proved of little consequence whenever the European officials moved to institute or collect the quit rents. In December 1796, elections were held for the Nova Scotian offices and a majority of those elected were anti-government. Europeans with votes were intimidated not to exercise their right of franchise. Quit rents again loomed on the scene early in 1797, forcing Macaulay first to plead emotionally with the settlers to change their attitudes in the light of the additional social services provided for them by the Company. Then, when outright rebellion appeared imminent, he threatened the dissidents with the use of force. The dropping of further mention of quit rents placated the settlers who returned less anti-government tithingmen and hundredors in 1797. Revival of the issue in 1798 brought strong anti-government forces back into office just as quickly as they had disappeared the year before. This time Thomas Ludlam, not Macaulay, was left to reap the whirlwind. Tithingmen and hundredors now became far more militant than in the past. Even when the government completely dropped the issue of quit rents, they forced new demands on the government. Their leaders, seeking to expand the power of the Nova Scotians, asked the government to appoint two Nova Scotians as justices of the peace. The Company's government refused and re-iterated the refusal when the demand was made for a second time. Methodically, the elected Nova Scotian leadership launched a general attack on Ludlam and the council during 1799. In September they declared that only the hundredors and tithingmen had the right to legislate since Nova Scotians owned the land in the colony. Europeans, they demanded, should pay taxes. Events moved with a certainty which led directly to the settlers' rebellion of 1800, directed by the officially elected Nova Scotians, intended by the Company to keep order.[51] The fortuitous arrival of the Maroons and the successful suppression of the rebels by the government ended the most dramatic revelation of independence among the settlers during the period of Company rule. Just as significantly, the arrival of the new charter ended the very institutions of tithingmen and hundredors which had given expression to the settlers' protests.

The economic life of the community provided further evidence of Nova Scotian independence, of the existence of their own province of freedom. From the earliest days of Henry Smeathman's dreams and Granville Sharp's first colony at the foot of the Sierra Leone mountains, agriculture had theoretically held a paramount place. It was to form the economic basis of the colony. In this the Company was no different from its predecessors. Indeed, schemes to make Sierra Leone an agricultural paradise providing produce for Europe and good returns for the settlers abounded throughout the colony's history. But in their plans for the agricultural development of Sierra Leone, the Europeans were also to be disappointed. Granville Sharp may have complained when the original settlers in Granville Town sold their equipment for food from their African neighbours, but their act indicated the really solid economic support for the colony: trade. Lack of sufficiently fertile soil, little knowledge of tropical agriculture, and continuing tax disputes dictated the drift of the Nova Scotian settlers to trade. By the end of the eighteenth century, only about one half of them were still engaged in agriculture; the rest were employed in trade or as craftsmen. Settlers engaged themselves for the most part in petty trade in Freetown. Many, however, entered the rivers and creeks to trade with the local population, mainly selling European commodities in exchange for agricultural produce of the more fertile lands in the interior. Long a site used by ships trading in slaves, Freetown developed in its first twenty years as an important *entrepôt* for goods from Europe. Realizing this, the Nova Scotian was able to build for himself out of the trade a firm economic foundation for his new society.

When viewed from the standpoint of the European in London, many dreams for Sierra Leone lay in ruins in 1808. But such was not the case in Sierra Leone itself. There the settlers had responded to the opportunity of living freely in Africa. Faced with considerable hardship and frustration, they had proved resilient and adaptable in their new situation. With a

43

spirit of independence shown in their churches, their governmental institutions, and in their economic life, they had given a new meaning to Sharp's original dream of a province of freedom. To them went the credit for the fact that as the Crown took over the responsibility for governing Sierra Leone, and as the first of a new group of settlers, the Liberated Africans, began to come ashore in 1808, there was a vital community of freed slaves upon which the subsequent history of the settlement would be built. In the independent actions of the settlers during the colony's first twenty years of existence, one may find in microcosm its subsequent history in the nineteenth century.

II

The Liberated Africans:
The Search for a Solution, 1808–1816

The Crown government that took over responsibility for the settlement in 1808 faced a formidable task. They inherited the problems left over from the earlier period of Company rule. Foremost among these was the fact that although the Nova Scotian settlers were quite capable of managing their own affairs, the colonial government was just as capable of ignoring this truth. The mutual suspicions and distrust of the earlier period between settler and government continued under the Crown. Moreover, as had the Company before them, the Crown wasted valuable time and money attempting to render the Sierra Leone venture into a profitable agricultural enterprise, and continuing to look down on those who quite correctly had found economic security in trade and commerce.

New problems were added which increased the Crown's difficulties. The same Parliament which had passed legislation taking over the Company's colony in Sierra Leone also legislated the abolition of the British slave trade. After twenty years of patient work in Parliament, Wilberforce's dream of abolition had come true. But now someone else had to face the real problems of abolition, and just as there had been serious and unforeseen difficulties with the earlier venture of the humanitarians to resettle freed slaves in Sierra Leone, there were to be serious difficulties with enforcing legislation abolishing the traffic in human beings. The most serious problem of all was what to do with the slaves captured on ships on the high seas and liberated by the British first in Vice-Admiralty Courts and later in

Courts of Mixed Commission in Sierra Leone. This formidable task fell on the four men who governed Sierra Leone between 1808 and 1816, Thompson, Columbine, Maxwell, and Mac-Carthy. They faced the responsibility of putting the reality of resettlement more in tune with the high humanitarian aims of the colony's founders and those who had legislated the end of the slave trade twenty years later. The first three failed as miserably as the Company; only one, Sir Charles MacCarthy, had any degree of success, but his accomplishments faded quickly after his bloody death at the hands of the Asante warriors a thousand miles away in 1824. Failure again came from a complex combination of factors. Plans too often were as poorly conceived as the earlier ones; when some chance for success seemed apparent, projects were dashed upon the rocks of poor administration. A further threat to the whole series of attempts to solve the problems of governing Sierra Leone were hazards of disease and early death for the larger percentage of Europeans who came to Sierra Leone.

The central aims of the earlier period remained dominant: to civilize and Christianize the African. The governors who ruled Freetown and its environs after 1808 conceived the civilization process as one in which the eighteenth-century values of order, neatness, and tidiness—the holy trinity of a society which still worshipped natural law and natural rights—were instilled into the population. From Thompson to Mac-Carthy they sought to make Freetown a far more regular place. To the governors the process of Christianization fitted neatly into this picture. Invariably they saw it as the means to rid the Nova Scotian settlement of its dissenting chapels and render the population safely into loyal Anglicans. Religion was thus consistently seen by the governors as an aspect of the overall orderliness which they sought to instil into the society.

Already, of course, a new sort of province of freedom had come into being. Noted first in the propensity of the Nova Scotian settlers to remain in their dissenting chapels, in the protests and rebellion which marked the Company period, and in their shift from agricultural pursuits to the more lucrative area of trade and commerce, these factors of independence grew and flourished in a situation of government failure and frustration. The growing numbers of new settlers—the Liberated Africans who came off the captured slave ships after 1808—demanded attention; again plans conceived in Britain proved insufficient to meet the crises in far off Sierra Leone. Increasingly it was left to the Sierra Leone population of settlers and Liberated Africans to work out the solutions to their problems of resettlement. That they were able to do this successfully confirmed the fact that in colonial Sierra Leone during the nineteenth century a province of freedom existed.

Still, the governors largely ignored this fact, and sought to solve the problems that faced Sierra Leone by themselves. In doing so they were largely reduced to reacting to the most glaring and immediate problems. Almost at once they faced the very large issue of settling the new arrivals, the Liberated Africans. Even before the first Crown Colony Governor arrived on the scene in 1808, the first shipload of Liberated Africans had been brought into Freetown harbour to be freed. Governor Ludlam, the interim administrator of the colony and former Company governor, thus initially faced the problem of how to deal with the growing number of new arrivals freed by the provisions of the Slave Trade Abolition Act. The problem arose because the humanitarians in England, exerting their energies in the cause of abolition, failed to anticipate the full human consequences of their programme. The wretched survivors of the slave galleys who found themselves on Sierra Leone's shore were those whom the Crown had felt obliged to free, but not yet to maintain. The act abolishing the slave trade provided only for the apprenticeship or enlistment of the recaptives, as the Liberated Africans were first known.[1] Ludlam apprenticed the earliest arrivals,[2] but before the end of the year both these means for handling Liberated Africans had proved inadequate. Many of those freed were unfit for either alternative and thus fell outside the scope of the act. Freetown officials felt moral if not legal obligations toward the recaptives; consequently, each successive governor devised different methods to deal with them. Over the next several years, governors and missionaries combined to evolve a plan by which the newly arrived Africans could be included under the original humanitarian objectives of the colony.

FREETOWN, 1808

Thomas Perronet Thompson, the son of a Hull banker friend of Wilberforce, who had secured his appointment, arrived in Freetown and became the first Crown Colony Governor in July 1808. Freetown had changed little physically since its rebuilding following the French attack. Gradually the town had begun to show certain minimal signs of prosperity by the time of Thompson's arrival. New houses were being built of stone, and well-to-do householders were beginning to substitute shingled for thatched roofs.[3] Thompson found the condition of the colony better than he had expected, but the independence of the population led him to observe that the settlers were not lacking in shrewdness. An old Maroon woman confided to him that '. . . in this country every where King, every where Governor, *not one so good as half a constable*',[4] and the new governor passed the observation on to Lord Castlereagh in London.

The Nova Scotians were independent. They had learned early in their experience to question the government and certainly not to depend overmuch on it. Religious dissent continued among the Nova Scotians. Although Methodist settlers had already made their first request to the British Wesleyans to send out a leader, their pulpit continued to be served by their own preachers, men and women alike. Still on occasion old blind and lame Moses Wilkinson would mount the pulpit and '. . . outstretch his voice . . . to terror and frightfulness'.[5] A four hundred seat Freetown chapel, built in 1798, testified to the fact that religious observance played a central role in the settler community.[6] Before Thompson's arrival, Ludlam had found it necessary to restrict religious services of any kind held after

8 p.m. and before 5 a.m. 'either in private houses or public places'.[7] Two English preachers, a few years later, confessed to London that the Nova Scotians in Freetown kept them so engaged that they had to ignore their mission outside the town. Each taught school one half of the time, and spent the other half holding various religious services for the settlers: two Sunday morning services, one at 5 and the other at 9, prayer meeting at 2 p.m., and preaching again at 6 p.m. Beyond this, church meetings were held each evening of the week except Wednesday. On Wednesdays prayers had to be conducted in private houses.[8]

The Freetown of 1808 remained primarily a trading centre and a reservoir of skilled craftsmen dependent on the public works. Government persisted in trying to encourage farming, and in making land grants earlier in the year, Governor Ludlam told the new landholders that they were responsible for keeping the country plot 'constantly . . . in good cultivation'.[9] The reality of the situation, however, discouraged the observant Thompson. His suppression of public works soon after his arrival caused considerable unemployment and consternation among the population. He ruefully remarked that the trouble with the settlement was that everyone was a craftsman of some sort in spite of the fact that there was little to eat: 'We are masons, and there is nothing to build, or carpenters, and there is nothing to frame; but very few of us cultivate the ground as we ought to do, because we have been apprenticed to easier callings'.[10]

The bright, smart, twisted headscarves and sky-blue bonnets of the women gave a colourful hue to the Freetown scene. Rings and beads of gold, coral, and cut glass adorned the necks, ears, and fingers of the ladies as they busily jingled through town on the way to market or chapel.[11] Freetown life was far from austere. Although the shock of the Maroon landing and the suppression of the Nova Scotian revolt meant that a definite tension still affected relations between the major groups of the town's population, numerous public houses and grog shops

49

D

allowed for plenty of gay enjoyment. The Nova Scotians had grown fond of the local palm wine. The most popular cuisine was a preparation of stewed rice liberally covered with a highly seasoned sauce, aptly named palaver sauce, made from fowl, palm oil, and cayenne pepper. Thompson could expect such a dish to be served him at the annual dinner for the governor prepared by the community's widows. Each woman prepared her special dish; collectively the widows provided the porter and wine to drink. Gaiety and dancing followed the gala meal long into the night.[12] Anticipating the greater prosperity that was to come with the Crown's assumption of responsibility, one could easily envisage Freetown in 1808 as a bustling town which within ten years was to make full use of a race track and adopt horse-racing as its prime attraction and pastime.

THE REFORMS OF GOVERNOR THOMPSON

Thomas Perronet Thompson's initial observations of Freetown revealed a basic dissatisfaction with the community and its population. They also exposed a burning zeal to change it. As with administrators before and after him, Thompson sought solutions in the principles of reason and order. An adventurous twenty-five upon assuming the governorship of Sierra Leone, Thompson had already secured his B.A. from Cambridge, rejected family pressures for a career in banking, entered the navy, then the army, and served meritoriously during the Royal Brigade's attack on Buenos Aires in 1807.[13] With such experience behind him, it was natural for him to see problems from the standpoint of a military man and to attempt to project on the community a certain sense of military order. Combining what he perceived as the two major threats to the colony—alleged libertine ideas among the settlers, and the indefensibility of the town from outside attack—he set about remoulding the community. Within his first month in office, he disbanded the volunteer forces which had long served the needs of the Company, and drafted all males between the ages of fifteen and sixty into a trained militia. Ignoring the settlers' protests, he justified his plan to Whitehall by assuring officials that his purpose was to build a strong feeling of allegiance to His Majesty's Government among the people.[14]

Thompson sensed that the very name of the town, Freetown, had been 'perverted to the Purposes of Insubordination and Rebellion', and so before the end of 1808 he changed it to the far more regal-sounding Georgetown. The streets of the town were similarly renamed with the intention of reaffirming the settlement's close connection with Britain.[15] No matter escaped his attention. Convinced that the dollar and cent currency of the Company reminded the settler of too many revolutionary American ideas, he issued a new specie in pounds, shillings, and pence.[16]

The first Crown Governor's purpose was to make the Sierra Leone settlement a more regulated place, an accomplishment which would assure prosperity. In Thompson's mind, the Company had failed because it had not paid attention to the details of administration, namely the regulation of its population. For this reason most of Thompson's activities were directed toward a general tidying up of what he thought was the confusion and disorder of the community. Legislation forced the impounding of cattle, previously allowed to roam the streets freely. The Governor provided settlers with directions for planting cotton seed in a vain attempt to introduce export crops to the settlement. He published a regular newspaper and began a regular postal service between Sierra Leone and Great Britain, the West Indies, America, Spain, and Portugal.

Buildings were of course essential. They would not only serve as important symbols of his new order, but also would end the unsatisfactory situation by which the Vice-Admiralty Court had to meet in a tent and the quarter sessions had to use the Methodist chapel. Thompson requested a Government House, a court house, a barracks, a church, and a hospital. He urged Castlereagh to consider building a church in order to assure a place for the Established Church in Sierra Leone. The old Company church continued to be the official house of worship for the English civil and military personnel. But a new edifice would attract the settlers to the Establishment and would, Thompson hoped, bring an end to the many sects. He felt sure that the settlers had merely created the chapels for their own amusement; at any rate, in his general plans for the colony there was no place for the dissenting chapels.[17]

The persistent problem of the Liberated Africans did not escape Thompson's attention. He was the first to perceive the difficulties of handling the newcomers. Investigating the consequences of apprenticing the new arrivals as suggested by the Abolition Act and practised by his predecessor, Governor Ludlam, he expressed utter dismay. Frustrated by the Act's inadequacy, he charged Ludlam and the Company he represented with aiding the cause of slavery by apprenticing the first recaptives. In transactions involving Liberated African labour, Thompson discovered that money was being paid by those settlers to whom the recaptives were apprenticed. Transfers of apprentices among the settlers were also effected by cash payment. Vindictively, Thomson turned on the Company, charging that Ludlam himself had sold the newcomers as slaves. The new governor released twenty-one Liberated Africans who had been apprenticed as labourers, had run away, had been recaptured and thrown into irons in the town gaol. Intent on getting all of the facts, Thompson demanded certain relevant papers from Ludlam, who had remained in the colony as the Company's agent. Ludlam refused. Angry, Thompson seized all of the slaves liberated before his arrival and declared their apprenticeships null and void. Next he threatened Ludlam with prosecution under the Abolition Act.[18]

Hidden behind these harsh assaults on the Company and Ludlam was Thompson's growing frustration with attempts to reform Freetown's settler population. The more he became involved with the strong-willed, independent Nova Scotians, the more he became inclined toward the community's non-settler population. This included both Maroons and Liberated Africans. He sought to increase their numbers by recruiting additional immigrants from the West Indies. Maroons told him that there were many Jamaicans who would eagerly settle in Sierra Leone. The energetic administrator believed such immigrants would be more easily worked into the population; they would more readily conform to his grand plans.

The Liberated Africans impressed Thompson for the same reasons; their advantage, of course, was that each month they were becoming more numerous. Those already in the community evinced two undeniably good characteristics: activeness and obedience. More importantly, the recaptives were untouched by those influences which had, in the Governor's mind, warped the Nova Scotians. With the idea, then, of making greater use of them, Thompson formulated a new plan for handling the increasing numbers of Liberated Africans in Sierra Leone.[19]

Abandoning the whole notion of apprenticeship, Thompson advocated the settlement of Liberated Africans in rural communities surrounding the main town. By putting them on the soil as free and independent agents, he hoped to protect them against falling prey to the 'constraint and perhaps oppression of a Colonial master': i.e., the Nova Scotians. He anticipated furthermore, that they would serve the original purpose of the colony and become the first wave of civilized Africans to penetrate the interior. They would provide a necessary agricultural base from which the town could draw a regular supply of food. Finally, their presence outside the settlement would protect it from the threat of attack from the interior. Thompson to the end was a military man, and, after all, the colony had in its earlier period been subjected to Temne attack. The young, idealistic governor regarded the Liberated African population as the colony's free peasantry.[20]

Whether Thompson conceived the plan in his fertile imagination or simply sought to harness a process of exodus from Freetown which was already in operation, cannot be discerned; nevertheless, he did put the plan into operation during his administration. He reported to London that the new rural communities were quite successful.[21] Although such communities, under his direction, might have developed according to plan,[22] the absence of any official approval for them from his London superiors guaranteed their independent growth once Thompson left the colony. Eventually the young governor's vicious attacks on the Sierra Leone Company proved too burdensome to those who remained in influential positions in London. They assured his own downfall. In challenging the Company's operations regarding the Liberated Africans, Thompson had been legally in error. The Company had apprenticed the recaptives and this method had been sanctioned by the Act abolishing the slave trade. Unfortunately for his plans in Sierra Leone, his attacks on the Company had also put a slur upon the work of the humanitarian group led by Wilberforce which had secured his appointment. In the end, the humanitarians gained his recall. The letter of recall from Castlereagh in April 1809, was the only answer Thompson ever received to all his mountainous correspondence.[23] Most of his reforms were abolished by his successor.[24] In later years, the first Crown Colony Governor, who went on to have a distinguished career in the army, in journalism, and in the House of Commons, could no doubt find some satisfaction in knowing that the government eventually returned to embrace his idea of settling the Liberated Africans in regular rural communities surrounding Freetown.

THE COLUMBINE REACTION

During his sixteen months' administration of the Colony Thompson's successor, Naval Captain E. H. Columbine, returned to the provisions of the Act, enlisting and apprenticing the Liberated Africans. As during Thompson's reform period, however, the provisions of the Act did not prove sufficient for the numbers of new settlers arriving in Freetown harbour. Thus, Liberated Africans themselves began to forge their own version of the province of freedom by continuing the process begun during Thompson's tenure. Those neither apprenticed nor enlisted trekked into the mountains surrounding the colonial capital and settled among their countrymen in village communities. Living in these settlements, which had neither official approval nor recognition, the recaptives showed the earliest signs of the influence they were to have after 1808 on the development of the colony during the nineteenth century. They lived independently of the government in rural communities circling Nova Scotian Freetown.

Columbine did not completely ignore the problems posed by the Liberated Africans. His efforts, however, were seriously curtailed by his instructions from London, his own desire to reduce expenditures, and his poor health. London sent Thompson's replacement with strict instructions to study, observe, and change such aspects of his predecessor's administration as he saw fit. Columbine was one of three to form a Commission of Inquiry in 1810; this responsibility alone took a considerable amount of his time. He concentrated on the institutions of government rather than continuing with the previous governor's desire to reform the population and to secure a new degree of order. Columbine's study of governmental institutions led him to the conclusion that government could be made more efficient. Within a month of taking control he wrote London that he could cut government costs in half. By doing so he would also end the inflation which had beset Freetown during Thompson's governorship, an inflation caused, Columbine felt assured, by large government spending. The simple facts that rents had increased 50% and that between a quarter and a third of a government clerk's salary went for house rent alone convinced the new Governor that inflation was a central problem.

The naval captain's solution was less government spending and more independent work from the population. He hoped to encourage agriculture. It was still a dominant panacea to most Europeans who came to the rocky, lateritic peninsula to solve problems and to govern. Although only 450 acres of land were under cultivation in 1810, the new governor found it encouraging that over one-half of the land had been cleared during the past thirteen months. Columbine found a direct correlation between reduced government expenditure and increased activities in the rural areas. That much of the new land was being cleared by Liberated Africans who would move as quickly into trade as had their predecessors, the Nova Scotians, escaped his attention.[25]

In addition to placing his hopes on increased agricultural production, Columbine instituted a system of careful accounting of existing stores and current expenditure. Reports by department heads lay unsigned on the governor's desk until he had been satisfied that such accounting had been done. He demanded weekly reports on government works, the number of workmen employed by the various departments, their work, and their daily wage.[26] Accounting procedures also characterized his relations with the Liberated Africans. He sought to regulate and control the recaptives by initiating regular weekly musters of Liberated Africans apprenticed to Freetown citizens. Government threatened to confiscate any apprentice not produced for the regular Saturday morning muster. Columbine also kept a regular file of indentures for those who had been apprenticed. In order to effect this system of counting, the governor found it necessary to delegate the responsibility for the new arrivals to the second member of his council. He thought that the fault in the system was that no single officer of the government had ever been charged with solving the problems caused by abolition and the Act of Parliament. Now entrusted with the care of the Liberated Africans, the second officer's responsibilities were to report to the governor on the 'actual condition of these people: their disposal, health, and the weekly expense of their maintenance'.[27] Fully satisfied that he had solved the problem by providing a new responsibility for a member of his government, Columbine patiently awaited the approval of Downing Street. It never came.

A far more serious problem to face Columbine was the unhealthiness of the Sierra Leone peninsula. Arriving in February, 1810, he had lost his wife and daughter by December, and had suffered three attacks of malaria himself. Despondent and discouraged, he requested a replacement, but when none came and he grew desperate, he left the colony on his own authority in May 1811, only to die at sea the next month of fever.[28]

GOVERNOR MAXWELL AND THE GROWING PROBLEMS
In April, a month before the naval captain had found it necessary to leave the colony in a futile attempt to regain his health at sea, Lord Liverpool had appointed Colonel Charles William Maxwell, the military commandant at Senegal, to the governorship of Sierra Leone. Maxwell reached Freetown and became governor on 1 July 1811. Undoubtedly reflecting the quiet stability of the Columbine period, Maxwell reported the town to be in a state of perfect tranquillity upon arrival. Provisions were plentiful and at moderate prices. Cultivation progressed although it was almost entirely restricted to cassava and other vegetables necessary for subsistence. Coffee cultivation, one of the few successful exports during the Company period, had again been encouraged. Farms continued to be cleared and Liberated Africans were building roads into the new agricultural areas.

The tranquillity which Maxwell noted during his first days in Freetown was more apparent than real. Barely below the surface, basic problems for the settlement's future continued unsolved. Trade with the interior, a hope first expressed in Company days, had not developed. Some camwood and a little ivory, in addition to food products to supplement the town's diet, was all that entered with any regularity. The persistent problem of land grants—ignored entirely by Columbine—still needed remedy. Moreover, mercantilistic Maxwell found it very unsettling that more supplies entered Freetown from America than from the United Kingdom.[29] Most troublesome of all, the settlement's greatest problem of what to do with the ever-increasing numbers of Liberated Africans remained unsolved. Again, in Maxwell, Sierra Leone had a governor who was more the man of action, the problem-solver, than a simple

57

reporter of conditions to Whitehall. Before he relinquished his post to MacCarthy, Maxwell succeeded in getting the London government to recognize the mounting problem of dealing with the human cargoes from the captured slave ships.

When he arrived, Maxwell found 360 Liberated Africans provided for by government subsidy in the form of rice rations. These came from among those who had proved unfit for either the army or apprenticeship and who had been forming the new communities in the rural areas. In spite of government aid, however, many suffered from bad health. The new governor also discovered that the village communities existed without government approval. Whitehall continued to ignore the problem and the challenge of separatist communities which defied government attempts to make of the Sierra Leone colony an efficient administrative entity.[30]

Experienced in administration, Maxwell moved more directly than either of his two predecessors in formulating a solution. He dispatched an administrative assistant, Lieutenant J. Mailing, to London to report on the problem first hand. He sought authority for a new programme as well as additional resources to ease the increasing burden of the rice subsidy on the Freetown treasury.[31] Maxwell, far more than Whitehall, realized that the numbers of Liberated Africans would increase. His observations along the West Coast had convinced him that the slave trade was not simply going to fade into the mist as a result of the Act of Parliament; the British government, however, was unprepared for such revelations in 1811.

Undeterred, Maxwell pressed ahead toward a solution. Like Columbine, he used the enlistment and apprenticeship provisions of the Act as much as he could. He selected the most healthy newcomers and sent them off for military training at Senegal or Goree; he envisaged an African army of three companies, a dream he more than realized by 1814.[32] He personally inspected the 360 on government assistance and selected those who could be apprenticed. But the governor knew all along that the provisions of the Act would still prove inadequate. Thus in May 1812, he again approached London and hopefully proposed his new plans.

His second approach proved more subtle. Obviously, in its earlier responses, the Crown had revealed that its humanitarian concern was counter-balanced by its more mundane insistence that costs be held to a minimum. Maxwell now hastily pointed out that since his arrival some Liberated Africans living in the independent rural villages had become self-supporting. Stressing this, he proposed that those Africans who could not be put into the army or apprenticed should be settled with official regulation on farms in the mountains behind Freetown. Mindful of Whitehall's budgetary concern, he promised 'to confine the number thus burdensome to the Public within the narrowest limits'. Earl Bathurst, who had succeeded Liverpool at the Colonial Office, replied in appropriately vague, but nevertheless negative terms. His Majesty's Government—confronted as it was with war on the Continent and signs of renewed hostilities in North America—was encouraged by Maxwell's assurance that he would decrease the financial burden. But Bathurst continued, 'I am not at present prepared to authorize any deviation from the mode adopted by Captn. Columbine of providing for those Negroes, who are unfit for the Army or Navy or for apprentices, but I trust that you will omit no exertions to reduce the numbers of Persons to be so supplied within the narrowest limits'. With this response, it became clear that unofficial and thus unregulated settlement of the vast majority of recaptives was to continue with government providing the occasional rice subsidy. Whitehall proved again reluctant to undertake any major deviation from the terms of the 1807 Abolition Act.[33]

Had British officials in London looked at the growing body of statistics from Freetown they would have seen the fallacy in their thinking. Even the roughest figures available for the period indicated that the Liberated African population needed greater attention. By 1811, a little more than 1,200 recaptives had been freed. More than half remained in the colony, the others had

been apprenticed elsewhere or put into the army.[34] The number of new arrivals nearly doubled in 1812 alone. Although
Maxwell succeeded in enlisting about half of these, a total of
about 600 settled freely in the colony.[35] Vice-Admiralty Court
figures revealed that nearly 6,000 had been emancipated by
1814.[36] Approximately one-third had entered the services,
3,500 were known to be in the colony and the remainder had
either returned to their home country, died, or been apprenticed
to the settlement at Goree. Over three-fifths of the colony's
population, including the surrounding Temne, were Liberated
Africans by 1814.[37] Beyond these simple statistics of population,
Whitehall surely did note that in spite of Bathurst's pleasure
with Maxwell's promise to reduce 'the Burden to the Public',
the cost of maintaining the newcomers had more than doubled
by the same year.[38]

Moreover, the growing concern of those who lived in the
colony underlined the cold, impressive statistics. Missionaries
reported that the poor state of health among those recently
liberated caused many deaths and increased the danger to other
colonists. Some newcomers died of starvation, a result, suggested the sympathetic CMS missionary Gustav Nyländer, of
the inadequate provision for them.[39] Maxwell himself admitted
that there were deaths among the new arrivals. Although he
attributed them to the generally poor conditions aboard the
slave ships, his reports nonetheless revealed the government's
inability to deal with even the most common sicknesses. Complaints came as well from the colony's few diligent agricul-
turalists. They accused the recaptives of robbing their farms of
produce. Thus, as had happened before, the frustrated farmers
sought the security of the main town.

The villages surrounding Freetown themselves provided
sources for complaint. They lay outside the government's control. A province of freedom for the newcomers, they contributed
to the older Nova Scotian settlers' fears and frustrations. By
European standards the new villages were disorganized. The
Liberated Africans living in them were alien to the Nova

Scotians and the robbing of the farms led the older settlers to fear an eventual attack on Freetown itself. Maxwell, without similar fears, wished only that they could be an integral and regular part of his Sierra Leone government.[40]

Like Governor Thompson before him, Maxwell sought to include the Liberated Africans in the original aims of the colony. More particularly, he desired approval for his regulation of the village communities. But Whitehall insisted on remaining bound by the provisions of the existing legislation. The home government refused to see any connection between freeing the slaves and assisting those who were freed beyond providing a small rice subsidy for the few. This became clearer when in 1811 Parliament passed a new Abolition of the Slave Trade Act. Its clauses only tightened the enforcement procedures. It did nothing to ease the resettlement of the Sierra Leone recaptives.[41] No amount of statistics or pleadings from governor or missionary forced London to modify its inadequate methods of dealing with the Liberated Africans. In the final analysis, it was the newcomers' lack of Christianity which moved the British government to include them in any ideal plan for the future development of Sierra Leone.

RELIGION IN THE YOUNG CROWN COLONY

Singing hymns when they arrived, indefatigable worshippers and preachers from the outset, the Nova Scotians had guaranteed that Freetown would know no scarcity of houses of worship. The founding population of the town had given it its Christian hue. Their society, however, had remained relatively closed to the newcomer. Although the Nova Scotians had been successful in some proselytizing among the Maroons, as late as 1811 they had made little attempt to convert the culturally alien Liberated Africans. In that year, at the Nova Scotians' request, the Revd. George Warren and three Wesleyan schoolmasters arrived from Great Britain to take over the direction of Methodist activities in Freetown. For seven years, the Nova Scotians had desired a more direct contact with the parent committee in London.[42] Unfortunately for their plans, Warren died seven months after his arrival. The three schoolmasters simply assisted the Nova Scotian leadership until a new preacher arrived in 1815.[43] The second preacher, the Revd. William Davies, and his wife, very quickly lost favour with the suspicious Nova Scotian congregation. The Davieses enjoyed the wine and good company of Freetown's public dinners and the quieter and more intimate hospitality of Government House. Within a year of his arrival, the Nova Scotians excluded Davies from their chapel.[44]

Davies's exclusion forced him into contact with the Liberated Africans and thus the work of the Methodist mission expanded to meet the needs of the newcomers. Davies had earlier noted the depressed state of the recaptives in Freetown. In 1816 a Methodist chapel was begun at Congo Town, one of the Liberated African villages near the town. The village, like the others, was purely an African venture. The land for it had been purchased five years previously by the recaptives themselves. Construction of the chapel was already under way when the Revd. Samuel Brown, the third Wesleyan preacher, arrived on the scene in 1816. The village headman turned the chapel over to Brown, who completed it and became its itinerant preacher. This chapel, and a similar one in Portuguese Town, another recaptive village, put the Methodists in direct contact with the Liberated Africans and served to make good the lack of Christianity among them.[45] The coming of Christianity to the Liberated African villages assisted in the cultural integration of the alien recaptives to the dominant Nova Scotian pattern. It also eventually served to bring the villages within the province of the Freetown administration.

Two factors, however, operated to the detriment of the Methodists' early desire to spread the word among the Liberated Africans. First, until Davies's arrival in 1815, they lacked sufficient leadership. Secondly, in a British colony in which the Crown was supreme the Methodists were undeniably dissenters. Though the Nova Scotians felt Davies had sought and won government favour, it was equally unpalatable to them that the favour of the chief occupant of Government House toward a dissenting preacher was always second to that awarded to the representative of the Church to which His Majesty's subjects implicitly owed their first allegiance.

EARLY COOPERATION WITH THE CHURCH MISSIONARY SOCIETY

The Methodist dissenter had to compete with the Established Church in Sierra Leone, and the Church, since 1804, had not ignored Freetown. The Church Missionary Society, an unofficial group of the Church of England which represented its more evangelical element, had entered the field in that year with two missionaries. One of these, the Revd. Melchior Renner, maintained continual service in the colony for seventeen years, but his case was not typical. The work of the CMS was hampered by the early deaths of its missionaries. By 1826, twenty-two years after its beginning in Sierra Leone, only fourteen of seventy-nine CMS missionaries, wives, and schoolmasters sent to Sierra Leone remained in service. The majority of the others were dead.[46]

In spite of such severe mortality figures, it was the presence of the CMS in Freetown which eventually led to the establishment of a more effective method of handling the Liberated Africans and a system of local government. Many problems had to be overcome before success came, the major ones being the need for the CMS itself to recognize the possibility of a Sierra Leone mission and for the government to accept the principle of cooperation with the mission organization. That each of these major barriers was overcome by 1816 stands in testimony to the perception and hard work of both the missionaries in the field and the successive governors sent to rule the colony.

In spite of the fact that the CMS first entered Freetown in 1804, it had not originally intended to establish a mission to the humanitarian colony. The town and its environs were not the society's primary fields of interest during the first twelve years of its activity along the coast. Following the advice of former Company Governor Zachary Macaulay, the CMS began originally to evangelize the Susu who lived one hundred miles north of the Sierra Leone settlement. Freetown served as the society's port of entry. As such it necessitated the presence of at least one missionary from 1804 onwards. Renner himself stayed in Freetown until the society finally succeeded in prodding him into his original assignment among the Susu in 1806. Nyländer, who had carried the message to Renner from London telling him to move on to the Susu country, immediately took his place in Freetown. With Nyländer's arrival, the first indications of government-mission cooperation became obvious. As Renner had before him, Nyländer became Company Chaplain, but his outlook was decidedly different. The new missionary looked around him and found the situation in the colony deplorable— 'as if there had been no missionaries sent out among the heathens at all'. In such statements he exposed a deep interest in the colony which grew during the subsequent ten years until the town eventually came to command the society's primary interest along the Coast.[47]

By 1806 Freetown needed a representative of the Established Church. Nyländer regularly preached in the company church, collected fees as the parish clerk, and baptized, married, and buried those at the top of early nineteenth-century colonial society. His most significant task, however, was as a teacher in the government-sponsored school.[48] As so often in the colonial missionary experience, schools and churches went together from the outset in Sierra Leone. It was hard to divide the functions of the earliest missionaries and certainly in the minds of the recipients of this form of westernization, the importance of the school was indiscernible from that of the church or chapel. The government-sponsored school under CMS guidance had pre-dated Nyländer's arrival. His teaching, however, made the educational work prosper. Finding twenty students enrolled upon his arrival, Nyländer doubled the attendance by early

Government House, Freetown

1808, and supervised over a hundred within four years. By 1810 Nyländer himself taught sixty boys while the remainder were under the tutelage of his Nova Scotian wife. Confirming the Crown Government's continued support of the venture, Governor Columbine built Nyländer and his wife each a new schoolhouse in 1810. The missionary, at the same time, expanded his educational work by opening an evening class for Maroon adults. Continuing to expand the day school, Nyländer reported late in the year, 150 regular scholars.[49]

Educational successes did not, however, blot out the frustrations and dissatisfactions of the missionary's life in Freetown. He grew weary of his duties late in 1811, shortly after the untimely death of his wife. He was left for a time in charge of both the schools. The promised assistance from the African Institution—an organization founded in Britain by philanthropists in 1807 to assist agricultural and educational development—proved almost absolutely useless. Of the three teachers they sent out to the colony that year, one entered the slave trade, one entered legitimate trade, and only one remained to divide the burden with the missionary. Nyländer's own health began to suffer under the strain. Unsuccessfully, he requested transfer to the Bulom Shore opposite Freetown where, he hoped, he might make a fresh start.[50]

The missionary society in London refused his request. Again, he married a Nova Scotian schoolmistress. He continued his Freetown work for another year. The impressive success he had had in the schools, however, was jeopardized when the Methodists opened their own school in 1812, and Nyländer began to lose pupils.[51] Old and in bad condition, the Company church had to be closed. Smallpox attacked the already weakened missionary; he renewed his pleas for transfer and finally the CMS gave in. Gustav Nyländer left Freetown, moved across the estuary and began his mission to the Bulom Sherbro.[52]

Nyländer's period in Freetown was crucial to the final settling of the Liberated African problem. Cooperation between the government and the Church Missionary Society had its

E

beginning during the German missionary's six year tenure in the town. When government paid Nyländer's salary as schoolmaster and built his school building in 1810, the formula for later cooperation was established. It developed between Nyländer and the succession of Company and Crown Governors largely on the basis of a personal relationship, a factor which became more evident after his departure when such cooperation lapsed. Government-Church cooperation of a far more significant sort resumed again at the first opportunity, with the arrival in Freetown of the Revd. Leopold Butscher. Much like the original cooperator except that he was far more aggressive, the Revd. Butscher had landed in Sierra Leone with Nyländer in 1806. Like all CMS missionaries before 1815, Butscher was German by birth. He had received his training at the Berlin Seminary, and had been ordained in the Lutheran orders. The Church Missionary Society had been forced to recruit its missionaries in Central Europe when it became quickly evident that none of its own nationals was forthcoming.[53]

An especially industrious and perceptive Swabian, Butscher had given early evidence of being somewhat different from his colleagues in the West African mission. Unlike Nyländer, he had gone directly to the Susu mission in 1806. While there he became aware of the strong economic foundations of the slave trade in African society. He realized more than the others the arduous work that lay before them if the complete abolition of the slave trade was to be accomplished. To those like Nyländer, who watched the increasing number of captured slave ships enter Freetown harbour, the slave trade appeared to be 'mortally wounded'. If it was 'not dead yet' this was because not enough of His Majesty's Ships were engaged in the work of the preventive squadron.[54] But Butscher realized that such a revolutionary change in the economics of African life as slave trade abolition was not so simple a matter. Abolition, he pointed out early in 1812, had taken away the one great source of commerce for the Susu. No other had replaced it. In order to avert economic disaster the Susu had either to trade in slaves or to discover new export products. By assisting the African to develop alternative commodities, Butscher felt the European would perform a major service.[55] Although not entirely unique, the German's insights were clearly ahead of the time in an abolitionist world that was not generally to accept them until Buxton's popular *The Slave Trade and Its Remedy* appeared in 1839.[56]

A bachelor, Butscher requested leave to England in 1812 in order to marry. CMS officials in London were anxious to have a first-hand report on their Sierra Leone mission and so approved of Butscher's leave.[57] Returning to Freetown the following year, the ship carrying the missionary and his bride crashed on to the rocks near Goree. When the couple went for assistance for the stranded ship, local pirates attacked the ship, killed the captain, and carried off much of the cargo. Butscher sought and received the help of the military superintendent at Goree, Major Chisholm, and his superior officer, the military commander at Senegal, Lieutenant Colonel Charles MacCarthy.[58] Most importantly, MacCarthy provided Butscher with the necessary credit to continue his voyage to Freetown.[59]

Naturally grateful, as well as impressed with the officers' efforts to educate their African troops in the British-held French possessions, the missionary wrote Josiah Pratt, the CMS Secretary, upon his return to Freetown and suggested that the society might be of some help in return. Pratt sent a supply of textbooks and, to familiarize MacCarthy with the society's work, a copy of their annual report. Butscher's shipwreck and the subsequent exchange of assistance proved crucial to the renewal of mission-government cooperation in the Sierra Leone experiment. Cooperative efforts resumed on Butscher's arrival in Freetown.[60] The resumption of the connection allowed the colony to move forward in its search for a solution to the Liberated African problem. Butscher returned with a letter of high praise for Governor Maxwell from the CMS President, Lord Gambier.[61] Maxwell replied immediately, indicating that he was pleased with the letter and assuring Lord Gambier that he, Maxwell, remained a zealous supporter of the missionary society.

Maxwell began almost at once, therefore, to use the CMS in London as a wedge to assist in a change in the British Government's policy toward the Liberated Africans in Freetown. Frustrated in his earlier attempts to get such a change, the governor now hoped to enlist the full force of the English abolition movement for the attack on Whitehall. His plans began in Freetown where almost at once he offered Butscher the colonial chaplaincy. The missionary accepted the post temporarily at first, mainly because his new bride was pregnant and he wished the baby to be born in Freetown. Cautiously, Butscher informed Pratt in London. Equally cautious, Pratt's reply none the less reflected some new thoughts in the society about their West African mission. The CMS's new thinking had been stimulated by the knowledge that since Nyländer's departure, Freetown had been without an Anglican representative. Earlier, Maxwell had offered the post to Renner who had refused, no doubt remembering the previous representations of the society that he should move on to his Susu work. Seven years of hardship among these people north of the Sierra Leone settlement had only proved to Renner the futility of the CMS's original choice. He sent a strongly worded dispatch to Pratt describing a 'godless' Freetown, a town prospering in everything except religion. 'Where', he asked, 'is the tabernacle of Zion?—who builds a house of God, a church for worshipping the good God who gives so much prosperity to the inhabitants'? Renner's letter implicitly challenged the assumptions of the CMS West African mission; why, he seemed to ask, ignore the town and concentrate only on the country to the north? His letter also allowed for a different sort of reply to the news from Freetown that Butscher had become temporary Colonial Chaplain.[62]

While Pratt refused to commit the CMS to a full change of policy, the amount of space devoted to a sympathetic understanding of the religious problems of the colony encouraged Butscher to think that it prefaced a complete reversal of the earlier insistence upon the maintenance of the Susu mission to the exclusion of Freetown. Pratt had particularly referred to the growing needs of the Liberated African population, and to the necessity of educating their children.

Thinking still in terms of Nyländer's earlier work, Pratt felt it was of primary importance for Butscher to become superintendent of schools in the young settlement. Instituting such an assault on the colony's difficulties, the C MS secretary hoped that 'the African Institution and Government itself . . . would aid us with money if we could bring all the Children of the Colony under a well-regulated system'. Such a plan would have decided advantages for the C MS in England. Pratt saw it as a way to enlist the support of more prominent private citizens to the mission's work in general. Thus far, they had remained aloof. Beyond that, Butscher's acceptance of the colonial chaplaincy on a temporary basis was important for it would provide 'a confidential medium of communication with our present and future settlements'. If Butscher had any doubts about Pratt's attitude toward his involvement in the religious and educational development of Sierra Leone, they were removed in Pratt's next communication which told the German missionary that the C MS secretary hoped he had understood the 'intimations' of his last letter and had accepted the government post.

Already impressed with the possibilities in Freetown, Butscher had of course accepted. Moreover, early in 1814 he became permanent Colonial Chaplain. Now confident that he was progressing in the right direction, Governor Maxwell asked the missionary society to send out a schoolmaster and promised that the Freetown government would pay the salary. The old formula thus revived: the missionary society provided the personnel and the government provided the money and the necessary buildings. Thus the mission and government together began the formal solution to the major problem of handling the Liberated Africans in Sierra Leone.[63]

Plans which emerged from the contact of Maxwell and Butscher in Freetown in 1813 did not reach fruition until after Edward Bickersteth's 1816 mission to the colony. Buttressed, however, with Pratt's encouragement of Butscher's remaining in Freetown, Maxwell aggressively moved ahead with plans to place the CMS in charge of the education of the Liberated African children. Early in 1814, he offered the society fifteen to twenty acres of land on which to build a schoolhouse, raising the amount to 100 acres later the same year. At the same time, Butscher's anxiety with the programme's slow progress assisted its eventual realization. He pleaded with Pratt to send out the schoolmaster at once if he had not already done so. He revealed that he had given his 'word, that the Church Missionary Society would supply this Peninsula with Schoolmasters and Missionaries, and should we delay or neglect this matter, I and the Society might lose our credit here and at home'.[64] Pratt's progress in London was thus further stimulated. Under his direction, the CMS began to extend its organization and initiated a separate school fund for Sierra Leone. Individuals subscribed £5 for the maintenance of one child for one year in exchange for the privilege of naming the child. Pleased with the early return, Pratt sent Butscher the first list of twenty-eight names in March 1814. He asked that the children should be placed under the supervision of the society, and Maxwell allowed them to be apprenticed to the missionaries at their various stations. Eventually, when the CMS school building was completed they were to be sent there. Butscher himself took four of the young children; six were sent across the estuary to live with Nyländer.[65]

Maxwell's own return to London late in 1814 encouraged further planning and closer cooperation. Soon after his arrival, the Sierra Leone Governor called on Pratt at the Society's Salisbury Square headquarters. There Pratt showed Maxwell more of the CMS's plans for the Freetown settlement. Among them was the dream of a new church building for the capital town. Encouraged by Maxwell, Pratt hoped to get the government to pay for it. If not, they would build the church themselves by private subscription, Pratt subsequently assured Butscher. But Maxwell did not drop in at Salisbury Square only to hear of the Society's plans. He had some plans of his own to tell.

He asked Pratt to undertake a formal mission to the colony itself, to go beyond the offer of providing for some Liberated African schoolchildren. Two things were foremost in the Governor's mind. First, 10,000 Liberated Africans were under British jurisdiction in Sierra Leone and, as he emphasized to Pratt, most were heathens. Secondly, the recent termination of the Napoleonic Wars signalled the resumption of the slave trade in West Africa. This meant that the Liberated African population of Freetown would surely rise. The exchange of ideas and hopes encouraged Pratt to press ahead with the plans in his own Home Committee, that group of crucial decision-makers which directed the missionary society's activities.

He soon secured their approval of the plan to form an establishment at Freetown.[66] Government-mission cooperation took another important step forward when, early in 1815, Whitehall agreed to finance the proposed CMS church building in the colony. Together with the school to be established on the plot donated by the government on Leicester Mountain, with Butscher as its superintendent,[67] the church edifice would symbolize effectively the CMS commitment to the colony and its freed slave population.

CONTINUING COOPERATION UNDER GOVERNOR MACCARTHY

So advanced were the society's plans and determination that they were unaffected by Maxwell's own resignation as Governor while in London. His successor, Lieutenant Colonel Charles MacCarthy, was well disposed to both Butscher and the society after the earlier events at Goree.[68] Indeed, MacCarthy developed government-mission cooperation to its finest level. He based his own particular contribution, the development of an effective system of local government, on the groundwork carefully laid out by Butscher and Maxwell before him. Most important of all, MacCarthy's ten year tenure, the longest of any governorship in nineteenth-century Sierra Leone, provided stability to the colony's development which had hitherto been missing. Like those who had governed before him, MacCarthy too realized the central importance of settling the Liberated African population comfortably into the Sierra Leone experiment. Building on the work of his predecessor, therefore, MacCarthy moved ahead with the arrangements made by Maxwell both in Freetown and London.

It was MacCarthy who gave Butscher the 1,000 acres on Leicester Mountain for the CMS.[69] Pratt enthusiastically wrote the German missionary that the school was to be the central headquarters for the society's work in the colony.[70] Named 'The Christian Institution of Sierra Leone', it was envisaged as 'a noble establishment . . . [calling] forth the blessings of the Christian world', by Pratt. 'In short, [the Institution], established and supported by the British Church Missionary Society, for the maintenance and education of African children, and for the diffusion among the Natives of Christianity and of useful knowledge would be an honour to Britain and to the Christian name, and an incalculable blessing to Africa'.[71] Pratt's message impressed Governor MacCarthy, who assured Pratt, after watching Butscher's work on Leicester Mountain progress, 'that I shall look on as the happiest moment of my life the moment I can see these Children placed under the Society's immediate protection.'[72]

Flattering words exchanged between the colony's governor and the society's secretary, however, did not in themselves solve the problem of settling the Liberated Africans. MacCarthy grew concerned when the CMS did not close its Susu mission and devote its complete attention to the Freetown settlement. He knew that the job in Sierra Leone alone was sufficient to tax the society's growing resources. The Susu mission continued to cause the CMS difficulty and to dominate its thoughts. For as the slave trade revived, problems at CMS stations in the north grew more severe. The Revd. Renner's Bashia settlement was burned. Outbreaks among the Susu confirmed the missionary's worst fears; they had failed in their endeavour and were unwanted. Fearful of further trouble and interested in receiving the society's undivided attention in Sierra Leone, Governor MacCarthy prohibited the society from transporting any more children to the northern mission stations. Renner himself virtually fled to Freetown and settled in a newly purchased house. He wrote Pratt encouraging the society to concentrate its entire effort on the Liberated Africans. Fear increased the tension among missionaries outside Freetown, which in turn led to almost incessant bickering as charges of drunkenness and profiteering were exchanged among them. In a wise move, Butscher suggested that the society send out someone from London to assess their work and to end the quarrelling.[73]

EDWARD BICKERSTETH AND THE 1816 MISSION TO SIERRA LEONE

The parent committee in London quickly decided to send Edward Bickersteth on this mission to Sierra Leone. Renner received the first indication of the plan when Pratt wrote that the society was going to 'send over a confidential friend . . . who may visit every Settlement, and report his views on the state of the whole Mission'. London had become particularly concerned over the increased cost of the mission in the north. News of Mrs. Butscher's death in Freetown led Pratt to postpone Bickersteth's journey; it would await more favourable reports on health conditions in Sierra Leone.[74] There were also considerable arrangements which had to be made before the relatively unknown Bickersteth departed early in 1816.

In selecting Bickersteth to undertake the mission, the parent committee went outside its own staff and picked someone whose only prior connection with the CMS had been as the founder of the Norwich branch of the society's supporters. He was a barrister and not an ordained clergyman until the very eve of his departure, when he insisted that not to be ordained would seriously jeopardize his study of the mission and its clergymen. Bickersteth's rise to prominence is a typical story of the Britain of the industrial nineteenth century. His life story, published by his son-in-law in 1852, is very much the tale of a self-made man.

His climb through the strata of English society exemplified those very qualities which in themselves became socially worshipped as the nineteenth century wore on. He had left school at the age of fourteen because of the large number of children in the family and worked for six years at the General Post Office in London in a minor position. During this period he began to read for the law and eventually entered the profession '. . . because it seemed the only path of advancement open to him'.[75] His entrance in 1812 into a relatively prosperous legal partnership with his brother-in-law in Norwich allowed him to develop his interest in Christian missions. His fervent belief combined with a certain genius for organization to produce the first successful local branch of the CMS just at the time when Pratt in London sought a more solid base in Britain. Thus, Bickersteth was noticed in Salisbury Square and when, in 1815, the CMS began to search for a new assistant secretary whose first charge would be to undertake the study mission to Sierra Leone, it was natural for him to be selected. With some difficulty the society met Bickersteth's terms, and he received priest's orders from the Bishop of Gloucester on 21 December 1815, only eleven days following his having been ordained deacon by the Bishop of Norwich. Leaving London in January, Bickersteth was told by the Society to examine the state of the mission and to suggest plans for its more efficient operation.[76]

When the Revd. Edward Bickersteth arrived in early March 1816, CMS work in the Freetown area was restricted to the new school for Liberated Africans at Leicester Mountain under the Revd. Butscher. The official visitor stopped in Freetown for a week before moving on to the Susu mission in the north. During the first week he met Governor MacCarthy, who naturally pressed his views that the CMS should concentrate its main efforts on the Sierra Leone peninsula. Impressed by the Governor and his plans for the colony, Bickersteth noted in his journal that it 'appears . . . very important to mark the indications of a providential leading. Among these I consider the protection of an established government, the facility and safety of intercourse with the people, the economy attending the mission, and the number that may be easily gathered together'.[77] In short, Bickersteth noted all of those qualities which Freetown provided and the Susu country did not. He wrote Pratt at the end of his first week that 'this Colony is the spot where we must spend our chief strength'.[78]

The official visitor's five weeks in the north did little to change his initial impressions of Freetown. It remained, in his mind, an open field, ready to be developed by the CMS. In contrast to this prospect, Bickersteth had to turn to the frustrations and failures of the Susu mission. While in the Susu country, he closed the Bashia settlement, moved one missionary, the Revd. Wenzel, to Kissy, a village three miles east of Freetown on the colony peninsula, and cleared up the many charges and counter-charges of the dissatisfied missionaries. He found little to show for the ten years of effort expended on the mission in the north. Returning to Freetown in late April, his impressions could only echo the earlier thoughts of the Revd. Renner about the utter futility of the first CMS venture in the mission field.

Almost at once he wrote Pratt that Freetown cried out for attention.[79] He remained in the settlement for the next six weeks, familiarizing himself with the area and its problems. Much of the time he stayed with Butscher on Leicester Mountain. Together with Kenneth Macaulay, he gathered important information on the Liberated African villages outside Freetown as well as some on the town itself. With a background of massive and thunderous clouds signalling the late beginning of the rainy season, Bickersteth finally sailed for England on 7 June 1816.[80]

Soon after his arrival in London he presented his formal report to the CMS committee. Although it had an important effect on the future of the CMS mission to West Africa, the report did not, surprisingly considering what he had seen, suggest the abandonment of the Susu mission. MacCarthy later criticized him for this omission. What Bickersteth did write about was the situation in the Sierra Leone settlement. He drew a vivid contrast between the pleasant and organized regularity of the

Freetown of the Nova Scotian settler, and what seemed to him the utter disorder of the Liberated African villages. The plain, grass-roofed mud and wattle huts of the villages compared unfavourably with the affluent stone and timber homes he observed in the main town. The simple, winding bush-paths of the rural areas did not match the planned eighteenth-century order of the streets of Freetown. In view of such contrasts, Bickersteth told the CMS that the Liberated Africans of Sierra Leone clearly remained outside any plan to civilize and Christianize the African.[81]

He applauded Governor MacCarthy's efforts to deal with the problems of the recaptives. Under him the Liberated Africans received clothing, food, and housing. Next, Bickersteth turned to the lack of Christianity among the newcomers. Again the villages stood in marked contrast to the religious activity noted in Freetown. By the time of his departure, regular contact with the CMS was available only at two villages, Kissy and Leicester. In reviewing the other rural settlements, the recent visitor left no doubt about their lack of proper direction and the vast amount of work that lay before the CMS. To him the society alone could fulfil the original aims of the colony's founders by providing Christian education for those growing numbers of representatives of many different African cultures who had been freed in Freetown. In this way the society would ensure that the Word would be spread throughout the continent. Bickersteth's report paralleled in tone the appraisal sent to Pratt after his first week in the colony. Two-thirds of the 10,000 people inhabiting the settlement in 1816 lived outside the main town. The peninsula therefore, Bickersteth concluded, 'calls for our chief attention and strength. . . . Here we have all the advantages of teaching in perfect safety, those heathens who feel under an obligation for the temporal benefits which they have received; and who . . . seem anxious to receive Christian Teachers'. The CMS accepted his report and agreed to undertake, with government support, the education of the Liberated African population.[82]

In approving of the Bickersteth report, the CMS did little more than increase the scope of their responsibilities. Long before the Bickersteth mission, Pratt, Maxwell, and Butscher had laid the foundations for the education of Liberated African children in the Leicester Mountain Institution. The acceptance of Bickersteth's report served only to increase the level of the CMS commitment to the colony and to focus more sharply on the problems of the settlement. An impartial observer, he simply confirmed what men like Butscher and Renner had been writing from the outset. If the CMS thought that the major solution to the recaptive problem in Sierra Leone lay in a Christian education, the Governor who had impressed Bickersteth, MacCarthy, certainly saw that the solution was far more complex than that.

THE MACCARTHY SOLUTION: THE PARISH PLAN

When Bickersteth sailed from Freetown harbour, he carried with him an official dispatch from MacCarthy which he delivered to Lord Bathurst in London. The letter contained MacCarthy's own plan for organizing the Liberated Africans, the plan under which the CMS would work not only as educators but also as administrators. Its long-term significance was far greater than Bickersteth's own report. MacCarthy's provided the first coherent and successful system of local administration for the whole colony.

Presenting for the first time a consciously thought-out scheme, MacCarthy showed his own genius as a planner. For although it revealed how the Governor benefited greatly from the long-developing process of government-mission cooperation, and although he borrowed heavily from the plans of former administrators, his proposals to Lord Bathurst clearly bore his own stamp. MacCarthy defined an organizational structure for the colony which dealt systematically with problems most urgently pressing for solution. Not unimportantly, it was a scheme which he would be able to supervise personally during the extended tenure of his administration.

Two considerations dominated MacCarthy's thinking. First,

he wanted to introduce a specific experiment in civilizing the Liberated Africans. Secondly, he recognized the need to make the increasing numbers of recaptives more useful to themselves and to the colony. Their daily increase, he noted, had retarded rather than advanced his earlier attempts to integrate them into the culturally more sophisticated population of Freetown. Between July 1815 and May 1816 alone, more than 2,500 newcomers had settled in the colony. Such an increase necessitated immediate steps to solve the long-existing problem of settling the recaptives, the majority of whom continued to fall outside the provisions of the original Slave Trade Abolition Act.[83] Only with a solution could MacCarthy or any other governor improve the colony.

In MacCarthy's view, the villages had failed to achieve their proper function. They lacked Christianity, but more practically, 'none of them raised a sufficient crop of Rice or Cassava for the support of its inhabitants [who] in a great measure received their maintenance by occasional employment at King's Works, and [by] bringing on their backs to the Market a small quantity of wood or lime'. Moreover, the numbers receiving a year's quota of food and clothing—the standard under MacCarthy— increased so quickly that the very continuation of the policy was threatened. The Governor found it imperative that those freed by the British Vice-Admiralty Court be put into a position of self-sufficiency as quickly as possible after their arrival. It was important and welcome that the CMS had agreed to begin its school at Leicester Mountain for Liberated African children, but it was far more significant, the Governor noted, that the recaptives themselves sought improvement.[84]

More had to be done than to open a new school. The adult population as well as some children not under the missionary group's care, needed immediate attention. Earlier MacCarthy had settled them into the villages and had 'devoted [a] great part of [his] time attempting to give them ideas of European Civilization'. Since he lacked a surveyor he had been hampered greatly in his efforts to provide the newcomers with properly defined allotments. Still, he had been able to extend and form four new villages. Basing his observation on this experience, the Governor wrote Bathurst in 1816, 'I am thoroughly convinced that in order to civilize the Captured Negroes and to induce [them] . . . to apply to agriculture it would be desirable to divide the Peninsula in Parishes, settling a Clergyman in each. I would propose to erect a dwelling House for each Curate with a Chapel which lasts for a number of years and would answer the purpose of a School Room [and to make] . . . small allotments of ground to each Settler with reserve for Public purposes'.[85] MacCarthy further proposed to pay the clergyman's annual salary which would be raised to £200 or £250.[86] According to MacCarthy's plan, the clergyman would be the government manager in his assigned village. He would represent the central government in a newly-defined structure of local administration. The Governor estimated that at least six clergymen were needed at once, but predicted that the number would have to be increased. Benefits would accrue from a careful application of his new plans. Increased educational training, particularly of a technical nature, would guarantee that future construction projects could be undertaken by locally trained carpenters, masons, sawyers, and shinglemakers. Then too, MacCarthy felt sure that the time would come when the trained Liberated Africans themselves would be responsible for directing the integration of the new arrivals in the Freetown settlement. Both results, the Governor promised would greatly reduce the expense of administration and eventually produce a considerable saving for the British Government.

The essence of the MacCarthy plan for Sierra Leone was its simple provision of an efficient system of local administration. With such a system the Governor solved the problem which had begun with the arrival of the first freed slaves in 1808—the need to make them self-supporting and contributing members of the struggling new colony. No doubt fully aware of the problems presented to them by a succession of colony administrators, and impressed with the thoroughness of MacCarthy's analysis as well as with the apparent simplicity of his solution, Whitehall readily approved of his plan. The Church Missionary Society agreed to the essential participation of its clergymen in the new system of local administration.

The plan as adopted in London in 1816 represented a long process of evolution. In this process, the instance of early and continuing cooperation on an informal basis between missionaries Renner, Nyländer, and Butscher on the one hand, and the succession of governors on the other, was of paramount importance. The essentials of cooperation, including the idea of using missionary personnel, had emerged long before the mission of Edward Bickersteth. What the former Norwich lawyer had contributed was his confirmatory observation and approval of an already existing procedure. His significant contribution, however, lay in adding his stature and objectivity to the argument in the London committee of the CMS that the society should enter wholeheartedly into the Sierra Leone scene. To MacCarthy himself fell the crucial job of giving earlier cooperation definite direction; he evolved the concept of cooperation between mission and government into a workable administrative system. Following on London's approval, he defined the parishes and appointed a missionary to each. The parish system of local government continued to operate during the remaining eight years of MacCarthy's tenure, and in modified form for much of the century. Through it the Governor freed the colony's government from the narrow restrictions and frustrations of the Abolition Act. Moreover, he succeeded in providing a regular and inclusive system of local government, and bringing the major focus of the Church Missionary Society to the colony. The success of this policy in the 1820's could be said to be a monument to Governor MacCarthy. More precisely, however, coming as it did after eight trying years of experiment and failure, the ultimate solution stood as a monument to time-honoured English empiricism, a faith in which MacCarthy, Butscher, Maxwell, and Bickersteth were only the most ardent disciples.

Street in Freetown

III

MacCarthy: Years of Success

The thought and events of the eighteenth century continued to influence the Sierra Leone colony long into the nineteenth. Conceived originally in the minds of men who perceived the world to be rational and orderly and who saw in the new settlement the answer to a serious eighteenth-century social problem, the colony's development was determined largely by the subsequent events of eighteenth-century revolution in America and Europe. The presence of the Nova Scotian settlers resulted from one of the century's political revolutions. The choice of Maxwell's successor, Charles MacCarthy, was not unconnected with the revolutionary upheavals in France during the last decade of the century. The new leader was secured not because of his particular knowledge of Africa nor for his ability to handle colonial affairs. He was simply an outcast from Europe, a former participant in the monarchist cause in France. Significantly, his remarkable service to Sierra Leone resulted from the fact that there was no place for a Charles MacCarthy either in a republican France or in an England ripe for reform. Born in 1768 to a French father and an Irish mother, MacCarthy had been brought up in France. He had joined the French army at the age of eighteen, but with the collapse of Louis XVI's cause and the beginning of the Terror, he had fled to Ireland. There he secured a commission in the British army and, after a brief period of fighting in Flanders, was sent to the West Indies in 1795. He remained in service in the New World until his recall and appointment in 1812 as military commander with the rank of lieutenant-colonel at the British-occupied French station at Senegal. When Governor Maxwell left Freetown to go on leave in 1814, MacCarthy moved his headquarters to Sierra Leone where he became acting governor during the early part of Maxwell's leave. When Maxwell resigned in London, Mac-Carthy succeeded him as governor in 1815.[1]

MacCarthy had not revealed himself to be a particularly spectacular figure prior to becoming Governor of Sierra Leone. His career had been varied and he was regarded as a generally capable officer. Precedent dictated his succession. All three of the previous Crown governors had been military men, and Maxwell, his immediate predecessor, also had been the military governor of Senegal before becoming governor at Freetown. When Maxwell resigned, MacCarthy was simply the most available and the highest ranking officer for the position. Once in office, he proved to be a brilliant administrator. On this fact alone rests his reputation as the ablest governor in nineteenth-century Sierra Leone. His early success in securing the agreement between the British government and the Church Missionary Society to guarantee the effective handling of the Liberated African population indicated his capabilities. Further, the development of the corresponding parish plan of local government assured for MacCarthy a special place in the history of the colony's development. With its effective application, success became the watchword of the MacCarthy era. This proved crucial in a colony which had not lacked plans in the past, but had suffered progressively from their lack of successful application. The success of both the CMS agreement and the parish plan provided early evidence of the Governor's forcefulness. The driving force of his personality allowed him to deal with the day to day problems of administration as well as to secure the necessary financial grants from the British government in London to effect his impressive plans. This was the important difference that separated MacCarthy from both his predecessors and his successors.

PARLIAMENTARY GRANTS, NEW BUILDING, AND EXPANSION

The success MacCarthy had in getting Parliamentary grants for Sierra Leone in itself marks him as an unusual figure in the colony's history before 1816. Unlike the others, he won the financial support of Downing Street. The total expense of administering the colony in 1815 was about £29,000. The next year, 1816, it rose to £41,000. Such expenses were covered by regular Treasury grants from London. The grants continued to rise steadily, reaching the high level of £95,000 for the year 1823. MacCarthy's personal role in this financial expansion was clear in 1825, the first full year following the end of his administration, when total expenditure dropped from £77,000 in 1824, to £39,000. The bulk of the new money sent to Sierra Leone at MacCarthy's request went directly into the growing Liberated African Department, the new government office charged with handling the affairs of the recaptives. Total expenditures for the new arrivals rose from £10,849 in 1815 to the high level of £59,629 in 1823, before dropping off to £19,091 in 1825. The annual average expenditure for Liberated Africans between 1816 and 1824 was £40,482.[2]

The increased expenditure that did not go directly for Liberated African clothes and rations went into an extensive building programme throughout the colony. In a real sense, MacCarthy built Freetown during the ten years of his administration. One missionary observed of the Governor in 1822, 'You know he is fond of buildings.' Under the Governor's consideration at the time was the consolidation of four Liberated African villages into two for the purposes of greater efficiency and economy. MacCarthy's Chief Superintendent of the Liberated African Department favoured the move, but, the missionary continued, MacCarthy 'bites his nails on account of the buildings which he has erected'.[3] Initially, MacCarthy secured an entirely unprecedented £5,000 annual building grant for the colony. The new English chaplain who arrived late in 1816 brought Treasury approval for MacCarthy's plans to erect new churches in the villages. By October 1817, however, the Exchequer complained to the Colonial Secretary that the energetic governor had exceeded his annual grant for building by £1,000.[4] MacCarthy's only response was to point out that the £5,000 was clearly insufficient for the needs of the colony. He requested, in addition to the new churches, a governor's home, and government quarters for the chief colonial surgeon. He asked that London double the building grant, and in 1819 the Lords of the Treasury provided him with the necessary £10,000. MacCarthy immediately announced plans to finish the church already under construction in Freetown and to begin building quarters for the colonial secretary, the chief engineer, the superintendent of the Liberated African Department, the chaplain, and the collector of customs. 1820 found none of these projects completed and so the Governor simply requested a three year grant of £10,000 annually. He assured London that he would reduce the requests to £2,500 per year after 1822. The Treasury approved, bowing again to the Governor's powers of persuasion. But in spite of the promise, MacCarthy's buildings were not completed by 1822; again he requested a three year extension at the £10,000 figure and again the Treasury approved. MacCarthy's final building grant lasted one year after the unforeseen end of his administration in January 1824.[5]

London's ready acquiescence to MacCarthy's requests came as a result of their realization that the Governor's buildings were essential to the effective working of his system of local administration. Much of the building took place in the rural villages, forming an integral part of his parish plan. A church, a school, and a house for the village superintendent were built at Regent. School buildings and a hospital rose on Leicester Mountain. School and superintendents' quarters were built at Gloucester and Leicester, and schools alone at Leopold and Kissy. The acquisition of more colonial territory and increased numbers of Liberated African arrivals necessitated the organization of new government villages at Kent and York along the colony's Atlantic coast and at Wellington, Hastings, and Waterloo along the eastern or interior side of the colony mountains in 1819. Each new village created the need for more government building. Moreover, the moving of the CMS Institution from Leicester Mountain to Regent in the same year called for the provision of additional school facilities.[6]

The intensity of the building programme brought increased population to Freetown and caused the town to expand. In 1816 the government bought some unused farm land immediately west of the town from Eli Ackim, a Nova Scotian settler. Mac-Carthy settled the increasing number of Kru who came up the coast on this new land. The Kru provided early Freetown with its work force, and thus facilitated the easier movement of the Liberated Africans into middle class positions as traders and merchants. With the settlement of the Kru in what came to be known as Kru Town, MacCarthy extended the western limits of the town to include the new section.[7] He also touched some extremely sensitive nerves among the Nova Scotian community. In buying the land from Ackim, the Governor forced the Nova Scotian to sell. Ackim entered into a heated defence of his right to retain his property, indicating the increased value of land in the town and the fact that the Nova Scotian settlers had invested heavily in property. In Ackim's arguments with Mac-Carthy, the old settler distrust of the government again reared its head. During the second decade of the nineteenth century this distrust was based on the belief that the new immigrant groups were securing too much governmental favour at the expense of the Nova Scotians. Although the Kru represented the immediate threat to Ackim, the words of his defence were to be repeated later by Nova Scotians seeking to condemn Liberated African purchase of Freetown property. MacCarthy's need for a steady and reliable work force to construct the numerous new buildings was unimportant to Ackim. To him the establishment of Kru Town meant simply that the government had robbed his children of the land that was to be theirs, and had given it to the 'thieving Kroomen'.[8]

Like many Nova Scotians, Ackim was a trader. Land in

Freetown represented the wise investment of savings earned in commerce. This was as true for the Nova Scotians in 1816 as it was to become for the Liberated Africans themselves less than a generation later. Land was the only bank known in early Freetown. As such it produced increasingly high dividends. This was especially true during the building boom of MacCarthy's administration. His construction programme brought a new level of prosperity to the town and its surrounding territory. The boom was reflected in rapid rises in the value of property. One missionary paid £36 for five acres of land outside Freetown in 1813. Three years later Ackim was offered £25 *per acre* for his land by a jury empanelled to evaluate it. Property inside the town also rose in value, and consequently so did rents. Butscher, the CMS missionary, bought a house and lot for £240 in 1813 and found that the value of such property had increased to £300 within two years. MacCarthy himself complained to Bathurst that the rent on his house rose from £250 to £350 in 1816. An advertisement in the *Royal Gazette* indicated most explicitly the increased value of Freetown property. Offering for sale a stone house on Wilberforce Street in central Freetown, the owner assured any prospective buyer that the property was an 'Excellent Opportunity for the secure and profitable Investment of Capital'.[9]

MacCarthy added to the territorial responsibility of the Freetown government in 1819 in an effort to eliminate any potential boundary disputes and to secure additional space for the increasing population. He acquired the left bank of the Bance river east of Freetown, land which included the low-lying plateau on which he would organize the new villages of Hastings and Waterloo. The following year the Governor secured the Banana Islands from the Caulkers.[10] In addition to the regular arrival of Liberated Africans and Kru labourers, the colony's population increased further in 1819 with the landing of nearly 100 former slaves from Barbados and over 1,000 discharged soldiers from the Second and Fourth West Indian regiments. MacCarthy settled the ex-soldiers in the outlying villages where their regular pensions added to the growth of a money economy and served continually to mark them out as a separate group among the dominant Liberated African population. Except for their relatively greater prosperity, however, the disbanded members of the West Indian regiments lived a life not unlike that of other rural Sierra Leoneans in the nineteenth century.[11]

FREETOWN LIFE

With new and dynamically successful leadership, increased government grants, intense building and greater employment, the consequent rise in the value of property and an increasingly diverse population, Freetown had grown both more prosperous and more cosmopolitan. Houses were larger and the variety of architectural styles began to reveal pronounced differences among the social classes of the town. The Parliamentary Commission of 1827, reporting at the end of the period of Mac-Carthian prosperity, spoke of four general *classes* of houses, representing four distinct classes in the population. At the lowest point in the social scale were the mud and wattle huts of the newly arrived immigrant groups, next those in which rough clapboard replaced the mud, thirdly, frame houses constructed entirely of squared timber with clapboard sides and shingled roofs, and finally, the houses of all stone construction. Since the latter two classes of houses were occupied chiefly by the older segments of the town's population, the Nova Scotians, the Maroons, and the Europeans, they naturally set the standard to which the lower classes aspired.[12]

In this period of prosperity the townspeople often turned to new pastimes and pleasures for recreation. Although the class structure could be easily perceived, mobility was not artificially curtailed. Classes as well as races mixed and participated in the town's social life. An observer of the period wrote many years later that Governor MacCarthy's 'hospitality was extended to persons of *all shades and colours*'.[13] Gala dinners were common. Horse-racing was a regular sporting activity. Many of the individual modes of entertainment were incorporated into an annual extravaganza, the Freetown Fair.

The Fair of 1819 was held in mid-January, at the height of the dry season, so that Africans from neighbouring lands as well as traders from the interior could attend more conveniently. At noon on the first day of the week's celebrations, the mayor and aldermen proceeded through the town on horseback, led by the resounding notes of the Royal Africa Corps' buglers and followed by a 'cavalcade of gentlemen'. The mayor proclaimed the beginning of the festivities from every street corner. At 3 p.m. he honoured the town's gentry with an elegant luncheon. On the following day a canoe race by the Kru in Freetown harbour provided the central attraction. First prize of an eight dollar hat went to the head Kruman of the Chief Justice while the second prize, a six dollar gun, was won by a Kru in the employ of Commissary-General Lefevre.

The entire week was filled with magnificent feasts and exciting sports events. There were pony races through the town and into the surrounding countryside, wrestling matches, a traditional rowing event with participants from ships in the harbour, and two days of horse-racing at the town's race-course. A packed and tense crowd watched on the fifth day as Lefevre rode around the course in a white surrey to announce the Grand Horse-race, the main event. Amidst thunderous cheering Kenneth Macaulay's entry won and the owner received the ten-guinea Governor's Cup. The main event the following day, the Sweepstakes, was won to the crowd's delight by Governor MacCarthy's Arabian, Sidi Ely, ridden by Surgeon Nicol. At the close of the week's festivities, the Governor gave a grand dinner in the large rooms of the Commissariat. Forty-five distinguished citizens joined MacCarthy and his senior government officials at the banquet table. Lefevre and several others from the government served as stewards. The splendour of the meal, the music and the patriotic toasts set a new standard for such events in Freetown.[14]

The gaiety of such occasions was considerably enhanced by

the presence of splendidly attired women, mistresses of the European officials. Many of the officials were bachelors. Those with wives often left them in England; there were rarely more than five or six European women in the colony at one time during the early nineteenth century. One Sierra Leone historian of the nineteenth century observed that 'the customs of the place . . . effectively preclude a white lady from accompanying her husband to the mansions of the unmarried man, where the coloured or black mistress might not show deference.' Generally the mistress was quite an integral and apparently accepted member of the bachelor European's household in early Freetown. The same historian gave evidence of the respect shown to the fifteen-year-old mistress of a later governor when she died in childbirth. The governor ordered a full dress funeral attended by all the chief government functionaries 'to give public pomp to her funeral'. A large and handsome monument stood over her grave at the Settler's Burial Ground.[15]

MacCarthy's mistress was Hannah Hayes, his housekeeper. Described in later years as a woman who had led the 'worldly life', Miss Hayes was housekeeper in turn to the Governor, to Walter Lewis, later Colonial Secretary, and to Nathan Isaacs, a wealthy European merchant. She bore MacCarthy one son for whom he provided in his will, several children for Lewis, and two sons for Isaacs.[16] In each household she performed the duties of wife and mother. She directed MacCarthy's home quite capably, and when he was killed in 1824, she moved eventually to undertake the same duties for Lewis. The missionaries usually took their housekeepers as wives in the more formal sense, having one of their colleagues perform the marriage service. For others, however, such a ceremony was not felt necessary. The housekeeper simply assumed the role of the wife of the head of the household.

The system caused very little difficulty. MacCarthy himself was generally not criticized for his relations with Miss Hayes. He only came into conflict with the missionaries when it was time to baptize his son. Even this was accomplished with only minor pangs of conscience on the part of the performing minister and some inconsequential criticism on the part of the Colonial Chaplain. The accommodating clergyman was the dutiful and accomplished Revd. William A. B. Johnson, the German Lutheran CMS missionary who was the superintendent of the mountain village of Regent. Johnson's increased duties at Regent had necessitated his purchase of a larger house costing him £45. Happily MacCarthy at this time saw fit to award Johnson an extra stipend in appreciation of duties he had undertaken at nearby Gloucester village during the previous three months. Neatly, the sum came to £50. The payment to Johnson, however, irritated the Colonial Chaplain, the Revd. Flood, who had had his eyes set on the additional stipend. Undoubtedly with the favour in mind, a few weeks later MacCarthy invited Johnson to the highest of expatriate rituals: Saturday lunch. Soon after Johnson had arrived, MacCarthy asked if he would do him the honour of baptizing his son. Johnson initially refused and suggested that Flood should be asked first. But the Governor insisted. He pulled back some curtains to show that everything was in readiness. Johnson 'replied that I did not approve of such a way of living to which he answered if the Child was to suffer for this'. The minister. was then seized with the fear that MacCarthy would hinder 'the progress of Religion in Sierra Leone' if he continued to refuse, and so he baptized the child. His defence to his London superiors was, 'anyone else would have done the same!' On hearing of the affair, the enraged Revd. Flood told Johnson that he had betrayed him for £50 just as Judas had his Lord for thirty pieces of silver. Although Flood threatened to 'expose' Johnson in England, he apparently never did.[17]

Actually, during the superabundant times of Governor MacCarthy, there were few who chose to judge the morality of the administrators by harsh standards. The exuberant development of the town was evident in the many diverse manifestations of its life. New social institutions such as freemasonry were introduced which made the town even closer to its European prototype. And although the Nova Scotian still tended to describe himself in letters to England as 'poor and oppressed', keen observers of the scene pointed out the deception. Most English goods could be purchased in Freetown at prices which were as cheap as those in England. The economy offered sufficient rewards to inspire a group of Nova Scotians to form a company of merchants in order to enter the wholesale trade.[18]

With greater prosperity came greater commercial abuse. Partly because expansion was not immediately followed by more resolute enforcement of necessary regulatory measures, the town's leaders were shocked to discover that most weights and measures in Freetown were shorting the customers. A correspondent to the *Royal Gazette* who signed himself 'Hard to Believe' suggested in 1817 that the merchants used separate weights for buying and for selling. The following year the mayor published a list of twenty-five merchants who had deficient weights and measures. Many had committed multiple offences.[19]

Other abuses reflected the tensions associated with the diversity of the population. Fights between individuals of differing tribal origin as well as several cases of arson were reported. An alleged case of cannibalism took place in one mountain village in 1818. The accused denied his confession in court, however, and although the Crown Attorney won the conviction, the Governor sought the advice of the home government. Since the whole case was clouded in questions of faulty interpretation and confused understanding, the Prince Regent acting for George III granted the accused a pardon.[20] The employer-servant relationship in Sierra Leone was also subject to abuse. At the General Sessions in March 1819, the Chief Justice requested new regulations which would govern both parties. The employer had to be kept from taking the law into his own hands; fighting and stripping had to be prohibited. Servants must be prevented from leaving without notice, an abuse which they always saved for particularly crucial times of the year such as Fair Week. The Chief Justice's warning was consistently and tragically ignored by Commissary-General Lefevre. His servants repeatedly complained to the government about Lefevre's abusive treatment. Finally Lefevre met a violent death in May 1820. In the process of beating one of his Kru servants, the gun with which he was inflicting the punishment fired and killed him instantly with a bullet through the heart.[21]

Not all of the grievances were so spectacular. The bulk of them were at worst simply annoying. The Revd. Collier, the Colonial Chaplain in 1818, wrote to London pleading, 'Please send some Locks, padlocks, not the common ones for boys can pick them with ease.' Hannah Kilham, the Quaker schoolteacher, reported the preponderance of dogs in Freetown. She was disturbed because they were often starved and neglected, and annoyed because their running and barking in packs at night kept her awake. While being shown through a merchant's new house she noticed that 'among other parts of the furniture he had a barrel of stones near his lodging room to throw at the dogs in the night.'[22] Missionaries complained about the sinfulness they found in Freetown. Moreover, their attempts to revive religion there were often frustrated. Freetonians would not attend meetings the way people in the villages did. In order to have a successful Bible meeting in Freetown, one missionary had to bring his own congregation with him from his mountain village.[23]

But abuses were observed not only by the expatriate missionary or official. The old settlers of the town themselves deplored numerous little changes and irritations. A writer signing himself 'Livery-man' called the attention of newspaper readers to an evil in Freetown that he observed was 'rapidly increasing.' Originally, he noted, the town had been laid out with the greatest regularity. Until recently it had been well maintained. But now, the writer reported of his travels around the town, one could find a staircase projecting on to one street, a piazza dangerously overhanging a second, and part of a house built on a third. Irregularities of this sort, he charged, were innumerable; fences were found projecting into streets 'which appear as if intended to represent the contorsions [*sic*] and writhings of a wounded serpent.' Streets were continually being choked with rubbish and stones, and the ruts were considered a menace to those who walked the streets at night. Periodically the town authorities ordered the streets cleared of all nuisances including weeds, which nearly always abounded. In 1820 MacCarthy ordered the mayor to act, pointing out that the health of the town depended upon the cleanliness of its streets.[24]

THE LIBERATED AFRICANS AND THE RURAL VILLAGES

Against this background of new prosperity and its consequent problems in Freetown, Governor MacCarthy turned his attention primarily to the Liberated Africans living in the surrounding villages. Between 1815 and 1820 he devoted his main energies to the application of the parish plan of local administration. Initially this necessitated the establishment or official recognition of new villages. Prior to 1815 there were only three villages recognized by the central government: Leicester, founded in 1809; Wilberforce in 1810; and Regent, two years later. MacCarthy established government authority at ten more villages before 1820. The process began with Gloucester and Kissy in 1816, and ended with the three outlying villages, Wellington, Hastings, and Waterloo, all founded in 1819. Although the last three were intended mainly for the disbanded soldiers, two of them quickly acquired a majority population of Liberated Africans.[25] The third, Hastings, was undoubtedly predominantly Liberated African from the beginning. The names given to the villages in all but one case, Kissy, referred to a famous English historical event, an important English city or county, or a prominent English individual. The marriage of Princess Charlotte to Prince Leopold of Saxe-Coburg in 1817, for instance, occasioned the naming of two mountain villages. When Charlotte died a year later and thereby rendered Leopold

93

no longer of importance in England, MacCarthy renamed the village of Leopold, Bathurst, after the Secretary of State in London.[26]

The central government provided Liberated Africans in each village with food, clothing, and various utensils which were assumed necessary for the new life in the country. By providing these necessities, MacCarthy hoped to ease the settling in process and to make the recaptive a productive member of the settlement. By 1819 the Liberated Africans received a regular government ration of rice, palm oil, and salt. Soon after he became governor, MacCarthy began to order the clothing and utensils directly from England rather than purchasing them from local merchants. Long order lists were sent periodically to the Colonial Office requesting such items as men's cotton shirts and women's petticoats, woollen blankets and girls' printed frocks, tin soup pans and pewter plates, and iron spoons and large iron pots. As the training of Liberated Africans progressed, carpenters' and blacksmiths' tools were requisitioned as well as large iron tanks for palm oil and sacks for corn. By 1823 well over two-thirds of the recaptive population was receiving direct government assistance of this nature. Only at Regent was over one-third of the population self-supporting. At three other villages, Wellington, Hastings, and York, the entire population was dependent on the government.[27]

The clothing and provisions did not always serve the purposes intended by the government. As early as 1815, MacCarthy sponsored legislation which was designed to prohibit the trading of commodities given to the Liberated Africans. But even though the informer was promised a sizeable percentage of the £5 fine for each offence,[28] the ordinance proved difficult to enforce. The goods came to the Liberated Africans free. Therefore, any return in trading represented a profit, especially when something more useful could be obtained. The local merchants were especially eager to buy since prices asked by the Liberated Africans were usually below the cost price of the articles in England. Thus the government assistance programme did more to stimulate trading in Freetown than it did to increase agricultural industry in the rural areas.

MacCarthy faced delays in implementing his parish plan. The home government was slow to approve his plans. He later wrote that the parish plan had been devised in 1814 and 1815, but he waited until mid-1816 before submitting it formally, no doubt with a desire to ensure CMS support from the outset. He had followed the same course on the matter of the schools. Downing Street, however, was busy, and approval even on the question of salaries for CMS schoolmasters was delayed until August 1816.[29]

The delays in approving both the provisions for school-teachers and the parish plan were not simply caused because the Crown government was busily engaged elsewhere. The opinion which the abolitionists had held as early as 1813 'that the African coast is now nearly cleared of slave ships'[30] had gained a certain acceptance in the government offices. Bickersteth reported from London to both MacCarthy and Butscher the prediction of Lord Bathurst that the number of incoming Liberated Africans would fall. As a result, the CMS chose not to erect permanent buildings at Leicester Mountain and ordered the temporary ones to be kept in repair. The assistant Secretary of the CMS confided to the Governor that Bathurst had said it was 'probable that the system of capture must, however reluctantly, be much limited'.[31] Governments interestingly take crucial decisions for the most curious reasons, and this case was no exception. Ironically, it was with a view toward limitation and in keeping with MacCarthy's promises that his plans would eventually reduce costs that the Treasury released funds for the school programme late in 1816. MacCarthy gained official sanction for the parish plan on the same basis, and a year later divided the colony into seven parishes and appointed seven superintendents. By mid-1818 he increased these to nine. All but two of the parishes were served by the CMS.[32]

The Governor, however, considered only four of the seven CMS missionaries as permanent superintendents. The other three included the two Colonial Chaplains in Freetown and Henry During, a CMS schoolmaster who was not ordained until later that year. These three MacCarthy hoped would soon be replaced by permanent English clergymen-superintendents. The Governor felt that the number of parishes was flexible and depended upon the influx of recaptives. He had used all of the personnel made available by the CMS and needed more. He had even used the Revd. William Davies, the Methodist preacher expelled from the Freetown pulpit, as one of his early superintendents. But Davies had since left the colony. The success of the system seemed assured by 1818 nevertheless, according to MacCarthy, because church attendance had risen four-fold, marriage and baptism were on the increase, and school attendance indicated that the newcomers were eager to learn.[33]

CENTRALIZED CONTROL

With the school system approved and beginning to operate, the parishes defined and superintendents appointed, the enterprising Governor next sought a permanent appointment for his chief superintendent of the Liberated Africans. The original director, George Macaulay, relative of the former Company governor, Zachary, had died while on leave in England in 1816. He was replaced two years later by an appointee of Lord Bathurst who, immediately upon his arrival, entered business as a trader. This action put him at variance with MacCarthy's Official Instructions which stated that he was to prevent civil servants from engaging in private trade. When MacCarthy asked the appointee to quit trading, he resigned his government position instead. Following several attempts the Governor finally received Bathurst's official approval in 1819 for the appointment of Joseph Reffell as Chief Superintendent, a post he had in fact held without salary since Macaulay left in 1816.[34] The Chief Superintendent under MacCarthy was to some extent a liaison officer between the different village superintendents and the governor. His main responsibility, however, was keeping an account of both Liberated Africans and their supplies.

Prior to 1820 the Chief Superintendent was more of a statistical officer than an administrative one. The latter responsibilities became more important when MacCarthy, by then Sir Charles, returned from London in 1821 as Governor-in-Chief of Britain's entire West African empire.

The individual superintendents, under the close scrutiny of Governor MacCarthy, made the parish plan effective in its early days. The Governor kept in close personal contact with the villages. The frequency of his visits to Regent was noted by the superintendent, the Revd. Johnson. Such visits led to trouble for the superintendent if everything was not in order. In the case of Regent, where Johnson happened to be a particularly diligent overseer, such trouble usually manifested itself in prolonged debates with the Governor regarding Johnson's conservative policy toward baptism. When MacCarthy's regular visits dropped off in 1820, Johnson remarked, 'I can assure you that we are here quite comfortable on that account'.[35] MacCarthy's concern with the less successful villages was directed to the lack of regular religious services, the failure to measure out regular lots, and the laxity of law enforcement on the part of the supervisor. MacCarthy conveyed to Pratt and Bickersteth his conception of an ideal superintendent when he wrote them that he was 'satisfied that it is nearly impossible for a Clergyman *residing* in the mountains with Captured Negroes to do much good, unless to that character he unites that of Magistrate & Superintendent:—by the authority of the two latter offices he can keep the uncivilized in due order and reward the industry of the well behaved'. The Governor moreover made it perfectly clear that the clergyman-superintendent had real and total power in his particular location. When new missionaries first went to their stations, the Governor accompanied them, introduced them to their villagers, and was seen 'leading the responses while kneeling in lowliness on the "mud-floors" of the humble out-post places of Divine Worship'.[36]

The structure of authority under MacCarthy was simple and clear to the African recipient of all this attention. At the top

97

was the Governor himself, the 'big' or paramount chief. Next was the superintendent, the 'village chief'. He operated in a remarkably traditional manner. According to MacCarthy's ideal, the village superintendent kept the unruly 'in due order . . . [while rewarding] the industry of the well behaved'. The image was reinforced since in his role as magistrate the superintendent settled palavers. Moreover, as long as he served as religious leader of the village he kept at bay any possible conflicting notions of the church and state being separate sources of power. The authority structure was completed when the village superintendent worked through the individual tribal headmen. These men represented the various tribal groups within a single village. The first CMS superintendent at Wilberforce, in a classical missionary manoeuvre, raised his church attendance from 4 to 150 by simply working on the headmen in his village. Once convinced, the headmen saw to it that their people attended.[37]

Since the supervisory personnel were missionaries and because conversion was a recognizable phenomenon by which a man's progress toward 'civilization' could be measured, the principal effort of the early superintendent was directed toward the establishment of religious authority. Thus the need to build churches was paramount. Since the principal religious agent in the villages usually represented the Established Church of England, the superintendents tended to operate the town's religious affairs in such a manner as to exclude the dissenting sects or independent preachers. This conformed to the Governor's wishes. That over three-fourths of Freetown's population were dissenters pleased MacCarthy no more than it had his predecessor, Governor Thompson.[38] The parish system could not be successful in MacCarthy's terms if it included religious sectarianism. In this area the historical connection of the CMS in Sierra Leone proved greatly beneficial to both government and church. The point was made explicit when the Revd. Wenzel was transferred to Kissy as superintendent in 1816. His arrival represented the formal introduction of the central government's authority in the village. With the government providing the material and the villagers the labour, a new home for the superintendent was begun. But Wenzel had not been in Kissy long before he encountered a potentially serious challenge to his authority. Prior to his arrival, a Baptist preacher had come each Sunday from Freetown to conduct services. When he presented himself the first Sunday after Wenzel's arrival, the superintendent asked him to leave. MacCarthy supported the expulsion. When the same Baptist preacher started a second meeting halfway between Kissy and Freetown in order to preach to his former congregation, MacCarthy closed the place on the ground that the preacher did not own the land.[39] The Establishment in Kissy prevailed. Periodical ceremonies guaranteed that it would continue to do so. Early in 1817, after Governor MacCarthy had laid the cornerstone for the new church at Kissy, several Europeans who had accompanied the Governor from Freetown marched in procession to the stone, each striking it vigorously three times with a hammer. After this stirring piece of symbolism few of the Kissy 'faithful' found it necessary to remember Wenzel's text for the occasion: 'Behold I am laying in Zion a stone, a cornerstone chosen and precious, and he who believes in him will not be put to shame.'[40]

The superintendent's power over lands and his control of the government assistance programme generally reinforced his authority. Wenzel reported in March 1818 that he was managing the collection of rice at the government store in order to ensure a stock for the rainy season. Rice, as well as other commodities, was doled out by the authority of the superintendent. Moreover, each of the superintendents busied himself measuring out regular town lots. One missionary observed that the purpose of this was 'that the town may be more like a town than it is when plan'd by Africans. In fact their *plan* is no plan for they build where and how they please'.[41] But in addition to making the village more closely resemble the formal rectangularity of Freetown, the superintendent's crude survey served to determine landholding rights and to give these rights official recognition.

The parish plan of local administration had its most complete application in two of the nine parishes established by Governor MacCarthy by 1818. This was at the two mountain villages of Gloucester and Regent. The remaining seven, however, were not unsuccessful. The strictly organizational requirements of the plan were generally satisfied. Certainly this was true at Kissy under Wenzel, and even to a greater extent when the Revd. Gustav Nyländer became superintendent after Wenzel's death. But it was only at Gloucester and Regent in MacCarthy's time that men were found who combined zeal for administrative detail with a compelling personal magnetism in the leadership of their village. Both Superintendents During at Gloucester and Johnson at Regent operated with a forcefulness on the local scene which was comparable to that of MacCarthy himself on a colony-wide basis. Both took the power given them and used it completely towards the goal of establishing an ideal community. Both secured their ordination as Lutheran preachers while in the colony largely as a result of MacCarthy's satisfaction with their work in the villages. Thus they owed their higher positions to the system itself. Finally, and of vital importance, both men had a sincere belief in the system as an effective means of raising the general standards of the Liberated African community.

THE REVD. DURING AT GLOUCESTER

During first entered Gloucester shortly before Christmas, 1816. He had come to the colony with Johnson earlier in the year and had served initially as a school teacher at the Leicester Mountain Institution. Like Johnson, During was Hanoverian and had been trained by the CMS in London as a teacher. MacCarthy's original intention was to let During fill the Gloucester post temporarily until the CMS could provide an ordained Englishman for the superintendency. The fact that none arrived and that During excelled led MacCarthy to make his appointment permanent by securing During's ordination in 1818.[42] At first During directed the activities of about 130 recaptives at

Gloucester. He found the setting of his new post 'beautiful, for I am surrounded on every side with small rivulets, the aspect of the surrounding mountains is Romantic, and on the whole I feel even here that pease [*sic*] which the world can not give'. The new superintendent quickly set about laying the ideal MacCarthian foundation for a Liberated African community. Schools were begun, the girls' school under the direction of the missionary's young English bride. By late 1817 During reported 99 individuals in school. A little more than a year later 345 were under some type of instruction in the village. Nearly 100 boys were taught by During in the day school while 20 to 30 more attended classes at night. Mrs. During taught over 100 girls in her day and evening schools. With so many under instruction, During began to use advanced Liberated African students like Mark Joseph Tamba as assistant teachers.[43]

Regular church services were conducted on Sunday and daily prayer meetings during the week. The services were well attended. The people responded emotionally; During reported that many services were interrupted by the weeping and crying of the congregation. Without doubt the Liberated Africans sought salvation as a result of During's work. As was the case with Johnson at Regent, During kept actual church membership restricted to the few with whom he had an especially close connection. The reasons, beyond the purely religious explanations given by the missionary at the time, were seen more clearly in the Regent experience. Generally, however, by keeping church membership select, the superintendent created a new elite group within the village community. This elite group was privileged to an extent easily recognizable by the other villagers. They served to highlight the intricate system of rewards which was an important part of the village superintendent's power. In a sense, the elite church membership set the standard in the village which the superintendent wished the others to follow. The church members, as a privileged group, often lived in the same part of the vilage,[44] usually in houses which gave evidence of their more advanced social and economic position. The first stone houses in Regent and Gloucester were occupied by church members.[45] The purpose of the plan—to ensure the advancement of the Liberated Africans toward the state of greater 'civilization'—was always borne in mind. The superintendent meant to keep the pathway narrow and controlled, with the limits clearly defined. By keeping church membership under thirty in a total population which had reached 450 by 1819, During kept things very much under his control.[46]

Though perhaps severe, the system did prove efficacious. An English Quaker, William Singleton, visited Gloucester for the Friends' African Instruction Committee in 1821. According to Singleton, During had no difficulty getting the Liberated Africans to work in the fields. The superintendent confided that at first the newcomers were reluctant to work for themselves. The recaptives would say to him, 'What for we work? King take all we make.' But, During added, they soon found 'by experience, that they can enjoy the fruits of their labour'. Singleton remarked that the Liberated Africans of Gloucester were industrious. They built improved huts on their four acre plots of farm land. The huts were mud and wattle with the added refinement of having been whitewashed. The visitor found them well adapted to the surroundings, especially since their thick walls kept out the wind and retained the heat inside. Farmland had been cleared of trees though not of stumps or rocks. Gloucester farms were planted in cocoa, maize, sugar cane, and cassava. Rows of pineapple were used as low fences. What Singleton witnessed at Gloucester was the result of the channelling of Liberated African industry through the application of MacCarthy's ideal plan. The success of the operation was due particularly to the effective superintendence of During, who ruled his domain according to the Governor's principles of punishment and reward. No more striking testimony of his successful application of power was given than when During opened a gri-gri or small charm purchased for a penny from a small boy trader. Inside the gri-gri he found among the usual seeds, bits of earth and tiny trinkets, his own signature written

on a scrap of paper. Much as charm-makers had incorporated quotations from the Koran to increase the potency of
the gri-gri against witches, so had one charm-maker turned
in an attempt to evoke the power of the superintendent himself.[47]

THE REVD. JOHNSON AT REGENT

The superintendence of the Revd. William A. B. Johnson at
Regent provided an even clearer example of the potential success that lay in MacCarthy's plan. The Regent experience has
been well documented both by Johnson himself and by the many
visitors whom the Governor sent to view the model community
in operation. The reports were glowing and falsely romanti-
cized what was in fact a profound administrative accomplishment. The CMS historian characterized this era as 'the period
of revivals' in Sierra Leone as a result of such reports. Both
American and English missionary visitors left impressed, and
William Singleton found Regent to be 'a favoured place; and
while there indulged in a wish that if the Friends should . . .
commence a settlement on the Gambia their success might
equal that of the superintendent of Regent's-town'.[48]

The reports of such visitors saw Regent as a spectacular
accomplishment for the missionary forces. It was surely that,
but also it was an extraordinary example of administrative
'neatness, regularity, order, and industry'.[49] These were the
very qualities of civilization which MacCarthy sought and the
ones which Johnson provided as superintendent. The Governor
often spoke highly of the missionary's work, and when his
widow applied for a government pension, MacCarthy supported the petition, affirming that Johnson's work made the
widow particularly deserving of the Crown's attention. Johnson
had performed both religious and civil duties attentively and
diligently. He had succeeded in spreading Christianity and
civilization. The Governor observed that 'the conduct and
improvement of [the people of Regent], their outward de-
portment, and real industry have been held as a Model of

emulation to the other Towns, and although many of them have made considerable progress in Civilization, and nearly approach them, yet Regent on a general view is yet at the Head'.[50] The Revd. Edward Bickersteth, in Freetown when Johnson was first assigned to Regent as a schoolmaster in 1816, observed that 'there seems [in Mr. Johnson] a deadness to the world, and a devotion of heart to the cause, which are likely to make him a blessing where God's providence shall place him'.[51]

Johnson's success at Regent was closely tied to his personal desire for betterment and his religious dedication. Although he never attained the administrative heights reached by Bickersteth, there was a similarity in their humble origins and their rise to positions of power through the CMS connection. Like the Assistant Secretary of the society, Johnson kept a record of his early life which revealed an intense concern with human weakness and an acceptance of the role of Christian religion in saving the spirit from complete and utter ruin. Johnson recognized the over-ruling hand of God in the discipline of keeping a journal. The fact that he had decided several times to begin a journal, but had failed 'showes me my weakness, that I can do nothing of myself; all determinations begun by self-strength will never come to perfection; a man may begin, and alter his life, change himself, but oh how long will it stand; as the morning dew passed away, so will also his self-determination pass away; nothing less than the Power of God operated through the Spirit of God, in the human heart will change man'.[52] As superintendent of a Sierra Leone village, thirty years after his birth in Hanover, he began to set down the story of his conversion and call to mission work.[53]

His most vivid recollections were the days of agony and hunger spent as a new immigrant in London in 1812. Johnson had come from Hanover to work. Shortly after his arrival he married but the picture of the early period of his marriage, as he recollected five years later, was hardly blissful. Instead, it was a study of a young couple who mutually suffered because of his unemployment. In one particularly vivid scene his wife lay on

the bed weeping with hunger, and Johnson, completely helpless, stood by her, fretfully thinking 'what I should do, "no
friend to go to" what to do, I did not know'. Johnson transposed
his physical difficulties into spiritual terms. He looked upon
himself as unworthy of God, a sinner, and wrote that this experience was 'as if a book was opened and I read all the sins I
had been guilty of. What shall I do? No worldly prospects and
an angry God!' After a night of suffering, he went out the next
morning and luckily found employment as a labourer in a
distillery. But the promise of betterment proved empty. He
simply could not maintain two people on his meagre wages.
Sadly, he reported that when the other labourers went home
for breakfast he could not for there was nothing to eat. He was
desperate. Nevertheless, in order to 'avoid suspicion' one
morning he did go home and found a happy wife and a full
breakfast table. Mrs. Johnson herself had found a job, and with
two incomes in the family their physical sufferings diminished.
Elated, Johnson tried to offer prayers of thanksgiving. Again he
found himself inadequate. He heard that the Moravian Brethren in London held prayer meetings twice weekly in a German
Church near the Savoy. He went on the first opportunity and,
at the first meeting, experienced salvation. He was, he wrote,
'called . . . out of nature's darkness into [God's] marvilous [*sic*]
light'. Shortly after his conversion he 'felt a great desire to convert those who were about me'. He tried to convert his wife,
but failed; attempts among his fellow workers were drowned
in their laughter.

At this time Johnson changed jobs and because of its near-
ness to both his new work and his home, he began to attend the
dissenters' Pell Street Chapel. While at Pell Street Chapel he
accepted the doctrine of 'the Free Sovereign Grace in Election'.
'By the Grace of God,' he wrote, 'I am what I am.' Late in 1813
his by now latent desire to convert others was again aroused by
the sermons of three missionaries from the London Missionary
Society. His own relative prosperity as a regularly employed
worker began to worry him. He thought about 'the misery and

wretchedness of the poor benighted Heathen'. But he suppressed his desire to become a missionary since he was married
and without ability. In his words, he returned to 'darkness,
prayerlessness, and carelessness'. The desire was renewed again
in May 1814, and again he was able to suppress it. One of the
major personal hindrances to Johnson's self-realization was
overcome when he converted his wife. Thus together they joined
the Pell Street Chapel. Before joining, however, they were
visited by two officers of the congregation, who examined their
religious beliefs. Only when they were satisfied were the couple
admitted to membership. This experience in joining an English
dissenting chapel was to be a keystone of Johnson's policy in
Regent. He personally examined anyone who sought membership at Regent church. The success of being accepted as a
member at Pell Street only initiated another siege of self-doubt.
A visit to his pastor proved decisive. The clergyman discovered
Johnson's suppressed desire to serve and sent him at once to
Charles Allen, who had personal connections with the committee of the London Missionary Society. Allen told Johnson
that so many had volunteered lately that there were no positions
available. A return visit a few weeks later brought the same
reply from Allen. Returning home greatly depressed, Johnson
met an old Hanoverian friend, Henry During. During told
him of his own training at the Church Missionary Society, and
that the CMS needed another school teacher to send with him
to West Africa. Johnson immediately applied, and the committee interviewed both him and his wife a few days later.[54]
In early August 1815, Pratt wrote to Butscher in Sierra Leone
that the society had 'three schoolmasters in preparation—
Johnson, During, and Jost.'[55] Johnson had been accepted and at
last had his chance to serve.

He began a period of training sponsored by the CMS. Although this training constantly reminded him of the inadequacy of his expression in the English language, he found re-
assurance one night in a visit to Pell Street Chapel. The preacher
told of a man who failed to master the English Grammar in

three years of schooling, but had nevertheless become a useful preacher. Relieved, Johnson turned his thoughts to Sierra Leone: 'It appeared to me a very dark spott—when Sierra Leone came into my mind a dark cloud appeared before me— but through this darkness the following promise glimpsed continually into my heart, (viz). "I will bring the blind by the way, that they know not, I will lead them in paths that they have not known. I will make darkness light before them, and crooked things straight. These things will I do unto them, & not for-sake them."' Johnson left Gravesend for Freetown in March 1816.[56]

After nearly six weeks at sea the ship anchored in Freetown harbour on the last day of April. The voyage had been difficult for Johnson and had given the earliest evidence of friction among the group, which in addition to himself and his wife included During and his wife, and Mr. and Mrs. John Horton. The Hortons were English and this fact alone helped to increase their separation from the others. Johnson found them too worldly, and objected to their marital squabbles, which at one point led to blows. The most offensive part of the voyage to Johnson personally, however, occurred when he preached to the sailors late on the afternoon of Easter Sunday. He had been disturbed by the fact that the Easter service during the day had merely been read. The young Hanoverian, determined to put things right, was appalled to find both Horton and During laughing at him during the sermon. Horton charged Johnson afterwards with insulting both the captain and his men by his remarks.[57] These and later differences between Johnson and other missionaries served to set him farther apart, and to increase the zeal of his work among his devoted followers at Regent.

The Sierra Leone committee of the CMS first assigned Johnson to Nyländer's station on the Bulom Shore. He remained there a little more than a month before being officially transferred to the mountain village of Regent. Bickersteth's letter of transfer told him to begin his work at Regent as soon as possible while MacCarthy's typically ordered him to begin the following day. Johnson expressed considerable pleasure at the new appointment although he initially found the people of the village 'so wild a race'.[58]

Johnson's arrival at Regent did not represent the first attempt by either the government or the CMS to control the village. Butscher had proposed sending the repentant Peter Hartwig to the community as a schoolmaster in 1814.[59] Nothing came of the suggestion. In 1815 Butscher himself had accompanied MacCarthy to the ceremony of laying the foundation stone of the church. Later in the same month, September, with MacCarthy out of the country, Kenneth Macaulay and the acting governor had found it expedient to send Thomas Hirst, the Methodist school teacher, to direct the affairs of Regent. On his return to the colony, MacCarthy found the appointment degrading to the Church, partly, no doubt, because he was well advanced in his negotiations with the CMS. The appointment proved shortlived. In May 1816, some people from Regent came to the Governor to complain that Hirst was failing in his educational mission. MacCarthy took the opportunity to transfer the Methodist back to Freetown and sent the immensely impressive Johnson to Regent.[60] The Governor wanted the community to be in especially good hands. Since becoming the chief administrator of the colony, he had sent hundreds of Liberated Africans to the small mountain settlement four and a half miles south of Freetown. The origins of the settlement were cloudy. It was one of the villages founded by the recaptives themselves in an initial attempt to establish order and regularity in their own lives following the ordeal of the slave passage. It represented one of their early attempts to carve out of their disaster something of their own province of freedom. Officially, the government recognized it as having been founded in 1812. Its population by 1816 was mainly Vai, Bassa, Wolof, and Ibo. Five years later a visitor reported over twenty tribes resident at Regent, and Bickersteth observed that it contained representatives of nearly all neighbouring Sierra Leone tribes.[61] Regent, by 1816, was the largest of the Liberated African villages. Visitor Robert Hogan estimated the population to be 1,200.[62]

Before Johnson's arrival MacCarthy had built a storehouse for government rations, and had begun a church, 'a decent and convenient Edifice which would not discredit any country town in England,' according to Hogan. A house for the superintendent was near completion, and, in addition, MacCarthy proposed to construct a gaol, a market place, and an infirmary. The Governor built entirely with stone since he had found that buildings of wood or mud with grass roofs offered 'but an inhospitable shelter against the heavy rains of this climate, and by letting in the wet and damp of the atmosphere cause fatal diseases'.[63] Johnson, accompanied by Chief Superintendent Reffell, visited Regent once before taking up residence. They went to observe the progress of the buildings and to provide the citizens with an opportunity to meet the new superintendent. Johnson fell into another state of depression as a result of this first visit. In his journal he wrote, 'But o how have I been cast down this day—if ever I have seen wretchedness it has been today. . . . These poor people may be indeed called the offscowrings of Africa . . . the greatest part have lately arrived from slave vessels and are in the most deplorable condition. . . . To describe indeed the misery of Regents Town would be impossible.'[64] But, the depression overcome, Johnson succeeded Hirst as superintendent of Regent on 18 June 1816. Two days later he was to be found in the centre of the village, surrounded by his people, distributing rations. His mission had begun.

Although officially only schoolmaster and superintendent, Johnson operated from the beginning also as religious leader. Using first his own house and then the completed church as his centre of operations, he quickly established control of the community. Within a month of arrival, he moved the prayer meetings outside his house because the numbers attending had grown so large. Sunday services began with two family prayer sessions at 5 and 6 a.m. Three divine worship services were held at 10 a.m., 3 p.m., and 7 p.m. Between the afternoon and evening services he often travelled to outlying sections of the town to conduct special meetings. Johnson's sermons at Regent were characterized by one writer as being in the 'style of Christian simplicity . . . from the heart *to the heart*'. They emphasized the mysteries and sufferings of Christ, the fall of man, and the necessity for man himself to endure a period of suffering. A result of the latter emphasis appeared continually in the individual religious testimonies of Liberated Africans. The period of slavery which they had endured was perceived as the necessary period of suffering. Johnson's use of the idea of 'blood-bought salvation' also helped to explain to the Liberated Africans how they were saved from slavery. The preacher once remarked that the speakers at a prayer meeting had expressed 'great joy . . . and . . . interest in the blood of JESUS'.[65]

CMS headquarters in London warned him at least twice about the excessively emotional content of his sermons. Bickersteth cautioned him in 1817 against carrying on 'revivalistic-type' meetings. The committee warned him to discourage anything like noise, cries and extraordinary expressions of emotion. Johnson's eventual solution to this problem was to have those who cried out continually carried from the church by the ushers.[66] In 1818 Pratt told Johnson to avoid preaching the doctrine of election. He asked the missionary to speak more of a loving God and to keep the truths of the scripture foremost in the minds of his parishioners, letting the phrases speak for themselves. The CMS Secretary asked him to 'remember what sort of people you have to deal with, and how dangerous and distressing would be the consequences if they were to get into high notions about doctrine'. The fact that Johnson was not ordained also bothered CMS officials at Salisbury Square. Pratt wrote him, after reading the initial reports of his success, that if he were to continue preaching he would have to be ordained.[67] MacCarthy, in Freetown, made an unsuccessful move to reward Johnson with a colonial chaplaincy. The Governor thought he was the best promoter of 'the Civilization of the Captured Negroes' he had. Pratt in the meantime arranged with Wenzel, Butscher, and Nyländer, all Lutherans themselves, to examine Johnson for ordination. Late in March 1817, his colleagues satisfied, Johnson received Lutheran orders.

By operating as religious leader, school teacher, and superintendent, Johnson greatly enhanced his personal authority in the village. Soon after his arrival the Governor sent some new clothing to Regent to be distributed to the Liberated Africans. The people assembled for the expected distribution one morning after family prayers. Johnson gave out some of the clothing, but then stopped. He explained to them that since he was not yet well acquainted with them he 'would come and see them at their respective Farms, and give them according to their industry'.[68] If initially he rewarded labour, he soon only rewarded labour and devotion. In 1818 he met with a group of schoolgirls to hear their testimonies. About twelve were present and all were very attentive. As a reward for their good behaviour he gave each girl one acre of land. Later he ordered some new clothing from the CMS in London and used it to reward his communicants. Johnson used assistants to extend and maintain control of the village. Two Liberated Africans who had been educated at Freetown were employed regularly to oversee rice shipments brought from the central storehouse there for rations. He also found four men who could spell and appointed them assistant school teachers. By employing this system he was able to open school within the first month after his arrival with ninety students divided into four classes.[69]

When Johnson enrolled the ninety students he also noted the names of the parents, their occupations, and their places of residence. He soon added to the class list the names of over forty adults who came to the evening school. Johnson's class lists became a formal record of part of his population, the part, most importantly, which he knew best. As he extended his authority, the record became increasingly valuable as a means of control. The superintendent could quickly single out and identify influential families or potentially helpful individuals by referring to it. Those men who became his later assistants were often discovered originally in school. Other assistants came from the church itself or from his own household. The latter were personal servants.[70] Johnson delegated considerable authority to his assistants. In his absence they would lead prayer services. Several entered the employment of the CMS, either leading missions to their home country or serving in the colony as school teachers. Three of his assistants, William Tamba, David Noah, and William Vivah, testified to Johnson's leadership training ability by serving the CMS long into the next decade.[71]

Johnson's efforts to establish control of Regent received an especially significant stimulus when the church building was roofed in and completed in August 1816, two months after his arrival. The church was full for the first time on the fourth Sunday of the month, and by the following year, the capacity of the building had to be doubled. Five times during his superintendency the church was improved and enlarged. At one point a balcony was added in an attempt to provide space for the constant overflow which usually heard the service from the compound outside through the opened windows. The congregations were estimated by Johnson and visitors as being between 500 and 1,000 at a single Sunday service.[72]

With the church building completed and attendance growing regularly, the close coordination of Johnson's efforts could be fully appreciated. He reported that the people became immediately more industrious. They strove to secure his attention in order to get new clothes in which to come clean to Sunday worship. The reward system, working in an efficient cyclical fashion, was now perfected. Its final refinement came a month after the church first opened. Johnson—not yet ordained himself—asked the Revd. Butscher to come to Regent to baptize twenty-one adults. Through baptism Johnson admitted citizens of Regent into the church communion. The elite group was thus initiated in Regent and defined as those who were church communicants. In fact, of course, members became important participants in Johnson's inner circle of administration. The group of communicants rose to forty-one by the year's end, and to seventy by October 1817. Like During at Gloucester, Johnson kept the number intentionally small by insisting on convincing individual testimony before baptism and admission.[73] In his whole ministry, the number of actual members never exceeded one-third of the total population of the village.[74] In his last report, in March 1823, Johnson reported a population of 2,000; there were 410 communicants. The most he ever admitted at a time was forty-eight and that occurred on the eve of his departure. Between 1820 and 1823, the number of communicants increased only by 110.[75]

In a purely social context it was important for Johnson to keep the number small. The communicants represented the highest level of the community's social strata. In addition to being the ranks from which Johnson's most trusted assistants came, the communicants themselves served as a group which he used to maintain order.[76] Any disturbance was reported to Johnson immediately by the communicants.[77] In regular Saturday night meetings with the superintendent from which all others were excluded, the communicants reported on village activities. They discussed the actions of citizens who sought membership in the group. A dissenting word from a communicant was sufficient for Johnson to exclude a prospective candidate. The actions of 'fallen members' were also reviewed at such meetings. The suspicion with which this inner group was regarded by the others was exemplified by the request of one female communicant to move from her house. She was surrounded by non-communicants who were threatening to fight with her. Such disturbances between communicants and non-communicants served as an outlet for the natural pressures resulting from what by 1819 was a severely stratified, authoritarian society.[78]

There were other advantages of church membership in addition to increased prestige. It has already been noted that communicants received clothing sent from England. Johnson also gave gifts of land, and adults received extra instruction in the evenings from the superintendent. Moreover, only those

113

baptized could enjoy a legally recognized marriage in Regent. One communicant who wished to marry a non-communicant girl, refused Johnson's counsel that the marriage could not be held until the girl had gone through a religious experience and had been baptized; Johnson had his name struck off the rolls of the church. Finally, communicants had the exclusive privilege of belonging to the Church Benefit Society. Similar to the benefit societies which abounded among the Liberated Africans in the villages, the official society of the communicants offered the advantages of lower cost and greater benefits. Johnson assured London that the benefit society 'has greatly increased love and harmony' in the village.

As the director of this efficient organization as well as superintendent of the village itself, Johnson was the patriarch. He once told the superintendent of the village of Kent, who was having disciplinary difficulties in his school, that he should act toward his pupils as a kind father.[79] One of the many visitors to come to Regent during this period wrote afterwards, 'I do indeed believe that the people love Mr. J. as their father. . . . Should there be a dispute amongst any of them they come to him to settle their palaver, and they abide by his decision satisfied that it is for the best.' A young communicant came to Johnson for advice when she had been asked to marry. She told Johnson 'You stand the same like my own Father, and I no want to do anything before I ask you.'[80] Johnson was the symbol of the oneness of the community, the all-centralizing force which MacCarthy had conceived in his plan. Styled by the villagers as the 'headman' or chief, Johnson, as pastor, teacher, mayor, judge, social welfare director, and the director of public works was, in fact, *the* leader.

He remained the leader of Regent with one brief leave until early in 1823.[81] Then, worn by his arduous labours and the effects of the climate, he began preparations to leave his beloved Regent. On 24 April, with everything in readiness, he and James Norman, his successor as superintendent, went to Reffell's home in Freetown for dinner. After the meal the Chief

Superintendent and Norman accompanied him to the boat. Norman noted that at the wharf Johnson 'complained of illness, and I began to suspect that he had caught the yellow fever which within a few days made frightful ravages in Freetown.' Johnson embarked, but Norman's suspicions proved correct. Johnson died at sea on 4 May of yellow fever, ten days out of Freetown.[82]

Explanations for Johnson's monumental success at Regent were varied. Governor MacCarthy was partially responsible, simply as the creator of the plan for the villages, and as the one who decided to send Johnson to Regent. The people of Regent certainly shared the responsibility. They sought improvement in the Governor's terms, and to a remarkable degree they accepted the subordinate position assigned to them theoretically by MacCarthy and actually by Johnson. The most relevant explanations, however, were to be found in Johnson's complex personality. The London period of his life was extremely significant. The periods of darkness experienced there were certainly manifestations of a deeply depressed state of mind. The light which almost constantly showed itself to him was the desire to serve, to spread the words of salvation which had initially helped him. Frustrated in his attempts in London and in his first wish to be a missionary, he turned to his new work for the CMS with an increased zeal. Transposed from London to the Regent setting, Johnson was given a challenging opportunity to prove to himself that he was a strong-willed labourer, working for what he would have termed 'God's cause'. He completely dedicated his efforts to the people of Regent. Everything he did was done for them. Perhaps chafing from the failure experienced in London and the laughter that greeted his sermons from more sophisticated colleagues,[83] Johnson restricted his contact with other Europeans. Personal contacts with Englishmen were particularly noted by Johnson as periods of distress or 'darkness'. Once, in 1818, he feigned sickness in order to avoid attending a banquet in Freetown given by MacCarthy in honour of the recently arrived English Colonial Chaplain. Instead,

Johnson walked to Wilberforce to preach to the Liberated Africans there. Occasionally he noted in his journal the feeling that he could not preach with full freedom on Sunday. The feeling corresponded to a time when a European was visiting. Johnson always expressed his appreciation of the visitor's praise for his work, but so long as the person was present he 'found not that comfort as when I preach to my own people'. Although he at first spoke with contempt about the people of Regent and experienced deep doubts in London about going to Sierra Leone—'the dark cloud', he had called it—he soon found his greatest satisfaction in Regent. The reason for this was simple. There was no ridicule for Johnson in Regent. Greatly appreciative of this, he wrote in his journal in 1818, 'Having been much tryed [*sic*] this week I found it good this evening to meet with my dear people. I was so fully convinced that the work of Grace was carried on in their hearts that I had no reason to doubt.'[84] On the eve of his departure in 1823, his thoughts again turned to his people. He wrote, 'the people among whom I reside have much endeavoured to make my burden easy. They have not only in an affectionate manner sympathized with me in my afflictions; but comforted me with many simple but striking expressions. Their behaviour has in general been peaceable; and they have been willing to serve me whenever an opportunity has offered itself. When I express a wish . . . they will . . . do it immediately. All these and other circumstances have formed an attachment between me and the people of my charge which is better imagined than expressed.'[85]

Missionaries in later years looked on Johnson's work with scorn. Their tasks were different; their powers restricted. They lost the power of superintendence shortly after Governor Mac-Carthy's death, when the government made a new agreement with the CMS. Unable to meet the personnel requirements of MacCarthy's administrative system, the CMS missionaries ceased being government managers. The Revd. Joseph May, a Liberated African who became a successful Methodist preacher, remarked that under Johnson the people came to church for 'the sake of loaves, and fishes while other attending arose from a fear of being fined or put in Gaol, by the miss'y who was also Magistrate'.[86] One of Johnson's successors, the Revd. William Betts, echoed May's words in explaining the decreased number in Regent Church in 1826.[87] The Revd. J. G. Wilhelm, however, one of Johnson's colleagues, admitted the importance of having temporal as well as spiritual authority over his people. He was faced with a serious revolt among the students at Leicester Mountain Institution in 1819. Defining the core of the difficulty to Pratt, Wilhelm wrote that 'there is a great difference between them and the captured negroes in getting them to attend religious instruction. The captured people are under higher obligations to obey all orders of the Missionary set over them; as he has the management of their temporal concern upon him as well as the care of their spiritual welfare'.[88]

The superintendence of temporal and spiritual affairs of the village, in order to centralize authority, was the intention of MacCarthy's plan. This Johnson had carried out. Although attendance weakened after he left, the organizational structure of administration did not.[89] In an era which was full of economic prosperity and gala celebration in Freetown, Regent proved to be a successful testimony to MacCarthy's ideal concept and Johnson's ability as a practical administrator. This was important for two reasons. First, Regent remained throughout the century as the highwater mark of British attempts to administer directly the affairs of the rural areas. Under Johnson, the European administration enjoyed its greatest success. Secondly, during the 1820's MacCarthy's plan was to enjoy diminishing success and eventually it was to fail. The memory of Johnson at Regent would long remain a touchstone in the colony's development, especially as responsibility for the development of Freetown and Sierra Leone society drifted increasingly into the hands of Liberated Africans themselves.

IV

The Return of Frustration and Failure

Robert Burns's lines about the plans of mice and men proved all too applicable to Great Britain's efforts in Sierra Leone during the nineteenth century. Until very recently those who have written about Britain's colonial venture in Sierra Leone have been led, largely through heavily ethnocentric frustration, to conclude that the colony itself was a failure. Shadows cast by those who in the nineteenth century sought at various times to abandon the experiment and close the colony have darkened the interpretation of later historians of the colony. But the colony did not fail, as Christopher Fyfe emphasized in his *History of Sierra Leone*. Nevertheless, one cannot write that the British succeeded in their plans for Sierra Leone. The boldest, most idealistic dreams—those of Sharp—lasted a mere four years and nearly brought complete disaster to the original settlers. The plans of the Company to make the settlement a viable economic entity ended in financial havoc and commercial bankruptcy for the Directors in London. The first attempts of the Crown to govern the colony were woefully inadequate, particularly in the manner of settling the growing numbers of recaptive settlers brought to the colony on the captured slave ships. Faced with a home government saddled with graver problems elsewhere, a succession of governors in the colony laboured arduously to effect a more humane scheme to handle the problems of administering the growing population. A relatively prosperous, but momentary success finally came to the British enterprise in Sierra Leone under Governor MacCarthy.

It also, however, proved incomplete; the burdens of daily life and the solution of problems fell once again to those who populated the mountainous peninsula. It was left to settler and Liberated African alike to develop in the course of their experience a pattern of living which, in the end, allowed some modicum of success to the Sierra Leone venture in the nineteenth century. The population, freed, as it were, by the frustrations and failures of British officialdom, developed its own province of freedom.

Nowhere was the problem of frustrated British plans more clearly illustrated than in the failure to handle the settlement of the Liberated Africans. Commissioner James Rowan, writing to Under-Secretary of State Hay in 1826, complained that 'the frequent change of measures which seems to be the invariable result of a Change of Men' was responsible for the general failure of British plans in the colony. The effect was obvious: 'there is nothing stable or permanent, nor does there appear to be any fixed system by which to form an opinion of the Departments [of Government] as parts of a whole, or to measure the conduct of the different individuals composing them'.[1] This was written two years after MacCarthy's death. Unfortunately, by 1826, his relatively successful design for the colony's administration had also gone astray. The order that the Parliamentary Commission of Inquiry found in the colony—particularly in the central government's relations with the Liberated African villages—was the result of MacCarthy's ten year administration. The order which remained, however, was merely a vestige of what had once existed, even at Gloucester and Regent. Three interrelated factors operated to ensure the ultimate demise of MacCarthy's plan. First, the Governor himself, after 1821, was drawn away from his primary occupation of administering the colony. Next, his relations with the CMS deteriorated, largely as a result of the society's failure to provide adequate or sufficient personnel. Finally, poor health conditions and a high mortality rate sapped away whatever trained personnel he had. These three factors worked against

MacCarthy's parish plan of central administration during his own tenure. When they were combined with a fourth factor—the extreme austerity placed on his two immediate successors by Downing Street, and their great zeal in paring colony expenditures—the eventual failure of the plan was guaranteed.

MacCarthy's Leave and Increased Responsibilities

Late in July 1820, MacCarthy left Freetown on a much deserved rest leave to the United Kingdom. He intended originally to be gone six months, but he did not return until November 1821, over a year later. He came back to Freetown with his much sought-after knighthood and greatly increased responsibility. Midway through his leave Parliament had passed legislation which withdrew the charter of the Company of Merchants Trading to Africa, and annexed its possessions. The act gave the administrative responsibility of the former Company possessions to the Governor at Freetown. Thus Sir Charles became Governor-General of all British possessions in West Africa, from the settlement at Bathurst, Gambia, to the trading forts of the Gold Coast. Freetown became the administrative capital of British West Africa.[2]

When he returned, Sir Charles at once visited the Liberated African villages. He found them in very good condition; the people were happy, content, and industrious; Chief Superintendent Reffell had carried on well during his absence. The foundations for colonial growth and prosperity—religion, morality, and agriculture—were all improving.[3] During his visit to Regent, the Revd. Johnson, the superintendent, staged an impressive show for the newly arrived, newly honoured Governor. As Sir Charles arrived at Regent, he marched through two lines of Liberated Africans, three or four deep, which formed along his way from the bridge over the creek up to Johnson's home and the church, high on the hill overlooking the town. All those along the road were neatly dressed and carried flowers. Twelve girls, wearing white dresses with green ribbons and decorated with roses, led the procession in honour of the

Governor. MacCarthy, overwhelmed with pleasure, as were those who had accompanied him from Freetown, immediately contributed £10 to the CMS to show his gratitude. Johnson trusted that the display had 'convinced [the Governor] that our Religion teaches a man to be loyal and not disaffected'.[4] More than ever before, the occasion was ceremonial. So, for that matter, were all the Governor's quick visits to the Liberated African villages after his return from London. In each case these visits proved to be commemorative ceremonies dedicated to that time when the Governor himself had maintained direct control over the villages. For if the period before MacCarthy's leave could be characterized by his direct control of Sierra Leone affairs, the time between his return to the colony and his death in 1824 was a period when his control was, for the most part, delegated to others. He had lost none of the drive which characterized the earlier period, but his energies were now spent in an effort to regularize the administration of the newly-acquired dependencies. The expansion of the Crown's interests in West African territories came at no small cost to the administration of its social venture in Sierra Leone.

A short time after his triumphant welcome at Regent, Sir Charles sailed for the Gold Coast. He did not return to Freetown for over three months. He remained in the colony only five months before leaving again for the Gold Coast in November 1822. Although he originally planned to return to Freetown the following March, he did not see the coastal mountains of Sierra Leone until July 1823. Again within months he sailed for the Gold Coast, and on this final journey he met his death fighting the Asante in January 1824.[5] During such extended absences, Sir Charles's Council administered the government of Sierra Leone.[6] Freetown suffered from all of those shortcomings usually associated with government by committee. Actions taken were indecisive, and the Members of the Council were beset by a host of minor squabbles and petty jealousies. The usually efficient attention paid to the arrival of Liberated Africans was absent during these periods of government by

Council. MacCarthy's response to the colony's difficulties when he was in Freetown was too often simply to seek more money from the home government. It was probably Kenneth Macaulay, a Member of the Council, who complained to his cousin Zachary in London that 'much evil arises from having extended the civil jurisdiction of Sierra Leone to the Gambia and the Gold Coast without sufficiently providing for its execution'. Macaulay characterized the new charter as being too loose and insufficient to implement the new responsibilities. Some of the difficulty was simply due to administrative oversight. Distance served to intensify otherwise minor problems. For example, when MacCarthy left the colony late in 1822, to be absent for more than eight months, he did not leave a Commission to hold the December quarter sessions. Therefore, prisoners held for committing a felony were detained until the Governor's return. The judicial establishment had not been able to function in his absence.[7]

MacCarthy's bloody death at the hands of the Asante[8] naturally added to the distress of the Freetown government. In 1818 MacCarthy had specified that in the event of his death the government should devolve upon the senior military officer in the colony. But in January 1824 MacCarthy had the senior military officers with him in the Gold Coast. The government should have then fallen to the senior member of the Council. However, a dispute arose between Macaulay and Daniel Malloy Hamilton, each of whom claimed to be the senior member. Reffell, the only other member of the Council present, was too ill to take part in the protracted discussions. Eventually Macaulay stepped aside and allowed Hamilton to become acting governor late in February 1824. Hamilton took office then, however, only because of the serious threat of trouble in Freetown. Both Hamilton and Macaulay feared that if one of them did not take office, the officer temporarily commanding the military garrison would. The commander had recently so antagonized the townspeople that the Councillors feared complete chaos if he became Acting Governor.[9] As Acting Governor there was little that Hamilton could do. He simply sat down and awaited the arrival of MacCarthy's permanent replacement, Major General Charles Turner, which did not occur until early in 1825. No doubt anticipating the extremely austere reaction of Downing Street to the latter days of Sir Charles's administration, Hamilton stopped all expenditure on buildings in the colony.

The disruption of the Freetown government occasioned by MacCarthy's absences and eventual death naturally affected adversely the development of the parish plan in the villages. Much of the success he experienced prior to 1821 resulted from his own personal attention to the details of administration. When this was missing, the villages, with a few important exceptions such as Gloucester and Regent so long as During and Johnson themselves were present, tended to escape from the central government's direct control. When bad health forced Johnson and later During to leave the colony, even these model communities which they had directed began to slip away into a more independent existence.

TROUBLES WITH THE CHURCH MISSIONARY SOCIETY

A second major factor operating against the realization of MacCarthy's plan was the deterioration of his relations with the Church Missionary Society. This was evident both in his contact with the CMS in London, and with the missionaries themselves in Sierra Leone. The beginnings of the difficulty with London were to be found in the CMS's continuing reluctance to relinquish the Susu mission. Their stubbornness, as MacCarthy viewed it, served to intensify the Governor's growing dissatisfaction with the Society for its failure to provide him with sufficient personnel. MacCarthy's objections to the continuation of the mission work in the north began in 1814, the first year of his administration. He found the mission unrewarding and unnecessarily dangerous. Objections gradually turned to anger when the admittedly vague promises of the society to close the mission never materialized. In 1815 CMS Secretary

Josiah Pratt wrote MacCarthy that the parent committee in London 'fully acquiesce in the just and benevolent views of your Excellency' regarding his fears of their continuing to work among the Susu. Interpreting Pratt's remarks as a promise to close the mission, MacCarthy read with astonishment Bickersteth's report in 1817 and its revelation that the CMS planned to continue the Susu mission.[10] Anger produced increased criticism of the mission's work. Specific remarks of MacCarthy to the Revd. Garnon, the Colonial Chaplain, about the Susu mission brought an angry reply from Pratt. Writing to Garnon, telling him to keep the contents 'entirely confidential', Pratt claimed that he could not account for MacCarthy's feelings. Defensively, he claimed that the CMS had always spoken highly of the Governor to 'an immense body of persons'. The government and the mission had always been fair with one another. Mounting an attack on the Governor, Pratt noted that MacCarthy owed 'to our exertions with Government that countenance to his plans, and to some conceived before he was Governor, which Government has given'. The CMS Secretary was willing to admit that errors had been made, but they did not justify the Governor's increasingly pointed criticisms. MacCarthy, in Pratt's view, had done the Society a grave injustice.[11]

A short time later, MacCarthy himself addressed Pratt directly. He explained his opposition to the continuation of the Susu mission, the reason being that until the slave trade was finally suppressed the money spent there could be more wisely applied to the problems of the colony. In reply, the CMS told the Governor that its responsibility in Sierra Leone represented only one part of the demands placed on it all over the world. Furthermore, they had very restricted resources. They agreed that the mission at Rio Pongas went slowly, but felt it was still important enough to keep. Finally, in an attempt to placate the Governor, the Society recognized that the colony was most important and promised to send personnel there whenever possible.[12] This pledge was aimed at the core of MacCarthy's antipathy toward CMS work outside the colony. By late 1817 the society, although accepting their responsibilities in theory, had sent out only two additional men since the arrival in 1816 of Johnson, During, and Horton, although the Governor had made it clear as early as 1815 that he needed ten to twelve men to work in the colony if his plans were to succeed. Even Kenneth Macaulay had conservatively estimated the need for at least seven new people including one dynamic leader. By 1817 MacCarthy requested an additional twelve school teachers. He stressed his growing dissatisfaction by pointing out to Garnon that he had had to send the Wesleyan Revd. Davies to administer Leopold. About this time MacCarthy revived his threats to seek the assistance of the Society for the Propagation of the Gospel in implementing his plans if the CMS continued to fail him.[13]

Five new people sent out since the 1816 agreement simply did not satisfy the Governor. Butscher reported in 1816 that he had quarrelled with MacCarthy about who was holding up the programme. MacCarthy bluntly told the director of the Christian Institution at Leicester Mountain that the CMS was rich and could afford the expense of the required added personnel. Similar charges were heard periodically by other missionaries and indicated the Governor's growing dissatisfaction and anger with the missionary society. At least twice he complained to Johnson. In 1818 he told the Regent superintendent that 'he would get missionaries from the society for promoting Christian knowledge; for the Church Missionary Society had long promised great things which they had not kept and he could no longer wait; and let the Villages be without Superintendents'. Far more pointedly, he later made the charge 'that the C. M. Society cared little about Africa; their attention was more directed to India and New Zealand'.[14] In time even the usually unsympathetic Johnson came to understand Sir Charles' frustration. Both men realized that the parish plan could work. The only thing it lacked was adequate supervisory manpower. Johnson began his own campaign to bring pressure on Salisbury Square in 1822. In a letter addressed to both Pratt and Bickersteth, he reaffirmed what MacCarthy had told them often: more missionaries and more schoolteachers were needed everywhere in the colony. Freetown alone needed three new workers. Most of the villages required at least one. The colony in all needed at least twenty-seven new missionaries and school teachers. From Gloucester, the more reticent During added his assent to Johnson's request.

Johnson wrote in terms the home committee could understand. Freetown desperately needed missionaries because it 'will be the only means of putting a stop to the many heresy's [*sic*] which have sprung up there. The longer the place is left as it is, the more will people's minds be prejudiced against the Church, yea against white preachers at large'. The expulsion of the Revd. Davies from the Nova Scotian Chapel and the resultant schism, even though involving the Methodists, bore an ominous warning to Johnson. Obviously dedicated to the unitary principle of church and state as desired by MacCarthy in Sierra Leone, Johnson observed that the 'Chaplains [in Freetown now] think it their duty to write sermons and preach them to the whites, and thus the blacks that would even attend cannot understand the preacher, who speaks in an unknown tongue to them. Who can blame them when they leave the Church and attend other places?'[15] Johnson's visits from time to time to villages other than his own convinced him of the need for more able superintendents. His visits to Gloucester while During was on leave in 1822 showed him how the number of 'backsliders' increased once a community lost its regular overseer. The higher number of communicants to be found in Regent when compared with villages without superintendents added convincing testimony to his request for more mission workers.[16]

Lack of personnel had yet another adverse effect on the realization of the parish plan. The scarcity of workers necessitated a constant shifting of missionaries and school teachers within the colony. After his arrival in the colony from the Susu mission in 1818, the Revd. J. G. Wilhelm served in three different stations during his first three years. Newly arrived school teachers were usually transferred several times during their first few months in the colony. Often they were appointed superintendents.[17] The Society's failure to provide sufficient personnel reflected its own recruitment problems. Missionaries of the Church cause were generally not forthcoming in Great Britain. It has been noted already that in its early years the Society had been forced by necessity to seek missionaries from the Berlin Seminary. Seventeen of the twenty-four missionaries sent by the Society to Sierra Leone during the first fifteen years were German. Moreover, only three of the seven English missionaries were ordained. Although the Germans proved to be generally excellent missionaries, their predominance was not acceptable to the society. Bickersteth particularly felt 'that we want and ought to have *English* clergymen. Much as we are indebted to our German brethren, their labours are our disgrace; their Christian courage and self-denial—our reproach. In an English colony also, they cannot (from their almost necessary ignorance of English language and habits) be so acceptable as Englishmen would be.' The fact that all seven Englishmen arrived in the colony after Bickersteth's visit indicated that a new effort was being made by Salisbury Square to recruit in England. That Englishmen were still reluctant to serve the CMS in Africa helped to explain the society's inability to fulfil MacCarthy's increasing demands.[18]

MacCarthy's difficulties with the CMS extended beyond the problem of insufficient personnel. They included differences on important questions such as baptism, which the Governor felt affected the colony's rate of development. Both the government and the missions were in Sierra Leone primarily to begin the civilization and Christianization of Africa. They both agreed on this. But they had serious disagreements regarding the relative importance of certain specific goals and the means to be followed in attaining them. The Governor debated with the CMS on the question of baptism during the whole of his administration. MacCarthy viewed the sacrament as a means toward the complete establishment of his plan to centralize governmental authority. No doubt recalling the rapid spread of Christianity from Rome northward among the pagan Gallic and Germanic tribes, MacCarthy desired a policy of general baptism in Sierra Leone. He called for the baptism of those who evidenced 'a good moral conduct, a Christian appearance, and an assurance of an anxious wish to become Christian.'[19] To him this meant almost all of his people. The missionaries, on the contrary, demanded that baptism had to be preceded by a recognizable religious experience. The recipient of the sacrament had to be able to testify to his own salvation. Few adhered to this principle more rigidly than the Revd. Johnson at Regent. During one of their many heated debates on the subject, Mac-Carthy pointed out to Johnson that the apostles themselves had baptized 3,000 on one occasion. Johnson contended that they had been all 'pricked in the heart', and that in Sierra Leone 'as many as believed were baptized'. The Governor replied that it was the duty of the missionary 'to make Christians' of Liberated Africans, but Johnson and most of the others believed that God alone made Christians and their job was to observe certain evidences of a heart that had been 'pricked'. At the end of this particular encounter, Johnson told MacCarthy that he was baptizing forty-six—a goodly number—on Christmas Day, and this showed how God's work was progressing naturally at Regent.[20]

Throughout such arguments, MacCarthy remained unimpressed. He interpreted the missionaries' conservative policy toward baptism as a threat to the Establishment. In 1819 he pointed out that CMS ministers in Freetown had baptized only about eighty people in the last three years. He knew that the various dissenting chapels had baptized more, and that a person baptized in a dissenting chapel had usually been refused the sacrament by a CMS missionary. This was most frustrating since one of the most critical factors in his plan for centralizing authority—having loyal receptive Anglicans populating the town and the peninsula villages—was thus seriously jeopardized. There could be no effective unity of church and state when the receptive population felt 'disposed . . . to look toward [the dissenters] . . . for Religious assistance'. The official position of the CMS in London varied somewhat but in essence it was to view baptism in its most narrow religious sense. This proved too conservative for the Governor. He wrote the CMS, and although the London body at one point in 1819 seemed to accept MacCarthy's argument and his underlying fear that the Establishment itself was being undermined, they left it largely to the individual clergyman in the colony to determine who had been 'pricked in the heart'.[21] The argument continued to chip away at the diminishing reservoir of goodwill between the Governor and the mission society.

BREAKDOWN OF COOPERATION IN THE VILLAGES

A more serious matter than either insufficient personnel or the dispute over baptism, however, affected the Governor's plans in Sierra Leone itself, namely the failure of most of the Sierra Leone missionaries to cooperate fully with MacCarthy's ideal scheme for the administration of the colony. Many questioned the workability of the Governor's plan. The consequent failure of certain missionaries to accept their defined role in the plan did as much to undermine it as any other single factor. Criticism of MacCarthy's parish plan ranged from the penetrating remarks of Revd. Gustav Nyländer at Kissy to pathetic revelations of incompetence by Wenzel at Kissy and Decker at Wilberforce. Far too many of the early Sierra Leone missionaries felt that to cooperate with the Governor was to make the religious interests of the mission secondary. Revd. C. F. L. Haensel, the first Principal of Fourah Bay College, expressed such a view ten years later when he wrote of the MacCarthy era: 'The friendly disposition which such men formerly in high stations in the colony used to manifest towards the mission, has been the occasion of secularizing the minds of the society's servants and drawing them off from fishing for souls to fishing for the Governor's applause.'[22]

Most missionaries, unlike Johnson and During, felt that it was not possible for a dedicated servant of God also to serve the

129

state. Not only did such a dual role set up certain conflicts of belief, but it established rigorous demands on the men. Most simply lacked the energy or desire to fulfil them. Wenzel complained from Kissy soon after his arrival that being justice of the peace in addition to missionary was 'a most arduous task'. He observed that he had 'more people to attend Wednesday in settling their quarrels, than on the Lord's Day when I preach'. He claimed, furthermore, that 'when I have to tell them they are wrong, they will immediately stay away from the Lord's Day'. The two jobs simply conflicted with one another in Wenzel's mind and could never be, as the Governor intended, complementary.[23]

When Wenzel died in 1818, MacCarthy secured the transfer of the Revd. Gustav Nyländer from the Bulom Shore to Kissy. Nyländer had served in Freetown from 1806 to 1812, when he had travelled across the wide estuary to begin his work on the opposite shore. Although he went to the Bulom Shore to proselytize, his main occupation and most useful accomplishment was a linguistic study of the Bulom Sherbro. He produced the earliest Bulom dictionary and grammar, but only a few converts. Nyländer was the earliest precursor of the great German linguists who came to Sierra Leone and West Africa during the nineteenth century for the Church Missionary Society. The missionary objected to his transfer to Kissy. A friend wrote that Nyländer often spoke with tears in his eyes about his having had to leave the Bulom Mission. Nyländer himself confessed that he had gone to Kissy only because of a desire not to be 'disobedient'; from the outset his heart was not in his new post.[24]

Because of his feelings, he never became a real part of the parish plan. Instead, Nyländer became its most reasoned and responsible critic. He began to reorganize Kissy after the ruin into which its church and administrative affairs had fallen during the latter part of Wenzel's superintendence. He fulfilled most of the outward requirements of his office. His day was as full as that of the most successful superintendents. He was up by 5 a.m., ate a small breakfast, went to church for morning prayer, settled palavers until a more substantial meal about 10, and then studied, if secular affairs permitted, until dinner. After his evening meal he again turned his attention to any pressing village affairs, led evening prayer, and used the remaining time to read before retiring early. His daily schedule fitted almost perfectly that set down by the visiting Quaker, William Single-ton, in 1822. Singleton offered the opinion that by following such a schedule a man could easily last twenty years in the tropics, a goal which Nyländer missed by only one year.[25]

The German missionary, whose greatest pleasure had been his work on the Bulom Shore, was 'of a quiet and sober turn of mind; and in general, very deliberate and circumspect in his dealings'. Hannah Kilham wrote of him that there was 'an air of sincerity and kindness, and gentleness about him that gives confidence, and a degree of rest to the mind in seeing him'. He reminded her 'of a venerable Moravian minister, or a good old Friend'.[26] Nyländer never lost the respect of his fellow CMS workers; his simple piety put him in the natural position of one to whom others in the mission came for advice. Though unlike Johnson's, his preaching showed little passion, he was 'sound in doctrine and affectionate in spirit'. He spoke each Sunday morning plainly and very predictably for forty-five minutes.[27] Early in 1824 he was seized by an asthmatic condition which everyone thought would be fatal. Although the series of attacks left him very weak, he soon resumed his duties. The London headquarters of the mission suggested he should come there on leave, but he declined, suggesting that the chill air of Europe might prove fatal. He would, he answered, remain in Africa where he had made his home for the past eighteen years. His remark echoed an earlier wish: 'now let me be buried with my people.'[28] A few weeks later he fell from his horse and was not discovered for several hours. Greatly weakened, he became seriously ill just when it appeared he would recover from his injuries. Still, he refused to remain quiet and, sure that he was about to die, Nyländer methodically set about preparing for his own end. He selected a grave within the

view of the front veranda of his home. He made the arrangements for his own funeral, and at the close of his last sermon he
told his parishioners that he would not speak to them again.
His prophesy proved true; he died before the week was out.[29]

None could question the thoroughness with which Nyländer
performed his duties as superintendent. Still, he lacked that
personal drive which seemed necessary to become the full participant in MacCarthy's village scheme. Content more often to
study and observe his people in the manner of his Bulom
linguistic studies, he never emerged as their leader as did
Johnson or During. He was not, however, detached from their
problems. His marriages to two Nova Scotian school teachers
no doubt brought him in direct contact with settler society and
made him aware of the abilities of Africans to manage their own
affairs quite capably. A Liberated African village never had a
more sympathetic superintendent. He never lost his ability to
identify with his people's problems. He reported in mid-1819
that he was in charge of 450 recaptives at Kissy. About one-
third of them attended morning and evening prayer, and two-
thirds the regular Sunday worship. Beyond this, however, he
confessed, the people of Kissy showed no real evidence of a
spiritual life or a desire for religious knowledge. 'It appears to
be alike to them whether they come to hear the word of God
or not; to some perhaps it is a burden that they are under some
obligations to come.' The superintendent had almost no contact
with the 500 people living around Kissy according to what he
called their 'country fashion'. Consistently Nyländer observed
that 'there is none as yet who has an ear to hear, nor a heart to
understand'. Nyländer's own experience at Kissy, coupled with
what he observed of the other missionaries, led him openly to
criticize the parish plan. Early in 1819 he admitted that Kissy
provided a useful field of work. 'But if you wish to know the
truth,' he explained carefully to Bickersteth, 'neither *I* nor *any
of our missionaries*, placed as superintendents to a Captured
Negro Town, are in our right sphere as missionaries.' The CMS,
he thought, had wanted them to 'devote their time and talents

to their ministry; but here we are encumbered with everything connected with our situations as *Superintendents of public works, clearing* and *repairing Roads, imprisoning* and *punishing—settling disputes* and *quarrels* between people.' Naturally all of these had to be done, but Nyländer wanted someone other than a missionary to do them.[30] The experience of two years at Kissy did not change his mind. Writing to Pratt in 1821, Nyländer criticized more specifically. He confessed, 'I am as averse to corporal punishment as any—and so averse that I have been censured for not keeping my people under greater subjection by those means; but I must freely confess that no Captured Negro Superintendent can dispense with it at present. . . . At present we have to consider them as Children of a barbarous uncivilized country where nothing but the fear of punishment keeps them in subjection. . . . When I wrote to you of the inconsistency of our being Ministers and Superintendents of Captured Negroes I mentioned no particulars: but now I must candidly tell you, that this is one of our burdens. None of us I am sure will make use of the rod without sufficient cause and in a degree consistent with the character of a tender parent.'[31] Other missionaries added to Nyländer's complaints. Renner wrote from the old village of Leopold in 1820 that 'many a time one is almost worn out with settling the different palavers amongst a rude people, and one gets almost out of humour to attend school-keeping'. Moreover, with such an overwhelming burden on the missionary, Renner admitted that the religion taught to the people produced only a 'light-headed', superficial result. The results in the administrative field were also often very tenuous. After death had removed Renner in 1821, Johnson reported that the superintendent-less village rioted when MacCarthy visited it on his return from England late that year. The Revd. Wilhelm also revealed difficulties with his dual responsibilities at Waterloo.[32]

In addition to those who seriously complained about the incompatibility of the two parts of their job, there were those who simply proved inept. Although the latter group tended to echo the reasoned complaints of a Nyländer, it was doubtful whether they would have proved successful had they had only one job to perform. Wenzel had come under criticism while he was with the Susu mission. He had been involved in the charges and counter-charges among the missionaries which Bickersteth had cleared up during his visit. Wenzel began effectively enough as superintendent at Kissy in 1816; MacCarthy had given him his complete support. But soon he fell victim of the climate and the too arduous responsibilities of his work. He turned for comfort to the wine bottle. He explained one absence from a Freetown CMS committee meeting by the excuse that the creek between Kissy and the capital was impassable, and his own health did not permit so strenuous a journey. Assuring his brethren that he would soon be better, he told them that he was resting on his veranda with the best medicine he knew: a bottle of red wine. No longer either a comfort or a medicine, the bottle of wine became an escape and before long Wenzel had to admit to Pratt what everyone in the colony had come to know. He had been drinking excessively. He protested defensively that there was no other refreshment in his village. By mid-1818 his condition became so serious that the other missionaries brought him to Freetown. Undoubtedly suffering from advanced malaria as well by this time, Wenzel was 'very dangerous, is delirious at times, and when in his right mind not comfortable'. The 'Enemy', added Johnson 'seems to have the upper hand—the world seems to be the all and in all.' Pratt suggested that Wenzel be dropped from the society because of his drunkenness, but before any action could be taken, Wenzel died. His initial work in Kissy was in ruins and it was left to Nyländer to begin again.[33]

Others that the mission society employed in responsible positions proved incapable from the beginning. In 1817 the CMS sent C. H. Decker to the colony and MacCarthy, eager for new personnel, almost immediately appointed him schoolmaster-superintendent at Wilberforce. Decker ran into difficulty with his villagers from the outset. When he measured out regular town lots with the assistance of Johnson, the people of Wilberforce simply refused to acknowledge the new boundaries. They continued to build how and where they pleased, and much to the superintendent's chagrin, they built houses on the central square which he had set aside for the new church building. To show their complete displeasure with him, they attempted to burn down Decker's house. From Freetown, MacCarthy watched the progress of Decker's superintendence with uneasiness. The real seriousness of his position only gradually revealed itself. Decker was unable to manage the financial side of his personal and government life. To cover up his extravagances, he soon became heavily indebted to two European traders of questionable character from Freetown. His debts also extended to villagers in Wilberforce. Things went very badly indeed for Decker. In an attempt to gain some success, and with a hope that it would correct some of his more glaring difficulties, Decker turned to the improvement of the religious life of Wilberforce. Here he also met disaster, for again, the villagers proved far cleverer than he; they soon had the upper hand with the simple discovery that by going to Decker with a story of hardship and by confessing to be truly religious, they could obtain just about anything they asked from the superintendent. His debts mounted. Such incompetence eventually rendered Decker completely helpless in his situation. Once it became known that he owed more than a year's salary to his various creditors, MacCarthy removed him from his superintendency. The embarrassed CMS sent him to be an assistant to the superintendent at Kent until his affairs could be straightened out. The local committee requested London to recall him, but before this could be done, Decker died at Kent. The effectiveness of the parish plan, as always, lay in the hands of its executors, and in such feeble hands no plan could hope to succeed.[34]

A further factor hindering the work of the missionaries was their constant bickering. Jealousies and personal quarrels were constantly eating at the foundations of the system; unfortunately the chief protagonists were often found among the system's most dedicated supporters. Thus Butscher's charges that Mrs. Johnson was illiterate only produced guarded admissions from Salisbury Square of her lack of certain abilities,[35] and bitter harassment of Butscher himself by the other missionaries in the colony. Johnson's own quarrel with the Hortons which had begun aboard ship led the quarterly meeting in Freetown to refuse the couple permission to leave their teaching posts at Leicester Mountain. When they left anyway and took a government position in Freetown instead, Johnson's barrage of charges grew more vicious. Largely because of Johnson's attacks on Horton's character, the Society was unable to accept as part of its record of accomplishments in Sierra Leone the glowing testimonial given by Chief Superintendent Reffell to the Hortons when they left the colony.[36]

All things considered, however, the greatest hindrance to the Governor's attempt to regularize the Sierra Leone government was poor health and the high rate of mortality. Had all other matters worked according to plan, because of the health factor there remains considerable doubt as to whether the parish plan could have worked. Death brought to a premature end most of the work which had been successful. Johnson succumbed to yellow fever, During was drowned in a shipwreck while on his way to Europe on a leave occasioned by his poor health, and Butscher, whose pioneering work with Maxwell and MacCarthy had done much to establish the mission itself and produce its first significant results at the Leicester Mountain Institution, was a victim of malaria. His death caused the ruin of the CMS Institution long before it could be the lasting credit to the society that Pratt had originally envisaged. The difficulty at Leicester Mountain was that, as elsewhere, success came only in personal terms. Just as success at Regent and Gloucester could not be separated from the influence of Johnson and During, so to the early success at Leicester Mountain was the reflection of Butscher's vigorous work. Butscher established the school and became its first director. The students respected him and worked hard for him. But after his wife's death in 1815, followed shortly by that of his infant son, Butscher grew despondent. Bickersteth brought Butscher's daughter to England with him when he returned in 1816. The missionary wanted her safe from the colony's unhealthy climate. He hoped to join her later. Butscher had been criticized prior to Bickersteth's visit for engaging in trade to the detriment of his mission duties. Allegedly he had made a £2,000 profit from the goods sold after the shipwreck in 1813. Bickersteth, however, had cleared him of these charges. There was, on the other hand, little doubt about Butscher's being 'more wordly' than the other missionaries. Intent on providing a suitable education for his children, Butscher had invested in potential income property in Freetown and the rural areas.[37] The charges of profiteering almost at once revived. That they did was an unfortunate example of some of the more petty jealousies in the colony.

Colleagues and even some who were not directly connected with the mission wrote London that Butscher ignored his responsibilities at Leicester Mountain. According to them, he spent most of his time in the Freetown market and attending to his property. Taking note of these charges, the CMS told Butscher to pay more attention to the school. The superintendent at Leicester Mountain answered that he would 'act according to the advice which I often heard many of the natives of Africa [give] to each other'. The advice was simple. When one received 'unpleasant news' or, as in this case, unwarranted criticism from relatives residing in another country, one did not answer immediately. Instead, the advice was to 'wait a little, do not send the messenger as yet, but let thine heart sit down first (be calmed), and then send the answer' because 'thy relatives are in another country, and [are] ignorant of the fashion in this country'. When 'thine heart can sit down thou canst then explain to them the whole Palaver and they will readily believe thee'.[38] The essential problem between Butscher and his colleagues was that he was too obviously a MacCarthy superintendent. Throughout the early period of the

Governor's disillusionment with the CMS, he continued to speak highly of Butscher's work. The Revd. Garnon remarked that MacCarthy saw only one side of Butscher. Butscher was one who planted and built, and this was the type of man Mac-Carthy respected. His being a MacCarthy superintendent, however, condemned him in the eyes of some of his colleagues. In their opinion, he lacked the proper spirit of reverence. The attacks on his personal life, the loss of his family, and the strenuous work on Leicester Mountain combined to weaken him. Early in July 1817, he suffered a severe malarial attack which was complicated during the second week by an intestinal complaint. Brought to Freetown where apparently little could be done for him, he grew progressively worse and died within a few days. Nearly everyone immediately recognized that his death was a great loss. But the Colonial Chaplain noted coldly that considering the low state of Butscher's spirit and his bad temper toward the CMS, 'perhaps then—respecting the great loss—the Lord has graciously interposed to prevent things happening which might have distressed all parties'. Undoubtedly he was referring to the fact that Salisbury Square had decided to pay heed to the attacks against Butscher and to dismiss him. The society only waited until a replacement could be found. Drawing a parallel between Butscher's death and that of King Asa in the Old Testament, Pratt and Bickersteth suggested that the late superintendent would now serve as an example to those who wished to indulge in pride and self-will.

Unfortunately for MacCarthy's plans, no adequate replacement was ever found for Butscher, and after his death the Leicester Mountain Institution fell into complete ruin. The missionary's assistant, Schoolmaster Horton, left in 1818 and was replaced by the Revd. J. G. Wilhelm. Wilhelm's only real distinction was the fact that he outlived all of the early missionaries. Arriving in 1810, he served twenty-four years in the colony. He was not, however, a particularly successful superintendent. Soon after his arrival at Leicester Mountain he confessed that the 'mechanics are a lazy and disobedient set of boys, who require a stronger hand than mine is over them to keep them usefully employed and in good order'.[39] Less than three months later the boys rebelled. Eleven students were gaoled by Johnson, whom Wilhelm called down from Regent to serve as magistrate. Subsequently, the boys drove Johnson from the Institute and he had to be saved by a constable. Wilhelm explained the affair accurately in terms of Butscher's death: the boys at Leicester Mountain had never transferred their loyalty from the original superintendent. To Butscher 'they were attached like children to their own father'. No one succeeded in gaining the trust of the boys after Butscher's death. By 1819 the situation had so deteriorated that Wilhelm himself was replaced. His successor wrote that 'the place is in a most ruinous state in appearance and reality'. Late the same year MacCarthy decided to move the Institution to Regent, where it began again under Johnson. He dismissed most of the former students and began with eleven of his own, ten of whom were already communicants.[40]

THE INSURMOUNTABLE PROBLEMS OF SICKNESS AND DEATH

Thus when insufficient, unconvinced, or inept personnel did not operate to hinder the progress of MacCarthy's plans, death did. The problem of poor health among the Europeans sent to the colony was central to the early failure to establish an effective and stable central government. The threat of death was so serious, almost so predictable, that potential missionaries could credibly speak about seeking martyrdom in Sierra Leone.[41] James Norman, Johnson's successor at Regent, sailed into the estuary in 1821, looked up from the deck of the ship, beheld the spectacularly verdant mountains, and returning to his cabin wrote, 'I was . . . much troubled with a fear that I should soon die in this unhealthy climate. I looked on the land as my burying place.'[42] Mrs. Hannah Kilham phrased the same fear more poignantly when she wrote, 'It is true, indeed, that the remembrance of what I felt the first evening we spent in Sierra Leone has been impressively before me, when, sitting with . . .

our kind fellow labourers in the African cause . . . my spirits were rather broken with the feeling of the very critical position in which we were placed, the constitution of each relaxed by the climate, and surrounded by mementoes of mortality; our state seemed comparable to that of sitting under a drawn sword, suspended by a hair almost indescribably slender.'[43]

Journals and letters throughout the first half of the century were filled with agonized accounts of the last hours of suffering, the frantic but ineffective attempts of the medical officers to save the afflicted, and elaborately argued post-mortem judgements as to whether the deceased had truly conquered death by accepting salvation. Although they varied somewhat, statistics told the story as simply as possible. In the fifty years between 1811 and 1861, the Wesleyan Methodist Missionary Society sent out fifty missionaries and fifteen wives. Of these, twenty missionaries and eight wives died in Sierra Leone.[44] During the first twenty years of CMS activity, the society sent seventy-nine missionaries and wives to the colony. No less than fifty-three died at their posts. Of five missionaries sent to Freetown in 1823, four died within six months. Even by 1840 the situation had not substantially changed. In January of that year thirteen CMS people arrived in the colony, but by July five had already died and five had returned to England because of poor health.[45]

Death's toll among government officials was no less severe. Late in 1814 MacCarthy left the colony to supervise the transfer of power to the French at Senegal. Less than a month after his departure in December, Major Mailing, acting governor at Freetown, died. Mr. Purdie, the senior member of the Council, took over but he was dead by March. Major Appleton, who succeeded Purdie, fell sick, resigned, and left the colony in June. His successor, H. B. Hyde, another Council member, served until MacCarthy's return in July. In seven months the colony had had four acting governors.[46] When MacCarthy returned from the Gold Coast in 1823, he found that the Freetown government had no lawyer, no chief justice, no secretary, no chaplain, only one writer, one schoolmaster, three medical men, three Council members, and a few missionaries. By July of that year, eighty-nine Europeans out of a total of 150 were dead, most of them from yellow fever. A workman in the King's carpenter's shop remarked, 'There is nothing but making coffins going on in our shop; three and four in a day.' It was understandable that by the end of the decade, a visitor took pains to record the following toast at one of Freetown's many elegant public dinners: 'To the most usefullest men as is in the colony,—I means the doctors.'[47]

The aptness of the toast was questionable for the doctors proved largely incapable in the face of almost incessant attacks from the two major killers, malaria and yellow fever, among the Europeans. In addition to these, dysentery, smallpox, and excessive drinking frequently weakened stronger constitutions or eradicated weaker ones.[48] Malaria was the most regular cause of illness. Nearly every European spoke about undergoing the 'seasoning fever' after his arrival. Usually, if the person survived the initial attack he could expect to endure subsequent ones with some degree of certainty. A few of the missionaries such as Nyländer, Renner, and Wilhelm remained in the colony long enough to build an immunity. Yellow fever visited the colony periodically. It lacked the predictability which enabled the colony to brace itself for its yearly bout with malaria during the rainy season. There were fifteen visitations of yellow fever in Sierra Leone between 1815 and 1885. The period which elapsed between the attacks was irregular. At one period they came three years in a row, but at other times there were from two to eight years between the attacks.[49]

The lack of medically precise diagnoses and the consequent failure to develop adequate means of protection combined to make malaria and yellow fever all the more dangerous to the European in Sierra Leone. By 1823 the medical men realized that they were fighting two different types of fever. Malaria, or as they called it, 'bilious remittent fever',[50] attacked regularly during the rainy season. If the infected person survived, the fever would remain dormant for a time before returning at regular intervals. What the doctors in nineteenth-century Sierra Leone termed 'malignant remittent fever', yellow fever, was unpredictable in its occurrence. When it did attack, it came in the dry season and produced almost certain death for the afflicted. Dr. William Barry adequately diagnosed yellow fever in 1823 and correlated it with the disease's last previous visitation in 1815. Although he considered his evidence insufficient, Dr. Barry suggested that infected ships entering Freetown harbour introduced the scourge to the town. The lack of consistency in the attacks supported his belief that at least yellow fever was not endemic. Yellow fever simply 'pursued a . . . rapid and fatal course.' The symptoms were explicitly noted, as were certain variations in the patient's behaviour during the hours immediately before death. But the doctors remained helpless in establishing a treatment. They could only note that as with malaria, yellow fever's most devastating attacks occurred in the low-lying sections of Freetown and that it was virtually unknown in the villages. Johnson remarked about his fear of going to Freetown during the fever season 'as I frequently bring [it] home.'[51] Various causes were suggested. During the 1829 attack of yellow fever, the Deputy Inspector of Hospitals, Dr. M. Sweeney, reported that he was 'inclined to attribute it to a peculiar state of the atmosphere'. Dr. William Boyle, the Colonial Surgeon, pointed to the unusually early beginning of the rains, the tornadoes and the hot sun, and the fact that this created a miasmic 'bad air' condition which hung over the town. The bad air, full of lifeless matter torn from trees by the tornadoes, could not escape. It enveloped the community. The evil atmosphere, according to Boyle, originated across the estuary on the Bulom Shore, and the careful observer, he contended, could see it coming slowly across the water. Bloodletting, he observed, was not a proper treatment for the fever.[52]

Most doctors observed more accurately than Boyle. But obviously their thinking was far too confined by the limits of their faulty assumptions. Their premises continued to prevent the development of an effective cure for either yellow fever or malaria. Although they had realized that they were dealing with two types of fever, their treatment showed that they often confused one fever with the other. The very names they used, bilious and malignant remittent fever, revealed their cloudy understanding of the differences. Yellow fever could produce the bilious characteristic, and conversely, malaria could be malignant. In attacking malaria, doctors spoke of two types of fever, remittent and intermittent. In actual fact, they simply described two stages of the same malarial fever. Such errors, which went uncorrected for decades, resulted from a complexity of reasons, but foremost among them was the insistence by the medical profession upon treating the symptoms of the diseases and never undertaking exploratory investigations of the cause. The very name fever indicated the dominant fascination with the pathological condition.[53] Frustratingly then, doctors struck out to discover the cure for the symptoms of the two major killers, yellow fever and malaria.

If, as Boyle pointed out in 1829, bloodletting was not an effective treatment for yellow fever, it continued to be used along with various other irrelevant methods to combat the more common malaria. Leeches were kept in constant supply and would be placed on the malaria patient's shaved head in the hope that the fever would be literally sucked out. The cures were, of course, very hard on the already weakened sufferer and often proved fatal in their own right. Doctors felt that if the patient salivated, the fever would reduce, so they administered large doses of calomel through the mouth to effect salivation. But this often only caused a loss of teeth, if and when the patient recovered on his own. Another means of stimulating the saliva flow was by the use of mercury or quicksilver. Quicksilver, however, usually produced more serious consequences than it remedied. The patient's mouth became seriously irritated and inflamed and, in the most extreme cases, swelling of the tongue from its contact with mercury caused death by suffocation. The application of steaming cloths to the shaved head of the patient or of large mustard packs to the stomach were other remedies. These were supposed to produce large blisters which, when they broke, would allow the fever contained within the body to escape.[54]

The use of quinine in treating malaria was known in Sierra Leone at least as early as the 1830's. Quinine, the sulphate of one of two alkaloids isolated from cinchona bark by Pelletier and Caventou in France in 1820, was used by doctors in West Africa by 1826, along with other less effective cures. After the British started to produce it commercially in 1827, the price gradually fell until the 1830's when its general use became widespread, and by 1840 it had become a popular substitute for the older and less reliable bark itself. If given in the correct amounts, cinchona bark itself could have been effective both as a treatment and as a prophylaxis against an expected attack. Known in England since the last half of the seventeenth century, doctors remained uncertain about its effectiveness throughout the eighteenth century. Too many variables presented themselves for the bark to be completely efficacious. Amounts of the relevant alkaloid varied in any given piece of bark; prescribed amounts of the bark to be used also varied; and most importantly, the doctors themselves lacked faith in the bark alone as a cure. Although it had been administered in the colony by Company doctors in the 1790's, it was not until the 1820's that the bark came in for another of its periods of popularity. Even by the 1830's the bark's isolated alkaloid, quinine, was not used exclusively nor as a prophylactic. One European doctor told the Revd. John Graf, CMS missionary at Hastings, in 1837, that his having had the seasoning fever very soon after his arrival had had more effect on his recovery than either the calomel or 'quenin' administered to him. Regular and more effective use of quinine waited until late in the 1840's.[55] In 1849 the Revd. Graf noted that he had been to Regent for a rest cure, and had visited three fellow workers who were afflicted with the seasoning fever. They all recovered, Graf gratefully reported, 'by a mode of treatment, hitherto untried in the colony, and by far not so undermining to the constitution as the mercury system is wont to do. I trust that the Bark (quinine) system of treating the fever . . . will go far in rendering this climate less injurious in the future.'[56]

Although the final confirmation of quinine's success awaited the dramatic expedition of the *Pleiad* up the River Niger under Dr. W. B. Baikie in 1854, mid-century itself became the great medical watershed in the history of the Sierra Leone fight against malaria. Fully two years before the Baikie expedition, the Wesleyan Methodist mission in Freetown, at its January 1852 district meeting, noted gratefully that it had not lost a single preacher through death during the preceding year. The society did not have any deaths due to malaria for a period of seven years beginning in 1850.[57] Europeans continued to die of malaria after 1850, but with the more and more regular use of quinine the toll was considerably reduced. When the anti-pyretic was used as a preventative later in the century, 'bilious remittent fever' was brought under even more complete control. Dr. Patrick Manson's theory in 1896 that mosquitoes carried malaria, and Major Ronald Ross's confirmation in India the following year, at long last opened the door for a completely effective means to control the once deadly disease. The discovery in Cuba by a team of US Army doctors three years later that yellow fever was also carried by mosquitoes and the development of an effective preventative technique in the 1930's finally rendered the colony safe for the European.

But it was much earlier that MacCarthy's Freetown faced the formidable task of preserving human life on Africa's west coast. During those times malaria and yellow fever remained what Surgeon John Shower called in 1824 'the dreadful scourge.' Since the doctors were helpless to find an effective cure, Europeans in general turned their attention to the matter of minimizing the threat of sickness to themselves. Hannah Kilham thought that the European community should move out of the town and live in the mountains, where she found herself much more healthy. Mrs. Kilham felt that the climate was not the only cause of bad health, but suggested in addition, immoderate living habits, the lack of capable housing superintendence, and the greater fatigue associated with working in the tropics. She wrote that 'this climate requires a cheerful disposition and good courage, as well as temperate habits'. She also pointed out that European styles of house architecture were not suited for life in Freetown. Such houses were not healthy, particularly during the rains when they had to be closed up. The occupant was thus forced to stay inside what became a dark, stuffy, and humid box. She noted the airiness of African quarters, and remarked that she would prefer houses for the Europeans which were built more on an African pattern or design.[58]

Governor MacCarthy, on the other hand, thought the maintenance of health in Sierra Leone was a result of proper exercise and good habits of cleanliness. He concluded in 1819 that he had survived eight rainy seasons in the tropics by keeping fit and dry. He took regular trips to the new outlying villages by either horse or boat. He always kept a dry set of clothing into which he would change whenever he got wet. Moreover, he remarked, 'By the use of shower baths I have accustomed myself to wet'. As if concurring with Mrs. Kilham's estimate of European housing, the Governor noted that 'I keep my windows open all night at all seasons of the year, and I am then less effected by exposure to a damp atmosphere'. Finally, since MacCarthy knew that the most dangerous aspect of the climate was its psychological effect, he 'dispelled all gloomy impressions as far as [he could] by keeping body and mind engaged, mixing with society, etc.'[59]

Other Europeans produced varied and generally less profound solutions. Butscher wrote meekly to Pratt after the death of his wife and son that he and MacCarthy had talked about the need for an establishment doctor. Major General Charles Turner, MacCarthy's successor, maintained that the fear of the climate was ill-founded. It would, he admitted, take some time to eradicate the idea, but new and weatherproofed houses with fireplaces would do much to help. Boldly he wrote, 'I find fires and port wine my best protection'. He died of malaria within six months. The Revd. Johnson gave his wife laudanum when she was seized with a severe pain connected with the fever. Colonial Chaplain Garnon had a portable sentinel box built for his use at the cemetery during the rainy season. With five or six corpses to bury in a single day, he simply had the box 'moved from grave to grave and read in it the services or wait[ed] in it if more were to be buried'. Unfortunately, Garnon also soon died of fever. The town fathers viewed the undergrowth in the streets and the overgrown jungle, particularly in east Freetown, as being a 'disgrace' as well as 'a fruitful source of the fever'. They ordered the removal of vegetation before the sun could destroy it and allow the dead matter to enter and contaminate the air.[60]

Although the observations of most people were usually precise, and their arguments well reasoned, the failure to find a solution stemmed from the original assumptions. People in general, and doctors particularly, complained at length about the *mal aria*. No one noted his annoyance with a mosquito bite. Though they came pitifully close with the observation that few contracted fever at the higher elevations, the tragedy of early Freetown was that the careful, or even the careless onlooker, never got to the heart of the difficulty. The element of the pathetic was never more clearly recorded than when Dr. A. Nicol, the Colonial Surgeon, wrote Thomas Morgan, a CMS school teacher who was returning to London in 1821 because of bad health: 'I wish I could accompany you. I am now tired of this place, and did I not wear a *red coat* I should instantly take my leave of a place so inimical to the health, and so destructive to the lives of Europeans as the peninsula of Sierra Leone is —*this place* is actually a hotbed to fever during the *long* rainy season—one attack but renders you more liable to others—This is a fact, and altho' the deaths are not so numerous amongst older residents yet their perpetual ill health renders existence miserable and destroys the best faculties of the mind. I draw a gloomy picture. . . .'[61]

The gloom overshadowed everything. Death and sickness continued to take enormous tolls. Lord Gambier, President of the CMS, cited poor health conditions when the Society successfully sought to free itself from the parish plan in 1824. Because of the many deaths and conditions of ill health the society simply had not been able to satisfy the colony's needs.[62] The Parliamentary Commission of Inquiry which arrived in Freetown in 1825 reported to the Colonial Office that one had to be in Sierra Leone in order to comprehend the difficulties of the colony. Henry Wellington and James Rowan, the two Commissioners, encountered difficulty merely investigating the immediate past since most of the people who had managed the colony's affairs were dead. With MacCarthy dead in the Gold Coast and the administration of the colony in a shambles, the Commissioners were forced to conclude in their *Report* that the older villages were in so neglected a state that little useful information could be gained from them, and the newer ones provided administratively 'few facilities for estimating their progress'.[63]

THE END OF THE MACCARTHIAN ERA

Four months after MacCarthy's death in 1824, the CMS asked to be relieved of the responsibility for superintending the villages. They promised to maintain their clergymen in the colony and to remain in charge of the Freetown schools. The government was left with the responsibility for education in the districts outside the town, and for the necessary religious, educational, and civic buildings. The British government in London recognized the ultimate failure of MacCarthy's attempt to administer the villages and so, with an overriding desire to cut its own costs, approved the new plan.[64] The MacCarthian era, which had ended for the energetic Governor in bloody death at the hands of the Asante, ended for Freetown with the signing of the new agreement and the coming of a new governor.

Governor Turner replaced superintendents with government

managers, few of whom had any connection with the CMS. Of the four managers first employed by Turner, only one was an English CMS missionary, and one of the remaining three, a Liberated African, had been trained by Johnson at Regent. Turner wanted new managers from the West Indies who were versed in coffee and cotton production. Civilization in Sierra Leone under Turner was measured by one's ability to produce crops for export, and religion was relegated to a secondary position. The most highly regarded manager in the next few years was Thomas Macfoy, the manager in Wellington, who was from the West Indies.[65]

Cooperation between the CMS and the government returned to the informal level of the pre-MacCarthy period. The missionaries, Anglican and Methodist, continued between them to hold a monopoly on education. Financial responsibility for education in the villages alternated periodically between the government and the CMS. MacCarthy's plan was dead. His own increased responsibilities as Governor-General after 1821, the Church Missionary Society's failure to provide sufficient and capable personnel, poor health conditions and a high death rate combined to cause its complete modification. This was assured when Governor Turner succeeded in cutting the colony's expenditures by half. With the parish plan the government had come close to controlling absolutely the destinies of the Liberated Africans. Reduced governmental expenditure and decreased official involvement combined to allow the independent Liberated Africans themselves to evolve the new society which was to dominate Freetown by mid-century.

V

Foundations of Liberated African
Independence

Freetown lost its administrative stability with the death of MacCarthy and his plan. In contrast to his ten-year term there were, during the next twenty-seven years, twenty-eight different administrations controlling the destiny of the colony. The effect of this could have been disastrous because, as the Liberated African historian, A. B. C. Sibthorpe, wrote shortly after mid-century, 'the Colony [was] grievously injured by want of a systematic plan or rule from the Home Government for its direction. Every governor [was] left to follow his own plans, however crude and undigested; and no two succeeding Governors . . . pursued the same course.'[1] What the English humanitarians had destined to become the cradle of African civilization, 'developed merely into a base of operations, judicial and naval, against the slave trade' after 1825.[2] The lack of systematic direction from Downing Street reflected the general attitude of liberal England toward the Empire. High mortality and the rapid deterioration of health on the Sierra Leone peninsula only confirmed the 'little Englander' in his anti-Imperial views. If the Crown had any single policy regarding its Freetown colony between 1825 and 1850, it was one of greater economy and hence of lesser involvement. The period of building had ceased. The era of MacCarthian prosperity was over.

Governor Turner arrived in 1825 to reduce expenses. His successors were also dispatched from London with instructions to cut the costs of operation. Those governors who had plans for the betterment of the colony found themselves tightly restricted by the budget and their instructions. Moreover, just as there was no compulsion to continue to pour vast sums into the colony, neither was there a desire to 'send forth the best ye breed'. The men who administered the colony after 1825 were generally mediocre. Only two of them exhibited the potential of greatness, but, unfortunately for the colony, both died prematurely. Gone from the records of this period were the succinct analyses of the problems of Liberated Africans and the reasoned attempts at solution which had characterized the administration of Sir Charles MacCarthy. Successive governors viewed the Liberated African increasingly either as ungrateful and degraded, and therefore unworthy of any further consideration, or as being perfectly able to manage his own affairs. Although the second opinion proved to be the salvation of the colony, the reasoning behind both views was tailored to fit the predetermined view of London: to keep the costs at a minimum. None of the governors sent met the call to greatness that his position demanded. Whereas the period of the colony's history prior to 1825 was marked by the central government's desire to build a more coherent structure to regulate the Liberated Africans, the period after 1825 was very much the story of the efficient management of affairs on the local level by the Liberated Africans themselves. The procession of mediocrities at Government House, coupled with the continuing difficulty which metropolitan mission boards found in securing and maintaining adequate personnel in the colony produced a situation in which the Liberated Africans themselves were able to determine the character of their own future. In this context Creole society of mid-century was developed.

When Parliament passed legislation in 1853 declaring that for legal purposes the Liberated Africans, like the Nova Scotian Settlers, were British subjects, the members at Westminster tacitly recognized the direction of social change in the colony. Low class villagers in the 1820's, the Liberated Africans had become in less than a generation active and independent participants in the life of the colony's capital city. Moreover, they had done so largely on their own terms. The methods which they used to attain this position were a combination of the ways of their African past and of the new society which they found on arrival in Freetown. Both the individual Liberated African and the initially alien culture which he encountered proved adaptable. The contact produced a new society through the constant interaction of peoples of diverse cultural origin. The cultural result is known in Sierra Leone history as Creole society. The foundations were laid in the second twenty-five years of the nineteenth century by the independent participation of the Liberated Africans in local politics, the growing commerce of the colony and its hinterland, and in the daily life of their own villages. Originally, the Liberated Africans had found independence in their villages around Freetown in the period before the MacCarthy administration; after MacCarthy's death and the consequent lessening of direct governmental involvement, what had been in effect a village or rural province of freedom for the Liberated African developed over the next quarter of a century into a colony-wide province of freedom for his Creole descendant. Controlling the colony's trade with the interior by 1840, recognized as British subjects by 1853, and admitted to the newly-constituted Legislative Council in 1863, the Creole had attained a level of independence and freedom not commonly associated with the histories of British dependencies in the nineteenth century. Unofficially, but still dramatically for the Creole, Sierra Leone had become his province of freedom.

GOVERNMENT RETREAT UNDER TURNER AND CAMPBELL
The European aided the Liberated Africans in their development of an independent status within the Sierra Leone colony. The expatriate did so mainly because of the budgetary cuts which necessitated a decreased involvement in the daily life of the recaptive settlement, and also because he gradually came to recognize the fact that Liberated African society, when left

to itself, proved quite capable of managing its own affairs. Still, Europeans never ceased to devise schemes for the betterment of the colony and its population. Some offered agricultural reform. Some suggested moving part of the colony's population to the Gambia or Fernando Po. Some thought official repatriation would prove beneficial, while others viewed the actual return of the Liberated Africans, particularly to their Nigerian homeland in the 1840's, with considerable misgiving. Most continued to place ultimate faith in education and Christianity since education remained largely in the hands of the missionaries. The schools' continued existence proved paramount for it gave a central focal point, a definable symbol for the newcomers in their quest for acceptance in Freetown society. Government itself played an important role in placing greater responsibility in the hands of the recaptive population. Greater economy of operation meant that government restricted the area of its participation. In a series of steps between 1824 and early 1827, the government gradually removed itself from the area of providing rations. In October 1824, even before Turner's arrival, Chief Superintendent of the Liberated African Department Thomas Cole cut rations to children of Liberated African parents living in the villages, and greatly reduced the beef ration.[3] Shortly after his arrival, Turner himself cut the number of Liberated Africans on direct rations, 4,000, by half. To reduce the number on direct governmental support further, Turner reinstituted the apprenticeship system. Under his administration, future arrivals were to be distributed among the colony's 'reputable' citizens who were to use them as farm labourers or house servants for a period of three years. Only the elderly and the very young remained under government support after 1825.[4] Further curtailment of governmental expenditure also served to put the Liberated African population on its own. Although he began the construction of the Army Barracks at Tower Hill, most other government building projects were halted. Government employment on construction sites fell by one-quarter by 1826.[5] Liberated Africans sought employment on the land or, more often, in trade, as their Nova Scotian predecessors had done under the Company and earlier Crown governments.

Early in 1826, Turner died, and in August, after a period of almost six months under acting governors, the colony welcomed its third new administrator of the year, Sir Neil Campbell. Under Campbell—the unfortunate officer who had been charged with keeping Napoleon on Elba in 1814—the policy of austerity continued.[6] Since the Liberated Africans continued to represent the largest single item in the government's budget, Sir Neil naturally turned his attention primarily to them. Within a month of his arrival, village managers were forbidden to buy anything for their villages without the prior approval of the government, 'except . . . the cotton for wicks for lamps used in the evening schools'.[7] Such prohibitions represented a temporary measure, however, for Sir Neil was busy devising his own schemes for rendering the Liberated Africans less expensive and more productive.

His own particular innovation proved highly important to the development of Liberated African independence although its motivation was purely to ensure for Whitehall the continuing economic operation of the colony. Beginning on 1 January 1827, the Sierra Leone government ceased providing the newcomers with the food and supplies hitherto thought essential. In place of the supplies provided abundantly to the recaptives during the era of MacCarthian prosperity, Campbell ordered that all new arrivals should be granted three pence per day for the first six months of their life in the colony.[8] After than, Sir Neil, and successive governments, expected them to provide for themselves. The new policy—known as the Plan of January 1st—was clearly progressive and with only minor modifications it became the standard policy for the future. The Governor's reasoning was sound. He had determined correctly that by ending the purchase of supplies in Freetown, he could save the government from large and unnecessary expense. By giving the newcomers money rather than goods, he served to stimulate the local economy. Increased circulation of money was effected through the increased purchasing power of the Liberated Africans. The policy provided a ready market for the agricultural produce of the rural areas, and increased consumption naturally led to increased production. Women and children were provided for separately under Campbell's Plan of January 1st, but the motivating principle of securing a permanent reduction of costs to the government remained the same. Women continued to receive food and supplies for the three months following their arrival or until they were married, whichever event occurred first. The government distributed children among those already established either in Freetown or the villages where they worked until they reached the age of fifteen. After that, they too had to provide for themselves.[9]

Progressive and theoretically sound, the benefits, nevertheless, of Campbell's plan eluded him during the remaining eight months of his tenure. He died shortly before the end of the year from an apparent attack of malaria. His own personal anxieties over proving himself as competent and trustworthy—the ominous shadow of Napoleon's escape from Elba bore heavily on his personality after 1814—coupled with continual bad health and persistent debate with his second in command, Lieutenant-Colonel Dixon Denham, no doubt accelerated the coming of his own death and rendered much of his administration ineffectual. The sheer numbers and length of his dispatches to Whitehall revealed a certain insecurity in his own mind. The presence of Denham rendered the insecurity into near madness. The Colonial Office, thought Campbell, had sent the famous explorer of the Sahara to check on him, a suspicion not unfounded. Denham was sent in 1827 to be Chief Superintendent of the Liberated African Department with separate but similar instructions to Campbell's, but with the opportunity to report directly to Under-Secretary of State R. W. Hay. The fact that he did so regularly no doubt served to antagonize the Governor as well as to undercut his own confidence. Previous superintendents of the recaptives had been virtual appointees of the governor himself; the mere fact that Downing Street had sent its own and had entrusted the position to one whose knowledge of Africa far exceeded that of the Governor himself proved a considerable threat to Sir Neil Campbell.

He began by totally ignoring Denham's presence, and then, after two months, switched to providing him with orders containing the most minute details, including the size, amount, and colour of clothing to be dispensed by the Department to the newly arrived recaptive women.[10] Very quickly the two men developed basic differences over policy. By the end of April Campbell began to worry that his Plan of January 1st was not producing the anticipated reduction of costs to the government. He thought the reasons were easy enough to explain—more new arrivals than anticipated, the necessity of taking over the cost of the schools from the CMS, and the additional cost of providing managers for the villages—but his anxiety led him to exceed the plan and to cut further. His new cuts brought him into a direct clash with Denham.[11] He ordered that arrivals be apprenticed to responsible citizens of Freetown and the villages, thereby reducing the total number on the three pence per day government subsidy. Furthermore, he told his Chief Superintendent to send some young Liberated Africans to the military station at the Isles de Los, and finally, to limit the children to three or four years of school between the ages of ten or eleven and fourteen. By the age of fourteen, he thought, they should either be ready to come to Freetown to work as servants or to remain in the villages as cultivators. Hopeful that the modifications would produce additional savings of £3,000 annually,[12] he turned his attention to other matters of state. He had not fully anticipated Denham's reaction. The Chief Superintendent accepted the first and second points, to increase the number apprenticed, but totally rejected the third, to decrease the number of children in schools. To Denham, the suggestion represented the worst streak in the Governor, his tendency to slash indiscriminately. Denham saw the schools as a guarantor of the colony's future. Understanding broadly the need to reduce expenditure, Denham nonetheless was a planner in the MacCarthy tradition who recognized the need for certain sound investments, such as in the recaptives' education. When he became governor himself a year later, he confessed, the 'Liberated Africans are my children and I shall not neglect their welfare'. To him, economy of operation in regard to cutting schools was of secondary importance. The future of the newcomer was of primary concern to Denham. If Campbell's desire to reduce expenditure was basic, to Denham it seemed that the Governor's attitude toward the Liberated Africans was more at fault. He objected to Sir Neil's characterization of the recaptive as vicious and disorderly. Neglect, he wrote privately to Hay in London, was the sole cause of the drifting and wandering of the Liberated Africans about the colony. He furthermore objected to the Governor's attempt to establish a system of military control over the population. Ordinary laws and ordinary police were quite sufficient to regulate a population of recaptives whose primary desire was to 'sit down quietly'.

Denham thus perceived Campbell's policy toward education as an attack on the long-standing humanitarian desire to Christianize and civilize the Sierra Leone Liberated Africans. Denham defended the educational system. It was 'the best we could afford'. More educational opportunity was needed, not less. But in spite of the debate, the Chief Superintendent eventually had to recognize his subordinate position to the Governor, and although he commented that the policy guaranteed 'the demoralization . . . of the Liberated Africans, Male and Female', he had the schools cleared and the children distributed according to the Governor's wishes. Again, however, the policy failed to make an appreciable saving for the government. Far more seriously, the policy led to considerable social disorganization in Freetown itself. The already substantial ranks of the town's prostitutes were enlarged. 'The elder girls,' wrote Denham, 'instead of being married, and settled in the Villages from the Schools, have after a short time left their adopted parents, from ill treatment, or neglect, and are living in a state of prostitution, in Free Town, generally with the soldiers.'[13]

Campbell died before such consequences of his modifications of the Plan of January 1st became evident. Lieutenant-Colonel Lumley who then commanded the garrison succeeded Sir Neil, only to be replaced by Denham himself in May 1828, when Downing Street at long last made its wishes known. Denham died from malaria within a month.[14] As one contemporary remarked, his death was 'a shock among all classes of people here'. Major J. J. Ricketts, later to be governor himself, confessed that Denham's work and plans 'were highly beneficial and useful, and would no doubt have produced in time the most desired effects'.[15] In spite of the friction with Campbell, Denham had accomplished much during his time in the colony. The new settlements were built during his tenure in the Liberated African Department. He had improved road connections between the villages and Freetown. He had perceived the future importance of moving produce from the rural areas to the town markets or to such secondary markets as those at Regent. Under-Secretary Hay, confessing his own shock at Denham's death, wrote to Lumley who again became governor that the former explorer had served the colony 'very much to his own credit and to the satisfaction of His Majesty's Government'. He had, in fact, provided the Colonial Office in London with its first systematic information on the Liberated African villages.[16]

ACTUAL ADMINISTRATION OF THE LIBERATED AFRICANS
That Downing Street had to send Denham in 1827 to find out such information reflected the tenuous control the British government exercised over the Liberated African community. The Crown had hoped that Denham could put the administration of the Liberated African Department on a sounder foundation. Wellington and Rowan, the 1827 Commissioners of Inquiry, had revealed the Department's inadequacies to Parliament. Their *Report* had been particularly severe on the De-

partment's lack of method in handling the recaptives. The Commission had found it difficult even to discuss the procedures for it had found 'no fixed code of regulations'. The individuals, like Joseph Reffell, who had been responsible for the Liberated Africans had not even an official digest of regulations for their guidance. There had been some uniformity in the allocation of food, clothing, and work, but otherwise the local superintendents had been in charge, serving for all purposes as autonomous agents. The Commissioners concluded that 'plans were chiefly adopted as the exigencies suggested them, and that their execution was entrusted to a succession of individuals, without any established rules for their guidance'.[17] Reffell himself led the Commissioners to conclude that there had never been any instructions for the Chief Superintendent. Reffell confessed to Wellington early in 1826 that the superintendence of the Liberated Africans had been ineffectual. MacCarthy, during his tenure as governor, had given orders directly to the local superintendents. Acting governors who followed him gave orders to the Chief Superintendent who passed them on to the local managers. Turner followed the latter procedure during his tenure. By then, however, the budgetary cuts had so reduced the area of responsibility that the orders often had to do only with the issue of provisions and stores, public expenditure in general, and the procedures for apprenticing, enlisting, and recruiting for the public works. Under Campbell most of these were eliminated entirely.

In addition to the absence of a system of administration, the Commission also found a serious lack of personnel. After completing its study, the Commission suggested a minimum number of fifty-one to staff the Department. The suggested number included those needed to staff an administrative centre in Freetown as well as personnel needed to staff each of the fourteen villages in existence by April 1826. Against this minimum figure of fifty-one, the Commissioners had found a total of fourteen actually working for the Department. The majority of the fourteen were still Church Missionary Society people who continued to serve in spite of the new agreements to the contrary signed by the London CMS Committee and the British Government.[18] A dim prospect was therefore rendered ominously darker by the death of Denham little more than a year after he had arrived in the colony to put things in order. The succession of governors, acting governors, and lieutenant-governors who administered the colony during the 1830's was barely able to keep abreast of the increasingly complex situation. What had once been an idyllic dream of civilizing the African, had become by the third decade of the nineteenth century merely an admitted struggle to maintain minimal control of a natural process of cultural change. From here on, the primary concern would be to contain within a certain acceptable limit the extent of actual liberty extant in the recaptives' society.

The government's new emphasis on simply controlling, rather than determining and directing the destiny of the Liberated Africans manifested itself in the late 1820's, the first indication coming in new instructions sent by the Department in Freetown to village managers and sub-managers. Gone from such documents was the older ideal of the superintendent as complete leader. The new manager was to be more of an inspector than a superintendent; his purpose was to regulate rather than lead. Chief Superintendent Thomas Cole told the new manager sent to the Mountain District in 1828 that he was to inspect the markets three times a week, school children and school teachers once a week, go to church every Sunday, settle any minor village disputes, and keep his town neat and orderly. Cole's instructions, in essence, were for the new official to oversee the activities of the Liberated Africans in his district.[19] Through such instructions the Liberated African Department resolved simply to keep up with the changes which were admittedly occurring, and to control the colony villages as policemen keeping the peace. If such orders admitted that the government could do no more, they also revealed that no more needed to be done. Liberated Africans were settling down quietly.

Village of Bathurst

The government's new system of inspection rather than super-intendence did not please some of those who continued to hold on to the older dreams. Its weaknesses were admitted and criticized. Joseph Reffell declared in 1829 that the villagers were so disorderly that it would take him 'twelve months' hard labour [provided he was the Governor of the Colony] to get them into anything like the order they were in [in] 1824.' He added, 'any change of system would be better than the present'.[20] Lieutenant-Governor Alexander Findlay frankly admitted that 'those with the position of Sub-manager[21] have been regarded by the Liberated Africans as having virtually no authority at all', and proposed a change of system in 1831. His alterations proved inconsequential for Findlay only changed the names of the responsible officials, upgrading the sub-manager to full manager. The duties of the individuals, and the manner in which they were regarded by the Liberated Africans remained unchanged. Such changes of titles did not hide the fact that, after 1825, the functions of the Department became essentially regulatory. Once thought of in higher terms, the recaptives themselves increasingly came to be viewed by the government as 'a supply of people', a phrase actually used in 1840 to describe the arrival of a recently-seized slave ship in the harbour.[22]

STABILITY AND SETTLEMENT BY TRIBE

Those who accepted the assumptions and desires of the original philanthropic group which established the colony, and of the enlightened government which succeeded it in 1808, found the post-1825 system hard to accept. They saw in it the failure of their hopes and plans. Uncritically also, they saw in it the failure of the colony. To them it came as a distinct surprise that no catastrophic collapse of society took place in Sierra Leone in the 1830's and 1840's. Their talk of failure foretold such a collapse and led to attempts such as that of Dr. Madden, the 1842 Commissioner of Inquiry, to convince the British Government that they should abandon the colony. Those who had dreamed the most about the colony in the early days found it hardest to realize that the settlement was not collapsing, the colony was surviving.

The desire to abandon the colony as a failure was relative to the whole mentality of the humanitarian Englishman interested in the colonies in the nineteenth century. When he talked about the failure of the Sierra Leone experiment and the lack of cohesion and stability in the colony, he really meant that change was not occurring exactly as he had predicted or desired. His plans had failed, not the colony. Those who were ready to write off Sierra Leone neglected to see or to understand the real elements of cultural cohesion and stability which had manifested themselves in Liberated African society. Largely in spite of the European's attempt to create a 'civilized' African, life was continuing to be lived in an orderly manner in both Freetown and the colony villages. Society was changing rapidly, but order did not break down. The African cultures represented in the Liberated African population proved resilient. Recaptives were able to adopt new techniques and to reinterpret old values. This fact proved to be central in the long-term success of the Sierra Leone experiment in the nineteenth century.

The government itself was instrumental in guaranteeing the effectiveness of the process. As early as 1822 it had recognized the greater stability to be found when Liberated Africans settled according to tribe. Chief Superintendent Reffell informed the village superintendents that[23] 'His Excellency [was] satisfied from actual observation that [the newly-arrived Liberated Africans] will more rapidly recover their health and strength and at the same time be rendered more happy by being settled with their countrypeople, [and] is pleased to direct that instead of their being confined to live together as heretofore (in some villages), the men until such time each can build his house, should be divided among the houses of the best conducted persons of their own country in the villages who it is hoped will feel a pleasure in instructing them in our language and the habits of civilized life.'[24] The policy did not, however, become standard. When Thomas Cole, then Chief Superintendent, answered the questions put to him by the Commission in 1826, he neglected to mention settlement by tribe at all. Curiously, when Reffell himself, seven months later, commented on the policy of settling Liberated Africans by tribe, he gave the impression that it was an innovation of Governor Campbell. Campbell had suggested the procedure to Bathurst as a means by which the Liberated African might be brought more quickly and by implication less expensively, to a state of civilization.[25] Colonel Denham wrote privately to R. W. Hay in Bathurst's London office that it was 'much better for the people themselves to be sent up to the mountain villages where they meet their Countrypeople and are fed on Cocoa's roots and other Vegetables—than for them to be kept here in Freetown within four walls idle and Sickening for want of employment.'[26]

By the 1830's the policy of settlement by tribe had been accepted as a relatively inexpensive and efficient method to maintain stability in the villages. A manager of Regent confirmed its continued use. By 1835 the government retained the newcomer on public works for the first three months in Sierra Leone. He was then sent to a village where he lived with 'his country-people', and began to build his permanent hut. He retained his twopence per day government subsidy until his sixth month in the colony. The payment was usually turned over to the people with whom he resided during this period. They provided him with food and shelter in return. Even after the sixth month, however, his countrymen continued to 'share their provisions with the newly-located Africans'.[27]

Because of this tendency to settle with one's countrymen, each village in the rural areas developed definable sections within its limits. People of one particular tribal or sub-tribal group lived in these sections. The area was usually known by the name of the group's tribal origin. Hastings comprised Aku-Town (Yoruba, Oyo), Egba-Town (Yoruba, Abeokuta), Ijesha-Town (Yoruba), Mocca-Town, and Crabba-Town (Calabari). Settlement by tribe also existed in Freetown and separate sections were readily identified with the dominant group making up its population. Foulah Town, on the city's eastern limit, was founded in 1819 by immigrant Fula traders from the interior. By the middle 1830's it had become predominantly Muslim Yoruba, as had also the section to the east known as Fourah Bay. The Mandinka traders settled originally on the town's western limits, but by 1850 they had moved into the section of the city along Destruction Bay known as Magazine Cut. The area took its name from the Powder Magazine which Kenneth Macaulay had built in the 1820's. The Mandinka settled in the area because of its proximity to the main Freetown market. There they specialized as butchers for the cattle which the Fula and Mandinka drove down from the north to supply Freetown's need for fresh meat. Thus both inside Freetown and the villages, settlement by tribe had come to be the accepted pattern by the third decade of the nineteenth century.

The pattern provided the colony with its cohesion and stability. In addition, it satisfied the government's need for economical operation. By 1830 the system of settlement by tribe had clearly won the endorsement of the government. Lieutenant-Governor Findlay informed London in September that he was 'convinced from [his] limited experience that by the manner in which the Liberated Africans generally conduct themselves . . . they have acquired such habits of industry and order as in [his] opinion qualify the major part of them to be left to their own unrestricted exertions'[28] Although such a bold declaration may have been met with some surprise in London, to many who were in daily contact with the Liberated African in Sierra Leone it was accepted as a simple statement of fact. The Liberated Africans had proved to be both independent and resourceful. Thomas Cole had admitted this five years earlier when he reported to Colonial Secretary Joseph Reffell that the Gloucester population was progressing quite well without any government supervision. The government, six months prior to Cole's report, had removed the Gloucester population from public works employment. While some of the residents had 'loitered nearly the whole of their time away . . .' most had in fact cleared new land, raised crops, and sold them for profit at the market. Cole suggested that such diligence, if turned to the production of export crops, could become a benefit to the whole colony. He concluded that the Liberated Africans did better on their own and suggested that the Department should end all rationing two years before Governor Sir Neil Campbell actually did so.[29] The diligent attention paid to agriculture by village recaptives did pay off for the colony before long. In 1831, one village manager credited the agricultural produce of the rural Liberated Africans with saving Freetown from 'the dire effects of Famine during the latter part of the last rains' when warfare in the interior cut off much of the food upon which the capital usually depended.[30]

The government therefore learned to appreciate the agricultural production of the recaptives. Some officials such as Lieutenant-Governor Alexander Findlay saw great hope for the future in such accomplishments in the rural areas. It led him to overlook the fact that the newcomers maintained 'the superstitions and Idolatrous customs and manners of their own countrys [*sic*].' He transferred his hope of civilizing Africa to the children of the Liberated Africans. Providing they received a 'christian and religious' education, they would surely advance western religion and culture throughout the continent.[31] Others were more willing to credit the security and stability found in a Liberated African village to their gradual advancement toward that state which most observers of Sierra Leone in the nineteenth century chose to call 'civilization'. Reffell himself, citing the ineffectuality of the Liberated African Department before the 1827 Commission, readily conceded that the recaptives had made progress toward civilization. The CMS Chaplain in Freetown, the Revd. John Raban, noted a slow advancement of the Liberated African manifested by the growing number of new houses being built in the capital by the more prosperous recaptives.[32] John McCormick, a European who had spent eighteen years on the West Coast and ten in Sierra Leone prior to 1826, confessed that although progress had been attended by great difficulty, many Liberated Africans had 'obtained that comfort which is essential to Freedom and happiness'.[33]

The Liberated Africans' ability to adapt quickly to their new environment explained the progress that had been made. The more observant Europeans recognized the resilience of the African cultures represented in the recaptive population. Such observers admitted that the differences between their own western culture and that of the Liberated Africans was not the result of mental inferiority or lack of natural abilities on the part of the Africans. The source of any difficulty which had prevented the African from advancing more rapidly was attributable to what the Quaker missionary Hannah Kilham called 'the lack of those advantages which are . . . made use of as instruments for the advancement and improvement of human beings'. Basically the African's technological disadvantage was little different from that of others in the non-European parts of the world.

The reduced level of technological development was apparent to any who sought to understand the nature of those societies from which the Liberated Africans came during the early nineteenty century. Even though most originated in what came to be called Nigeria, they represented a variety of traditional African cultures. Koelle at mid-century analysed the languages of one hundred different linguistic groups represented in the Freetown Liberated African population. He estimated that in all there were two hundred different languages spoken in colonial Sierra Leone. His figures alone attest to the variety present. The relatively high level of political and social stability evidenced in Liberated African life, moreover, could be understood best from the standpoint of the settled communities from which the recaptives came. A sampling of three different West African groups, the Yoruba and Ibo from the interior regions of the Bights of Benin and Biafra, and the Asante from the interior of present-day Ghana, should give an indication of the cultural variety represented in the resettled African population of Sierra Leone in the 1820's.

The third decade of the nineteenth century found the Yoruba states of western southern Nigeria embroiled in the first of a series of major civil wars. These were to characterize the history of the Yoruba during much of the nineteenth century and ultimately lead to British annexation before the century was out. The wars naturally upset the stability which had characterized Yoruba life prior to the nineteenth century. Political life had focused on the ancient capital at Old Oyo. A vast empire stretching from the Niger westward as far, at times, as contemporary Dahomey and Togo centred in Yoruba proper. Although the oldest history of the Yoruba remains clouded in the myths of origin and migration, it is clear that by the fifteenth century the rudiments of the Yoruba empire had been set at the city of Old Oyo. The empire which eventually came to dominate most of Yoruba as well as a vast area to the west developed around the institutions of a limited monarchy. The Alafin was the monarch. Two major institutions served to limit his power, the Oyomesi, a seven member aristocratic Council of State, and the Ogboni Society, a body through which the freemen of Yoruba effected the destinies of their empire. All elements of Yoruba society theoretically participated in the government of their state: the monarch, the aristocracy, freemen and slaves. The most powerful check on the power of the Alafin, however, came from the Bashorun, a virtual prime minister and leading member of the Oyomesi. In his position was vested the power to deliver to the Alafin the parrot's eggs, a traditional sign of the people's displeasure with the Alafin, an act which was followed by the disgraced Alafin's suicide. An indication of the vast power which rested in the hands of the Bashorun was to be found in the brutal usurpation of authority in the latter part of the eighteenth century by Bashorun Gaha, one of the factors which led to the eventual decline of the Yoruba empire.

The power of the Oyo empire was to be found in its political institutions, its army, and its ability to generate wealth through trade and tribute. As the empire spread from its base at Oyo, its local institutions adapted to the needs of imperial administration. To an important extent the institutions of Oyo became those of the imperial areas. The nature of the empire was flexible. Power was in the hands of a provincial administrator who reported directly to the Alafin. Through this administrator came tribute to Oyo and orders to the local people. The army of the Alafin was a powerful instrument in the acquisition of imperial territory. It was composed of infantry and cavalry with an elite 'praetorian guard' of the Alafin at the centre. The military commander of the Old Oyo army was a minor Alafin in his own right. In the event of a defeat he and the Alafin had to commit suicide. Through the effective use of this army, the leadership of the Oyo empire was able, during the eighteenth century, to extend its dominance westward over the entire Dahomean kingdom. The fundamental, long-term power of the Oyo empire, however, was to be found in its economic roots. Just as the foundations of the older medieval kingdoms to the north and west had been in their ability to control and dominate the trans-Saharan trade, those of the Yoruba were to be found in the ability to control trade routes to the sea during the seventeenth and eighteenth centuries. With the routes to the sea continually open, the riches of the Atlantic trade could be focused on Old Oyo. Once this could be effected no longer, the empire began to crumble and a series of civil wars ensued with the various Yoruba cities vying for control of the trade routes and the right to succeed Oyo as the dominant city among the Yoruba people. In the more stable days of the past, wealth generated from trade had allowed for the expansion of power from Yoruba proper, the group of core cities around Old Oyo. Such expansion produced a further economic support to the empire in the form of tribute. That from Dahomey alone amounted to £32,000 annually.

Another distinguishing feature of Yoruba society at the beginning of the nineteenth century was its cities. The Yoruba remain unique in traditional sub-Saharan Africa for the urban nature of their life. Although the Yoruba cities were more akin to agricultural communities or market towns than to the modern westernized cities of the West African coast, they nevertheless provided the Yoruba with a pattern of urban living which no doubt contributed advantageously to those who were recaptured and resettled around Freetown during the early part of the nineteenth century. Yoruba cities were large. Population estimates of Ibadan in the nineteenth century ranged from 70,000 to 150,000 and those for Old Oyo from 25,000 to 75,000. The circumference of the walls surrounding Ibadan at the middle of the century was twenty-three miles.

The architecture of the Yoruba urban dwelling with its solid walls facing the paths and only a single narrow entrance into a central courtyard spoke of the protective function of the city. The markets gave evidence of the economic function of the cities. They were regular establishments. Their interior organization and arrangement indicated the self-governing element and organized condition of the people. Markets were arranged symmetrically and were carefully regulated by an officially appointed master. Each market was divided into distinct sections which provided different places for each type of produce or manufacture. Craft specialization was readily apparent. Visitors reported finding the very fine cloth manufactured at Old Oyo throughout the markets of Yoruba country. Cities provided the focal point for Yoruba life, and joined together as they were in a political empire, they formed the basis of power throughout the period of Yoruba ascendancy.

The Yoruba wars which broke out early in the nineteenth century provided Sierra Leone with a dominant Yoruba group in its Liberated African population. A secondarily large number of recaptives came from Ibo country, a territory to the interior of the Guinea coast to the east of Yoruba, beyond the Niger as it descends to the coast at the Delta. Ibo culture stood in marked contrast to that of the Yoruba. The basic unit of Ibo political life was the single village. Centralized political institutions or control were never a part of traditional Ibo culture. The village was composed of several households scattered in close proximity around the countryside. These households were joined together by kinship ties. The largest political unit was a grouping of such villages which shared a single deity and a central market-place. Sovereignty rested in the individual village unit, and although the people recognized the leadership of the head of their particular lineage, they did feel an allegiance to the larger village group which was manifest in certain annual rites as well as in maintaining the market place.

The unifying aspects of Ibo culture were to be found outside the area of political institutions. In a most elementary way language itself unified the peoples east of the Niger. Furthermore, elements of the social structure served to provide a common denominator. Although each village comprised members of a single lineage, the lineage structure pervaded all of Iboland. Religiously, the Ibo recognized Chukwu as their supreme being. This latter factor was of singular importance as an integrating feature in Ibo life. The Chukwu Oracle at Arochukwu served as a final court of appeal in the legal structure of Ibo society. Respect for this oracle allowed the people of Aro to dominate trade throughout Ibo during the high point of slave trading just as the common respect for the oracle at Awka allowed for the domination of travelling blacksmiths from that community. The market places which dotted the countryside naturally served to integrate the otherwise isolated life of the Ibo village. Of final importance was the particular nature of Ibo marriage custom. Ibo exogamy necessitated that a man find a wife in a village group other than his own. By this practice otherwise separate village groups were intertwined with one another. This proved beneficial to inter-village trading as well as in the reduction of potential rivalry and tension between the villages. Such an intertwined fabric of kinship provided a degree of unity to Ibo life which was highly sophisticated and of ultimate benefit. The 'pure democracy' of Ibo political life could survive with such a variety of integrating elements in the culture.

In other parts of West Africa, the lack of such integration even among peoples with common origin and a common social structure led to the growth of large political empires for the purposes of protection. This is an aspect of the story of the growth of the Asante empire in the seventeenth and eighteenth centuries. People from Asante were to be found among the Sierra Leone population both among the returned Maroons from Jamaica and the nineteenth-century recaptives. The former group in fact added the distinctive folk tales of the Cape Coast interior to the rich folk heritage of the Sierra Leone Creole.

The Asante of modern Ghana formed an important segment of the Akan-speaking peoples of that nation. Together with a common linguistic origin, the Asante shared with other Akan speakers similar customs, religious beliefs, and domestic and political institutions. Most importantly, they held the eight matrilineal and eight patrilineal lineages in common with their language relatives of the Gold Coast. Throughout the history of the Akan peoples, clan allegiance and particularly taboos remained mutually more important than allegiance to one of the several different Akan states. In fact, the rise of the various states to domination represented the imposition of the power of a particular lineage on the other clan groups.

A variety of reasons served to stimulate the rise of separate and competing Akan states from the sixteenth century onwards. The rise of these states gave to the history of the Gold Coast interior its distinctive character. The reasons leading to the rise of the most famous of these states, the Asante, serve as a useful example of the history of the Akan in general. Of primary importance was the geographic location of the Akan states at the confluence of the two major trading routes from the Western Sudan which connected with the main routes from the south bringing gold and kola to be trans-shipped northward. A second factor was the subjection of the Akan peoples of this area by the Denkyira at the middle of the seventeenth century. This stimulated other Akan states to form an empire for the purpose of ending the tyrannical rule of the Denkyira. A third reason for the rise of Asante was the growth of the Atlantic trade. That trade in particular strengthened the Asante by providing a constant source of guns and gunpowder. Furthermore, it eventually brought the Akan peoples of the interior to the coast where they traded directly with the Europeans.

With these reasons as background, the arrival of the Oyoko clan in the Kumasi area by the 1670's provided the leadership for the rise of the Asante empire. Of crucial importance was the individual leadership of the first three Oyoko rulers at Kumasi: Obiri Yeboa, Osei Tutu, and Opoku Ware. Together the three forged the Asante empire out of the Akan states subjected to Denkyira overlordship. During the period of Osei Tutu, the empire received its most potent symbol, the Golden Stool, which served as the embodiment of the soul and unity of the Asante people. From these beginnings in the seventeenth century, the Asante empire spread throughout central Ghana and eventually reached the sea. It was this empire's further attempts to control trade to the sea in the nineteenth century together with the rise of the Fante empire which led to the eventual clash between the British and the Asante. This clash, by the 1870's, produced active British involvement in the Gold Coast interior and the eventual annexation of the territory to the Empire.

In each of the three groups considered, the Yoruba, the Ibo, and the Asante, the force of circumstances—geographical, political, economic—had brought about dynamic responses and growth. By the beginning of the nineteenth century each group had evolved a complex and viable culture. Each culture served the changing needs of its people. The view that the peoples of the West African coast had sunk into a period of retrogressive development following the fall of the medieval empires of the Western Sudan only to be saved by the coming of the European in the nineteenth century is simply not supportable by the history of these and other coastal peoples between the seventeenth and the nineteenth centuries. Each group proved resilient and adaptable to the changing challenges of the shift of trade, the introduction of new products, and the rise of new political empires. With a firm foundation in their own cultures therefore, it was not surprising that the recaptives from these territories who were resettled in Freetown should prove themselves able to adjust to their dramatically changing circumstances. What distinguished the Liberated African from the European who had come to administer and to rule him was what distinguished the culture of the first from the second. The technological differences were major.

In Sierra Leone the Liberated African's position was even more desperate because such technological differences were compounded 'by that oppression, which wherever exercised, had a natural tendency to fetter, to depress, and to blunt the powers of the mind'.[34] Slavery and the slave passage had clearly taken a toll beyond the simple statistics of those who died in transit.

The stability and security evident in Liberated African villages were seen as a remarkable achievement to someone with the sensitive mind of a Hannah Kilham. The great dislocation occasioned by the slave trade was severe. The Liberated Africans lived in Sierra Leone as expatriates themselves. In effect, the colony was as foreign to the majority of them as it was to the European missionaries or government officials. By 1836 the vast majority of the slaves emancipated at Freetown were being shipped from trading stations far down the coast, in the Bights of Benin and Biafra.[35] Although the trade had gradually shifted down the coast toward the close of the eighteenth century, operations of the British Naval Squadron sent to prevent the illegal trade in 1808 lagged behind. Not until after 1813 did it become clear that the Naval Squadron's activities had also shifted southward.[36] In the seven years between 1819 and 1826, the masters of sixty-nine ships were tried before the various Courts of Mixed Commission at Freetown. Only four of these ships had been captured north of Sierra Leone. The remainder had secured their human cargoes at such trading points on the coast as Lagos, Calabar, and Popo. Tribally, these captured slaves were mainly Yoruba, Ibo, and Dahomean. By 1830 the first two groups represented the dominant cultural groups among the Liberated Africans.[37]

THE SLAVE TRADE

The reasons which lay behind the capture of individual Africans were as complex as the reasons for the trade itself. It quickly became apparent to even the most unseasoned observer that the Act of Parliament which abolished the trade did not in itself lessen the trade or reduce its horrors. Astute politicians pointed out these facts to abolitionists in London. Even an occasional abolitionist expressed his dismay 'that our measures for the suppression of the Slave-Trade not only increase its horrors . . . but its very extent'.[38] Unfortunately for those who sought a simple answer, the causes of the slave trade were so intertwined with the political, economic, and social systems of the West African peoples involved, that complete abolition of the trade had to await not only the more effective suppressive measures of the naval squadron, but also necessary changes within the African societies themselves. To a large measure the business of such political entities as the Oyo Empire in eighteenth-century Yoruba had been the slave trade. The wars of this empire had produced prisoners who often found their way into the complex system of the international slave trade. In later years the wars which arose from the gradual loss of the Oyo empire's hegemony in western Nigeria similarly fed the slave trade. As social dislocation reached an advanced stage throughout the territories to the interior of the Bights of Benin and Biafra, more and more prisoners were captured and eventually found their way into the international commerce in human beings. Very simply, the increasing number of prisoners meant that more slaves were transported in the international trade, and more slaves were recaptured, adjudicated, and freed in Sierra Leone.[39]

Warfare clearly emerged as the primary cause of capture from the many stories told by recaptives in Sierra Leone. The young Ajayi Crowther, later destined to return to the country along the banks of the Niger as a great missionary bishop, was captured during one of the wars in the Oyo country at the beginning of 1821. A much lesser known Liberated African, John Wright of Hastings, was captured at the age of six when his birthplace, Ilaro in Yoruba country, was taken quietly one night by an enemy force while everyone slept. The entire countryside 'was . . . thrown into the wildest consternation and confusion. In the midst of this bewilderment families upon families rushed from their homes and in that dark and troublous night madly committed themselves to the bush for concealment.' In the mad rush of the flight, John Wright was separated from his mother and never saw her again. Wandering about lost and frightened, the crying boy was seized by the enemy and spent the next eight years of his life serving various masters as a slave before he was finally sold into the international trade and began the long voyage to the New World. Seized on the high seas by a British cruiser assigned to the Preventive Squadron, the ship carrying John Wright was brought to Freetown where its human cargo was freed. The emancipated Wright was sent at the age of fifteen to the school at Waterloo in 1838.[40]

Crowther's capture was a result of the politico-religious struggle raging in northern Yoruba country between the Fulani, their Muslim Yoruba allies, and the decaying Oyo Empire of the Yoruba. Crowther's town, Oshogun, fell within four hours of the Muslims' initial attack. Completely surrounded by the superior numbers of the enemy force, even the relatively large and prepared militia of Oshogun could not withstand the attack, and most of the town's population was taken prisoner. The story of Crowther's capture as a youth, like that of Wright, was typical of many such catastrophic events throughout Yoruba country during these years. Women and children tried to flee into the surrounding countryside during the attack. Flight proved a false hope. All were seized and bound together to be carried off by the enemy after the battle. With the lingering memory of a burning town scorching its own indelible mark in their minds, the once free citizens of Oshogun were marched off to Isehi, a town twenty miles distant, where the enemy mustered its prisoners. As prizes of battle, the captives went to the several chiefs of Isehi, among whom they were divided. The chief who claimed the young Crowther soon after bartered him for a horse, but finding the horse unsuitable, ordered the young slave returned two months later. He was thus reunited with his mother for the next three months when he was again led away and sold to a trader who put him into chains and took him to the market town of Ijelu. There a Muslim woman bought Crowther and took him with her own son into the Popo country to the west.

Popo country proved completely foreign to the young Yoruba. Both the people and their language were strange. His mistress gave him considerable freedom to move about as a consequence. There was little risk to the owner in allowing the young slave such liberties since Crowther could have hardly found his way back to his own people without, as a foreigner, falling prey to someone else. In addition, he feared the local people, their 'enormous devil-houses', and the numerous witches. Most of Crowther's time was spent with the woman's young son. He found considerable security in his situation, and when she began to talk of going to the coast to buy tobacco to trade, Ajayi feared the worst: that she intended to sell him to the Portuguese traders. He stopped eating, and within a short time he had dysentery. He considered suicide, but when he tried to strangle himself he found that he lacked the courage to close the noose tight enough. Realizing her young slave's mental state and fearing that if she did not do so quickly she would lose her investment, the Muslim woman sold Crowther to another trader. The young Yoruba was grieved and dejected. Traders sold him twice more before he eventually arrived at a slave market near Lagos on the banks of a large river. Then, for the third time since he left the woman and her son, Crowther was sold. Eko traders from the opposite side of the river purchased him. Ajayi greatly feared crossing the water, writing later that

Christ Church, Pademba Road

it was like 'the thought of going into another world'. Finally the Eko traders carried him to the canoe which took him to their trading station. There he met two nephews who had been captured at the same time as he, but who had filtered down to the coast by other routes.

Since water surrounded the trading station at Eko, the traders allowed slaves freedom of movement. The area was divided into three separate sections. The Spanish and Portuguese traders occupied one, the free Eko the second, and the slaves the third. Crowther remained at Eko three months before he saw his first European. Then, 'one evening [some European traders] . . . came to the street of the house in which I was living. Even then I had not the boldness to appear distinctly to look at them, being always suspicious that they had come for me; and my suspicion was not a fanciful one; for, in a few days after, I was made the eighth in a number of the slaves of the Portuguese. Being a veteran in slavery, if I may be allowed the expression, and having no more hope of ever going to my country again, I patiently took whatever came; although it was not without a great fear and trembling, that I received, for the first time, the touch of a whiteman, who examined me whether I was sound or not.' The Portuguese traders who purchased Crowther kept him in their factory for four months awaiting transportation. Reports of British naval cruisers in the area prevented an early departure. Eventually a Portuguese slaving vessel loaded at Eko with 187 slaves, including the young Crowther. That evening, following the ship's departure, and while it was still near the Lagos area, two cruisers from the Preventive Squadron seized it. Crowther to date had spent over a year in slavery.[41]

The essentials of Crowther's experience were repeated thousands of times in the stories of capture told by other Sierra Leone recaptives. The burning of a town, and the seizing of the fleeing inhabitants in the night proved typical. Captured people were sold several times, and passing from trader to trader they eventually reached the sea. European traders bought them at one of

177

M

the many slave factories along the coast and then loaded them aboard the slave ships. Only on rare occasions was the slave freed before embarking for the New World and then most commonly by a wealthy relative who could afford to ransom him.[42]

Warfare was by no means the only manner by which Sierra Leone recaptives were enslaved. Some were sentenced by tribal courts to slavery. Ba, a Bassa from the Sierra Leone interior who had been brought in on the slave ship *Eliza* in 1819, told the Mixed Commission court that he had been until only recently a free man in his own country. He had had the misfortune of being caught sleeping with another man's wife and having the outraged husband bring him to trial before the village elders. They had found him guilty and had ordered him sold to a local trader who within a short time began the process of trading by which Ba, moving from trader to trader down the creeks and rivers of the Sierra Leone interior, eventually reached the sea and became the property of the Spanish captain of the *Eliza*. The Spaniard's ship, however, never embarked. The British man-of-war, *Thistle*, captured it as it rode at anchor off the coastal trading town of Bassa, less than a hundred miles south of Freetown.[43] A Calabari from the coast east of the Niger reported in 1821 that he had been sentenced to slavery instead of death by a court at Old Calabar for 'ravishing' his father's wives. The presence of a slave ship at Old Calabar saved him from death. Sometimes the one enslaved proved to be a dissident political rival of a local chief or the son of a chief whom rivals thought best to remove from the scene.[44] The existence of the international slave trade most simply provided African societies with a ready means of ridding themselves of their least desirable members.

THE RED WATER CEREMONY

Complex judicial procedures developed within the tribe to provide a steady supply of slaves. K. O. Dike has detailed the sophisticated development of the Aro Chukwu Oracle in southeastern Nigeria in his *Trade and Politics in the Niger Delta*.[45] Other tribal groups throughout West Africa had similar phenomena. Among the coastal Bulom-Sherbro to the north and south of Freetown, the Red Water Ceremony was extensively used. The ceremony was described by Dr. Afzelius, the Swedish botanist, in his journal during the 1790's, and again by the Revd. Gustav Nyländer in 1819. Ostensibly the Bulom sought to discover witches among their tribe by the ceremony. Nyländer correctly pointed out, however, that as soon as a slave ship was known to be in the area, 'our business [i.e. his mission work] is upset and witches are produced from all quarters, even by such of them of whom we had reasons to entertain a good opinion'.[46]

The Red Water Ceremony took place in front of the *Bankeleh*, a representation of the Mighty Spirit of the Bulom. The *Bankeleh* appeared in the form of a round stick, about three inches in diameter and about eight inches long. The bottom end of the stick was tapered so that it could be stuck into the ground. The stick was covered with black cloth which had a few cowry shells sewn on in order to represent a face. The 'head' was orna-mented with different coloured feathers. Once the adorned symbol was placed in the ground at a particular place reserved for the performance of the sacred ritual, small strips of leather covered with bunches of feathers and small calabashes contain-ing white beads were put on either side. The *Bankeleh* had special power to discover witches. Acting through the red water, the *Bankeleh* had power either to kill a witch outright or to discover him so that he might be punished. After the place had been made completely ready the ceremony began. An elder of the village laid himself down before the *Bankeleh* and begged that if the accused be a witch he might be able to discover it, but if not, that he might occasion the red water to make the accused person vomit. Next another elder, sitting on his heels, addressed the idol, '*Bankeleh* thou art the one that does us good. I beg thee if this man have killed *Pa Nam* [the victim] by witchcraft, let us know it now; if he be not guilty, make him vomit.' A third elder then stepped forward and placed two brass kettles before the *Bankeleh*. Each contained about one gallon of liquid. One contained clear water; the red water was in the other. An old man then lay down on the ground in front of the kettle containing the red water. With his face to the ground he hit the kettle with a small stick. As he struck the kettle he related the whole accusation against the individual charged with being a witch. He concluded by repeating the charge to the Mighty Spirit that if guilty the man was to be killed by the red water, but if not guilty, he was to vomit, spitting up even the rice he had had that day.

Following the accusation a mat was spread before the *Bankeleh*. Three bags were placed on the mat. Each represented lesser Bulom spirits, called *Suru*. At the same moment, the elders placed a horn, an axe, and a sword as an offering to the *Bankeleh*. Their contributions continued until it included two rusty hoes, an axe without a handle in a small brass pan, a country knife, and a small horn stuffed with trinkets of magical value. Next a man, again sitting on his heels, sprinkled rice flour on the three *Suru*, and pleaded that they assist the *Bankeleh* in his important business. During this period the friends as well as the accusers of the alleged witch pleaded to the *Bankeleh* for his assistance. The tension increased as the old man who had prepared the red water and was coming to administer it entered the area. He was followed immediately by the accused, who was brought before the *Bankeleh* for the first time. The accused sat on a scaffold, his right hand held high above his head. The hand held a stick which was quickly driven into the ground. A small bell hung from the stick. His left hand remained limp on his left knee, and his feet rested on sticks so that they did not touch the ground. His friends and relatives assembled behind him; he faced his accusers. Now the ceremony had reached its climax. The whole area remained still and quiet as the old man stepped forward with the brass vessel full of the red water. He handed it to the accused who took it and drank.

If the accused vomited, he proved himself not guilty and was freed. Originally, if he could not vomit, the red water poisoned him and he died. By Nyländer's time, however, most did not vomit. Neither did they die.[47] For, as the slave trade developed, the Bulom had found that it was to their advantage to sell the condemned witch to the Europeans as a slave. It successfully rid the society of its undesirable elements, and brought in return tobacco, rum, and other especially sought after commodities from the western world.

As late as 1862 one Dahomean woman related how she had been refused twice as a sacrifice at a great feast day because she was considered to be a witch. Eventually her people sold her to the Portuguese as a slave. Other Sierra Leone recaptives were kidnapped individually as they walked between villages or as they went on errands within a large city. Some became slaves as a result of the indebtedness of their parents or other relatives. One ten-year-old boy, freed when he came to Freetown in the 1870's with his master, had entered slavery as the collateral in a loan secured by his uncle. The loan was not repaid so the boy was bartered five different times during his lifetime; he had travelled throughout the northern parts of the Sierra Leone interior before his last master, the son of the paramount chief of Port Loko, brought him to Freetown on one of his frequent trading trips and the boy fled to become a Sierra Leone Liberated African.[48] Occasionally, the story of capture was one with Freetown itself as the setting, the teller being, in effect, a recaptured recaptive. More than once, the freed African asked to be returned to the place at which he had resided as a slave, on one occasion to exchange his status as an unemployed freeman in Freetown for that of a lucrative slave cigarmaker in Havana.[49]

RECAPTURE

Recapture, then, did not necessarily end the ordeal of the former slave. Even for those who settled satisfactorily in Sierra Leone, recapture itself carried with it considerable fear and danger. Reactions among the Liberated Africans to being recaptured varied as much as the stories of their original enslavement. Ajayi Crowther reported little initial difference between the British seizure of his slave ship and the many other transfers he had undergone during the period following his original capture. To many it must have seemed that they had exchanged masters yet another time. Crowther's recapture initially proved terribly frightening. Two naval cruisers seized his slave ship but soon afterwards several others appeared. The British captors divided the slaves among the several ships. Crowther was assigned together with six others to one cruiser. The future bishop boarded the ship in the second of two groups of freed slaves. He was shocked when, upon boarding, he found no sign of the earlier group. His shock turned to horror when he and the others in his group 'saw parts of a hog hanging, the skin of which was white—a thing we never saw before, for a hog was always roasted on fire to clear it of the hair in my country; and a number of cannon shots arranged all along the deck.' The re-captives 'soon came to a conclusion of what had become of [their friends] . . . The former we supposed to be the flesh and the latter the heads of the individuals who had been killed for meat'. A quick reunion with their countrymen proved ex-tremely reassuring. Together they proceeded to Sierra Leone, working as sailors. They entered Freetown harbour to be freed on 17 June 1822.

Not all of those slaves on board Crowther's slave ship were so lucky, for dangers to the slave freed by the British did not cease merely when he was recaptured. One hundred and two of the recaptives seized with Crowther never reached Freetown. They were drowned when their cruiser sank during a severe storm. As in Crowther's case, furthermore, the ships carrying slaves were often captured nearer to Nigeria than to Sierra Leone. This meant a long sea voyage of several months before liberation in the freeman's colony. Crowther's voyage after re-capture took two and a half months.[50] It was not untypical. Seventeen of the sixty-nine ships adjudicated at Freetown be-tween 1819 and 1826 had been seized about 1,200 miles from Sierra Leone. The average distance was 790 miles. One ship reportedly was captured 1,500 miles away and had taken 209 days to arrive. The 1827 Commissioners doubted these figures, but did cite two other cases where ships took over 200 days to reach Freetown after seizure. Sixty-two days was the average period which passed between seizure and adjudication. Death naturally took its toll from the recaptives during such long passages. Two hundred and seven of 1,889 captured between 1819 and 1822 died before the vessels could be condemned at Freetown. Sir George Collier, the Commander of the Preventive Squadron in 1821, reported that forty-six died out of 266 captured on board the Spanish schooner *Anna Maria* during its two months' passage to Sierra Leone. Fifty-seven of 424 died in passage aboard the *Perpetuo Defensor* in 1826. They succumbed to dysentery and smallpox. Those who were landed continued to be threatened with the diseases. In addition, they posed a serious threat to the entire Sierra Leone population.[51]

During the same year the Portuguese ship *La Fortune* was captured ten days out of Freetown. The return trip took 21 days because of adverse winds. During the trip forty-six of the 245 slaves on board died. *La Fortune* remained in the harbour six weeks awaiting adjudication. Seventy-seven more slaves died while the ship rested at anchor. Thus, one more than half of those originally recaptured were never liberated. Delays awaiting adjudication at Freetown were common, but few had to wait the six weeks of those aboard *La Fortune*. Sometimes delays resulted from the death of one or more of the judges; at other times a judge was absent from the town. In many cases the trial had to await an interpreter sent from one of the villages to question the recaptives. Before 1827 the usual delay was from twelve to fifteen days. On occasion the slaves on board a ship in the harbour rioted and thus had to be removed to the shore. Later, the ships were unloaded before adjudication in order to lessen the chance of death while the ship rested at anchor. Even then, however, a medical doctor's order was necessary to satisfy the legal minds at the Courts of Mixed Commission.[52]

Once the slave ship entered the harbour, the slaves became

the responsibility of one of the Courts of Mixed Commission. The master of the ship was brought before the court, tried, the ship and its cargo were condemned, and the slaves were freed. Once they had been liberated—later once their ship had anchored—the slaves disembarked and entered a large, walled area near the court which was known as the King's Yard. In the yard the recaptives awaited resettlement. One visitor to the yard in the early 1830's reported that 'when the momentary gratification of setting foot on land . . . had passed away, [the newly-arrived recaptives] looked sullen and dissatisfied, but not dejected. It struck me that on landing they expected to be allowed to go wherever they pleased, and were consequently disappointed and angry when they found themselves still under control.'[53] Although the King's Yard was directed by the Liberated African Department, the recaptives remained the responsibility of the capturing naval ship until after adjudication. All expenses incurred before adjudication were charged to the naval ship.[54] Such expenses naturally varied according to the number of recaptives and the length of time they awaited adjudication. It cost one naval ship £9. 5s. 6½d. to maintain 253 Liberated Africans from the *Fanny* in the King's Yard for one week in 1828. This included the cost of 116 bushels of cocoa, eleven bushels of rice, and twenty gallons of palm oil.[55] The government did not allow the recaptives to do any work during the period between landing and the trial. They only cut wood and carried water for their own cooking. Each twenty-five recaptives had one overseer who took them to a nearby brook to bathe. This was the only time they left the yard. All reports agree that none ran away. Although no work was officially required or allowed, the yard was alive with activity. Everywhere recaptives congregated in small groups around a fire if it was during the cold rainy season. Stories of capture were exchanged. In one corner someone pounded snuff between two stones. In another corner of the yard, a group of craftsmen from one tribe had established a simple but efficient system to produce knives. One man sharpened pieces of old iron hoop which he had found about the yard. Another shaped odd pieces of wood into a workable shape which still another, more skilled, carved into handles. A final man took the blade and the handle, joined them together, and placed an iron ring around the handle to hold it tightly. Others ground down the ends of broken cutlasses which the Liberated African Department had supplied for cutting undergrowth in the yard. They fashioned these into broad swords, and fixed them into handles carved by others awaiting final liberation. Prior craft specialization was also indicated when someone attempted to set up a forge in the yard. The man was undoubtedly skilled, but could not perform all of the tasks required. His job in the complex operation had been to know 'when to take the iron from the fire, and when to replace it there'. In order to pursue his craft he had to await a later reunion with countrymen in the villages.

Everywhere in the yard recaptives were busy. Some made baskets and straw hats. One man shaved the heads of his fellow recaptives with broken pieces of glass. Some made small bags called *cootacoos*, from small pieces of duck or canvas. They tore the material from their own waist cloths. They sewed with nails found lying about the yard, and thread which they also took from their waist cloths. Others passed their time playing the traditional game of warri with pebbles collected from the beaches and holes dug in the ground.[56]

The sounds of various musical instruments nearly always arose from the yard. Drums were most common. They took various shapes ranging from that of a sugar-loaf to that of an hour-glass. Most were small enough to be held under the arms. Another common instrument was one which has come to be known in Sierra Leone as the *kwande* or *kalangi*. Its nineteenth-century version was 'a hollow box about six or eight inches square, with four pieces of bamboo resting at about two inches from their extremities upon a bridge, while their other extremities are secure to the box—something similar to what would be represented if the strings of a violin were extended continuously, projecting over the bridge without being secured to the tail-board'. The player pressed the pieces of bamboo down, and by releasing them quickly he produced a mellow vibrating tone, The calabash or hollow gourd provided another musical instrument. A hole was made in the calabash and a covering was placed tightly over the opening. Small cowry shells were attached to the covering which produced a resonant percussive sound when the calabash was shaken. To make another instrument the recaptives used a long fibrous string taken from a piece of bamboo and attached it, in a state of tension, to a very flexible stick which was bent in an arch. By using another small stick, the musician struck the string which caused a vibrating sound. He modulated the sound with two fingers which he moved up and down the string. Occasionally the player took the string to his lips, and thus intensified the tone, which was normally extremely low.

The dance, like music, was an important part of life in the Liberated African yard. The nature of the dance differed according to which tribal groups were represented. At times, as one European visitor noted, only the women and children danced. The men provided the music. The dancers assembled first 'in a circle, with one person in the centre who [was] for the time the leader of the dance and music; the dance consist[ed] in walking . . . at a slow pace, round the circle, the principal action not being the feet, but in the hips, body, arms, and shoulders'. The head moved gracefully toward either shoulder. The men who surrounded the dancers rhythmically beat drums, shook the hollow gourds, sang, and clapped their hands.[57]

The work, music, and dance of the King's Yard indicated the strong desire on the part of most Liberated Africans to pick up life where it had left off in their own home countries before capture. The degree to which this was possible in the yard depended upon the number of countrymen the individual was with or whom he found on arrival. The yard was crowded at times with recaptives from more than one ship awaiting liberation.[58] Reunions among countrymen were not uncommon in the yard itself.

After the trial was held the recaptives became the complete responsibility of the Liberated African Department. Each one was entered in the registries of both the Mixed Commission Court and the Department, and received a small metal ticket which was tied around his neck. The ticket carried the individual's registry number. Once registration was completed, recruiters from the army entered the yard and secured enlistments. The remaining men were apprenticed, after 1830, for three months to one of the government departments. The women were taken directly to the villages, where they were placed with 'responsible married persons . . . to learn domestic duties prior to their own marriage'.[59] Most of the children were enrolled in one of the village schools. Invalids received an immediate pension of 2d. per day. Those who recognized relatives among the already settled Liberated Africans who constantly mingled around the yard were sent to live with them, according to the established custom, if not the official policy of the Liberated African Department.[60] Reactions to the process again varied considerably. For the most part, the Liberated Africans found the promise of a new life in Freetown initially encouraging and quickly settled into its pattern. For a few, the many changes proved to be too much of a burden. A suicide was occasionally noted. Sometimes it occurred while the slave ship rested at anchor; at other times someone took his life in the yard itself. Suicides in the villages were not unknown. On the other hand, one is curious to know how many of the Liberated Africans felt like the old Ibo woman who told the Revd. Johnson at Regent in 1820 that she felt as if she had been brought to heaven itself. Those who easily associated transportation on a slave ship with the death penalty for crimes committed in their own country, were certain that liberation at Freetown was some form of a 'rebirth'. It was the beginning of a second life.[61] Eventually, most newly-arrived Liberated Africans made the long journey to one of the several villages in the rural areas around Freetown. In these villages the new life really began. The new life acquired its cultural meaning in the political, economic, and social functioning of the people of the Sierra Leone rural villages. There in the villages Creole society began.

VI

The Politics of Independent Liberated African Life

Creole society could begin in the villages because in nineteenth-century Sierra Leone they existed as the Liberated Africans' own province of freedom. Certainly not unaffected by the efforts of government and mission to determine their nature and to control their development, these villages surrounding Freetown in the rural areas had nonetheless remained largely what they had been from the beginning: havens for the recaptives in which they could maintain themselves according to a pattern which bore a remarkable resemblance to their life before capture. It was the large measure of independence existing in the Liberated African villages which guaranteed their persistence as provinces of freedom for the recaptives. The measure of freedom which prevailed was the most significant result of the continuing failure and frustration of specifically British plans to civilize the Africans freed from the slave trade. In any society, the factor of independence is largely determined by the limits, legal or otherwise, which are placed upon its everyday life. In a colonial situation, the dominant power determines the legal limits. Conceived as the necessary means by which a people is governed, these limits, in varying degrees of effectiveness, curtail the independent functioning of the members of the subject society. For several reasons, the degree of effectiveness was greatly limited in Colonial Sierra Leone. British laws were sporadically and badly administered. As a result, the colonial power, rather than controlling society, left an administrative and legal void. The existence of this void was what gave the

Liberated Africans their large degree of independence and rendered the several villages into a province of freedom vastly different in character, but certainly not in intention, from that originally conceived by Granville Sharp for his first settlement in 1787.

The cultural result of such a province of freedom—the emergence of one of the earliest Afro-European groups on the West Coast of Africa by the mid-nineteenth century—and its apparent similarity to the earlier dreams of the European colonialists of creating a Christianized and civilized African society to spread the word throughout the continent, should not prevent one from recognizing the significance and excitement of the process of change which took place. For that change was largely the result of Liberated African choice, just as surely as the order found in nineteenth-century Sierra Leone society was that established by the recaptives themselves in their rural villages. Acting independently of government, Liberated Africans developed a new culture which was relevant to their Sierra Leone situation. Liberated African self-sufficiency revealed itself at each level of their society. The recaptives' province of freedom included control of local politics, trade and commerce, and their own forms of voluntary association. For all practical purposes, Liberated African control of local politics was assured by the 1830's. By then they had also exhibited their economic independence. The first Liberated Africans had moved back into Freetown where, with capital acquired from farming and petty trading, they had begun to buy property, open shops, and knock for the first time on the hitherto exclusive Nova Scotian and European door of the capital's society.

By mid-century, Liberated African society had gradually transformed itself into something resembling the Creole society of Freetown during the latter half of the century. The success of cultural transformation which had taken place by the period between 1850 and 1870 was due to the resilience and adaptability of the Liberated Africans. Such qualities had always been present in the society of the recaptives. They exhibited themselves early in the century. To a great degree they had contributed significantly to the early successes of Governor MacCarthy's plan. The individual success of any one of the early Church Missionary Society missionary-superintendents depended largely on the effective organization of the majority of the population on a tribal basis. Religious dynamism on the part of the village's leader alone could not have accounted for the success. If this had been true, the expected chaos would have occurred when a Johnson or a During left. In fact, it did not. Organization by the villagers on a tribal basis guaranteed that it did not.

RESETTLEMENT AT REGENT AND WATERLOO

The social transformation began initially in the villages where the first steps were taken in the formation of Creole society. The early nature of the fusion was indicated by the activity touched off in the mountain village of Regent when the captured slave ship *Anna Maria* anchored in Freetown harbour in 1821. Chief Superintendent Reffell sent a message to Regent informing the Revd. W. A. B. Johnson of the ship's arrival. He told the missionary that the 238 recaptives awaiting adjudication in the Liberated African yard would become his responsibility as soon as the Court of Mixed Commission liberated them. The newcomers were Ibo and Calabari, two groups already heavily represented in the mountain village's population.[1] Reffell ordered Johnson to come down to the capital the next day and to bring some of his villagers with him in order to help march the recaptives to their new home. News of the anticipated arrival of additional Liberated Africans spread quickly and brought excitement to the people, who at once began to plan a gala reception and celebration feast. Preparations were well advanced when Johnson left the following day for Freetown.

The court took an extra day to condemn the *Anna Maria*. Johnson noted that the judges were rigorous even when slaving

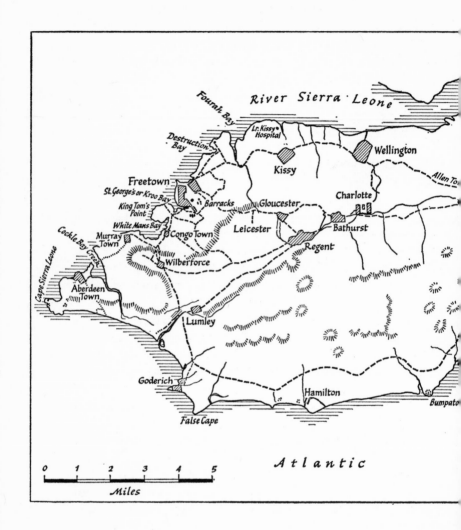

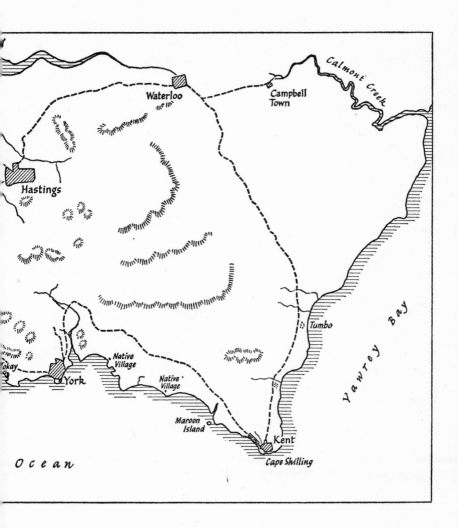

N

operations were obvious. Viewing the recaptives in the yard, the missionary remarked movingly about their thin and emaciated condition. Several were sick. When the legal proceedings were finally completed, Reffell decided to send twenty-one of those originally assigned to Regent to the hospital at Leicester Mountain. They were too weak to be sent immediately to a village. Two hundred and seventeen began the long march with Johnson up into the Sierra Leone mountains to their new home. The superintendent surrounded them with those who had come from Regent to assist as they marched along, a necessity to protect the newcomers from the desires of the 'soldiers of the Fort [who] were on the lookout to get some of them for wives'. As a further protection, Reffell himself accompanied the party as far as the mountains. In the meantime, considerable activity and preparations had taken place at Regent during the superintendent's two day absence. The preparations for the meal, although delayed, had continued. Johnson confessed that the scene when the newcomers arrived, led by their European superintendent, was indescribable. Everyone came out of his house as the party came into sight, and ran down the road to meet them. There were loud shouts of greeting; many recognized friends and relatives among those who had just come to Sierra Leone; people cried out: 'My mother!' 'My brother!' 'That man lived in the same town.' Those in the new group who were in an especially weakened condition were helped along by Regentonians already settled. The newcomers were startled by such a reception. Some of those who now greeted them, they had long presumed to be dead. Fear mixed with joy in their reaction. They had travelled thousands of miles and yet, strangely, they seemed to be entering again a village not unlike their own. With the initial greetings over, householders entered their compounds and returned with the traditional foods to celebrate the occasion. Newcomer joined those already settled for a feast of cocoa, yams, cassava, and rice, in addition to pineapples, oranges, bananas, and groundnuts. The festivities continued long into the night when the flickering fires and oil lamps illuminated the scene of reunion, happiness, and thanksgiving.[2]

None could deny the Christian meaning which Johnson ascribed to the event. It was certainly significant also that on the first Sunday all of the newcomers were taken to church by their fellow countrymen. Only one new girl hesitated before entering the church, fearing that all the people had in fact gathered for a slave sale. The welcoming, the festivities, and the dinner which followed were, however, also part of the traditional systems of the Ibo and Calabari located at Regent. The generosity shown to old friends and relatives was an important part of their life before capture which they had retained and made a vital part of their existence in rural Sierra Leone. Changes were occurring in village Liberated African life, but a solid base of traditional culture remained significant. This was shown particularly in the independent activities of the people in Regent during Johnson's two day absence in Freetown, and by the nature of the celebration when he and the new people arrived. Life in the villages, even for those in relatively prosperous Regent, was difficult. Nearly fifty of the two hundred and seventeen new arrivals died before the end of the first rains. Johnson attributed the loss to their poor health on arrival. Two women from the group, however, died in childbirth, pointing out the basic inadequacy of medical facilities in the villages.[3]

Grieved over the deaths in Regent among each group of newcomers, Johnson nevertheless suspected that conditions in other villages were even worse, and the Revd. J. G. Wilhelm's report from Waterloo a few months later confirmed his suspicions. Wilhelm had only recently received 163 newly arrived recaptives, also made up of Ibo and Calabari. But Waterloo was not as well prepared as Regent to receive the newcomers. There was only rice and cassava in the distant village for them to eat. They were accustomed to cocoa, but this was in short supply in the eastern village. Within the first week ten of the newcomers were dead. Wilhelm lamented that as 'soon as [they] were taken into the sick house we could not get them to eat anything but boiled Cassadas dipt [*sic*] in cold water'. The missionary's wife prepared cassava and groundnut soup for them every day, but to no avail. 'In this condition', the missionary continued, 'they lie till nothing but the mere skeleton with the mere skin is left of their bodies, and thus they starve themselves to death with the food before them.'[4] Waterloo had few Ibo and Calabari already settled there. The Yoruba comprised the majority of the population together with discharged soldiers from the West Indian regiments. Therefore, not only was the food different, but at Waterloo there was no traditional welfare system for these new arrivals as there has been at Regent.

The system used later of keeping the newcomers in Freetown for the first three months to work as labourers for the several government departments modified some of the extreme difficulties of immediate settlement. A certain element of cohesion developed during this initial period, and intensified the sense of independence among the new arrived Liberated Africans. One manager in the early 1830's noticed that the men, during the three months in Freetown, created a definite organization among themselves. When they were subsequently transferred to the villages, such an organization eased the immediate problems of rural settlement. This could be of crucial importance where there were no already-settled countrymen to be of assistance. Associations formed among the newcomers during their months of labour in Freetown continued to exist during the early days in the villages. Sometimes as many as seven men would live in a single hut and share the various household duties until they found wives for themselves. These associations, developed by the recaptives themselves, tended to overcome the hardships resulting from the official government policy which was to insist—unsuccessfully—that each individual erect a hut for himself when he came to live in a village.[5]

VILLAGE LIFE

Once the new arrival settled into village life, a fairly common pattern could be seen emerging. Stability certainly came more quickly to the newcomer in the villages where a familiar pattern of life could be followed. For this reason the new recaptive preferred to settle among his countrymen and eventually the government came to approve of this technique. Except for the obvious colonial symbols such as the church building, the rare stone building of European architecture, and the occasional intrusion of the government manager, the focal points of the Liberated African's life in the Sierra Leone village were similar to those of his environment before capture. The life of the re-captive centred around the fields, the market, and his compound. Particularly in the eastern villages the foundation of the vil-lager's livelihood was agriculture. The men went to the fields each morning shortly after dawn and did not return until the sun neared the western horizon in the late afternoon. Although he had been assigned an individual plot of land by the govern-ment and had been encouraged to till it by the sweat of his own labour, the wise Liberated African tended to band together with countrymen or members of his own benefit and welfare society to farm his land if not communally at least cooperatively. It was customary and common for the recaptives to share the tasks of planting, cultivating, and harvesting among themselves. Not all of the men were engaged in agriculture. A few in each village earned their living by working as labourers, craftsmen and mechanics in the tiny service industries.

While the men worked in the fields or in the village, the women congregated around the second important focal point of the rural villages, the marketplace. As was the case in so many of the traditional societies represented in the Liberated African population, women dominated the trading life of the village market. Every village included at least one market where the main produce of the countryside, plantain, banana, cassava, rice, groundnuts, beef, and pork were traded alongside certain prepared foods such as *agadi*, the Yoruba equivalent of a quick snack which was made from pounded corn, bread, fufu balls, dried fish, and various soups. In the villages more distant from Freetown such as Waterloo and Hastings, the market-places included stalls where women sold printed cottons, hand-kerchiefs, shirts, thread, tape, flints, pocket knives, iron utensils, and smoking pipes. Prices and profits fluctuated throughout the nineteenth century, but generally, the livelihood squeezed from the petty trade of the market place was meagre. Some women preferred to ignore the market altogether and instead set up single stalls in front of their own compounds or at some important road junction where they sold small quantities of salt, groundnuts, and fruit from their own gardens.

Like the men in the fields, the women tended to stay in the market trading throughout the day. The main activity was concentrated in the early hours of the morning, however, and much of the remainder of the day was spent in conversation among the women. Eventually the women picked up their produce and headed for their own compounds where activities were focused for the rest of the day. Before the men joined them in the compound, the women would already have begun the preparation of the evening meal. In most cases this meant that they would have overseen the host of relatives, apprentices, and other helpers who also made up most village compounds, and often did the actual work of preparing the food. Most commonly the evening meal would be a substantial portion of cooked and prepared cassava, usually in the form of fufu balls. To go with this, the cooks would prepare a sauce, aptly called palaver sauce, which was sometimes poured over the cassava and sometimes placed in a separate bowl into which the diner would dip the rolled and pounded cassava. In the more prosperous compounds, rice would be the base over which the sauce was poured. This was rare, however, for more often the rice when cultivated was reserved for the premium price fetched at the Freetown market. The ingredients used to prepare palaver sauce varied from village to village and from time to time in the nineteenth century. Palm oil usually provided the base to which were added various vegetable greens such as cocoa leaves. Other greens were used and in a village like Hastings, for example, most retained their Yoruba names. During their season, yams and corn might be added to the sauce. Meat or dried fish completed the mixture and their presence or absence testified to the relative prosperity of the individual compound.

Fresh from a rest following their arduous day in the fields, the men awoke for the serious business of satisfying their hunger and the enjoyable conviviality which accompanied the evening meal in the compound. The meal usually was informal, European observers noting that although eating utensils nearly always graced the walls of the Liberated African home they were only rarely used actually to assist the process of eating, fingers being far more often used. The quiet conversation of the meal continued into the early hours of the evening. When the sun had set and while other members of the household washed out the pots and returned them inside the house, the man and his wife would find a log or stone by the entrance to their compound and sit, smoking their pipes, greeting friends as they passed, and relaxing after their long day. After a while the woman, sometimes accompanied by her husband, would get up and go off to the church or chapel for evening prayer, a solemnly fitting close to a day in the Liberated African's new life.[6]

Not all of the recaptives ended their day in the chapels of the villages, however. Some congregated together after the evening meal to listen and dance to the music of the drum and the cowry-decorated calabash. Despite the pleas of successive missionaries, the drum and the dance continued to provide the most popular pastime of the villages. Once the missionaries lost their power as village superintendents, the dancing went on without restriction. Although some of the missionaries thought that the dancing was calculated to thwart or undermine their position in the rural areas, actually it continued as a vital part of Liberated African life. Hannah Kilham, who established a school at Charlotte in 1831, reported that there was hardly a moment during the day and night when the village was not without the sound of the highly active recaptive life. In the evening the cries of the children arose from nearly every house.

Later it was the noise of the palavers brought before the government sub-manager for settlement, and finally—on into the morning—the noise of the dancers, singers and drummers.[7]

The independence of life among the Liberated Africans took many other forms. Samuel Ajayi Crowther commented on the early reluctance of the recaptives to attend school. He wrote that some early Liberated Africans felt that they were too old to learn. 'Booklearning was for white people, and was rather a boyish employment.' For the most part these recaptives attended evening school merely to please their missionary-superintendent. Often if a hundred assembled at the beginning of the evening for lessons, only fifty remained at the conclusion. The others had 'slipped away to their homes'. In some villages they proved even braver. At Wellington the people all came at the sound of the bell and assembled. Before school began, however, they 'all with one accord tumultuously rushed out of the (grass) Chapel, through the doors and windows in the utmost confusion possible. To crown the whole, they shouted (in their country languages) as soon as they got out with an expression of victory over the Schoolmaster.'

Wilhelm complained about another sort of Liberated African self-sufficiency. The recaptives in his village successfully devised a way to make money on Governor Campbell's Plan of January 1st. According to the Plan, the women were to be sent to the villages where they would be kept on rations for three months or until they married. The false assumption in the Plan was that they would marry quickly. Between June and early September, 1826, the government sent Wilhelm eighty-six women who were to be kept on rations until married. Late in September he wrote Freetown that none was yet married, and there appeared to be no prospects. Joseph Reffell replied from the capital that thirty of the women should be sent to the far-distant village of Kent where the prospects were much better. Wilhelm instead announced in Waterloo that all eighty-six were to be sent to Kent, a deception which stirred the entire village to action. He spent the next two days marrying all but seven of the new women. 'Thus,' the proud Wilhelm afterwards wrote, 'by this simple means I got them all settled and struck off from Government Rations.' He admitted that all had in fact been married, in the 'country fashion', long before the busy two days, and in that way they had been able to continue to collect their rations.[8]

The government itself recognized the resourcefulness and independence of Liberated African society. Even Governor Sir Neil Campbell, who more than once had expressed his deep disgust for the Liberated Africans,[9] confessed that 'they possess the same faculties and propensities as white people'.[10] Thomas Cole in 1830 criticized a magistrate for having a citizen of Hastings publicly flogged.[11] By 1834 it had become clear that the occasional harsh actions of a superintendent of a decade earlier were no longer either proper or necessary. If the villages did not look physically like the model communities envisaged at an earlier date, they were for the most part adequately organized, quiet, stable, and relatively prosperous. Governor Octavius Temple was willing to render such a verdict on the colony and its development when he wrote in June 1834, 'Thus there is established in the very land of slavery and infidelity a nation of free Black Christians (32,000 Souls) settling with complete triumph the superiority of Free over Slave Labour, giving the lie to the calumny of their unfitness for all the duties of social life, increasing in numbers and with means adequate to this increase, and whose religion, knowledge and habits must extend with themselves to the blessing and civilization of their country. . . .' While 'the old [consoled] themselves for the loss of their country in the freedom of their children, . . . the children [exulted] in their freedom as their first Birthright'.[12] By the middle of the 1830's, even the governors recognized the extent to which the Sierra Leone venture had come to be a Liberated African province of freedom.

HEADMEN AND POLITICAL ORGANIZATION

A key factor in the stability of the Liberated African villages was their political organization. Almost every group in a village had its own headman who served the community as its chief. Even the casual groups of labourers during their first three months in the colony developed their own leadership.[13] Michael Banton has written of the importance of the headmen to the tribal administration in late nineteenth-century Freetown.[14] The traditional leader was of much earlier importance, however, to the organization of the Liberated African villages. The institution of the headman, in fact, appears to be the earliest form of Liberated African political organization. The earliest missionary-superintendents had, of necessity, to work through existing institutions.[15] In the most successful government villages, the headmen were brought into the governmental administrative structure itself by carrying the orders of the superintendent to the people. The headmen also took charge of the prevention and punishment of crimes in some villages. In 1818 a Kosso was brought to trial in Wilberforce for murdering a fellow countryman. The superintendent—the inept Decker—was unable to take charge of either the burial of the victim or the trial. The Kosso headman therefore substituted for him. He brought back the body of the victim from the bush where the crime had taken place, and saw to the burial. The burial ceremony went on for three days, much to Decker's annoyance. The Kosso tribal members danced and 'played' in the traditional celebration. Then the headman saw to the punishment of the offender. Eventually the Kosso headman came to control village affairs so well that Decker had to have him removed.[16]

In the village of Leicester in 1819, the Revd. Wilhelm tried to end a Jolof family dispute which was disturbing the whole village. The wife only scoffed at the missionary when he threatened to put her in gaol. 'Gaol,' she shouted, 'pray Sir, for who is gaol made?—is it not made for people to live in?—me no mind Gaol!' The Jolof headman heard the woman, interrupted the proceedings, and told the crowd of people who had gathered that the woman had to be flogged. Wilhelm told the headman to make the necessary preparations to see if she would quiet down without having to endure such a severe punishment. The headman assured Wilhelm that if he left the scene he would quiet the woman within a minute. Before the missionary had reached his house, quiet had returned to the village thanks to the firm power of the Jolof headman.[17]

Theoretically, the laws of England were in force in the Sierra Leone colony. However, the presence of the Liberated Africans as well as increasing numbers of people from the Sierra Leone interior meant that English laws could be administered only in a modified form.[18] Within the villages, for the most part, traditional systems of law prevailed. In fact, certain specific areas of legal procedure were reserved for the headmen. The Wesleyan preacher at Hastings in 1840 reported that 'country fashion' trials were held for persons suspected of theft, revealing tribal secrets, lewdness, and murder. The suspect was tried by ordeal. If the person was unable to dip his hand in hot oil after the headman uttered his incantations, he was found guilty. If he could, he was innocent. The rubbing of cayenne pepper in the eyes was sometimes used as a substitute for the hot oil. The Chief Superintendent of the Liberated African Department himself made use of headman's justice. In 1830 he returned an 'incorrigible thief' to her village with instructions for the manager to turn her over to her 'country people'. He hoped that they would be able to handle her, but if not, he wanted her put into the manager's school. As late as 1859, the manager of Kissy informed the Freetown administrators that 'if any dispute arise amongst any of the members, it is referred to the leaders of the district, who are generally able to settle the matter. If not, I am applied to, and my decision is generally considered final.'[19]

The most telling indication of the effective power of the headmen occurred in one of the early villages. It was embodied in a written contract which missionary-superintendent the Revd. William G. E. Metzger entered into with five Wilberforce headmen in 1823.[20] By this document, Metzger sought the type of cooperation from the five tribes which the Revd. Johnson had enjoyed at Regent. The contract defined the extent to which the Liberated Africans would follow Metzger. At one point in the document they called him 'our Chief-headman'. The headmen conceded much to Metzger. They agreed to 'obey all his commands and submit ourselves to all the regulations he shall make'. They specifically promised to keep the Sabbath Day holy by preventing noise and ceasing to walk about the village during the morning service; to stop performing tribal rituals in the town, and shooting guns within the town limits; and to begin to keep houses, yards, and streets clean. They agreed to stiff fines and gaol sentences for any offenders. It was to cost one shilling and one day in gaol for anyone who refused to leave the street during Sunday worship, and one shilling for each shot fired from a gun. In addition, the five headmen agreed to make their people settle in an orderly fashion. If anyone refused, after a fourteen-day warning, the headman could pull down the person's house and forcefully drive him from Wilberforce. To prevent anyone from going to Freetown with a complaint against Metzger, the contract gave the headmen power to remove any complainer from the village. Anyone who ran to the Freetown government to complain would be prevented from returning to Wilberforce. Metzger recognized the judicial system of the headmen and they in turn recognized an individual's right to appeal to him. From him there was to be no appeal. The headmen accepted Metzger's right to call them together 'should [the superintendent] desire to consult us'. Metzger promised to provide the use of the village constables in apprehending debtors. Lastly, the document empowered Metzger *and* the headmen to act as the final judges of who was to settle in the village and its immediate area.[21] This provision was particularly important to the headmen. If an individual headman had the authority to prohibit someone from settling in the area, he had an important lever by which he could retain and extend the power of his position. Until Metzger proposed the contract, the headmen had been *de facto* leaders of the five communities which made up the village. They were, nevertheless, entirely extra-legal. Metzger's contract made them a recognized part of the local administrative structure. In the tradition of the eighteenth century, it was a social contract to Metzger.

The Governor, Sir Charles MacCarthy, found it abominable. He removed Metzger from his superintendency at once. The Freetown government, as the contract suggested, had been besieged with the complaints of Wilberforce villagers against the superintendent. The contract proved to be the last straw. MacCarthy sent Metzger to Kissy where he was to serve as Nyländer's assistant. The Governor told Nyländer to watch Metzger constantly.[22] The contract was unacceptable to the central government because it attempted to make a regular and legal institution of the headmen. The government, in 1823, was satisfied only to recognize their existence informally, and hope that its own administrative policies would eventually succeed and render the use of the tribal headmen unnecessary.

Of course the headmen did not fade in importance. Indeed, they continued effectively to rule the individual villages throughout the nineteenth century. A petition to Lieutenant Governor H. D. Campbell in 1835 revealed at least three headmen at Wilberforce. They were even called chiefs on this petition, a title for which the less distinguished word headman was usually substituted. Eleven headmen, representing eleven tribal groups, signed a similar petition in Waterloo less than a month later.[23] By the latter half of the 1830's the government had become less sensitive regarding the recognition of headmen. In fact, in 1838, the government itself proposed to appoint a headman for every ten families in the rural villages, and a 'chief-headman' or centenary over every ten headmen. The Freetown government sought to use the headmen as a better means to be informed of vital statistics, the condition of agriculture, and the movement of population. The plan failed to come to any consequence, but it did reveal the extent to which the government was willing to go in order to incorporate the effective headman system of administration into its own.[24]

Separatist Villages

The Liberated Africans, meanwhile, continued to exhibit their self-sufficiency through the effective management of their own affairs. This was shown most significantly in the tendency of some Liberated Africans to establish separate village settlements outside the jurisdiction of the colonial government's administration. This was a repetition of earlier patterns of Liberated African expansion and settlement. Most of the original villages had been founded in this manner and only after their existence had been discovered were they brought under the control of the Freetown government. The earliest example in fact predated the abolition of the slave trade in 1807 and the first use of Freetown as a place to settle recaptives. The 1794 *Report* of the Sierra Leone Company told of a group of 100 slaves aboard a Danish vessel anchored in the estuary some five or six years earlier. They escaped to the shore and fled into the mountains where they built a village four or five miles from Freetown. They continued to live in their village, Deserters or Danish Town, quite separately from the Company settlement on the shore below and were very reluctant to accept visitors, being constantly on their guard lest they should be captured again.[25] When the French attacked Freetown in 1794, at least three of the Nova Scotians fled to Danish Town where they were welcomed and protected.[26]

This tendency to seek safety away from the main centre of European control persisted once the Liberated Africans began to arrive in Sierra Leone. Some years before 1815, three separate groups of recaptives moved out of three separate settlements, Regent, Kissy, and one near the present site of Goderich on the colony's Atlantic coast, on to the low-lying plain to the east of the main town along the Bunce River where they founded two new villages. The founders were of the Congo people, and of the Yoruba tribes of Ijesha and Egba. Their two unofficial communities survive in the historical tradition of the village of Hastings and are known to those who retain the tradition by their Yoruba-sounding Krio names, Aréoster and Abekola.

Each name referred to the main commercial or agricultural function of the settlement for at Aréoster, oysters were taken from the river, and at Abekola, the Yoruba recaptives cultivated and traded kola. In 1815, as a result of a shortage of water, the settlements merged at still a third location, closer to the protection of the mountains and near a rushing brook. Here where the Temne village of Robump had stood,[27] the recaptives remained and four rainy seasons later the village was officially recognized, named Hastings, and brought within the administrative system of the central government.[28]

The pattern of the founding of Hastings was repeated throughout the 1820's and 1830's and caused the central government considerable concern and effort in its attempt to regulate and control the independent tendencies of the Liberated Africans. The Revd. William A. B. Johnson reported the existence of separatist communities around Regent for the first time in 1818. He and the Colonial Surveyor discovered some of them one day when they set out to find a shorter route between Regent and Freetown. Barely two miles from the village they came upon a small village of Bassa who had earlier fled from Johnson's superintendence at Regent. Johnson tried to convince the Bassa headman that he should lead his group back to the official mountain village; the headman, on his part, tried to explain that they had left Johnson's village because they had been ill during their time there. They were more comfortable by themselves. The headman apparently did not present the missionary with a convincing case, and in the end promised to return to Regent with his people.[29] The village disappeared but the people did not return under Johnson's wing, finding, no doubt, more comfort in another place better secluded or perhaps by joining together with other Bassa in a larger separatist community. By 1826, five such independent villages existed between Freetown and Regent, populated for the most part by those who had been originally settled in Johnson's Regent.[30]

Twice during the 1820's the government tried to contain the formation of separatist villages by regulating the movement of

Liberated Africans within the colony. In 1821, the Chief Superintendent merely requested his village superintendents to return any strangers they found among Liberated Africans to their assigned villages. By 1829, the government revealed its increasing frustration by announcing a fine of five shillings for anyone who harboured or entertained a runaway Liberated African in his house. The government also provided for the movement of Liberated Africans from one established village to another as long as those who moved had first secured the manager's approval.[31] Such regulations worked no more effectively than other governmental plans. Visitors reported seeing many new settlements all over the colony, formed by recaptives once they had been freed from government control. The Liberated Africans simply chose to set out on their own.[32] In 1827, one group who had started a village on the road between York and Kent on the west coast of the colony told the government representative sent to investigate that their crops would not grow where the government had originally settled them. They sought a place away from 'the Mountain Rats and Rocky ground about York' where they could grow enough food for their subsistence. Hearing their explanation Chief Superintendent Dixon Denham ordered the manager of York to let them remain where they had settled, to give each man a lot, and to include them in his next village report. The settlement was later named Ricketts, after a subsequent governor. Reports continually filtered into Freetown concerning such separatist villages. The Chief Superintendent asked the manager of Wilberforce to investigate complaints that the headman of one such village was exacting labour from his fellow countrymen in the village. The same Freetown official had to write another manager a few months later to criticize him for arresting three Liberated Africans who had illegally lived in his community for four years before being discovered. 'If they had been allowed to absent themselves for so long a period,' the Chief Superintendent wrote, 'and no notice taken of them . . . I do not think it right to disturb them now.'[33]

Some left their assigned lots because the soil was unproduc-
tive. Others left to be nearer their countrymen. A Regent
manager in the 1830's wrote that it was 'useless to persist in
making [Liberated Africans] erect a line of huts, which it is
certain they will *not* continue to inhabit, as well as cruel to
compel them to remain in a location, or in the exercise of an
employment, for which they feel no inclination: and we should
not be surprised at the line of conduct pursued by these people,
if we consider the circumstances and situation of a captured
Negro. Settled in a strange land, without a friend, or a relative—the nearest intimate within his reach is a countryman;
every person and thing around him is novel. . . . He is driven,
absolutely driven, by the want of society and friends, to domicile
with his neighbors or country-people.'[34] Considering why a
group left Waterloo to establish a village three or four miles to
the southwest, the 1827 Commissioners offered another important explanation. They completely discounted the search
for more fertile soil or the desire to be with their countrymen.
These Liberated Africans had moved instead 'solely with a
view of secluding themselves from interference and control;
an object which . . . they have effectually attained'.[35]

SERGEANT POTTS'S 'SECRET' SOCIETY

Independence from government control gave crucial political
meaning to the many benefit societies which arose among the
Liberated Africans. Primarily, the benefit societies developed
to assure the welfare of the individual recaptives. But as the
societies grew and situations changed, the functions of the
societies broadened into areas which posed a threat to the
colonial government. In some such situations the apparent distinc-
tions between groups of Sierra Leoneans, such as that between
Liberated Africans and discharged soldiers from the West
Indian regiments, faded. This proved to be the case in the so-
called 'Secret' Society founded by Abraham Potts, a discharged soldier of the 4th West Indian Regiment, in Freetown
in 1824. By 1827, it had spread to six colony villages. In the

beginning the society was purely and simply a benefit society. Potts's objectives were to collect a fund by monthly subscriptions and to apply the proceeds to the relief of distressed members of the society. The society also imposed small fines in cases of drunkenness and misconduct among its members.[36] As the society's founder, Potts naturally became its headman, with headquarters in Freetown. The time of the society's founding was crucial to its later development and its broadened function. This was at the end of the MacCarthy era and during a period when government control, after having reached its heights during the days of Sir Charles, Johnson, and During among others, quickly diminished. An administrative and legal void became readily apparent and into this void Potts's society moved. The society assumed an entirely new dimension as it spread quickly among the Liberated Africans in the villages. Before long it had its six branches in colony villages. Each branch had its own headman, and Potts, in Freetown, with his expanded responsibilities came to be regarded as the society's chief headman or 'king'. The society not only spread geographically through the villages but also took on a political and judicial function. It developed into an extra-legal, colony-wide government. Although the local headmen did not have any absolutely defined responsibility to the Freetown headquarters, the connection in actual practice was extremely close.[37]

The society remained secret only because the government for a long time seemed completely unaware of its existence. Soon after Sir Neil Campbell became Governor, a man belonging to the society came to Freetown from Kent to complain about the society's activities. With his complaint the government received its first real information about the extent and scope of Potts's benefit society and its power. In its development, the society had evolved its own police and judicial systems. Specially appointed members of the society's hierarchy called on delinquent members. If the delinquent protested, as the man from Kent had done, he was taken to a local house and tried before the society's headman. Although some later charged that they had been detained, a gaol sentence was not a usual penalty to be inflicted. Some were flogged, but more often, the guilty delinquent was sentenced to endure the silence of all his fellow members for periods which ranged from two to six months. Although apparently tame, such a sentence in a society which depended heavily on trade for its economic livelihood could spell financial ruin for the guilty benefit society member.[38]

The revelations of the man from Kent left Governor Campbell fearful. His own subsequent investigations confirmed his worst fears that the apparently harmless benefit society had been expanded to create what was in actual fact an extra-legal government for the rural areas. Quickly, he moved to suppress the society in July 1827.[39] King Potts was removed and sacked from his minor government position. The village headmen were tried in civil courts and those who were discharged soldiers lost their pensions. Campbell allowed for the continuation of the welfare funds on a local and voluntary basis only under the strictest supervision of the village managers. He forbade any further associations on a colony wide basis. In an effort to prevent the development of such a phenomenon in the future, Chief Superintendent Denham suggested the creation of a government savings bank for the recaptives. Denham felt that Potts's society had flourished because Liberated Africans had savings, but no place to put them. He himself knew of several cases where recaptives had come to their village manager with from £5 to £30 with a request to care for it. Denham's understanding of the success and spread of Potts's 'Secret' Society was correct only as far as it went. The lack of a savings bank did not explain the political nature which the society had assumed. In the area of politics a more potent reason for the group's expansion was the relative administrative and legal void which it filled. Many of the rural villages had no manager during the period between 1824 and 1827. Regent was without a manager in 1825 and no doubt the society, under John Thomas, provided a crucially important administrative and judicial cohesion to the village which it otherwise would not have had.[40] Sir Neil

Campbell's suppression of the Potts benefit society proved successful, for its existence was never again mentioned officially or unofficially. Potts's early success, however, laid the framework for future movements toward unity in the rural areas. Furthermore, it provided the government with a fearsome and potent example of the extent to which the colony citizens would go to assume control of their own affairs.

THREAT OF REBELLION AT WATERLOO

Other dissident political movements among the Liberated Africans proved more difficult to control. The Yoruba, or Aku as they are called in Sierra Leone,[41] were particularly troublesome. Part of their successful opposition to the government derived from their high degree of tribal cohesiveness. Countrymen tended naturally to bind together in groups in the villages. With the Aku 'this feeling of compatriotism [was] carried so far, that if a new man [was] apprehended and brought before the magistrate for petty theft, and punished by a small fine, they paid the imposition amongst themselves, rather than see their countrymen committed to the house of correction for default'.[42]

For seven years, beginning in 1826, a group of Muslim Aku proved to be a continuing problem to a succession of Freetown administrators. They settled in an area outside the colony, to the east of the village of Waterloo. From there they threatened the whole eastern district of the colony and presented the central government with the first organized opposition to its policies. The first indication of any difficulty came early in December 1826, when the Revd. J. G. Wilhelm, the Waterloo superintendent, reported that runaway Liberated Africans, armed with cutlasses and some firearms, were regularly passing through his village. Rumours spread quickly that the runaways were forming ranks to plunder the village. A headman from a nearby settlement told Wilhelm that about twenty armed Aku had passed through his territory bound for the interior. The frightened missionary immediately sent for Chief Superintendent Cole who, upon arrival, notified the governor of the tense situation.

Governor Campbell dispatched troops to Waterloo and a local militia was formed for additional protection. All was in readiness to defend the village from the threatening Aku. As tension grew, thirteen armed but otherwise unsuspecting Yoruba entered Waterloo and were seized by Wilhelm. He sent them to the capital where they were put in gaol as 'suspicious characters'.[43] Wilhelm's fears were not imagined. Cole told Campbell that he certainly thought there was trouble brewing. The armed Aku force had been seen nearby. Wilhelm feared an Aku attack at Christmas when the discharged soldiers, the bulk of his militia, would be in Freetown to collect their pensions. By mustering the Waterloo Liberated Africans, Cole found that some Aku were missing and concluded that they too had joined the dissident rebels.[44] The missionary had every reason to fear the Aku. His superintendence at Waterloo had not been successful. As early as 1822 he had sought the advice of the other missionaries because 'we see ourselves insulted and put to shame—yes, we are troubled on every side'. In 1824 he had had to endure a village riot occasioned by an argument with a recaptive about his illegal rum-selling. A year later he wrote the London CMS Committee that there was less and less regard for Christianity in Waterloo, and more and more idleness. After Governor Campbell himself viewed the scene late in 1825, he removed the missionary-superintendent from Waterloo and assigned him as missionary to the village of York.[45] The Governor's private secretary noted the missionary's fear of the Aku as the reason for his removal.[46]

Wilhelm's removal was an important victory for the assembled Aku force. Whether or not they had ever intended to attack Waterloo was immaterial. The disturbing nature of their activities had succeeded in eliminating the CMS from the area. The village remained without a missionary for more than five years. When Governor Campbell asked John Pierce, a CMS schoolmaster, to go to Waterloo as a catechist in 1827, he refused, explaining to the Governor that the village was unhealthy, the people were irreligious, and his presence there would be an insult to Wilhelm, a man to whom the people had shown their ingratitude.[47]

THE COBOLO WAR

The crisis of 1826 at Waterloo passed quickly after Wilhelm's removal. A new one arose four years later which led to the first real bloodshed between the government and the Aku. In August 1830, Lieutenant Governor Alexander Findlay issued an order which prohibited sacrificing to idols. But wherever a government official attempted to enforce the order, another flight of Aku from the colony resulted. The ranks of the dissident force swelled. By mid-1832, complaints were increasing from neighbouring chiefs that the escaped Aku were plundering their traders.[48] The Governor grew restive. Rumours again spread through the colony that the Aku were massing to strike at Waterloo. Taking the rumours seriously, C. B. Jones, Assistant Superintendent of the Liberated African Department, sent an urgent message to the manager of Hastings on 12 November 1832. He informed the manager that gangs of Aku from the villages would join the rebels that night. The obedient manager called up all the volunteers at both Hastings and Waterloo. The volunteers began to patrol the areas east of Waterloo. Four days later, on 16 November, word reached the assistant superintendent at Freetown that one of the volunteers had been killed and four others had been wounded in a skirmish with the Aku on the Maharra road, east of Waterloo. Jones ordered another company of discharged soldiers from Wellington to join the force already gathered at the easternmost colony village. The following day, Governor Findlay ordered the force at Waterloo to move eastward toward the village of Cobolo on the Ribbi river where the Aku had established their base. He sent word to a second force, commanded by a naval lieutenant, to move up the river in a boat as a diversionary manoeuvre. Findlay estimated the Aku force at Cobolo to be 1,000 and feared that more from the colony villages would join them.[49]

A second Sierra Leone militia force penetrated the area and lost seven volunteers. The government forces increased their pressure on Cobolo. This provided the temporarily subjected citizens of Cobolo with enough confidence to rebel. Before Findlay's combined offensive could reach the village, the Cobolo population overthrew their Aku masters. The Yoruba losses were devastating. More than fifty were killed or drowned as they attempted to escape across the river. Ojo Curi, the leader of the rebellion, did escape and fled southward to the Sherbro country opposite the Plantain Islands. But he found no security there. Chief Caulker, the Sherbro chief, led a group of warriors against the escaped Aku, and in a final desperate skirmish, the Aku leader was killed along with two others. Caulker delivered the prisoners and the ears of the slain Ojo Curi to the Governor in Freetown.[50]

The suppression of the Aku rebellion did not fully satisfy Governor Findlay. He remained deeply troubled. He needed a scapegoat for his recent difficulties and seized upon the Fula and Mandinka migrants in the colony. Blaming their Muslim influences on the Yoruba recaptives for the colony's troubles, he ignored completely the fact that the great majority of Muslim Aku were already converts to Islam before they reached Sierra Leone. They had become followers of the Prophet while still in Yoruba country, converted for the most part by the Fulani *jihad* of Uthman don Fodio during the early years of the century. These facts were ignored by Findlay. The Governor was convinced that the Fula and Mandinka in the colony had converted the Aku to Islam, persuading them that by leaving the British settlement they could eventually reach their Yoruba homeland. The Aku's ferocious fighting at Cobolo resulted from their having placed great faith in the gri-gris and fetishes 'purchased from their Mahomedan teachers'. Findlay's simplified view of causation led him to renew his attempt to isolate the Liberated Africans from the Muslim Mandinka and Fula. When pressure had increased after 1830 in the eastern regions of the colony, the Governor had prohibited the Mandinka from the village of Waterloo. Now, in 1833, with the rebellion suppressed, he extended his prohibition, forbidding Muslim priests to settle in any village and ordering conformity with the European pattern of dress.[51]

Findlay did not stop there in his attempt to rid the colony of what he perceived to be an Islamic menace. He took the captured Aku to court. But in court the government's attempt to suppress the dissident Muslim Aku received a sharp setback. At the Quarter Sessions of Oyer and Terminer in December 1832, and January 1833, he sought indictments against six of the prisoners on charges of high treason. The grand jury issued true bills against only four of the accused. The other two went free. The Acting Chief Justice, M. L. Melville, appointed William Henry Savage as counsel for the Aku. The trial began on the first day of 1833 with Savage immediately challenging the jurisdiction of the court. Cobolo, he argued, was outside the colony and thus outside British jurisdiction. Furthermore, Savage continued, since the Liberated Africans were not British-born subjects they owed no allegiance to His Majesty. They came under the authority of the Crown only so long as they remained in the colony. Melville found Savage's argument intriguing and admitted that the court's jurisdiction was, in fact, questionable. A dejected Findlay himself confessed that when the judge confirmed the doubts planted by the defence counsel, the jury could do nothing but acquit the Aku, which they did in due course. Despondent, but not defeated, the Governor promptly secured a second true bill against the four Aku participants in the Cobolo war. It charged them with the wilful murder of the dead militia members. Findlay, restive about the implications of Savage's argument, wrote London that if what the lawyer said were correct, he could foresee the threat of a Liberated African revolution organized outside the colony. Calm and unmoved by such fears, Melville postponed the trial until the next sessions. When it was finally held in March 1833, it only resulted in more frustration for the Governor. The jury again acquitted the four Aku. The lack of any material witnesses for the Crown combined with Savage's old argument concerning the court's lack of jurisdiction to spell defeat for Findlay this time. His own bright idea to try the four in an Admiralty Court under an 1832 Royal Commission would not work either, the Acting King's Advocate Robert Dougan patiently explained, since it covered acts of piracy committed on the high seas. Under no circumstances did the waters of the Ribbi river qualify under a series of acts dating back to the twenty-eighth year of the reign of Henry VIII. With no doubt some embarrassment to Findlay, Dougan himself supported Melville's opinion in favour of the court's lack of jurisdiction at the second trial.[52]

W. H. SAVAGE AND THE FOUNDING OF FOURAH BAY

The second acquittal ended Findlay's attempt to suppress the Muslim Aku. W. H. Savage had proved to be the central figure in both trials. His role in court indicated his rising prominence in Sierra Leone life. An English mulatto, he had arrived in the colony in 1810 as a schoolmaster, having secured a patronage appointment from Lord Barham,[53] a man who had earlier assisted the Committee for the Black Poor to make their arrangements at the British Admiralty. Governor Columbine had ended Savage's brief career as a government servant in the schools as part of his economy drive. Savage then took a job with John Ormond, a slave dealer in the Rio Pongas. Although the connection with Ormond lasted only for five months, it was later used by a Methodist missionary in Freetown in an attempt to discredit Savage. Soon after taking office, Governor Maxwell re-appointed Savage to the government service and he remained attached to the government until 1821 'when finding there was no chance or hope of getting advanced and that color seemed to be an insurmountable objection even in Africa he quitted the service'.[54] Savage then returned to England, took out papers as a notary public, and sailed again for Sierra Leone. He was admitted to the bar on the basis of his notary's papers, joined in a commercial partnership with Samuel Gabbidon, a Nova Scotian, and became a prosperous merchant. He traded in timber and was a supplier of goods to the Liberated African Department in the 1820's. Savage also prospered as a lawyer. Freetown had but two lawyers in the 1820's, Savage and a white Englishman. Neither had been professionally educated. Combining trade and the law, Savage consistently improved his position. He moved in the top circles of Freetown society, numbering among his friends and associates Kenneth Macaulay, Gabbidon, John McCormick, and Robert Dougan. From 1826 to 1828 he was Freetown police clerk. As a lawyer his clients included naval claimants and Havana commercial firms in cases before the Courts of Mixed Commission. Many whom he defended had no doubt continued to maintain a close connection with the slave trade. Apparently in 1836, he nearly became the official Brazilian representative at Freetown.[55]

In 1821, he offered to assist the Wesleyan mission at Freetown to establish a station in Temne country at Port Loko. Five years later he donated a new clock to Freetown's Maroon Chapel. By 1836, however, his relations with the Wesleyans had badly deteriorated, largely because he had represented the Nova Scotian Wesleyan congregation in their successful attempt to remain autonomous from the European Wesleyan missionaries. In doing so he particularly earned the wrath of the Revd. Edward Maer, the missionary in charge of British Wesleyan activities in Freetown. The indirect relationship between Maer's charges and Savage's failure to secure the post of King's Advocate in 1836 was readily apparent, in spite of Governor H. D. Campbell's testimonial. Nonetheless, Savage had prospered by the 1830's. He owned his own home on Cross Street in Freetown where he lived with his wife and their ten servants.[56] By the time he represented the four Muslim Aku at the 1833 trial he had also acquired a country estate near Fourah Bay. Proving to be a lawyer with a feeling for both individuals and groups which extended beyond the courtroom, Savage allowed several Aku to settle on his country estate after the trial.

The Muslim Yoruba community at Fourah Bay originated with this settlement. An Imam, Alfa Yada, was brought from the village of Hastings to lead the community which, as its first task, built a small mosque.[57] The settlement became permanent with Savage's death. The lawyer left no heirs, but numerous natural children.[58] His claims to the Fourah Bay estate fell to Henry Garel Savage who collected rent from the other Muslim farmers.[59] By 1862, the younger Savage had sold the land to E. A. Bell who in turn resold it two years later. This initiated an involved and intricate dispute which continued for the next hundred years, developing in the 1870's into a religious struggle among the various local Muslim factions.

The pacified Aku who had fought bitterly in open rebellion at Cobolo settled peacefully at Savage's Fourah Bay estate. They established a Yoruba village, farmed plots, and sold produce at a market near the present Clinetown quay. Maintaining their contact with Mandinka and Fula Arabic scholars, the Aku established Koranic schools. After the long day spent in the fields the men would gather in the evening in groups of from fifteen to twenty around a fire to learn long passages from the Koran.[60] The Aku exodus prior to the Cobolo war had been occasioned partly by their intense desire to go home to Yoruba country. The settled Aku at Fourah Bay did not relinquish this desire in spite of their success in establishing a community in Sierra Leone which was both Yoruba and Muslim. The Revd. Samuel Ajayi Crowther received several requests to allow Aku Liberated Africans to accompany the CMS mission to Yoruba country in the 1840's. Stories of shipwrecks which frustrated early attempts to return to Nigeria were told to the author when he was collecting material in the Fourah Bay community in 1959 and 1960. By 1844, the Aku at Fourah Bay had their own ship, the *Maria*, which travelled between Freetown and Badagry.[61] It was no doubt aboard this ship that one group of fifty Fourah Bay Muslims left for Badagry in 1844. Among the emigrants was a fourteen-year-old, Mohammed Shitta Bey, who after prospering in commerce in the Niger regions built the first substantial mosque in Lagos in 1885.[62] Continuing religious persecution contributed to the Fourah Bay Aku's natural desire to return home. Lawyer Savage had provided them with a place to develop their community independently, but no one could provide them with the religious toleration which was absent. Freetown was Christian almost by definition. Not until the twentieth century could the average Muslim from Fourah Bay or Foulah Town venture forth into Freetown's commercial and educational life without the protection of a Christian second name.

KING MACAULAY AND THE SEVENTEEN NATIONS
The political dissent of the Yoruba had succeeded by 1833 in allowing them to exercise that element of independence which characterized the life of the resettled Liberated Africans in Sierra Leone. By mid-century the increasing desire for independence had manifested itself in a final important form. The development of the political structure known as the Seventeen Nations during the 1840's proved to be of the greatest long-term significance. With it the Liberated Africans found a way to govern their own province of freedom. The specific idea of the Seventeen Nations began in Waterloo as a result of civil riots between Ibo and Yoruba in 1843, but its roots lay in the whole experience of the Liberated Africans with the broadened judicial and political functions of their benefit societies. Through their voluntary associations, they had, in large measure, governed their own affairs. Crisis in the 1840's pushed them to a more specifically defined institution to carry on with their judicial and political business at a local level. This was the Seventeen Nations.

Tribal divisions among the Liberated Africans provided the immediate stimulus. Throughout the early half of the nineteenth century the tendency had been for tribal groups to secure the loyalties of their Liberated African members in Sierra Leone. Beyond the obvious elements which proved important to the recaptives, such as common language, there was the key matter of social welfare. The tribal group invariably took prime responsibility for the welfare of its members. As the number of recaptives continued to grow, villages in the rural areas like Waterloo and Hastings increased both in tribal diversity and in the size of the individual groups. Each group tended to develop its own official representatives, and its own internal structure. Each group tended also to compete with the others for the favour of the government manager. As population increased, the competition developed into intense rivalry. In Waterloo in 1839 and 1843, as well as in Hastings in 1851, intense rivalry either turned or nearly turned into inter-tribal rioting. In answer to this threat of civil war, the government sent John Macaulay, the 'king' of the Freetown Aku, from the capital to Waterloo in 1843 and to Hastings in 1851. Macaulay, a Liberated African who served in various government posts from policeman to overseer in the Liberated African Department, was dispatched to establish peace among the rioting tribes.[63] His answer was to initiate a super-tribal organization in the villages which became known as the Seventeen Nations, after the seventeen tribes at Waterloo.[64] The organization at Waterloo was specifically geared to end the Ibo-Aku difficulties. To effect this Macaulay created a council which represented all of the tribes. A member from each group sat on the council. Its function was to redress 'all petty grievances and [to assist] in the administration of justice and the maintenance of order'.[65]

In Hastings eight years later, the dispute pitted the Yoruba against nine other tribes, including the village's discharged soldiers. The Aku opposed the government overseer who was managing the village. One report alleged that the overseer had bribed the other tribes in order to secure their support. Matters became so intense that 'a petty quarrel of two market women or a little bickering between two School children, would instantly have been taken as a signal for the Soldiers to sound the bugle and the Akus to blow the horn for a general uproar against each other'. John Macaulay entered the Hastings dispute before it could develop into an actual riot. He counselled the Aku 'to keep themselves sober for the time being'. Within a month a government commission had arrived from Freetown. It broke up the nine tribe opposition to the Aku and dismissed the overseer. An inter-tribal organization was founded shortly after on the model of the Waterloo one.[66]

Macaulay's ability to mediate these disputes derived from his role as a powerful and unofficial spokesman for the Liberated Africans. His government positions, minor and inconsequential for the most part, represented the British administration's re-cognition of his powerful position. The highest post he held, Chief Overseer in the Liberated African Department yard, came to him because of his position as king of the Yoruba, and from his own shrewdness in convincing Governor Pine that he could effectively assist the much frustrated ambitions of the British Government in making the scheme of emigration to the West Indies successful in the 1840's. Pine regarded Macaulay as an intelligent and honest man who represented the senti-ments of the Yoruba 'over which [group] he possesses almost un-bounded influence'.[67] The appointment came to Macaulay in 1849 because of 'his great usefulness in promoting Emigra-tion . . .',[68] paid him £48 per year, and lasted until 1853 when a later Governor, Arthur Kennedy, who regarded Macaulay's appointment in the Yard as a perfect sinecure, abolished the position altogether.[69] In the meantime, Governor Norman Mac-donald had tried unsuccessfully to get Macaulay removed from his job in the Department. Macdonald, while admitting that it was the king s pre-eminent position among the Aku which had secured his post, considered that the appointment was unwise. Pine's was an 'unsound policy' because it gave 'the native population . . . ground for supposing that, as Headmen or otherwise, they possessed greater power or influence than the local Government'. With remarkable candour, Macdonald continued, revealing the extent to which Liberated Africans controlled their own affairs: 'It is . . . a sufficiently disagreeable and embarrassing fact for the Government itself to know that those under its charge do, in a certain measure, possess superior

influence to it, over a portion of the community; but it appears to me . . . [imprudent] to let that fact . . . become public . . . As Macaulay himself knew that he did possess a certain amount of influence over his Country people, he was not backward . . . in coming to the conclusion that his appointment was due entirely to the fact that he possessed more than the Government, and that the local Authorities could not do without him. . . .'
Macaulay had discouraged emigration during Macdonald's term of office. The king never cooperated with the Governor. Moreover, he also signed petitions to London calling for Macdonald's removal, an act that clearly did not ingratiate him with the Governor.[70] The Colonial Office answered Macdonald's charges against Macaulay with words which clearly showed London's understanding both of Liberated African independence and the power of the recaptives' headmen.[71] Macaulay stayed as chief overseer in the yard.

It was then as Yoruba king that Macaulay rose to his powerful position. Throughout the colony people regarded him as King Macaulay or King Atapa, the leader, strictly speaking, of the Freetown Aku, a post he acquired on the death of Thomas Will in 1840.[72] As Aku king, he was recognized also as the virtual representative of all Liberated Africans. His assumption of the Yoruba kingship was unusual since Macaulay himself was Hausa, 'of the pure Bornu tribe'.[73] Perhaps the relationship between the Hausa and the northern Yoruba in the Niger regions, a relationship based on the common religious faith, Islam, carried over to the connection in Freetown between Macaulay and the Freetown Aku who were mainly Muslim. Macaulay himself was a Muslim until five years before his death in 1868. In 1863, the Revd. James Johnson, Liberated African pastor of Christ Church on Pademba Road, succeeded in converting him.[74] Macaulay's religious defection did not adversely affect his powerful and respected position. Several tribes vied with one another to honour him at his funeral. The main market as well as the large shops of Freetown closed. Hundreds of people, crowding into the church, came to pay final honour to their leader, the one who had often served as their mediator in disputes with the government. In addition, Macaulay had proved liberal and generous, oftentimes to his own financial loss. The people had brought all their disputes and petty quarrels to him. His compound had remained open at all times, and he had often been seen sitting and patiently listening to rivals arguing their cases. His immediate followers, the king's closest supporters, had detected gangs of night robbers, and had assisted the government in their apprehension.[75]

Macaulay had come to Sierra Leone as a recaptive sometime about 1822. It is possible that he was the John Macaulay who was listed as the Freetown headman of the 'secret' society of King Potts in 1827.[76] By the late 1830's he had secured his first minor government position, rising to the post of Head Overseer in the Liberated African Department yard in 1849. Of greater relevance, however, to his role as an important man was the fact that he had prospered in business. When he left the government service in 1853, he ran a grog shop, traded, and owned property.[77] In 1854, he co-owned a brig, the *Nunez*, which was engaged in the palm oil trade between Badagry, Lagos, and Freetown. The ship also carried much more profitable cargoes of tobacco and rum, and was seized at least once by Customs officials for importing these items illegally. Macaulay prospered through his trading ventures, and his economic prosperity as a merchant reinforced his powerful political position.[78]

King Macaulay's innovation for the Waterloo and Hastings disputes, the Seventeen Nations, spread throughout the colony. Each village established a comparable institution, and by its use, the Liberated Africans more completely secured the control of village affairs for the remainder of the century. In the 1880's the power of the Hastings Seventeen Nations stifled the attempt of William Grant, a successful Creole publisher from Freetown, to take over 1,000 acres of land near the village. The action of the local committee came after the governor had given his permission.[79] The value of the organization was heralded in an

Samuel Ajayi Crowther

1881 account which pointed out that in Hastings 'the custom of clanship was most rife . . . in former years, but of late the practice is being less adhered to and is now become extinct, for the people of various tribes have . . . formed themselves into one powerful association called "the Seventeen Nations," in this association such petty disputes and quarrels as are not considered worthy of law suit are determined and disposed of to the satisfaction of all concerned'.[80]

Described in 1872 in Wilberforce as 'a secret government within a government', the Seventeen Nations served as the effective government throughout the colony after the 1840's, particularly in those places where government supervision was ineffective or non-existent. The Seventeen Nations Association supervised village affairs in the manner of a government, settling disputes, keeping roads and streets open, and 'preventing social disorder in communities where the spirit of insubordination largely predominates, and where disputes frequently arise from trivial circumstances'.[81]

The first indication of the formation of a 'legal company' to settle disputes in the western village of York came in 1860, when the Acting Governor asked the Acting Manager of the district, stationed at Kent, to visit York to look into the existence of such a company.[82] The company proved to be the earliest form of the Seventeen Nations at York. By the late 1860's the organization was run by an administrative committee to which each tribe sent two or three representatives. One of them was the headman of the tribe. The committee intervened in all 'hard cases' in the companies of the different tribes, and settled all disputes and quarrels. They dealt with private arguments as well. The committee acted with speed to suppress any threatened dispute between tribes, disputes which often included threats of bodily harm, poisoning and witchcraft. To resolve such disputes, the committee usually held a public trial in the village market.[83] With its organized structure and several responsibilities, the Seventeen Nations at York had become the virtual governing body of the village.

In eighteen months of residence at York, the Revd. Joseph May, a Liberated African Wesleyan preacher, became a keen observer of the Seventeen Nations. He witnessed three trials for witchcraft or poisoning during this time. Anyone found in possession of a poisonous ingredient was publicly driven out of town, and his house was pulled down and 'made a dunghill of'. Anyone even suspected was brought immediately before the committee. The committee's power increased so rapidly and so completely that May felt obliged to call together its members as well as the community's religious teachers and ministers to preach to them on the 'evils of this system'.[84] The York committee of the Seventeen Nations was the town council to May. Macaulay's innovation had become their effective government. Moreover, the government at Freetown recognized the town councils as the agencies through which the people maintained contact with the central government. Appeals from the council went to the manager and eventually, if necessary, to Freetown. On occasion, the council communicated directly with the governor in the capital who then informed the district manager.[85]

INEFFECTIVE VILLAGE MANAGERS

Ineffective or non-existent official systems of local government set the stage for the rapid spread of the Seventeen Nations. What its spread indicated was that the particular system of having district managers oversee the affairs of the largely independent Liberated Africans had proved ineffective. Since even before the original outbreak of difficulties in Waterloo, governors had expressed considerable dissatisfaction with those who served as managers. Governor Doherty wrote in 1838 that 'the half educated managers, unobserved and independent, neglect their duties, oppress their villagers, and are tempted by the hope of impunity to the commission of peculations'. Such a situation 'called for an anxious and incessant control of their conduct. . . .' Governor Norman Macdonald in 1846 had had to forbid managers and sub-managers from leaving their districts without prior approval because the officials, especially those who lived close to Freetown, had been spending long periods of time in the capital rather than doing their jobs in the rural areas. Seven years later the condition of the managers had not improved. Arthur Kennedy, looking over their situation soon after becoming Governor, confessed that 'some are without character, and all without capacity. They have little or nothing to do, and that little is done without regard to common law or Common Sense'. In later years, governors only occasionally turned their attention to rural area affairs, but when they did they had to deal with the managers at an extremely elementary level. Governor Rowe specified in 1879 that he wanted managers to visit their villages at least once a month; in 1881 the manager of the Mountain District had to be asked to provide the governor with information on the frequency of his visits when it appeared that he had not visited them at all between January and August.[86]

The spread of the Seventeen Nations to York after 1860 resulted from the fact that the village was without the direct influence of a manager. The responsible official, John Bucknor Elliott, of Nova Scotian descent, resided at Kent between 1864 and 1883. Kent was at the extreme south of the colony's Atlantic coast. His visits were infrequent and brief because, after 1870, his most important duties had little or nothing to do with the administration of the area under his control. He maintained a vigil at sea to capture slaves being moved along the coast between the Sherbro areas to the south and Bulom and Temne areas to the north. Elliott was also the important communications link between Sherbro and Freetown, seeing to it that messengers who arrived from Freetown were cared for and that their dispatches were forwarded on to Bonthe. On occasion Elliott himself was sent to Shenge or some other southern post to report to the governor on developments in the newly annexed territory. Such responsibilities became the dominant consideration in the eyes of the central administration in Freetown. Growing old and infirm, Elliott in 1882 moved his headquarters to York. The government objected once they discovered the move, and ordered the manager back to Kent. York again had no contact with the central government. Elliott went on leave in 1883, and was pensioned by the government in 1884. Twenty years of service to the colony government as manager of the Western District received terse notice at the Executive Council meeting approving his retirement; the government thought Elliott's combined pension of nearly £200 per year was too high 'seeing that Mr. Elliott was never a valuable public officer'.[87] The harsh summation for the individual nevertheless provided an appropriate epitaph for the whole system of district managers. The continual difficulties of defining their duties, finding suitable candidates, and ensuring effective performance of their responsibilities proved insoluble to the central government at Freetown. The villages were therefore left without an effective system of local government provided by the colonial power. The administrative and judicial void allowed for the development of the Liberated Africans' own province of freedom; the freedom allowed a Liberated African to innovate the Seventeen Nations, a system of local government for the recaptives in the rural areas, as well as allowing the Liberated Africans themselves the opportunity to control their own affairs.

Thus, beginning with the early use of headmen, the establishment of separatist villages and colony-wide benefit societies, through the successful settlement of the Cobolo Aku at Fourah Bay, and the innovation of the Seventeen Nations, the Liberated Africans had accepted the challenge presented to them by the failings of the British colonial government. They proved to be capable administrators in their own province of freedom. The effective use of their political independence assured the creation of stable and secure village communities. To a large measure, their unheralded contributions in the field of politics saved the British experiment along the rocky coast of Sierra Leone from utter and complete failure.

VII

Liberated African Society: Independence in Religion, Welfare, and Economics

Independence of action became the theme of Liberated African life in nineteenth-century Sierra Leone. Just as it had allowed for the development of political groupings in the rural areas, independent activity continued to characterize the growth of recaptive voluntary associations in general. Such activity in the society at large gave dynamic meaning to the otherwise empty phrase, province of freedom. In the Liberated Africans' province of freedom they had the opportunity to innovate freely in areas besides politics. To investigate the recaptives' religious life and their economic and social associations is to discover again the manner in which the persistent failure of the colonial plans for the settlement was overcome by the Liberated Africans' resilient and independent abilities to develop what came to be Sierra Leone's Creole society by the latter half of the century.

The growth of voluntary associations was crucial to this development. Their independence, although it varied in intensity, was constant. In religion, the vast majority of the Liberated African population did not conform to the Established Church. Many of those recaptives who became Christian joined the numerous dissenting chapels or formed new ones which more specifically represented their interests. The factor of independence from the Establishment dominated. Some Liberated Africans remained or became Muslim, while others continued to worship their tribal deities. The key welfare organizations in the colony were the benefit and welfare societies developed by the Liberated Africans. Their services to the population varied, ranging from saving for future investment to burying the dead. The economic growth of the society depended significantly on either *ad hoc* or long term trade associations among the recaptives. This variety of voluntary associations served to confirm the independent action of Liberated Africans in the field of local government. The successful activity of the non-political associations contributed significantly as well to the nature of the emergent Creole society of mid-century and after.

RELIGION AND FREETOWN SOCIETY

Freetown was, in conception and to most by implication, a Christian community. The original settlers and the Nova Scotians had been Christian before their arrival in Sierra Leone. Their early interest in converting the Maroons and their activity among the Liberated Africans indicated their adherence to Christianity and their wish that the community should provide for all the gift of redemption. To Briton and settler alike, the conversion of the heathen was as much a part of the settlement's collective purpose as was the wish to civilize the so-called barbarian. The purposes were inextricably interwoven. In spite of the many hardships facing the missionaries in the early years, they had established themselves and had assured that Christianity would be an important part of Sierra Leone society. Aspects of the Christian faith became as important a determinant of Creole-ness as did European names, dress, and education. But the victory of Christianity, particularly as interpreted by the Church's own missionaries, was far from complete. There persisted within the Christian church in Sierra Leone a strong element of prior, non-Christian belief which tended to fuse with the religion of the European. In addition, Islam was to be found flourishing both in the villages and in Freetown. Then too, another strong and troubling minority continued to worry the Christian missions. These were the many recaptives who successfully maintained belief in their tribal deities without embracing Christianity at all. Thus, religious belief among the Liberated Africans in the first half of the nineteenth century included groups of Christians, Muslims, and pagans. These three basic groups, moreover, remained distinct in the Creole society of the latter half of the century. Even at the earliest period there was some correlation between social class and religious affiliation among the Liberated Africans. The more economically prosperous, who invariably became the social elite by the early decades of the second half of the century, were almost without exception Christian. As Arthur T. Porter has pointed out about a later period,[1] the social elite tended to be members of either the Anglican Church or one of the more prosperous Freetown Wesleyan chapels.[2]

The percentage of such a social elite in the total population was never large. The estimated number who were religious conformists was even smaller. For, like his Nova Scotian predecessor, the Sierra Leone recaptive who embraced Christianity remained steadfastly a religious dissenter, the member, more often than not, of one of a variety of Wesleyan groups. In spite of the consistent wish of the British governors for a church monopoly, Freetown and its surrounding villages remained dissenter's territory. Governor MacCarthy's report in 1818 that over three-fourths of the Freetown Christians were dissenters was repeated by others throughout the century. Many of the dissenters were even independent of the Wesleyan Methodist Missionary Society's European leaders in the settlement. A judge of the Mixed Commission Court contended three years after MacCarthy's report that no more than 600 of the 5,000 who comprised the Freetown population attended Sunday services at Established Churches. Moreover, most of those who were not European went to service because of some sense of personal obligation. He estimated that more than twice as many attended services at Methodist chapels.[3] Thus, exhibiting the same characteristics of independence which were evident in other areas of their lives, most Christian Liberated Africans were dissenters.

RELIGIOUS DISSENT AMONG THE LIBERATED
AFRICANS

Those who were Methodists, moreover, were not content simply to remain under the direction of the English missionary society. By mid-century the Liberated Africans had made themselves an independent religious force within the general Wesleyan movement in the colony. Again they had followed in the footsteps of the Nova Scotians. In 1822 the Nova Scotian settlers broke with the British Wesleyan Methodist mission and began an independent church which they called the West African Methodist Society. Their main chapel was on Rawdon Street in Freetown, from whence their separatist movement spread throughout the colony. It naturally attracted many Liberated Africans who became members.[4] The Nova Scotians wanted recaptive members in order to ensure the success of their own independent church. Liberated Africans sought membership because it freed them from the European overlords of the English Methodist movement in Sierra Leone. However, the mutual attraction of Liberated Africans and Nova Scotians also revealed serious problems within a short span of years. Anxious to have the recaptives as members, the settlers were intent to prevent them from rising in the movement. Nova Scotian fears of domination by the numerically superior ranks of the Liberated Africans in the community in general led them to adopt a policy of discrimination within their own Methodist society. Rawdon Street Chapel contained both a reading desk and a pulpit. When a Liberated African lay preacher delivered a sermon he found himself barred from the pulpit; Liberated Africans had to use the reading desk. This was but one example of the many forms discrimination took, but it proved one of the most pointed and eventually decisive manifestations. The recaptives found the discrimination increasingly difficult to accept and began to object to their second-class status in the chapels of Nova Scotian Methodism. By the 1840's the Liberated Africans far outnumbered the Nova Scotians in the West African Methodist Society. A recaptive lay preacher, Anthony O'Connor, reflected long and hard on the many forms of social discrimination built up over the years by the settlers, and decided to lead the Liberated Africans from the Rawdon Street Chapel in 1844.

O'Connor's schism spread quickly throughout the colony chapels of the West African Methodist Society; when the dust had settled almost all of the Nova Scotian society's Liberated African chapels were under the banner of the West African Methodist Church, the name chosen by O'Connor's group. The new church had 2,000 members and forty-three preachers, an abundance of resources which allowed the recaptives under O'Connor to open almost immediately three small wooden chapels in Freetown and to begin to build a large stone edifice to seat 800. The stone building was pointed to by the Liberated Africans 'as a specimen of what *Liberated Africans can* do and what they *will* do'. Five years later a European Wesleyan, reviewing the group's rapid growth, suggested in explanation that it was 'emphatically the People's Society. It is what they themselves began and have carried on. It is not the Wesleyan—not the Settlers—not the Church—but emphatically—"the Liberated Africans'" own Society.'[5]

O'Connor's split and the formation of an independent Liberated African religious society in Freetown merely confirmed the religious independence shown by the recaptives earlier in the villages. As early as 1829 the villagers of Wellington had built their own church building. When government objected, the villagers negotiated with the Church Missionary Society to secure a regular preacher. If the pulpit fell vacant for a year, however, according to the contract, the English society lost its privileges.[6] Similarly, a group from the already established dissenting chapel in Hastings asked Freetown leaders of the British Wesleyans to include them in the regular Methodist circuit in 1836.[7]

By the 1850's prosperous Freetown Liberated Africans dominated the Wesleyan chapels. The increasing prosperity of the congregations was reflected in the many new chapels which were being built. Buxton Chapel opened in 1854. Its opening immediately caused the trustees of Bathurst Street Chapel to begin preparations to replace their building. Four years later, the colony's governor laid the foundation stone for the new Wesleyan chapel on Trelawney Street. Long before its completion, Wesley Church had become the obvious symbol of the newly prosperous Freetown Liberated African and Creole. Iron windows were forged in Britain and the materials for the roof came from North America. No expense was spared by the trustees who directed the subscription drive and succeeded in securing a £1,000 donation from the British Wesleyans as well as £200 from the Colonial Government. The trustees themselves included the top people of mid-century Freetown society, Liberated Africans such as John Ezzidio, W. H. Pratt, and William Lewis, those who had already risen by their commercial prowess. The affluence of the Freetown Wesleyans reached such heights that by 1862 the Revd. Charles Marke, a Liberated African preacher, found it necessary to preach against those who would join the society merely for prestige.[8]

OLDER SURVIVALS IN A CHRISTIAN CONTEXT

If top Freetown society by mid-century chose to exhibit its continuing sense of independence in the form of larger and more substantial dissenting chapels, the lower elements continued to manifest such qualities in other ways. They tended to retain elements of prior belief systems or to reinterpret elements of Christianity in order to make them more compatible. The use of the charm to protect its wearer from evil persisted, particularly in the villages. The Revd. J. F. Schön at Bathurst reported finding a charm around the neck of the son of a family belonging to the parish church. He called the boy to his house and tried to persuade him to take it off. The boy refused and left, but soon afterwards he returned to the missionary with his parents. Both parents were enraged; the father became abusive. He argued that the charm was not a gri-gri 'because he had not bought it with an intention of killing or injuring any person, but as a medicine to cure the child, and . . . to secure it against the influence of witches. It was in his opinion just as much as if he had given some medicine to the child to drink, or had [had him] vaccinated'. The Revd. Graf told of a similar case in Hastings in 1844. The parents in this case wanted to protect their son from 'bad luck' and witches. Most of the charms contained seeds, grass, dirt, or a piece of paper with some saying on it, usually in Arabic. The Hastings charm contained also 'a small pair of iron stocks, such as used on feet of criminals.' The mother explained to Graf that this meant that sickness of every kind was 'tied and fettered' to keep it from attacking her son. The Bible itself was used as a charm in some cases. An African school teacher at Waterloo was dismissed from the CMS because he used the Bible to discover 'evildoers'.[9] Contrary to the belief of most missionaries that the gri-gris were imported into the colony by Muslim teachers from the interior, some were made in the rural areas themselves by recaptive Christians. Moreover, the making of charms persisted late into the nineteenth century. One such Liberated African manufacturer of charms who was a professed Christian was discovered swearing oaths before a sacred tree in the bush near Charlotte in 1886. He threatened to kill his fellow communicant who had found him practising his craft and who also discovered that the charms he was at that moment making were intended to kill three of the villagers. Unwilling to hide his discovery, the man who had found the charm maker went to the village elders who held a trial and found the gri-gri maker guilty. They destroyed the charms found in the man's house and fined him forty shillings. The man disappeared from Charlotte, but those who continued to live there did so in considerable fear that he would return in the dark of the night to bewitch them.[10]

The use of charms as well as libations and other forms taken from traditional ceremonies pertaining to death were almost universally incorporated by the Liberated Africans into their new life. In 1846 a communicant at Gloucester demanded that an offender come to pour libations in a case of 'woman damage'.

The traditional wakes and mourning celebrations, called *awujo*, became integral parts of Creole life. Their origins were in the traditional death celebrations of the Yoruba and other tribes represented in the colony. The wakes usually shocked the European missionaries. Their descriptions, however, revealed how the recaptives modified the celebrations in order to make them more compatible with their present needs. Schön wrote of one in 1846 that it produced 'the most shocking scene of revelling and drunkenness and went on not only that night, but for a whole week. And the most distressing thing to my mind is their giving these occasions a religious appearance by singing and praying at intervals; and members of the church always justify their presence on this account.'[11] The recaptives vehemently defended the necessity of having the wakes. If missionaries continued to regard the wakes as the worst carry-over from the recaptives' past,[12] the Liberated Africans themselves thought of them as the most important. Schön was told on another occasion that the drumming and singing comforted the widow. The missionary tried to stop the celebration anyway but was firmly rebuffed. One recaptive explained to him that 'We were born in another country, this fashion we learned from our fathers. What they did we do too. This fashion no fit for white man, white man's fashion no fit for black man; you do the fashion you see your father do, we do the fashion we learn from our fathers. Suppose our fathers go to hell, we cannot tell; suppose they go to heaven, we cannot tell.' Schön tried to refute the argument, but suddenly another recaptive intervened and told him, 'Sir, it no fit for you to come to we tell we so, suppose you have any thing to say, you must call headman to your house, and must speak to him alone, and the headman fit man to come to the company to bring work and the company say now, no other person ever done like you.' The Liberated African rather neatly told Schön the procedure to follow if he cared to protest further. Schön left the celebrants and returned home.[13]

The Wesleyans, later in the century, attempted to control the wakes by enforcing a rule which threatened expulsion for any member found guilty of attending a wake. The Wesleyan missionary at Wilberforce in 1867, however, confessed that 'amongst professing Christians I have found those who take delight in "Oru", Last Burying and other such . . . relics of heathenism'. He discovered that Wesleyans from Freetown and members of the Anglican Church in Wilberforce joined his local membership to perform the ceremonies.[14] What he refused to acknowledge was reported by the Liberated African Wesleyan preacher at Wellington in 1870, the Revd. Charles Marke. He explained to the English officials of the society in London that the practice of wake-keeping, particularly by the relatives of the deceased, was an integral part of their religious belief system. Any departure from the practice of remaining in the home of the deceased relative for two weeks was 'considered as an absence of love for the deceased . . . [and] in direct contrariety to established usage'.[15] Integral too were the practices of providing food in yards, streets, and on the tombs of relatives and friends in order to feed the dead. The regular trips to the graves of departed relatives 'to talk to them' also became an entirely integrated part of Liberated African and Creole Christianity.[16] Although it continually brought negative comments from the European missionaries in the colony, such a fusion of religious belief among the Sierra Leone Liberated Africans was no more significant or surprising than the same type of fusion which had taken place centuries earlier when Christianity had moved northward from the Italian peninsula into northern Europe. Nonetheless, missionaries persistently echoed the protest of the Revd. J. G. Wilhelm in 1828, 'now for me to be their priest, would make me a complete greegree man!'[17] The recaptives retained much of the past and reinterpreted much of the new doctrine presented to them by the missionaries. In this fashion, by 1870, the dominant element of the society was oriented more toward Christianity than it had been fifty years earlier.

The Growth of Islam among the Liberated Africans

Neither Liberated African society nor the Creole society into which it developed, however, was universally Christian. Some Liberated Africans turned instead to Islam. The quite erroneous tendency has developed among writers on Sierra Leone and its history to treat this Muslim element of Liberated African society separately, and not to include it at all in the development of Creole society. Michael Banton, in *West African City*, used a too particularized definition of the term Aku—which to him meant a Muslim of Yoruba descent—and Arthur T. Porter wrote of the Muslims, 'Until about the eve of the Second World War, they were a community who did not share or contest a share in the status-reward-power system of Freetown'.[18] While the points made by both authors contain some truth, neither makes allowance for the extremely similar pattern of development contained in the histories of Freetown Creoles who were Christian and Muslim. In everything but religion, the Freetown Muslim Creole developed similarly to the Freetown Christian Creole, a fact which seriously calls into question the complete validity of the use of religion as a means to describe a Creole. In the nineteenth century the descendants of Muslim Liberated Africans were called Muslim Creoles. The practice continued into the twentieth century, even using Banton's apparently exclusive term Aku as a measure. As late as 1960, Freetonians were careful to modify such terms as Aku and Creole with the adjective Christian or Muslim.

Not to see the similarities between Muslim and Christian Creole development in Sierra Leone is to ignore the fluidity of religious belief in the colony in the nineteenth century. Liberated Africans changed their religion with relative ease. John Macaulay was converted from Islam to Christianity five years before his death in 1868. The obituary of Mrs. Elizabeth Shaw in 1885 revealed that when her first husband, Mr. Shaw, died she married a Muslim and became a Muslim herself. Although she had belonged to Christ Church, Pademba Road, she moved, after her second marriage, to Foulah Town where she became one of the community's leading citizens. The CMS missionary J. G. Wilhelm reported as early as 1833 from Freetown that he discovered the wife of one communicant to be a member both of his congregation at Gibralter Church and of a mosque where Mandinka Muslims prayed to Allah.[19]

Muslim society in Freetown did develop separately. For the most part, Christian and Muslim Liberated Africans lived in different sections of the town. Nevertheless, in language, food, and numerous customs, the Muslim showed himself no different from other recaptives. Developing separately for a long period in the nineteenth century, the Muslim Creole community, by the last decade of the century, began to make a concerted effort to reintegrate itself into the mainstream of Freetown society. This it did through the development of a Muslim reform movement within the community concentrated in Fourah Bay and Foulah Town on the town's east end. Such reintegration proved to be a long process because of the Muslims' reaction to the government's attempt at suppression in the early 1830's, and its blunt persecution in the later part of the same decade. This resulted in a tendency among the Muslims to withdraw, and caused many actually to leave the colony. Muslims comprised a significant part of the Liberated Africans who emigrated to Nigeria in the 1840's.[20] Those who remained in Sierra Leone turned inward in order to secure their own village communities, and to perfect their understanding of Islam.

The history of the development of a specifically Muslim Creole community in Sierra Leone provides the most significant example of the extent to which the Liberated Africans went on expressing their independence. Confronted by military defeat at Cobolo in 1832, and antagonized by the burning of the Foulah Town mosque—explained by the governor of the day as a mistake—in 1839, the Freetown Muslim took up a religiously defensive position by strengthening his own understanding of his faith. Governor Richard Doherty was himself irritated by the presence of Muslims in the colony. His suggestions to the

Colonial Office in 1839 revealed a conscious policy of strict discrimination against the Muslim recaptives. Their 'ostentatious observance' of the rite of Islam together with their polygamous family life offended him. He feared their spreading throughout the colony and noted that they dispatched 'emissaries' to other parts of the capital as well as to the surrounding villages. To Doherty, 'terror . . . charms and incantations' formed the basis of their conversion movement, a movement which had had its success among children and apprentices. The Governor advocated a policy of breaking up the Muslim communities and moving them beyond the colony's borders. He felt he could do this successfully because the land upon which the settlement at Fourah Bay had been built remained Crown Land. In Foulah Town, where the mosque had been burnt to the ground, Muslims expressed the desire to move on if the government were able to provide them with alternative land. From Fourah Bay came a politely worded petition, signed in Arabic by Mammado Savage, Henry Macaulay and James MacCarthy—all thoroughly Freetonian—who called themselves 'Your Excellency's most dutiful and loyal Liberated African subjects'. The petitioners expressed sorrow and regret that they would have to move because the original Lawyer Savage did not have a deed to what now was discovered still to be Crown Land. They pointed out that two prior governors had approved of their settling on Fourah Bay and that they continued to be a respectable community of sawyers, carpenters, blacksmiths, tailors, labourers and farmers. Finally they asked Doherty to change his mind. Whether it was because of the tolerant thinking of James Stephen and Vernon Smith at the Colonial Office in London or the fact that Doherty himself left the colony before any such policy could be implemented, the Muslims remained in Freetown at Foulah Town and Fourah Bay and by 1841 two mosques had replaced the one destroyed by the police.[21]

Their presence continued to be a source of irritation to the missionaries, who referred to them as 'the deluded followers of

James Johnson

Mahomet,' and to the government, which on occasion imagined the deft hand of Fourah Bay Muslims behind embarrassing set-backs to its policies in surrounding areas. Governor Norman Macdonald sought to implicate them in the burning of his newly-established settlement across the estuary at Clarkson when, in fact, he had been caught interfering openly in Bulom-Susu politics outside his own territory. In a maliciously false dispatch to cover up his own errors, he showed the extent to which some would go to malign the Muslim minority in the colony. Calling them the '. . . blisters on the face of our Society' he repeated Doherty's proposed solution by suggesting that he be allowed to break up the dissident communities; the Colonial Office pondered Macdonald's recall, its only reaction. Macdonald remained, however, and in 1849 announced that he was determined no longer to apprentice new arrivals to the Muslims.[22]

While the government worried about the embarrassing existence of a Muslim minority in Freetown, the Muslims themselves largely ignored the government's charges, and seemed content to restrict their contact with the rest of the community to trade. The more important task remained to perfect their own faith. The reasons for this were sound. Islam presented a somewhat ambivalent picture in early nineteenth-century Freetown. Such ambivalence resulted in part from the different origins of the faith in the colony. Of the approximately 2,000 who professed Islam in the settlement in 1848, a large number were Mandinka, Susu, and Fula, while many were Liberated African Aku.[23] The Mandinka, Susu, and Fula had introduced Islam to the peninsula before the settlement of the Black Poor in 1787. They had been coming to trade in the area since the fifteenth century when the Portuguese had first appeared on the scene.[24] With the founding of the settlement at Freetown and its rapid development as a good source of European goods, the trading Muslims from the interior settled in permanent communities near the capital. One of these communities was Foulah Town, founded in 1819.[25] The immigrant Fula and Mandinka represented

241

a western Sudanese form of Muslim orthodoxy. Converted before the middle of the eighteenth century, they had accepted Islam not only as a faith but also as a way of life by the time they settled in the Freetown area in the nineteenth century. One distinctive feature of their communities was that their leader, the *almami*, tended to have spiritual as well as temporal power. Recaptured Mandinka and Fula joined these settlements of Muslim countrymen once they had been freed from government control.[26] A third tribal group of some size in Freetown, the recaptive Hausa, also belonged to those who could be generally classified as the orthodox Muslims of early Freetown.

A large number of Muslims in the colony by mid-century, however, had different origins. They were the more recent converts from Yoruba country in Nigeria. Most were from the northern parts of Yoruba and had been converted during the Fulani *jihad* of Uthman don Fodio early in the nineteenth century. Those who were in Freetown had been captured in the slave wars, recaptured on the high seas by the British naval squadron, and liberated by the Mixed Commission Courts in Sierra Leone. These Yoruba were devout Muslim believers, but their belief differed from that of the more orthodox Mandinka, Susu, Fula, and Hausa. The recentness of their conversion explained such differences. The Sierra Leone Aku tended to be Muslim only in religious belief. Their pattern of life remained essentially Yoruba and was still little affected by the new belief. The clearest indication of this difference was the fact that the Yoruba, unlike the others, maintained a clear distinction between political and religious leadership and power. The Aku maintained a headman in addition to an imam.[27] Beyond this, as a recently acquired religious belief, Islam had superimposed itself on many indigenous customs and institutions among the Yoruba. A strong Muslim minority among them insisted on the continuation of the *Agugu* (*Engungun*) secret society within the new religious context. As many Yoruba themselves grew more orthodox during the later part of the century, this extreme group of Yoruba Muslim was gradually ostracized and eventually prohibited from worshipping in the mosques of Freetown.[28]

Early Yoruba Muslims depended heavily on Fula and Mandinka teachers and religious leaders for instruction. Their religious education, tragically interrupted in their home country, resumed once they settled safely in their Sierra Leone communities at Foulah Town and Fourah Bay. The Fula and Mandinka alfas led Koranic schools to which the Muslim Liberated Africans went. The crucial Muslim occasions, holidays, and celebrations were observed under the watchful eyes of these more orthodox elements in the community. Travellers in the 1840's reported on the observance of the fast of Ramadan and of the parade and dancing which marked the feast of Eid-el-Fitri at its close.[29] Gradually, the Muslim Yoruba themselves became more orthodox in their belief. The beginnings of such orthodoxy date from the visit to the Mandinka community in Freetown early in 1856, of the brother of Hadj Omar, the great Muslim leader of Futa Toro in the north. Freetown Mandinka tradition says that Omaru himself visited the city, although confirmation exists only for the visit of his brother. A leading Aku Muslim from Fourah Bay called on the visitor and asked him to take his young son back to the north with him so that he could be educated at the school at Dingarawe. Omaru's brother agreed and for the next twenty years Legally Savage, the young Fourah Bay Aku, remained under the guidance of the Arabic and Koranic scholars to the north. Some time about the middle of the 1870's Legally Savage returned to Fourah Bay and became an assistant imam at the mosque.[30] In this position he emerged as the leader of Muslim orthodoxy in the Fourah Bay community. The prestige of his Muslim education, coupled with the fact that he was a Savage, guaranteed his position. The tiny community of Muslims never forgot the original beneficence of the lawyer, W. H. Savage. With authority, Legally Savage reformed the pagan influences contained in the Islamic beliefs of the Aku in Fourah Bay. By doing so, he alienated some of the older elements in the east end community.

But Freetown was Freetown, and almost at the same time

that Savage was making Fourah Bay Islam more orthodox, another new tendency was developing among the followers of Mohammed. This was the group of Muslim modernist reformers who sought to integrate Freetown Islam more with the dominant elements of Freetown society. Specifically, they sought to modernize Muslim education. Savage at Fourah Bay quite naturally resisted the pressures of the growing numbers of modernist reformers within his community. To resist both groups, however, left Savage with little numerical support. His followers, the Tamba, were clearly in a minority. His eventual involvement in the persistent land dispute led to his downfall in 1889, when both he and the imam of the mosque were removed from power. For the next ten years he and his supporters prayed privately away from the Fourah Bay mosque. His eclipse came in part from his insistence on maintaining Muslim orthodoxy. He consistently fought against every attempt to reform Islam in Freetown. The Alfa viewed this correctly as an attempt to reintegrate the Muslim Aku into Freetown society. The movement was all-pervasive. He objected to the design of the new mosque built in the 1880's as being too much like that of a church, and to the fact that many Christian labourers worked on its construction. Next he protested against the invitation sent to Governor Hay to attend a wedding at the mosque. Ignoring the problem of gaining government recognition for Muslim marriages—which would at least have been secured symbolically by the Governor's presence—Savage stood by the simple view that to have a Christian witness a Muslim ceremony was wrong. Finally, Savage mounted a successful attack against the great defender of West African Islam, Dr. Edward W. Blyden. Allying himself with the forces of modern Islamic reform at Fourah Bay, Blyden had begun classes at the mosque. Savage would have none of it, particularly since Blyden himself was not Muslim. There was no need for an English education in the mind of one educated by the leading Muslim teachers of the north. The Fourah Bay alfa succeeded in ending Blyden's teaching at Fourah Bay in 1889.

The struggle among the factions continued. The Jamat, the congregation of the mosque, finally forced Savage's removal and that of the imam, when Alfa Legally solemnized a marriage only to discover that one of the parties had not been properly divorced. Although the marriage provided the immediate cause for the removal, the continuing land dispute in the community also played its part. The Tamba and the Jamat differed over who owned the land on which the mosque was built, the Tamba, Savage's followers, contending that it belonged to the Savage family while the Jamat insisted that it belonged to the whole community. More basic than either the marriage or the land dispute to the dissensions at Fourah Bay, however, was the question of what was to be the nature of Islam in the colony.[31]

The period during which the Muslims of the Sierra Leone colony sought to perfect their understanding of Islam lasted from about 1840 to about 1870. Then, led by men like Mohammed Sanusi, a Foulah Town Muslim Creole of Aku parentage, the Muslim community gradually began to take a more modern position and to seek a more relevant place in Freetown society. A government interpreter, Sanusi had had contact from his earliest years in Foulah Town with English officials of government and mission. He used to come regularly to the CMS missionaries at Fourah Bay to read their latest English newspapers. Educated by a Fula teacher near Futa Jalon, Sanusi was skilled at Arabic, able to speak it fluently and to write it sufficiently well to secure his living as an Arabic writer for the government. Blyden himself thought that Sanusi's Arabic library was very respectable. His English, moreover, was excellent and he knew the Bible better than most missionaries knew the Koran, a fact which made him a popular visitor to missionary quarters. One who maintained as well an active interest in commerce and trade, Sanusi was then a new sort of Freetown Muslim, one who had a dominant interest in the rest of the community. This was what made Sanusi and others modernist reformers within the east end Muslim settlements.[32]

During the later half of the nineteenth century, young,

literate Muslims such as Sanusi became the alfas of the Muslim Yoruba communities in Freetown. Their influence reached an important summit in the early 1890's when the government agreed to assist the Muslims in maintaining their own primary schools.[33] The schools taught essentially the same curriculum as the older mission and government schools, but with the addition of Arabic and Koranic studies. The Muslim Liberated African and his Creole descendants sought the same benefits of western education, but without the sacrifice of religious belief. Thus, even with the adoption of western education by the Muslims of Freetown, the persistent tendency to remain in some manner independent of the Christian-oriented governments of the day continued.[34]

With the emergence of the forces of modernist reform, the Freetown Muslim grew closer to other Liberated Africans and Creoles. The integration was assisted by the government which, unlike Governors Doherty and Macdonald, became far more tolerant toward the Muslim Liberated African minority during the last half of the nineteenth century. Muslim petitions were acted upon. One governor contributed £5 'in the Queen's name' to the building of the Foulah Town mosque in 1882. Another entertained a large gathering of Muslims at Government House at the close of Ramadan in 1879. Missions themselves were not unaffected by the process of integration noted among the younger elements of Freetown Muslim society. Long having had Muslim students in their secondary schools, the CMS reported in 1876 that they now had a Muslim studying English authors at Fourah Bay College.[35] Thus, because of the new Muslim leadership and a more tolerant attitude among the dominant Christian hierarchy, the tendency toward integration in Freetown received a significant impetus. Muslims increasingly took their place in Creole society. The tendency could be noted in several ways. Schools were most significant. The architecture of the Muslim sections of Freetown resembled that of the rest of the city. Homes in the Fourah Bay and Foulah Town areas reflected the same gradations of economic prosperity and social status as those in the central and western parts of the capital. The mosques built in the 1880's resembled church buildings, the only concession to Islam appearing to be the substitution of a single or double minaret for the Christian bell tower. Muslim weddings had a distinctive Freetown flavour. Both bride and groom entered the mosque and the bride was often attired in a long, white wedding dress much as if she were going to be married in a church. From the traditional photograph taken after the ceremony it was difficult to know the religious persuasion of the newly married couple unless some specific note were included to identify the building in the background as mosque or church.

The most revealing indication of Muslim-Christian Creole integration in the nineteenth century in Freetown came at the end of the century when a single Creole association was formed. By the 1890's, the Freetown Creole had begun to face the problem of working out his relationships with the immigrant population from the Sierra Leone interior. Fears in the Creole community led the settled Freetown population to suspect that they were no longer heard at Government House and that they were in fact becoming sacrifices to the less sophisticated African from the interior on the altar of British imperial rule. These fears led Creoles to explore the possibility of forming a new association the purpose of which would be to secure the ear of the government. The movement began early in 1889 and had a strong element of Yoruba nationalism in it. Described in the press as both 'A Novel Gathering' and 'A New Feature' the first meeting of Christian and Muslim Creoles took place at the Methodist high school where Abayomi Cole lectured to a gathering of Christian Creoles and Muslim Aku from Foulah Town and Fourah Bay on 'Olorun—the King of the heavens.' Cole, a clergyman and a professor with connections with the American Wesleyan movement, told his listeners in Yoruba that 'the Redemption of Africa depends on all irrespective of religion . . . [and that] all minor differences should . . . sink to dust . . . and all should unite for the salvation of Africa and leave the event to God who has made all men of one blood'. Mohammed Sanusi praised Blyden because it was he who had taught the Muslims about Christianity and the Christians about Islam. In a manner which certainly marked the culmination of Muslim modernist reform, Sanusi told the audience in the Methodist Hall, 'Both the Mohammedans and Christians of this country are of one race. . . .' J. B. M'Carthy, voting thanks, called the meeting a mark of new progress in the colony, and asked for further contact with the settlement's Muslims. James Taylor seconded the thanks, Cole's choir sang the doxology —earlier they had opened with hymns—Cole himself pronounced the benediction, and Muslim tracts were distributed after the meeting.[36]

M'Carthy's wish for further contact was granted two years later when the Aku Creoles formed an association and elected a 'king' or headman to serve their interests. Appropriately enough they elected George Metzger Macaulay, the son of King John Macaulay of Seventeen Nations fame. George Metzger Macaulay himself had traded in the Sherbro country to the south and had, on occasion, acted as a government interpreter and 'Protector of Strangers' in Freetown. He was a man of some substance, being named together with T. J. Sawyerr and J. B. M'Carthy as directors of the Sierra Leone Sugar Manufacturing Company in 1879. He owned his own large home on Circular Road in Freetown. He died there at the age of 61 in 1899.[37] The organizational meeting which crowned Macaulay as the king of the new Creole association took place in April 1891. The association's avowed purpose was to reinstitute the communication between the Liberated African and Creole community on one hand and the government on the other. The speakers at the occasion again revealed that Muslim and Christian were pulling together. Cole delivered the main address, telling his audience that 'our atmosphere is filled with words, words, words; we are living artificial lives. We fail, not because our civilization is precocious, but because our existence is false. . . . It is the aim of those interested in the present movement . . . to resuscitate those virtues common to us as a nation, but which have been long swept away in Sierra Leone by the blast of "civilization".'[38] His words were followed by those of the aged Imam of Foulah Town, Almami Amara, who told the gathering of between 7,000 and 10,000 that the movement was dedicated to peace and intended to prevent '. . . too much quarrel'.[39]

The government took a dim view of what seemed to them to be another government within a government. The governor told the leaders that such a thing would not be tolerated.[40] The main stimulus, protecting Creole interests, was largely answered a few years later with the introduction of an elected municipal government to Freetown. The association died out with this development and Macaulay's own death in 1899. Nevertheless, for its duration, it had brought together Muslim and Christian in Freetown for the longest sustained period of cooperation during the nineteenth century. It marked the most significant landmark on the path toward reintegration which the Muslim communities, under their modernist reform leaders, had taken. The often strained alliance of Christian and Muslim Creole continued into the twentieth century. It was not extraordinary in the 1950's and 1960's to find Mandinka young men in the east end of Freetown who proudly carried National Council party cards. Some also supported the Settlers' Descendants Union, another supposedly exclusive Creole supremacy organization. Elders of the Fourah Bay community looked forward in 1960 to the day when the National Council would rise again. A leading member of the Foulah Town community, Ahmed Alhadi, alone took up the pamphleteer's pen in defence of Creole interests in 1956 when he authored *The Re-emancipation of the Colony of Sierra Leone*, complete with the emotionally-charged farewell sermon of Governor Clarkson, and including a foreword by Dr. Bankole Bright, the last leader of the National Council.[41] The basis of such cooperation in the twentieth century was that the Muslim's land-owning and business interests made his concerns strikingly similar to the more conservative Christian Creole elements of Freetown society. The background to such cooperation was to be found in the concerted effort of Muslim Creole society to integrate itself into the mainstream in the period after 1870. Such an effort served finally to ensure the growth of Islam and the development of a settled Muslim community within Freetown as well as emphasizing the resilience and resourcefulness of Liberated African society in general.

THE WORSHIP OF SHANGO AND OTHERS

If many Liberated Africans were Christian and some were Muslim, there were still others during the last half of the nineteenth century who continued to maintain prior systems of African belief. The persistence of beliefs in the various deities of African tribal pantheons provided a further example of the general level of independence in the recaptive group. Generally those elements of Liberated African and later Creole society which worshipped according to older, indigenous forms represented the new arrivals. As such they formed the lower strata of the class structure. This was not absolutely universal, however, since there were several instances in which Liberated Africans who had been converted to Christianity returned to the former systems of belief. This was caused by disgust with the Christians in the society or with the Europeans who tried to maintain absolute control of the missions. In other cases the individual had decided that Shango or Oduduwa really provided better answers to his religious problems than did Jehovah. Moreover, at least one report indicated that one old Hastings couple had simply avoided the conversion pressures of the missionaries although they had lived in the colony for thirty years.[42]

The majority of the so-called idol-worshippers, a term which was generally used in the nineteenth century to describe those who were neither Muslim or Christian, lived in the villages. The greatest number appeared to live in the village of Hastings. The Revd. Weeks counted four different types of Yoruba idols there in 1831. There was a predominance of twin figures. These were rough wooden figures, intricately carved on the head, which stood eighteen inches high and which were considered to afford effective comfort in the time of sickness. If a woman gave birth to twins, and one died, the parents went to a 'greegreeman' and obtained a figure to serve as a substitute for the dead child. The idol was thought to protect the living twin. If the living child fell ill, the parents prayed to the idol to restore the youth's health. Belief in the efficacy of the idols was strong. The Revd. Graf reported from Hastings in 1844 that one of his oldest women communicants had given birth to twins, but both had subsequently died. She indicated that the Christian prohibition which had prevented her from having twin figures to protect her children had led to their death. The funeral ceremonies showed a return to the safety and security of Yoruba belief as the woman 'got a sheep, some fowls, rice, rum, etc., and on an appointed night she had the most notorious idolaters of this town at her house, who killed the creatures and made the requisite religious mummeries'. In other cases, when parents did pray to the idol to restore health, they were naturally concerned to know the gods' reaction to their offering and sought the answer in divining by throwing kola nuts. One of the parents would divide the kola into four parts and throw them on the ground in front of the idol. If the round part of the majority of the pieces remained upwards on the ground, the answer was favourable, and the worshipper would then sacrifice a goat or a sheep to the idol in gratitude. Divining through kola was a fairly widespread activity among the Liberated Africans. At times only halves of the nut were used rather than quarters. The Revd. Charles Marke, the Wesleyan recaptive pastor, noted the occurrence of divining through kola during the smallpox epidemic at Fourah Bay in 1859.[43]

Among the idols found by Weeks at Hastings were those to Shango, the god of thunder; Ellebar, described by the missionary as the devil; and Orchung, the god of water. With these and many others throughout the colony continuing to receive the attention of the recaptive community, it was not hard to understand that the persistence of idol worship engaged a considerable amount of the missionary's time. Nearly every missionary to the villages reported about at least one attempt to break up a meeting of Liberated Africans worshipping idols. In the village of Sussex in 1851, Mende idol worshippers met to perform sacrifices at eleven on Sunday mornings in order to avoid the suspicious prying of the Methodist missionary. They knew that he would be engaged in his own worship service at that time.[44] Generally, however, those who continued to sacrifice to African deities were unimpressed by the attempts of the missionaries to convince them otherwise. If the missionary persisted with his interruptions some groups eventually allowed the European to see what they were doing. They knew that after the European had seen, he would preach to them, and, after that, he would retire to his own house. The missionary would be disgusted, but the worshippers knew that he would afterwards leave them alone. Some of the more aggressive missionaries began programmes of collecting the idols from the villages. This represented a more serious threat, but one for which the Englishman's own law offered sufficient protection. On one such expedition collecting idols, the Wesleyan Revd. Fletcher forcefully entered a village house to gather up a particularly large example made from clay. The owner assured Fletcher that he would destroy it himself the next day, but instead of doing that he went to the local magistrate who issued an arrest order for the missionary. Fletcher was tried, found guilty and fined for breaking into and searching the man's house. Although the missionary himself thought the fine small in comparison to the great amount of good done by collecting idols, and although the man afterwards apologized to Fletcher for taking him to court, idol worship throughout the colony continued.[45]

These religious observances and rituals continued because they were related to some crisis which had afflicted the participants. Someone had fallen ill, and a sacrifice was necessary in order to effect a cure. Thus a smallpox attack in Aberdeen in 1857 necessitated the sacrifice of sheep.[46] The worship of Shango, the Yoruba god of thunder and lightning, was tied in part to the sight of lightning and the sound of thunder. These represented Shango's displeasure. Ceremonies in his honour noticeably increased with the coming of the annual rains. Sacrifice was a central part of these observances. A chicken usually sufficed, but if the circumstances were particularly serious or if the person affected was especially important, a goat or sheep was killed. The priests of the group then bathed the idol in the blood of the slaughtered animal. Sacrifices of this nature were used by individuals who simply wanted work or desired greater prosperity. Similarly, if someone wanted to discover a thief, he often sought the help of the idol rather than that of the European officials.[47]

The nature of the specific idols varied greatly. Most were constructed either from wood or clay. Europeans generally described them as being ugly in appearance. They varied in size from the small eighteen-inch twin figure to large pieces of sculpted wood or clay that dominated the whole corner of a room. A wooden image of Shango seen by the Revd. Weeks in Hastings in 1831 was the size and shape of a mortar; it was about three feet high. A figure of 'Ellebar, the Devil' was smaller and made of clay. The wooden idol of the god of water, Orchung, had a basin carved in it in which a small quantity of water was constantly kept. The large idol which Schön and Metzger saw in Kissy in 1833 dominated a large part of the room. It had the usual bloodstained face, two horns, and a large bowl in front of it half full of the blood of a chicken.[48]

Although the largest number of idol-worshippers resided in the villages, they were by no means absent from Freetown. As was the case in the villages, the dominant gods who were worshipped in the capital were Yoruba in origin. The Yoruba occupied the eastern and southern fringe of the growing city by mid-century. They lived in Fourah Bay to the east, and westward along Fourah Bay Road as far as the junction with

Kissy Road. From there they spread southward along Mountain Cut into Foulah Town. The majority of these Yoruba were Muslim, but pagans were interspersed. Southward from Foulah Town, the Aku lived along Circular and Pademba Roads as far as Portuguese and Congo Towns on the western fringe of the city. The Yoruba of these latter sections tended to be what the Revd. Samuel Crowther called 'gross idolaters'.[49] The major mission work in these sections between 1840 and 1870 was done for the Church Missionary Society by an educated Yoruba recaptive, the Revd. Samuel Ajayi Crowther, and a Colony-born Creole of Aku parents, the Revd. James Johnson. Both later distinguished themselves in the Niger mission of the CMS. Both reported at length about the nature of Yoruba religious belief, for they particularly believed that the Christian mission had to work through the existing religious knowledge of the people it sought to convert. Crowther especially attempted to show why the older forms of religion persisted among the Yoruba. He was on close terms with the pagan worshippers in his area. The idolaters received Crowther with considerable respect; he was seen as a Yoruba who had succeeded in the new environment that was Freetown. Crowther reported that they 'always acknowledge[d] the worship of the only true God as superior to any other, but [could] not resolve to give up their gods whom they believed were created for the good of mankind, and therefore ought to be worshipped'.[50] Preaching to the idol-worshippers in Yoruba, Crowther received cogent replies from the priests. One old Ife priest told him that he could not give up his god 'because he was a doctor; that he could not consent to give his medicine to anyone who applied to him without consulting his god whether he should give it or not, and according to the direction of Ifah, so he acts'. Later the same priest told the missionary that he lived by being a doctor. For him to forsake his god would be to put himself out of business. Another Ife priest who lived in a house behind that of Crowther and Schön assured them that he had recently incorporated Jesus Christ into his own belief

system. He told those who came to him for advice 'that whenever they wished to offer any sacrifice to their gods, *they must
first . . . call on . . . Jesus Christ'*. The fact that he had heard in
Sierra Leone that God had given his son to mankind sufficed
for his inclusion with the other lesser deities of the Yoruba. The
man did, however, remain an Ife priest.[51]

Both Johnson and Crowther reported that the worship of the
Yoruba god, Shango, continued in Freetown. One house of
Shango worship was located on Circular Road. On a visit to
the house, Crowther was met by three drummers at the opening
of the compound. They sat on the ground facing the idol which
was located immediately inside the house. The idol rested on
a mound of earth which was 'raised a few inches in a semi-
circular form about two or three feet from the centre of the
circumference, touching the walls at both ends'. There was a
smaller semicircle inside the larger one in which they placed a
large white-washed calabash. The banks of earth were striped
with red clay and white chalk. They placed several small
calabashes, pots, bottles, and a club which they used to make a
thunderous noise alongside the banks. The Yoruba had begun
their worship the night before Crowther arrived and had
drummed and danced all night. Crowther reported that they
also had occasionally 'offered a ram, an animal particularly
dedicated to him'.[52] Crowther naturally tried to convert the
Shango worshippers to Christianity. Undoubtedly some were
converted, but the Revd. James Johnson noted twenty years
later that every Friday there was 'a . . . parade of idolaters;
they walk about in large numbers; a man goes before as a
leader; he is dressed in a female's attire, carries on his shoulder
an axe, the weapon of the god of thunder. He has in his hair two
or three feathers of white, red, and black colours; his followers
dance and sing wildly in praise of Shango.'[53] In 1866 Johnson
tried to preach to a similar group of marchers who had paraded
to George's Brook. An old Yoruba told him that his longer
experience had made it clear to him which form of worship,
Yoruba or Christian, was more effective. He dismissed the

young Johnson as a small child who spoke the way he did because the mission paid him to do so. Johnson painfully observed that five of the drummers were Creole, colony-born children of Liberated Africans. The transference of Yoruba systems of belief to the Creole generation distressed the missionaries. They had long placed hope in the second generation. Nevertheless, the older pattern persisted into post-1850 Freetown.[54]

Johnson also visited a 'Creole idolatress' in 1863. She kept a long pole at the gate of her yard from which a small flag flew. The flag was made from pieces of white and red cotton. She told the Creole missionary that the flag 'was a special gift to her dead twin sister, whom her parents, before their death, used to worship in order that they might live long in the world and enjoy peace and prosperity'. She gave the flag and the pole to Johnson, but kept a second idol which she had in her house. Made of cloth, white beads, and two iron rings, she prayed to it so that 'she may be lucky in her trade'.[55]

Illness and the fear of illness and death provided potent reason for the continuation of worship of such deities as Shango. Careful statistics concerning sickness and mortality among the Liberated Africans were not consistently kept, but it was fairly evident that such government institutions as Kissy Hospital or the recaptive medical dressers stationed in the villages were not sufficient. Death met many recaptives in the colony soon after settlement, primarily due to the poor conditions on the slave ships. Thomas Cole, after more than twenty years in the colony, confessed in 1840 that about one-third of the Liberated Africans died within a few weeks of arrival in the colony from illnesses contracted on board the slave ships. Consistently throughout the first half of the century reporters noted the poor condition of the new arrivals. Although the government attempted to provide for the health of the recaptives, the success of the Liberated African Department's medical efforts was questionable. One village manager in the 1830's suggested that for every hundred men employed, 'there are at least one hundred others unavailable, through sickness, accident, or

Fourah Bay
College

other causes, and this *after* the Africans have been recruited with three months' good living, and easy employment, in the yard at Freetown....'[56] The colony itself on occasion proved unhealthy to the Liberated African population. Visitations of smallpox, yellow fever, and influenza combined with persistent maladies such as dysentery, dropsy, opthalmalia, and ulcers to render recaptive life decidedly insecure.[57] Smallpox provided the best example of the dangers one faced. Unlike most illnesses which afflicted human beings in Sierra Leone in the nineteenth century, doctors knew how to diagnose, treat, and prevent smallpox. Still, hundreds if not thousands regularly died from new introductions of the disease. Liberated Africans sacrificed sheep and goats to placate the angry gods and to protect themselves from the dreaded death from smallpox. In 1859, the frustrated government issued a proclamation for '... general fasting, and humiliation, on account of the dreadful epidemic which is taking away so many of the colonists'. Going without food, even at the government's wish, did little to alleviate the suffering or correct the situation which allowed smallpox to be a continuing problem after sixty years. The government had simply failed to institute a consistent and conscientious programme of vaccination. Even when regular supplies of vaccine did arrive during periods of the century, it was oftentimes of such poor quality or so old that it was useless. On occasion, ordered vaccine never did arrive. European doctors knew how to prevent the scourge, European missionaries supported their efforts, but inattention and inefficiency produced the situation in which the recaptive found consistently more security in traditional sacrifice to the gods.[58]

Such mortality statistics as are available confirm the grim picture of Liberated African chances of a healthy life on the Sierra Leone peninsula. Of the 1,500 recaptives treated at Kissy Hospital during 1841, over 500 died while just over 750 recovered. Dropsy proved the biggest cause of death, 159 having succumbed to it; while next in order came dysentery, 125; ulcers, 61; diarrhoea, 44; and remittent fever, 18.[59] The

R

situation in 1842 showed some improvement with the mortality figure falling to 24·9%, but the causes of death remaining approximately the same.[60] Death at Kissy Hospital became an expected event throughout the period. Over 250 patients died there during one five-month period of 1853.[61] This represented about one-half of the hospital's capacity at its most crowded period.[62] There was little need to explain why the recaptives 'manifest[ed] the greatest reluctance to be taken into the hospital under the charge of the African Department . . .' and preferred to be treated by their own countrymen in the villages.[63] To them the medical facilities provided by the government proved to be inadequate.[64]

In these conditions the recaptives naturally turned to medicines and techniques which had proved effective in the past. They also developed new medicines to meet the specific health problems of Sierra Leone. Since the potency of the medicines often depended upon one's belief in the higher powers of a deity, the maintenance of the African religious beliefs was guaranteed. The Revd. Schön admitted that he lost some potential communicants when their countrymen promised better health if they did not become Christian. Even within the church itself, many communicants continued to use gri-gri and local medicines to cure their illnesses. None, however, put the problem so clearly as an old Yoruba woman in the Pademba Road District in 1865. The Revd. James Johnson went one day to see some Shango dancers at Oke Muri, at the base of Mount Aureol. The old woman's daughter had recently become insane. Everyone in the area thought it was the punishment of the god Shango. The dancers had come to the woman's compound to try to placate the deity. Johnson had come with his Yoruba testament and hopes of converting the woman. When she saw him, however, she simply told him to go away. She told him that she had entered the church three times during her lifetime in Sierra Leone. She admitted that she had 'found peace' on each occasion, but she had not found good health. Therefore, she told him, she would remain with the

Shango dancers who did provide good health. She told Johnson to leave and then danced off with the others.[65]

An important element in the association of good health with African forms of religion was the Liberated Africans' understanding of the causes of illness. Illness continued to be regarded by them as having been caused by the 'instrumentality of [one's] enemies'. It was therefore clearly of an advantage to remain within the system which alone provided certain cures. Commenting on such beliefs among the Liberated Africans in 1850, the Revd. Graf of Hastings wrote that many '. . . look upon Europeans as absurdly sceptical for disbelieving what to them appears to rest on the plainest evidence'.[66]

BENEFIT AND WELFARE, AND BURIAL SOCIETIES

The continuation of old forms of associational groupings as well as the creation of new ones was closely tied to both the areas of religion and health. Most villages abounded with 'compins', local voluntary associations of Liberated Africans which had a variety of functions. Benefit and welfare, economic, and funeral societies were the most common. Although such organizations had an important political potential which for the most part was exploited, their main function was to assist their membership in times of need. Dr. Madden's report in 1841 indicated that the assistance of the recaptive's associations allowed them to move into the Freetown trade, as well as providing for them when they first arrived.[67] In most cases each member of the association contributed a certain amount to its common fund either weekly or monthly. If a member became ill, the society made sure that he and his family received care and assistance. If a member died, the society supported his widows and children, and provided him with a proper funeral.

These societies developed from the needs of the recaptives in Sierra Leone. A Creole woman, searching for the origins of the societies, suggested quite correctly to a Freetown newspaper in the 1880's that the societies had begun 'when our fathers and mothers found themselves alone'. Finding it necessary to protect themselves against personal disaster, the 'first cultivated attachments . . . among those of the same street or neighbourhood. Secondly by recognizing . . . those who were brought here from the same slaver. Thirdly, [they formed] tribal companies.'[68] Far more pointedly, a Calabari headman told Revd. Schön at Bathurst in 1836 that such societies were necessary because nothing was done for them [by the British] to improve their condition'. The only thing that was better in Sierra Leone, in his view, was the recaptives' freedom from being sold again as slaves. The companies provided not only welfare assistance but purpose and cohesion to the life of the Bathurst Calabari. The companies or societies catered to every need of the Liberated Africans' life. One benefit society in Hastings specialized in marriages. A member joined before his marriage, and contributed regularly to its fund. When the marriage took place, the 'compin' purchased food and drink for the wedding celebration.[69]

The idea of benefit, welfare, and funeral societies became so general in the colony that the missionaries had to incorporate them into their own Christian context. When the Revd. W. A. B. Johnson was superintendent of Regent, the communicants formed a benefit society for the relief of the sick and distressed members. The seventy members of the society in 1817 established the promotion of brotherly love and harmony as their goals. News of the society spread through prayer sessions to the countrymen of its members. Soon the society took on a new dimension as it turned its resources to the building of prestigious stone houses in the village. It set out to build fifty new houses, a figure it never reached. Nonetheless, many of the stone houses of early Regent were built by the society.[70] The general importance of the church benefit society in Regent was indicated simply by the fact that it continued in existence when Johnson himself went on leave in 1820 whereas the church's missionary society did not. Johnson explained that the benefit society continued because it 'was kept in order by themselves'.[71]

During his tenure at Gloucester, the Revd. W. K. Betts

introduced a 'church compin'. His company was an adaptation of an already existing Yoruba funeral society. He had become disturbed by the drinking which accompanied the usual Aku funeral observance and so determined to introduce the idea of temperance to his society and then gain members by making the subscription lower than that of the competing organization. The success of Betts's experiment in introducing temperance to Gloucester was uncertain, but the society itself continued to operate for several years. Membership in the 'church compin', however, did not interfere with tribal allegiance and obligation. In 1834—two years after the formation of the company—the Ibo membership also contributed to the funeral of a 'heathen countryman', and to the support of another who had lost a child. Two years later the communicants built a house for a widow and provided her with a weekly pension.[72]

The church company at Regent, however, ultimately ran into difficulties. Weeks reported in 1842 that rum-drinking and wake-keeping were breaking down the church's discipline. He decided to rid the village of the numerous local companies which he blamed for the growing difficulty. His task, however, proved impossible. Regent alone had from nine to ten separate companies at the time. Unable to get rid of the societies, Weeks finally compromised and became their nominal overseer. Rather ingeniously the companies themselves had suggested this compromise as a solution to the difficulties with the missionary.[73] Similarly, the Revd. Graf began a Church Relief Company at Hastings in 1842 in an attempt to subvert the abuses of the existing societies. Until 1849, however, he was forced to accept two customs which, if suppressed, would have led to the total collapse of the society. The members of the church benefit society were allowed to slaughter several bullocks every Christmas and to share them among the membership. In addition, the company provided a 'frugal' supper at every funeral for those members who had stayed up all night for a week with the bereaved survivor. The Revd. James Johnson founded a Christian Young Ladies Association in Freetown in 1869. Its purpose was to improve the poorer class of women living in his district. In reality, it was a simple benefit society intended to offer the women a substitute for 'their burial and other relief societies [which were] . . . the very hot beds of sin'.[74]

ORGANIZATION OF BENEFIT SOCIETIES

Regardless of the evaluations of the missionaries, benefit societies proved to be a crucial part of Liberated African society. The growth of the companies by 1840 reflected the changing nature of recaptive life. J. B. Hazely, a Wellington magistrate, defined two distinct types of companies: the so-called 'big company' was a general society comprising members of several tribes while the 'little companies' were much smaller in number and were restricted to members of one specific tribe. The titles of the administrative officers of the societies also reflected the changes that were taking place. The leader was no longer called simply chief or headman. Instead, he took the title of king, probably from the earlier society of Abraham Potts whose headquarters had been in Freetown during the 1820's. The next officer was called 'queen', and the third, 'king's son'. In descending order of importance the remaining officials of the company were: governor, judge, Macaulay, Reffell, Commissary, Dougan, Savage, and Constable. Each officer performed an essential function for the society. Both in titles and functions, the hierarchy of the companies found their parallel in the hierarchy of the colonial government. The inclusion of personal names such as Macaulay, Reffell, Dougan, and Savage represented a recognition of those who had served the Liberated Africans particularly well. Macaulay was no doubt Kenneth Macaulay, the prosperous merchant and twice acting-governor. Reffell had been Chief Superintendent of the Liberated African Department; Dougan had been a lawyer and judge; and Savage, the English mulatto who had helped the Muslim Aku after Cobolo, had long been a defender of the

Liberated African cause. The title Commissary referred to the officer at one time attached to the Liberated African Department who had provided the recaptives with rations and supplies. In the companies which Judge Hazely described in Wellington, the Commissary was the treasurer, the one who dispensed funds from the Company's savings.

The regulations of the groups operating in the Wellington area indicated the all-inclusiveness of their authority and functions. Not only did they serve those who were sick or those who survived, they also provided more generally for the welfare of the individual and the community. If the village manager fined a member because his yard or fence was untidy, the society made a loan to him so that he could make the necessary repairs. If someone's house burned down, the society advanced funds so that a new one could be built. If a member wanted to begin a new farm, he notified the society, and it arranged to have its members come to help him clear the land. The member, in return, provided two meals a day for the society's labourers. The society's offer came as a result of its belief that every member should have a farm. Indeed, its regulations stated that anyone not having a farm or anyone not giving sufficient reasons why he did not have a farm would be reprimanded and forced to select some land. If the person completely refused to farm, the company eventually expelled him.[75]

The all-inclusiveness of the societies assured their control of the villages. The Revd. Weeks reported that one company efficiently controlled justice in the village of Regent. It brought 'charm-men' from Freetown to discover thieves when their own techniques for discovery failed. On one occasion when the first diviner from Freetown did not succeed in discovering a criminal, the company invited another who had complete success. The society paid the two diviners six and a half dollars or well over one pound. They were satisfied that justice had been done. Most of the missionaries objected to the governmental and judicial functions of the companies. The Revd. Graf of Hastings felt that by encouraging the companies the government ran the risk of making the Liberated Africans disloyal. In his opinion, 'the influences [which the companies] exercise in a *civil* point of view is . . . destructive of all order and loyalty'. He felt that the public list of regulations of the companies served 'only as an ostensible instrument wherewith to screen their real rules and practices'. Graf suggested that the promises of the companies to punish church and civil offenders, for example, were most often ignored.[76]

SECRET SOCIETIES

If the attitude of the Hastings missionary toward the Liberated African societies seems unduly severe, there was good reason for it. Hastings was a village in which the societies thrived. The reasons for this were not clear except that the most successful societies usually were Yoruba in origin, and Hastings was predominantly Yoruba. Another reason was the fact that not all of the societies among the recaptives were simple benefit and welfare or funeral societies. Others had a more mysterious function to perform. Such groups were the secret societies whose origins were to be found in the distant past of the tribes which comprised the Liberated African population. The most widespread secret society was the *Agugu*. The strongest *oje*, the name by which a local branch of the *Agugu* society is known, was at Hastings. Some believe that Hastings was the headquarters for all the *Agugu* in the colony. *Agugu* had been brought from Yoruba country by Aku recaptives. Known in their homeland as *Engungun* or *Egun*, the society had its origins among the Nupe. They had introduced it to the Yoruba during the time of Ajiwough, a Yoruba king who entitled himself *Obba ni Igbogi* or king of Igbogi. Eventually both the king and his subjects fell under the control of the *Egun*. The *Egun* was believed to be an inhabitant of an invisible world, the spirit of a dead man. He made his appearance on earth again as a 'heavenly messenger'. No one could touch his clothes on pain of the immediate punishment of death from the spirit. The *Egun* carried with him charms which would hurt anybody except one who believed

264

in and practised *Egun* himself. The spirit danced and performed various magical tricks before his audience, and spoke with a deep, hoarse voice which was noticeably different from that of a man. After the spirit had performed, he was given several cowries, goats, and sheep in payment. Then he returned, presumably, to the grave.[77]

Spirits of the society who danced in Sierra Leone in the nineteenth century covered themselves with loose clothes such as a pair of sheets sewn together. The gown was covered with different coloured strips of cloth which gave the appearance of a patchwork. The face was also covered, but with net decorated with cowries. This allowed the spirit to see as he danced, while at the same time remaining anonymous. A guide usually led him through the streets. The spirit of the society knew all that had occurred in the village and thus the dance of the *Egun* often became the occasion for the punishment or chastisement of local offenders. The spirit knew all of the secrets of the community and his revelations during the dance often caused considerable personal embarrassment to individuals. The overall effect was to keep the villagers under strict control.[78] In a village like Hastings, where *Agugu* was particularly strong, the influence of the society was considerable. As in Yoruba country itself, the *Agugu* in Hastings was the virtual power behind the throne. It no doubt effectively controlled the operations of the Liberated African companies, and this helped to explain the hostility of the Revd. Graf. The CMS missionary survived in Hastings tradition as an 'uncompromising enemy of the Egugu Dance and superstitition begotten of or connected with it'.[79] Many of the forays out of his home to break up a dance, an illicit sacrifice, or a general disturbance were directed against *Agugu* members. He mentioned them often, commenting once about the death of one of the two Hastings *Agugu* 'devils'. He was particularly concerned about him for he had been a Christian at one time. The missionary noted with regret that the widow allowed the 'devil's' company to perform 'a heathen ceremony' at her home after his death.[80] The missionary's accounts of suppressing the activities of *Agugu* did not include the amusingly revealing tradition about which J. S. T. Davies reminded his fellow townsmen at the Centenary Celebrations in 1919. One day Graf went out with a whip in his hand to end an *Agugu* dance. He 'began to castigate [the dancers]; but he only flogged a mass of empty Egugu clothes. The bodies inside the clothes had mysteriously and inexplicably vanished. The [missionary] marched back to the Parsonage; his whip had dropped, but a broom belonging to one of the . . . Egugu escorts, followed him to the Parsonage, gyrating in fact executing a little dance of its own behind the worthy Cleric's back. However, when [he] turned round flourishing a Bible, it disappeared.'[81]

The intent missionary made it difficult for *Agugu* during his long tenure at Hastings. Graf did not, however, even approach the point of complete suppression. *Agugu*, like Shango worship, maintained a strong appeal in Sierra Leone because of its apparent efficacy. It was a facet of Liberated African life prior to settlement in the colony which successfully adapted itself and provided for a real need. It provided a means of keeping order in the community which was both effective and fearsome. It prospered and maintained its control simply because those who found security in it at one time in their lives feared the personal consequences of leaving it later on.[82] It thrived partly on the simple mysteries of death. Again, like Shango, *Agugu* offered a traditional and credible answer to those who sought to know about man's fate after death. Beyond this it provided a very practical answer to the local problem of health. The medicines of *Agugu* were central to its success. Each *oje* leader controlled two types of medicine, vindictive and curative. Vindictive medicines were used both as punishment and as a technique by which the *oje* increased its membership, and the society itself spread throughout the colony and Freetown. Curative medicines were also used as an appeal; they apparently proved very effective for the common disorders affecting the recaptive population. In each case, the intelligent use of the medicines assured the continuation of power in the hands of the secret society.

Agugu established branches in Freetown among the Yoruba initially, and later among other tribal groups. According to local tradition the earliest known *oje* was at Oke Muri, to the south of the Yoruba community at Foulah Town. No date can be attached to the founding of the first *oje*, but it was certainly before mid-century. *Agugu* did not spread to the Yoruba at Fourah Bay until sometime after 1850.[83] At Fourah Bay it enjoyed far greater success than it had earlier, and from there it spread to neighbouring non-Yoruba Muslim communities. Eventually there were *Agugu* branches among the Christian Creoles, the Susu, the Mandinka, and the Temne.

The secret society, moreover, followed Yoruba Liberated African merchants into the interior where, along rivers such as the Great Scarcies, they established branches in nearly every village. The power of the society increased as it spread, and in many colony villages as well as in some sections of Freetown 'the religion of the Egung' became as closely connected with local politics as it had been in Nigeria.[84] In some cases the *Agugu* connection served to maintain tribal allegiance among separate colony communities in spite of such things as religious differences. This proved to be the case between Muslim Fourah Bay and the largely Christian village of Hastings. As late as 1960 Yoruba residents of each of these communities preferred their children to marry Yoruba, regardless of religious affiliation. A Christian Yoruba of Hastings would have liked his son to marry another Christian Yoruba, but a marriage with a Muslim Yoruba from Fourah Bay was preferable to one with a non-Yoruba.

Agugu was not the only successful secret society in the colony. Its efficacy in the urban areas did make it unique among the men's secret societies. *Poro*, a man's secret society prevalent among the Mende, for example, never succeeded in Freetown on a similar scale. On the other hand, *Bundu*, a women's secret society among the Mende and Sherbro, did prove successful in the colony and Freetown. It apparently entered the colony villages for the first time in the late 1850's. The Revd. Joseph May, a Methodist Liberated African preacher, recorded its introduction at Hastings in 1858. *Bundu*'s introduction and spread was also related to illness among the Liberated Africans, particularly the devastating outbreaks of smallpox in the late 1850's. May wrote that the two leaders who began to operate near Hastings in 1858 convinced numerous Liberated African women that *Bundu* was a 'system of Purification and a remedy against bodily disease'. Seeking protection from the rapidly spreading smallpox, several women from Hastings and Wellington entered the *Bundu* bush for the traditional operation and confinement of from two to three months.[85] Beginning in Hastings, *Bundu* spread to other villages and eventually to Freetown. *Aro*, *Agemo*, and *Gelede* were other secret societies which enjoyed some success on the Sierra Leone peninsula. *Aro* was strong in the western district, particularly in the village of Murraytown. Like *Agugu*, it operated on the mysteries of death and the power of its strong medicines. *Agemo*, like the other two, was Yoruba in origin, while the origin of *Gelede* was Popo.[86]

Not all of the societies originated outside the colony. As Creole society emerged about mid-century, new secret societies were formed. They catered more for the changing needs of the population. The Hunters grew out of the village recaptive's need to hunt. It developed into a distinctly Creole secret society which for many served as a more sophisticated replacement for *Agugu*. In the nineteenth century the Hunters at Hastings had special days during the week on which they went out to hunt. When they returned, the Hunters deposited their kill in the compound of the headman. The kill usually included some large deer, some fawns, wild bush pigs, and guinea pigs. They were skinned at the headman's, chopped up, and distributed among the members. During the distribution, the Hunters drank a soup made from the entrails of the animals.[87] As the Creole became increasingly a Freetown-based person, and as the wild life in the colony grew scarce, the Hunters society transformed itself into more of a social association. Eventually it developed into a secret organization of Creole civil servants with the governor as the society's patron. Annual hunt days were organized to remind the members of the society's first function and a portion of the kill each year was brought to Freetown and given to the patron at his residence at Government House. By the twentieth century, the Hunters became a society about midway on the stratification ladder between the extremes of the *oje* at one end and the successfully revived Masonic Lodges of Freetown on the other.

ECONOMIC ASSOCIATIONS

Liberated Africans who lived independent lives politically, religiously, and with regard to their many benefit and welfare societies could be expected to have had a fairly independent economic existence as well. They did. A final type of voluntary associational grouping which revealed the independent nature of recaptive life was economic in nature. The existence of small economic and commercial groups contributed significantly to the development of Liberated African society both during the first half of the century and in the later Creole part. Such economic and commercial 'compins' were closely related to the benefit and welfare societies, but their contribution was of singular importance. Invariably the commercial groups brought village Liberated Africans into the economic world of Freetown where the larger fortunes were to be made. Governor Fergusson, in his published letter to Thomas Fowell Buxton, mentioned the recaptive practice of banding together in the market place in order to buy or trade in larger quantities than the individual alone could do. The Liberated Africans used the same technique at the auction sales of the captured slaving ships, the so-called prize sales. They joined together in groups of from five to seven in order to buy goods from these ships. By the mid-1830's these groups were able to underbid the highly competitive European merchants in Freetown who were gradually forced out of business entirely. Eventually these *ad hoc* companies of traders were able to buy a whole ship and its stores at the prize sales. The capital formation potential of such 'compins' is realized in the fact that the ship alone could cost as much as £600. Through these companies and their successes at the slave ship auctions, many of the early Liberated African and Creole commercial empires of the nineteenth century were established.[88]

The prize sales were particularly good for Freetown commerce. When captured, the ships often had their holds filled with European trade goods which always found a ready if unintended market in Freetown. The Liberated Africans developed an efficient system of distribution through a network of some 400 to 500 hawkers and traders in Freetown and the villages by 1840.[89] The goods that were carried by Liberated African traders in the interior met the demand of these tribes for European products, a demand which had been initiated by the slave trade itself. Interior peoples found that Freetown had become a good source of supply in the nineteenth century for those items of European commerce such as cloth, rum, and guns, which they particularly desired. The interior produced metals, timber, and ivory in exchange. As early as 1824 one group of Fula traders from the north spent £5,000 worth of gold at Freetown.[90] By the 1830's Liberated Africans began to replace the few earlier Freetonians engaged in trade with the interior. Recaptives had actually expanded such trade by establishing themselves in the interior villages within another decade.[91]

The independent action of the Liberated Africans in trade and commerce resulted from their considerable prior experience in both trade and in the formation of the small economic companies. The latter made large scale trade possible for the recaptives in Sierra Leone. The majority of the traders appeared to be Yoruba. Yoruba country in Nigeria had been an area of highly developed trade and commerce. Within its expanded territory there was a good deal of craft as well as agricultural specialization. The large cities which arose among the Yoruba included numerous specialized market-places. The accompaniments of trade such as credit, banking, and simpler forms of savings were understood. Thus the Yoruba Liberated Africans were firmly grounded in the world of commerce long before their arrival in Sierra Leone. The same tended to be true for those Liberated Africans from the neighbouring territories such as Dahomey, Benin, and Ibo. Once the Liberated Africans had acquired sufficient capital, they could continue their lives as traders in their new setting. The importance of their past experience as a determinant of forms operating in Sierra Leone extended to the area of capital formation itself. The *Asusu* as it was known in Freetown had its roots in the trading techniques of the Yoruba. It was a simple system of savings which proved successful as a means of capital formation. Each of the members of the *asusu* contributed a certain amount each week. One of the five to seven withdrew the aggregate each week and used it as his own. He could not withdraw again until all of the others had done so. Societies similar to the *asusu* were described by travellers to Yoruba country in the nineteenth century. Although the function of the *asusu* was not contrary to the goals of the European colonial government in Sierra Leone, its origins were clearly not European. Not until 1885 was the *asusu* recognized officially as a part of Freetown's economic life. In that year a Freetown court upheld the legality of an *asusu* contract. The newspaper article reporting the decision defended it by invoking the principle of the Golden Rule. Accepted within a Christian context, the *asusu* had really arrived.[92]

TRADE AND LAND

Trade provided the transitional key in the economic field by which Liberated African society gradually became Creole. Those Liberated Africans who became prominent had, for the most part, prospered in commerce. The economic system of the villages remained predominantly agricultural. A few of the larger villages had shops in addition to a market place, and skilled craftsmen such as carpenters and blacksmiths.[93]

Naturally, however, the larger and more specialized shops and greater concentration of craft specialists were to be found in Freetown. The capital city of the colony generated the real wealth of the area. Through participation in the more abundant and prosperous trade in Freetown, the Liberated Africans acquired relatively large amounts of capital. They invested such capital in land, the one secure item in an otherwise greatly fluctuating economy. The land was primarily in the form of Freetown real estate. One's social position in Creole society, to a large extent, was governed by the location of one's real estate holdings within the city. Property in the central part, near the main shops and the Government Wharf, was of first importance. A piece of property and a house on Oxford Street or Westmoreland Street usually assured its owner a place of prominence in the society of the city. In trading and gradually securing Freetown property, the Liberated Africans followed the path set out for them by their predecessors, the Nova Scotians. Investment in land particularly had proved to be a temporarily secure investment for the earlier settlers. Moreover, the pattern continued to have relevance for the later history of Sierra Leone. As tribes from the interior of Sierra Leone began to arrive as permanent settlers in the city late in the nineteenth and throughout the first sixty years of the twentieth century, they also turned to land as a safe form of investment. The private ownership of Freetown real estate continued, moreover, to carry its important implications for securing one's social status.[94]

There was no set timetable for such changes in the development of Liberated African society. Recaptives were buying Freetown land as early as the 1820's, and other recaptives were still selling their farm produce in the Freetown market in the late 1860's. Generally, however, by the late 1830's the process of migration from the villages to Freetown was well under way. Prior to this time the village Liberated African had gone daily to Freetown to trade where possible and then returned to his rural home. The daily migrants to the Freetown markets from the villages numbered about four hundred during the 1830's. One observer reported them passing his house on the way into town as early as four o'clock in the morning.[95] Agricultural produce provided the basis of the village trade with Freetown. The produce could be divided into two distinct types: that grown for home consumption and that intended specifically for the market. The rural farmers grew yams, cocoa, plantain, maize corn, cassava, and rice. The farmer took his yams and rice to the Freetown market where he would trade them for general articles from a ship or for other, cheaper food products. The varying nature of the colony's landscape meant that certain areas specialized in certain products. Mrs. Kilham recommended the excellent palm wine tapped at Wellington. By the late 1850's two-thirds of the estimated monthly consumption of 9,000 gallons of palm wine came from the eastern villages of Kissy and Waterloo.[96] Along the ocean, Western District Liberated Africans specialized in fishing. By mid-century approximately 120 boats and canoes engaging the labour of about 850 men fished the ocean waters around the colony. They used circular casting nets for the most part. The industry was concentrated in the villages of Aberdeen, Murraytown, York, and Kent, from where the large amounts of dried fish consumed with rice and fufu in Freetown were sent. Some of the fish was smoked and salted and then packed for shipment into the Sierra Leone interior where it became an important article in the colony up-country trade. The owner of one boat was thought able to make a monthly profit of between £10 and £15 in the fish trade.[97]

The rural area farm plot of the Liberated African was small. As late as 1869, no one cultivated a holding larger than ten acres. The soil in most of the colony was rocky, and did not lend itself even to the simplest forms of nineteenth-century western mechanization. Tilling continued to be done by hand, by the cutlass and the short hoe. The Liberated African did transfer earlier forms of simple specialization to the Sierra Leone setting. Numerous laws supporting monogamy, coupled

273

with the methodical work of the missionaries, presented a problem to the Liberated Africans who were used to the agricultural and economic advantages provided by systems of polygamy. Plural wives had quite simply meant extra farm and market labour. In certain situations, restrictions were overcome by new innovations. One such innovation was the widespread use of apprentices or newly arrived countrymen as farm and market labourers.[98] A village missionary complained in 1833 that the apprentices were too weary to attend evening classes. They were sent to Freetown daily by their Liberated African masters, carrying trade goods to and from the market, a round trip of fourteen miles.[99] Such a job in some indigenous societies had been performed by additional wives.

When a farmer increased his operation, he began to prosper on a small scale. Dixon Denham noted the results of such prosperity in the three-fold increase in more substantial housing in the villages of Regent and Gloucester in the mid-1820's. The houses were either frame on a stone foundation or entirely of stone. They represented an investment of between one hundred and two hundred dollars each. Although some had acquired such wealth as carpenters, tailors, coopers, and blacksmiths, many had done so as farmers. At Wellington where seven stone houses were constructed between 1825 and 1827, one farmer had made 160 dollars in two years by selling his crops. Another built his house from the money made from his crops of maize corn. Regent's population of 1,300 in 1827 boasted thirty Liberated Africans who were each worth over 400 dollars.[100]

In spite of such rural prosperity, the movement of people was, even in Denham's time, to Freetown. The paths into the city were crowded every day. In the capital city some women secured positions as seamstresses and laundresses while others prospered as vendors of gingerbeer, palm wine, and sweet cakes. Living initially on the fringe of Freetown, along Circular Road or near Barracks Hill, they attended the market daily, and traded in rice, palm oil, meat, bread, mangoes, grapes, poultry, and eggs. The main suppliers of meat to the Freetown market were two women traders, Betsy Carew and Nancy Hughes. One reporter of the Freetown scene remarked that each 'possessed the distinguishing characteristics of their brothers of the trade in England—portliness of person'. Both were extremely wealthy as a result of their trade. They were two of many such women who acted as entrepreneurs, buying produce in the rural areas at extremely low wholesale prices, transporting it to the city, and selling it at a large profit in the main Freetown market.[101]

In addition to producing for local consumption, the rural area farmers grew varying amounts of ginger, arrowroot, and pepper for export. Around this trade, a regular system of brokerage developed. The farmer would sell his crop for an extremely low price—it was 3d. to 4d. per pound for pepper in 1838—to a Freetown merchant who would then sell it at a profit for export. The farmer was rarely paid in cash, but instead received goods in return for his crop. The merchant would also regularly exact a 50 per cent surcharge on the goods to protect himself from the risks of climate and the fluctuations of the international market. In fact, of course, the surcharge simply added to the merchant's profit. Gradually, the farmers grew critical of the system. The goods given to them in exchange, for the most part cloth and crockery, were hard to get rid of and too often ended in storage in their own homes. Then, by 1868, the ginger farmers discovered that the Freetown merchants had proved 'deceitful'. The brokers had taken advantage of the farmers' relative ignorance of current prices and had been making quite large profits from the nominal prices paid. To add to the situation, the farmers felt insulted by the merchants' comments on the high level of profit made by the growers, which they felt was largely non-existent. The farmers, long exploited by the system which had grown up, decided to retaliate and in 1868 refused to sell any ginger until a fair price had been agreed upon. Some in the village of Kissy went further and burned the local house of a Freetown broker, a traditional expression of displeasure and rejection.[102] The broker himself retaliated by having the offending farmers put in gaol and their headman tried for bringing an illegal combination against him. These difficulties between the farmers and the brokers combined with falling ginger prices to bring the trade to an end as the century wore on.[103]

Not all Liberated Africans remained farmers; some like the brokers and the women meat entrepreneurs were distinctly better off. A few others entered manufacturing although most such enterprises remained necessarily small due to the relative minuteness of the markets. Most of the fishing boats were built in the colony. The craftsmen trained by government and missions from the beginning of the century assured the development of a competent building construction industry. Skilled carpentry produced much of the ornamental woodwork gracing the interior of a Freetown Creole home, and most of the furniture. Leather workers congregated near the meat market and along Fourah Bay Road where they produced good quality shoes. The colony's first factory, begun by the European trader, R. A. Oldfield, in the 1840's produced groundnut oil used for lubricating the heavy machinery on the steam ships along the coast and for lighting the lamps of Freetown.[104]

The money gained in trade and manufacture by the Liberated Africans went into city property. The process had begun by the later half of the 1820's. William Macaulay's dispute with Governor Sir Neil Campbell in 1827 revealed his ownership of land along Kissy Road. The Governor was involved in over forty land dispute cases at the time. They resulted from his attempt to expel settlers from the vicinity of Barracks Hill where they sold spirits to the soldiers. Campbell's actions affected at least two other Liberated Africans, Edward Fitzgerald and George Randall, each of whom had recently acquired Freetown land.[105] Many more Liberated Africans bought Freetown property in the 1830's. African school teachers and pastors who had earlier concentrated on rural landholdings began also to turn to the capital city for invest-

276

ment. Samuel Crowther defended his purchase of a Freetown lot in 1838 to the CMS. By the time he had married he and his wife had saved nearly £40 from their positions as school teachers for the government and the missionary society. They had been able to maintain the level of their savings during the early years of their marriage, but when they began to have children they spent faster than they could save. Because of this, they decided to 'secure (their savings) by purchasing with it a good spot of ground in a suitable and convenient situation which will be of use, if not to ourselves . . . to our children after us.'[106] The continuing rise in the value of Freetown real estate not only guaranteed the security of such savings but also a sizable profit over the years. One Hastings Creole bought a lot on Fourah Bay Road for £27 7s. 9d. in 1862 and soon after built a house on it at a cost of £42 7s. 8d. His total investment was slightly less than £70. A few years later the owner sold the property to another man for £200. Another Creole mortgaged a Freetown lot in order to improve his business and eventually sold it at an £80 profit to pay for his son's English education.[107]

The slow but persistent drift of Liberated Africans from the rural areas into Freetown between the 1820's and the 1860's marked the emergence of their society and the gradual development of the distinctive Creole society of the latter half of the century. The farmer and trader from Hastings, Regent, and York came to the city to prosper and as he did he settled down in the city itself, buying property, opening a shop, sending his children to Freetown schools and English universities, and generally assuming a more active and dominant role in the life of the city. His life as a Liberated African had brought him to the city, a life through which the dominant thread of independence had run. In the rural areas he had come to be his own political master. In religion, he had expressed his actual freedom through his dissenting chapels, his adherence to Islam, and his insistence on maintaining faith in a host of tribal deities. He had provided his own system of social welfare through a complex multitude of benefit and welfare societies.

His very movement into Freetown trade was financed by small, *ad hoc* economic companies to which he belonged. An adaptable, innovative, resilient human being, he had sculpted from a rock of opportunity and dreams, neatly placed but unused by the British, through failure and frustration his own province of freedom. The main theme of the finished product, independence, came with the Liberated African to Freetown and continued to dominate the Creole life which followed.

VIII

Freetown, 1870: Cultural Diversity and Unity

In April 1869 the Revd. James Johnson surveyed his district, the Christ Church District, Pademba Road, on the southern fringe of Freetown. It stretched from Brookfields, Grassfields, and Soldiers Town on the south to Kroo Town, the Cotton Tree, Tower Hill, and around to Foulah Town on the north. The district's population was a mixture of new immigrants and old settlers, representing the complexity which Freetown had attained by the end of the seventh decade of the nineteenth century. It included Liberated Africans from the villages, Creoles born in the city, Kru immigrants from the Liberian coast, and soldiers of the West Indian regiments, often with their wives from across the seas. Religiously, it encompassed full Christian communicants, Christian probationers, Muslims, Shango worshippers, charm and idol makers, as well as 'a goodly number of worldly minded young men and women'. The peal of the church bell competed with the rhythmical sounds of the drums of Shango, the noise of the dancers, those who sacrificed chickens and goats, and the melodious call of the horn to the Foulah Town mosque. A walk along Pademba Road or Circular Road brought one in direct contact with the wide variety of people in the district. Christian communicants lived in the house next to the Shango shrine, which in turn bordered the compound of those who carved and worshipped the figures made in honour of twin children. Drunkenness in Soldiers Town compounded the sins of heathenism in the sensitive mind of the Creole who was pastor to such a varied flock.

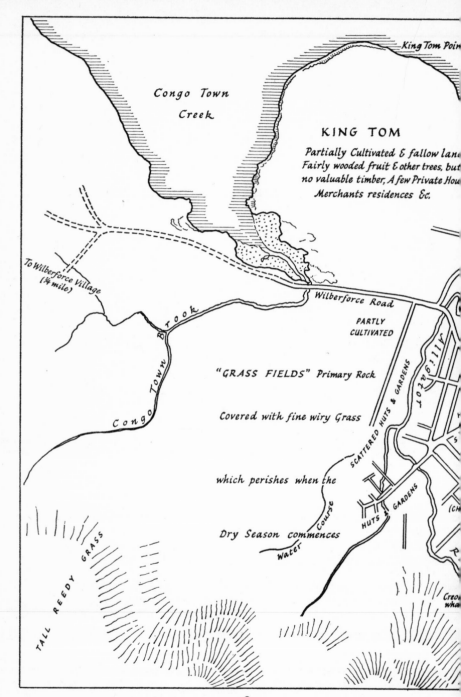

King Tom Point

Congo Town
Creek

KING TOM

Partially Cultivated & fallow lan
Fairly wooded fruit & other trees, but
no valuable timber, A few Private Hou
Merchants residences &c.

To Wilberforce Village
(¼ mile)

Congo Town Brook

Wilberforce Road

PARTLY
CULTIVATED

"GRASS FIELDS" Primary Rock

Covered with fine wiry Grass

which perishes when the

Dry Season commences

Water Course

SCATTERED HUTS & GARDENS

ALLIGATOR

HUTS GARDENS

(CH

TALL REEDY GRASS

Creo
wha

R

280

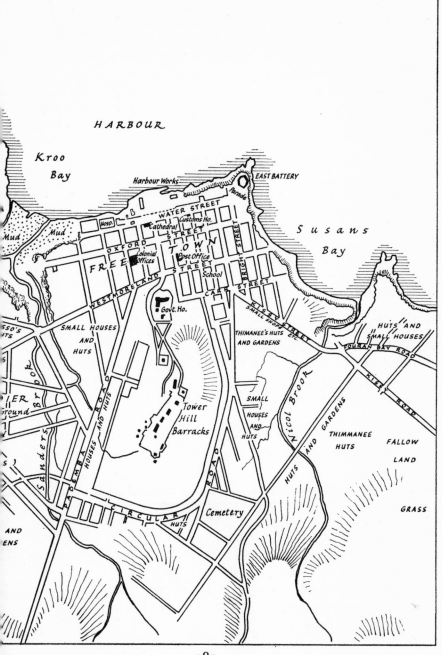

HARBOUR

Kroo
Bay

Mud

Mud

Harbour Works

EAST BATTERY

Parade

Hosp.

WATER STREET

Customs Ho.

Cathedral

OXFORD

Colonial
Offices

FREE TOWN

STREET

Post Office

School

Susans
Bay

WESTMORELAND

Govt. Ho.

CARR STREET

RIGHT STREET

SMALL HOUSES
AND
HUTS

Sanders Br.

Ground

HOUSES AND HUTS

PADEMBA ROAD

KIZZY STREET

SMALL SHOP STREET

THIMANEE'S HUTS
AND GARDENS

Nicol Brook

HUTS AND
SMALL HOUSES

FOURAH BAY ROAD

KIZZY ROAD

SMALL
HOUSES
AND
HUTS

Tower
Hill
Barracks

ROAD

CIRCULAR

HUTS

Cemetery

HUTS AND GARDENS

THIMMANEE
HUTS

FALLOW
LAND

GRASS

AND
ENS

281

A walk into Kroo Town brought a confrontation with the mysteries of the Kru Dance of Death, in which death emerged as the Kru hero. Death, dressed in extravagant attire high-lighted by rough goat skins, sang low and monotonously as he played on a gunbay, producing a simple sound made by a beadstring striking the side of a calabash. Two Kru dancers, each with a knife, first approached death, individually intent on mortally wounding him; each backed away as the crouching, singing figure took a quick step towards them; they returned together, trembling before the persistent, unending power that the singer held, and when he stepped unafraid toward them again, their daggers crossed above his head and instead of shattering his skull, they framed the never-ending conquest of death over them. The dancers limped away to die and Johnson was left with the implications of the dance to his own religious message.[1]

Further along, out of his district, beyond the cotton tree, Johnson would pass along the wide avenues of the oldest section of the city, the twelve intersecting streets of the original Nova Scotian Freetown. To this part the Liberated African had moved as he had prospered economically; here he had con-firmed in homes and shops along Westmoreland Street and Oxford Street his own enhanced social position in the town. Johnson's stroll from Christ Church down Pademba Road, through Kroo Town and back to the city's centre had brought him past the compounded elements which comprised Freetown society by 1870. There was no doubt that what he saw, and what the English read in his report once it reached CMS head-quarters in London, was in some ways depressing. Christ Church District was a long way from the realization of the dreams of those Englishmen who had wished for the creation of what they called a civilized and Christianized Africa eighty or ninety years earlier. As something of a microcosm of the city itself, the district in which Johnson ministered to the Sierra Leoneans did represent a far more exciting and relevant deve-lopment. In Freetown one found in 1870 the full fruits of cultural contact and cultural change. The Liberated Africans themselves had governed the nature of these changes. Progressing far beyond the intentions, imaginations, and expectations of the Europeans who had come to rule and to convert, the recaptive population had determined what to change and how to change, so that by 1870 the cultural result to be seen in Freetown society was the product of their choice and not something imposed by others. This factor explained the variety to be found in the settlement's population, and the disappointment expressed by those who held too tightly to preconceived and unrealizable notions of cultural change in the nineteenth century.

SOCIAL CLASSES OF FREETOWN

Along the streets where Johnson walked, he found representatives of each class in the city. Governor Fergusson in the 1830's had first defined the city's class structure for the large audience which read Sir Thomas Fowell Buxton's *The Slave Trade and Its Remedy*. Increased mobility within the social structure guaranteed the fact that it remained relevant throughout the subsequent decades of the century. Fergusson's class structure was divided into four distinct groups represented by the different types of house architecture. Pademba Road district together with the city centre in 1869 contained examples of each. The lowest classes lived in mud and wattle huts around the fringe of the district where their occupants engaged in small-scale farming and trading. The second class comprised those who lived in houses of frame construction. They dealt in small, inexpensive items of trade such as nails, needles, and thread at the Freetown market. Some also traded agricultural produce brought from the colony or the surrounding country of the interior. They would buy such commodities as oranges or fish by the whole load and then proceed to retail them throughout the city. They were the ubiquitous petty traders who often crowded the busy streets of Freetown. Some craftsmen also belonged to this second class. The third class showed their relatively higher position by having their larger frame houses raised six or eight feet above the ground on stone foundations. Their homes were painted throughout, contained some pieces of European furniture, and usually had a few religious books lying about. The occupants were most often storekeepers or general merchants. From this class came, most often, those who would join together to buy a whole prize ship at auction and those who offered the European merchants their stiffest competition. Many owned boats in which they traded up the rivers into the Sierra Leone interior. At its most successful extreme were to be found those who bought central Freetown property and began to enjoy its social and economic advantages. The highest class of Freetonians was composed of those who were the wealthiest and most prosperous and who lived in houses built entirely of stone, filled with fine European furniture, and financed from their own large mercantile profits. They carried on their business in neat shops located on the ground floor of their own homes. Such Sierra Leoneans were extremely wealthy and regularly educated their children in Europe.[2]

THE CREOLE AND EDUCATION

The regular migration of the sons and daughters of wealthy Liberated Africans and Creoles to English schools, universities, and Inns of Court represented their wish to ensure a position of high social status in the future. An overseas education became second only to the purchasing of land in the city as a form of sure investment. With an economic future assured by the increasing return of a sound investment in property, the astute Creole businessman sought also the ultimate security of a professional training for his children. From the beginning of the colony, the Liberated Africans had been impressed with the importance of education. An indispensable part of early Freetown, primary schools became a part of nearly every rural village. Butscher's Christian Institution on Leicester Mountain represented the earliest effort to introduce higher education. When his successors proved incapable for the task, the Institution moved to Regent where it remained in operation until Johnson's departure in 1823. It lay dormant until 1827 when the Church Missionary Society reopened it at Fourah Bay. There it soon attained its place of prominence all along the western coast of Africa as Fourah Bay College. The CMS opened necessary secondary schools in Freetown in the 1840's. Liberated African parents sacrificed much in order to secure both a general and professional education for their children at the CMS Grammar School, opened for boys in 1845, and the Female Institution opened in 1849, renamed the Annie Walsh Memorial School in 1877. From these and other secondary schools opened later in the century by the Methodists, the path to professional training invariably led to Britain itself. The future Sir Samuel Lewis, son of the prosperous Liberated African businessman William Lewis, went to London and the Middle Temple in 1866. Earlier, in the 1850's, James Africanus Horton left Fourah Bay College at the request of the War Office, who sought to train African doctors for the West Coast, and entered London and Edinburgh, returning in 1859 with an M.D., the first of two Sierra Leoneans to enter the government medical service. The prestige of an English degree became so high that in 1876 the CMS initiated a connection with Durham University whereby Sierra Leone and West African students could take the Durham degree without travelling to the northern English city. University education had come to Freetown.

The granting of English university degrees in Freetown marked the high value placed on western education by the Creole population of Sierra Leone. The importance of an education had been stressed by the missionaries, and the Liberated Africans had accepted its necessity. It represented the most important adoption in a host of cultural values transported to the west coast of Africa. Even Freetown Muslims at this time were changing the nature of their traditional system of education by the addition of English subjects. Together with the community's Christians, they had found that education ensured a continuing position of prominence in the society and successfully insulated the latter-day Creole from the vagaries of British imperial policy in Sierra Leone. Training in the law particularly allowed the Freetown Creole to hold his own with the European and to do so exclusively with the white man's own tools. Education gave Creole society a distinctly European orientation. In other cultural areas such as clothes and, for some, attendance at church on Sunday, the European stamp was also plain to see. But not all of Creole society was so western in its nature. Just as James Johnson found a variety of peoples, houses, beliefs, and religions when he walked out among the residents of Pademba Road district, so too did one find a distinct diversity existing in the total Creole society of 1870. To some observers of the scene, contrasts between Christianity and Shango worship, or Christianity and Islam, between large scale commercial ventures run from shops on Westmoreland Street and small *asusu* companies, between education in the most highly developed school system on the West African coast and membership in the *Agugu* society or the Hunters, and the continual necessity of holding an *awujo* to mark the death of a relative, represented cultural confusion or conflict. In Sierra Leone such elements of diversity did not represent conflict at all, but simply the way things were done in Creole society.

CULTURAL UNITY: LANGUAGE AND FOOD

There were many areas of cultural fusion in Creole society of 1870. Among the most representative were language and food. *Krio*, the language of the Creole, had developed from the Liberated African's earliest contact with the English language. No doubt the poor facility in English of the early German missionaries also played its part in the development of *Krio*. Initially this produced a simple pidgin English. The pidgin developed in a parallel fashion to the newly developing society. By the 1860's there was clear indication that *Krio* had developed not only as a lingua franca, but also as a written language. Newly converted Methodists at Murraytown wrote the Revd.

Cultural Unity: Language and Food

R. Fletcher in 1860 in a *Krio* which was very close to the language of a hundred years later. The letter as written in 1860 is in column A, while a 1960 translation of it into the *Krio* of that period is in column B. The Murraytown Methodists wrote Fletcher:

Column A	Column B
School Masser. O, for true	School Master. O, for true
na God made we. Why we say	nar God meke we. Waitin doo, we say
so, when that white man	so, way da waite man
take we country fashon we	bin take we contry fashin, we
thought say him go die;	bin member say he go die;
when we look him for sum	but way we look for some
day, him na die, and we	day we see say he nor die, en weseff
too na sick, we heart	nor sick, we heart
tronger, we say na God	tronger, we say nar God
made we and all thing for	meke we en all ting for
true. Then we na fraed	true. Den we say
again, we say country fashon	contry fashin
him na true God. Then we	nar from God he camm. Den we
give our heart to true God.	gee we heart to de true God.
O Scroo Masser, we heart	O School master, we heart
good now, we heart sweet	don good now, we heart sweet
now, we heart laugh now,	now, we heart gladie now,
we heart happy now.	we heart de laff.
We poor in the body, but	We poor nar de body, but
we heart gentle (rich),	we gentry nar heart.
a long time we fraed to die	For long tem now we de fraid for die
but now if dead come we can	but now if die camm, we go
glad to go. Ah, Scroo	gladie for go. Ah! School
Masser, we heart good.	master, we heart don good now.
We thank dart white man, o	We tell dar wait man plenty tenki, nar
Scroo Masser, God go make	School master, God don mek
him good, he go make him	am good. He go mek am
high na this world in	high nar dis worl en
another world. O Jesus	de oder worl. O Jesus
God son have mercy upon	God im pikin sorry for
our white man, we want you	we wait man, we want you
make him high, make him	mek am high, mek am
tronger in this world to	stronger nar dis worl for
do your work, and when him	do you wok, en wei he
die put him to good high	die put am pan good lite
happy place na heaven. O	happy place nar heaven. O
God you make dart white man	God you mek dar wait man
good, make we good. We	good, mek weseff good. We

287

free from slave for devil
now, we no buy goat this
time, no sheep, no Colar,
no fowls, but we eat our
money, we take our money
buy clothes we give money
to meeting (class), Glory
to God: for long time we
no savey say God live there
but now we savey say God
live there, Glory to God.[3]

don free from slave for devul
now. We nor get for buy goat dis
tem, nor sheep, nor kola,
nor fowel, but we eat we yone
koppoh, we take we yone koppoh
buy klos, we gib we collection
nar class. Glory
to God. Because for long tem now we
nor bin sabi say God day, day.
But now we don sabi say God
day, day. Glory to God.

An article in 1885 in *Sawyerr's Circular* recognized *Krio* as neither a patois nor a dialect of English, but rather as a Sierra Leone vernacular. The author correctly pointed out that the 'ideas it embodies are not English but native; it is the collection of means whereby Sierra Leoneans express their thoughts *naturally* and without effort.' *Krio* was learned by the child 'from the lips of [the] parents'. It evolved as a 'composite native language' made up of an English, German, French, Ibo, Yoruba, etc., vocabulary and a West African grammatical structure.[4] The process of evolution has been most concisely defined by Eldred Jones, who has pointed out that, unlike the earlier Nova Scotian and Maroon immigrants to Sierra Leone, the Liberated Africans came to the colony during the early nineteenth century with no prior knowledge of English. In the struggle to communicate they used all means at their disposal. 'The new settlers acquired as much of the new vocabulary as they could, and used these newly acquired words, often in a corrupt form, along with their native vocabulary, while often thinking in the style of their original languages.' *Krio* was the result, and as a language it reflected appropriately what had occurred in the whole area of culture change: 'a part of all it had met, and yet different from each.'[5]

The Creole staple food, fufu, developed in a similar manner. Over a span of about thirty years, fufu took on its particular Sierra Leone Creole form. The name itself was a borrowing, for the Maroons brought with them a prepared food called fufu. But Creole fufu developed in the colony itself. The regular cultivation of the cassava plant began around Hastings in the 1820's. Initially the roasted roots of the plant were used to feed the apprentices. This allowed the Hastings Aku, for example, to sell their more valuable crops at the market place. Gradually, however, as the other crops began to fail due to soil infertility, more and more Liberated Africans turned to cassava as a staple food. They began to experiment with new ways of preparing the cassava. They adopted, where possible, methods used in the preparation of other foods. At first the double skin was cut off and the root was sliced into pieces which were then laid on a wicker-work to dry. The Liberated Africans stored the dried pieces in a tightly sealed shed from which daily amounts were taken and cooked for eating. Eventually someone thought of using a European nutmeg grater to produce a rough flour. The drying process was eliminated and the cassava root was skinned, washed, grated, and cooked immediately. Difficulties arose over the tendency of the starch to cling to the flour. This was eventually overcome by adding small amounts of palm oil to reduce the effects of the starch. Later innovations included soaking before grating and cooking the cassava wrapped in banana leaves on hot buried ashes. In order to make the cassava marketable, by the late 1830's Liberated Africans began to grate the root immediately after immersion and washing. They then rolled the cassava into little white balls which, when dried, were taken to the market and sold. These small balls acquired the name fufu at the markets. The name derived from the process of preparation, particularly the grating, which produced a susbstance not unlike that of a 'fu' prepared from pounding. The specific additions in the preparation such as grating and the addition of the palm oil came from the needs of the Liberated Africans on the Sierra Leone peninsula. The specific development of fufu resulted, then, from the innovations of several of the tribal groups in the recaptive population. The Liberated Africans, in the course of their experimentation with cassava, developed other products such as starch, which was also marketed locally.[6]

T

Such developments as *Krio* and fufu contributed to a certain cultural unity among the population of Freetown and the rural areas by the 1870's. *Krio* had become the language of the Creole. Even that top stratum of the society which prided itself on its English education, its English character, and its English dress spoke *Krio* when they left their shops at the end of the day and entered their homes for the evening meal. It was *Krio* that their children learned first, leaving the mastery of English to their later years in school. Certainly in the rural villages the Ibo recaptive who spoke to his Yoruba colleague on the committee of the Seventeen Nations did so in *Krio*. The Arabic prayers of the mosque were interpreted to the congregation in *Krio*. Similarly, by the latter half of the century nearly everyone in Sierra Leone society ate a meal of fufu some time during the week. Together with its usual companion, palaver sauce, it had become a staple for those from all levels of the emerging Creole society. Both the language and the food had developed over a seventy year period of culture change during which the diverse cultural experience of over one hundred different African language groups met and intermingled with the culture of Western Europe in the form of British government officials, and British, French, German, Swiss, Portuguese, Spanish, and Irish missionaries and traders, as well as with the already Europeanized African influences of the Nova Scotian settler. The product was the Creole culture of Sierra Leone, a cultural fusion in which the European influences appeared to dominate, but in which there were many functioning and vital elements taken from the recaptives' cultural past. Many of these were reinterpreted into a largely western context such as the *awujo*, which became an integral part of Christian burial, yet others existed quite independently of any outside, dominant influence. The resultant Creole culture was not a culture which copied intentionally or thoroughly the culture of the West. The aspirations of its members may have been to attain the status represented by the large stone houses which graced the broad streets called Westmoreland and Oxford in the city centre, but its character and breadth could not be so easily stereotyped. Creole society was Freetown, and Freetown encompassed a cultural experience which ranged from the village farmers who trekked daily to the city market in ever increasing numbers, to the Muslim of the east end who sought to make his faith more adaptable to the dominant hopes and aspirations of the city's leaders, to the Liberated African petty trader who sought with diligence and hard work to buy a shop and a house and educate his children, to the second generation recaptive, the Creole trading from his shop along Kissy Street, sitting with the governor in the Legislative Council and writing Arabic letters to chiefs north of the settlement for the British administration.

CULTURAL DIVERSITY: FOUR SIERRA LEONEANS OF 1870
Four Sierra Leoneans of 1870 represented the wide diversity which existed in the culture of the settlement. In Foulah Town lived Amara, an Aku brought into the colony aboard a captured slave vessel shortly before Queen Victoria mounted the English throne in 1837. In 1875 he would become Imam of the mosque in Foulah Town, succeeding Imam Musa. Amara was already in his thirties when he entered the colony for it was thought that he had been born in Yoruba country in 1805. He settled first among Yoruba countrymen in Grassfields and there was converted to Islam by Alta Musa, commonly called Musa Ojay. Musa presided over the few faithful of Grassfields and each week he would gather together his students to go off to the Foulah Town mosque to pray. Musa named Amara. After some time Amara himself went to live in Foulah Town and there acquired the sound knowledge of Muslim law necessary to become a religious leader in the devout Muslim community. His excellence secured for him first a place on the Imam's council and then, upon the death of Imam Musa, the imamship itself. His tall, stout, majestic stature combined with his mastery of Muslim law to ensure him a respected place in the Foulah Town community; he was one to whom others came to settle disputes, for advice, and for consultation on matters of

importance. He closed a schism which had previously existed in the community, not unlike the one which persistently fragmented the other community of Muslim faithful at Fourah Bay. He managed the affairs of the community and the mosque skilfully and due to his work a permanent mosque was erected in Mountain Cut during the 1880's.

Amara may have been the Imam of Foulah Town, but his vision extended to the total community. He supported the reform programmes of younger Muslim Creoles like Mohammed Sanusi to broaden the dimensions of primary education in the Muslim schools and to unite with other, non-Muslim Aku to form the Creole association under George Metzger Macaulay in the early 1890's. The prayers of Imam Amara were usually heard at the public meetings of the association along with the speeches of Abayomi Cole and the music of the Methodist choirs. He fell ill in May 1898, and at first refused medical treatment. When he finally did see a doctor, it was too late. Amara died on 25 June 1898. Those who had respected him throughout his life in Foulah Town came in great numbers to his funeral. Christian and Muslim alike joined such Freetown dignitaries as Mayor J. B. M'Carthy in paying their final homage to the Yoruba slave boy who had been freed at Freetown and had become the honoured Imam of Foulah Town.[7]

During the same year that found Amara a member of the Imam's council in Foulah Town and still five years from the imamship himself, 1870, the strange and mysterious death of another recaptive was recorded in the distant village of Hastings by the Liberated African Methodist clergyman, the Revd. D. W. Thorpe. The death was that of John Wright, the Aku who had been captured at Ilaro at the age of six and who arrived in Freetown aboard a captured Portuguese slaver in 1838. Wright had been sent first to the school at Waterloo, but was eventually apprenticed to Thomas and Harriet Wright of Hastings. He came under the influence of the Wrights, who regularly attended the services at the Methodist chapel across from their house. Thomas Wright, who gave John his own surname, also persuaded him to join the Methodist chapel. John Wright became a devout Christain and took advantage of the chapel's evening classes for adults where he learned to read. He remained in the Wright's employment for eight years and then took up farming on his own. He bought a town lot, built a house, and married in 1853. He became the father of five children before his untimely death. Married and settled in Hastings, John Wright rose in prominence within the local Methodist chapel. He became one of three elders of the local chapel and was a lay preacher. The nature of Methodism in a Sierra Leone rural village at mid-century was such that much of the administration of the chapel rested in the hands of the local elders. The preacher rode a circuit and although the Revd. D. W. Thorpe, the preacher at Hastings in 1870, resided at the Mission House in Hastings, he was away ministering to other chapels in his territory much of the time. He felt the affairs of the Hastings chapel were in good hands, however, and certainly in John Wright he had a loyal and trusted worker. Thorpe knew that Wright read his Bible regularly and when he spoke during evening prayer sessions or at a Sunday service, he did so in a manner which all could understand and which revealed the strength of his own inner piety.

Wright learned the lessons of Christianity well. His knowledge and sense of responsibility led him to a course of action late in 1869 which resulted in his own tragic death the following year. Wright found funds missing from the chapel treasury and soon after discovered that the other two elders were guilty of the theft. He brought them before the government manager who found them guilty and sentenced them to gaol. Wright had acted quickly and forthrightly to correct a wrong. The tragic implications of his actions became manifest in August 1870, when, on the 24th, he fell seriously ill. In spite of all attempts to save him, including those of a Freetown doctor, he died on 31 August 1870. The cause of his mysterious illness lay locked in the secrets of the Hastings *oje* of the *Agugu* society. John Wright of Hastings had been the victim of poison. Each of the three elders involved, the two who had stolen the money and Wright himself, was a member of the *oje*. The *oje* did not sanction theft any more than the colonial government. They did, however, find Wright guilty of taking the culprits to the wrong authority; the *oje* itself should have been called upon to deal with the case of the stolen funds. In Wright's death the Hastings *Agugu* reminded the villagers of the power of the society in the village. Few would afterwards forget.[8]

A third and far more prominent Liberated African left Freetown in 1870 to try to recover his health in England. Sick, discredited, but still a resolute man of strong principles, John Ezzidio remained in many ways the very apex of recaptive life in Freetown by the end of the seventh decade of the nineteenth century. Although he was to die within two years, he was still, in 1870, the first Liberated African to serve on the Legislative Council, elected by the mercantile community of the colony in 1863. Born in Nupe, he had been enslaved and sent to the Yoruba country in the south as a child. Put aboard a Portuguese slaver in 1827, he began the long voyage across the ocean to Brazil. Instead of completing it, however, his ship was captured on the high seas by the British naval squadron and brought to Freetown where Ezzidio was freed by a Mixed Commission Court in October. Unlike most Liberated Africans, Ezzidio, like Amara, was apprenticed in Freetown and was not sent to one of the surrounding villages. Ezzidio's master was a French shopkeeper in Freetown, and from him the young Nupe acquired a name—Isadore, which was first spelled Ezzido but eventually became Ezzidio—and considerable training in the skills of business in a colonial capital. When his first master died, Ezzidio gained employment from two other European concerns in succession before opening his own shop within a decade of arriving in the colony. By 1839 he had begun to acquire Freetown property, and in 1841 be bought the house in George Street opposite St. George's where he resided and carried on business for the rest of his life. In 1835 he had joined the Methodist church and during the 1840's his connection proved beneficial for his business when the head of the mission introduced him to English wholesalers in London and Manchester. From then on he could order directly from England without going through a European middleman. His prosperity was matched by his sincere Christian piety, evidenced both in his daily prayers at home and in his progressively responsible positions within the Methodist church in Sierra Leone. Ezzidio's prominence in the community led Governor Fergusson to name him for the largely ceremonial posts of alderman in 1844 and mayor of the city in 1845. Far more significantly, when Governor Blackall revived the Mercantile Association in 1863 to elect an unofficial member for the newly instituted Legislative Council for Sierra Leone, it elected the leading African merchant in Freetown, John Ezzidio. No other recaptive 'arrived' quite to the extent of the recaptive Nupe. As a member of the Legislative Council, Ezzidio remained a representative of the commercial community. His house was open to all and, in character both with his large stature and his 'big man' status, Ezzidio's premises became the gathering place for the city's unemployed who used it as something of an employment exchange.

Ezzidio's work for Methodism increased with his greater prominence in business and government. For much of the later 1850's and early 1860's he was effectively the superintendent of the mission's work in the colony. He supervised the Sunday School at the Bathurst Street Chapel and raised funds for Buxton Chapel. His dream was Wesley Church, the construction of which was begun in the late 1850's, but which was not finished until long after his death. Ezzidio's monument to Sierra Leone Methodism, Wesley Church, was sacrificed for a time on the altar of British sectarianism. Unknown to the largely independent and certainly cooperative Christians of the settlement, sectarianism was introduced with a viciousness seldom known in the colony by the darkly bearded dictatorial zealot, the Revd. Benjamin Tregaskis who became, largely at Ezzidio's own request, the head of the mission in 1864. John Ezzidio, like most recaptive and Creole Christian non-conformists of mid-century Sierra Leone, was on friendly terms with the Anglicans. Tregaskis, from Britain, was not. The dispute grew in emotional intensity over the years as the British superintendent on one hand warned against the evils of the Established Church while Ezzidio on the other voted for the government's annual grant to the Native Pastorate in the Legislative Council. Livid with rage, Tregaskis regarded Ezzidio's support of the Establishment as treason, and successfully turned many Sierra Leone Methodists and certainly the English mission group itself against the determined recaptive legislator. In 1867 all work stopped on Wesley Church. No further money for the project was forthcoming from Britain. Business losses totalling £3,000 added to Ezzidio's isolation; he fell ill and was ordered by his doctors to take a rest cure in the Banana Islands. In 1870 he sailed for England, but again fell ill and had to be carried from the ship which brought him back to Freetown. Coarsely, Tregaskis predicted his death, but Ezzidio lived through 1871 and into 1872, attending the meetings of the Legislative Council and voting in favour of the grant to the Native Pastorate for the last time in November 1871. Death came to the reduced but highly principled figure in October 1872. As Christopher Fyfe has pointed out, the two real monuments to Ezzidio were the interdenominational church friendship which prevailed long after Tregaskis had ceased to cast his shadow on Sierra Leone Methodism, and his work on the Legislative Council. The latter was unspectacular, but solidly responsible. He did not use his position for personal benefit or for the welfare of a small or private group within the community. What Ezzidio evidenced on the Legislative Council proved '. . . to a barely appreciative government that he and his fellows were worthy of the confidence they were slowly and grudgingly granted.'[9] Ezzidio showed the same qualities in his legislative work that hundreds of other Liberated Africans had revealed for decades in their ability to manage their own affairs whether in the government of the rural villages or their business transactions in the market places of Freetown.

As seen in the biographies of Imam Amara, John Wright of Hastings, and the Honourable John Ezzidio, M.C., great cultural changes in the lives of the recaptives had taken place by 1870. The world of the Liberated Africans was slowly merging with that of their children, the Creoles of Sierra Leone, who dominated the culture of Freetown for the rest of the century and on into the next. The fourth Freetonian to represent the breadth of the culture of the city was himself a Creole, born in the village of Hastings, whose rise to prominence in the community parallels the story of John Ezzidio. Joseph G. Wright was born on 16 March 1840, to Thomas and Harriet Wright, the employers of Liberated African John Wright.[10] In 1870, Joseph Wright opened a shop on Kissy Street in Freetown, from which he traded. His life to that point fairly well fitted the pattern usually thought typical of the mid-century Creole. He spent the first four years of his life in the village with his parents. They then moved to Freetown, where he was educated for eleven years. In 1857 he joined John T. Williams at his shop on Fourah Bay Road and began to learn the shoemaker's trade. By 1860 he had finished his training and had begun to work for himself. Within two years he had acquired sufficient capital to buy a lot, and in 1863 he began to build a house in Freetown. Prosperity had come not only from making shoes, but also from his participation in the very profitable ginger trade. A few months after his new house was completed he proposed to Miss Mary Ann Coker and in June 1865 they were married at Zion Chapel in Soldiers Town. The engagement party in November 1864 was typical of such events in Freetown. Wright purchased bottles of brandy, old tom, Madeira, ale, gin, porter, and a gallon and a half of rum, in addition to kola nuts and other foods for the event.

Shortly after the wedding Wright left Freetown for Lagos, eventually settling in Badagry. His bride followed early the next year. They stayed in Nigeria until sometime late in 1868 or 1869. On the first of January 1870, Wright opened a new shop in Kissy Street. The shop marked Wright's rise to prominence and he continued to prosper on an even larger scale after 1870. Within four years he moved to larger, rented quarters along the same street of shopkeepers. He stopped making shoes and in December bought half of a lot on Kissy Street, built a shop, and rented it to another trader. Predictably, money earned in trade and in his craftmanship was securely invested in city property. In 1881 he tore down the shop and built a house on the lot. Wright's investments assured his continuing affluence. His property increased as did the number of his commercial enterprises. His position in the generally prosperous Creole community was secure. He became a prominent member of the city's merchant associations and active in church work serving as a lay preacher in the Methodist church.

On several occasions he revealed this growing prosperity and subsequent increasing demands made upon him. In 1888 he paid his lawyer, Samuel Lewis, £350 for legal fees. The same year he sent his twenty-six-year-old son, Claudius, to England to begin his training for the bar. He had already seen him through Fourah Bay College in Freetown. The young Wright arrived back in Freetown in 1891, having passed his examinations at the Inns of Court and received the B.C.L. degree from the University of Durham.[11] The elder Wright's rise to social prominence was clearly reflected in Claude's 1894 marriage to Miss Laura Davies, daughter of the successful Creole doctor, W. B. Davies. The event was heralded as the social occasion of the year, taking place as it did in St. George's Cathedral. The Canon of the Cathedral performed the ceremony. Newspaper descriptions of the wedding left no doubt about the fact that the Freetown Wrights had reached the heights of Creole society. They described the bride's white satin gown trimmed with white silk chiffon, white silk lace, and pearls; the five brides-maids in pink crepon and white spotted net; the large gathering inside the Cathedral; the police who stood at the entrance to prevent the even larger crowd of spectators outside from breaking in. Official witnesses, in addition to the two fathers, included the lawyer Samuel Lewis, Frederick Dove, the wealthy merchant, and Major J. J. Crooks, Colonial Secretary and author. After an equally gala reception, the couple left for their honeymoon cottage on Leicester Mountain.[12] Joseph Wright's prosperity continued until he retired in 1906. He lived on quietly for another two years before succumbing at the age of 68 in 1908.[13] By then, his success was enriched by the knowledge that his son Claude had become Mayor of Freetown.

SIERRA LEONE SOCIETY: CONCLUSION

The four Sierra Leoneans of 1870, Imam Amara, John Wright, John Ezzidio, and Joseph G. Wright, represented the society of the settlement in 1870. There was quite a cultural gap between the death of John Wright in Hastings and the opening of Joseph Wright's shop on Kissy Street the same year. If John Ezzidio's departure for England represented the trend of the development of the society, so too, in its way, did the rise of the majestic figure of Amara within the Foulah Town community. The particular events of the year and the lives of the four men in general revealed more than just the extremes of Sierra Leone society sixty-three years after the first recaptives were landed at Freetown. They disclosed the entire scope of its development. One extreme was not conquering the other. Each showed an aspect of the world of the Sierra Leonean of 1870. By then Liberated African society had become Creole society, the culture of the second generation recaptives. In 1853 the Liberated Africans and their children had been declared British subjects by Parliament, a fact which served to give a certain legal credence to A. J. Shorunkeh-Sawyerr's pronouncement in 1893-that the Creole was a 'Black Englishman'.[14] It was true that the society of the Creole was visibly European in its orientation. But it was far more than it visibly appeared. Its members could appreciate a wide variety of cultural experience. The society's development, its very growth, depended as much upon the huge reservoir of past African experience as it did on the new European forms. Creoles understood the frightening pathos of the Kru Dance of Death; they enjoyed the pleasures of the formal ball and its revelation of the current styles abroad. Joseph Wright's provisions of drink for his own engagement party included rum and brandy; it could have easily included palm wine and a few years later Bass Imported Ale on tap from Porter's hotel. Those who accepted the secret power of the *oje* were increasingly coming to understand the intricate secrets of the Masonic lodge. Christian burial included the *awujo* for the bereaved survivors. As with the language, *Krio*, the society of the 35,000 to 40,000 who comprised the population of the mountainous settlement in 1870 was 'a part of all it had met, and yet different from each'. Neither entirely African nor entirely European, the society was Creole and, as Creole society it would make its effect felt all along the West African coast in the next fifty years.

The Sierra Leone Creoles emerged as they did because their fathers and mothers had been able to establish their own province of freedom in Sierra Leone. The plans envisioned by the founders and the host of British administrators who came to the colony in the early years had simply failed in application. Some of the fault lay in the incompetence of those who sought to manage the affairs of the colony and its recaptive population. Much of the failure resulted from the unhealthy conditions of the colony for the European, which meant that there was pitifully little continuity of either personnel or programmes. Against this general picture of failure and frustration was contrasted the resilience, adaptibility, and innovative skills of the recaptive immigrants themselves. They did, for the most part, settle down quietly to mould a new life in the settlement, something they had the opportunity to do because the British had saved them from the rigours and horrors of the international slave trade. Thus, provided with their freedom and conscious of the administrative void into which they had been thrust, the recaptives of Sierra Leone set about establishing their province. Social welfare and security came from their benefit and welfare societies; political and judical stability came from the broadened functioning of the social voluntary associations as well as from the secret societies; necessary economic prosperity came from such phenomena as the *asusu* and other forms of *ad hoc* commercial companies. Independence was the key word to describe the attitudes and activities of the Liberated Africans during the first seventy years of nineteenth-century Sierra Leone history. Wherever one investigated their culture, independence was to be found. Those who founded the first villages, those who left the government villages to live isolated from the social community envisaged by the colonial power, those who fought Governor Findlay's forces at Cobolo in 1832 and who settled in Fourah Bay in a Muslim community afterwards, those who built their own dissenting chapels in the villages and then contracted for clergymen with the missionary societies, those who told the missionaries they were better off worshipping Shango, those who were Wesleyan and yet supported the annual grant to the Native Pastorate of the Established Church, all gave evidence of independence, all in their way defined Sierra Leone's province of freedom. The independence assured the success of the Sierra Leone colony. The Liberated African people themselves gave to the very name Freetown its true meaning in the nineteenth century.

Notes

ABBREVIATIONS

PRO—Public Record Office, London

CMS—Church Missionary Society Archives, London

MMS—Methodist Missionary Society Archives, London

ASS—Records of the Anti-Slavery Society and the Aborigines' Rights Protection Society, Rhodes House Library, Oxford University

SLA—Sierra Leone Government Archives, Freetown

LALB—Liberated African Department Letter Books

CSLB—Colonial Secretary's Letter Book

Notes for Chapter 1

1. Philip D. Curtin, *The Image of Africa: British Ideas and Action, 1780–1850* (London: Macmillan, 1965), pp. 16, 96–7. Hereafter cited as: Curtin, *Image*.

2. Christopher Fyfe, *A History of Sierra Leone* (London: Oxford University Press, 1962), p. 15. Hereafter cited as: Fyfe, *History*.

3. Edward Fiddes, 'Lord Mansfield and the Sommersett Case', *The Law Quarterly Review*, Number CC (October 1934), pp. 499–511.

4. Prince Hoare, *Memoirs of Granville Sharp, Esq. Composed from His Own Manuscripts, and other Authentic Documents in the Possession of His Family and of the African Institution* (London: Henry Colbourn, 1828), 2nd edition, I, 11. Hereafter cited as: Hoare, *Sharp*, 2nd Ed. Curtin, *Image*, p. 54.

5. Granville Sharp, *A Short Sketch of Temporary Regulations (Until Better Shall be Proposed) for the Intended Settlement on the Grain Coast of Africa near Sierra Leone* (London: H. Baldwin, 1786), p. 13.

6. *Ibid.*, pp. 14–15.

7. N. A. Cox-George, 'Direct Taxation in the Early History of Sierra Leone', *Sierra Leone Studies*, new series (December 1955), number 5, p. 21. Hereafter cited as: Cox-George, 'Taxation'.

8. Hoare, *Sharp*, 2nd Ed., I, 240.

9. *Ibid.*, II, 157. Curtin, *Image*, p. 101.

10. G. M. Trevelyan, *History of England* (New York: Doubleday Anchor Books, 1954), III, 130. Hereafter cited as: Trevelyan, *History*.
11. Eugene Stock, *The History of the Church Missionary Society: Its Environment, Its Men, and Its Work* (London: Church Missionary Society, 1899), I, 41–2. Hereafter cited as: Stock, *CMS*.
12. Paul Edwards (editor), *Equiano's Travels: His Autobiography, the Interesting Narrative of the Life of Olaudah Equiano or Gustavus Vassa the African* (London: Heinemann, 1967), pp. 160–9.
13. PRO: T.1.643/487, Lists of Black Poor embarked on *Atlantic, Vernon*, and *Belisarius* transports, 27 February 1787. J. J. Crooks, *A History of the Colony of Sierra Leone Western Africa* (Dublin: Brown and Nolan, 1903), pp. 28, 30–1. Hereafter cited as: Crooks, *History*. R. R. Kuczynsky, *Demographic Survey of the British Colonial Empire* (London: Oxford University Press, 1948), I, 43.
14. Hoare, *Sharp*, 2nd Ed., II, 83.
15. *Ibid.*, II, 92.
16. *Ibid.*, II, 117.
17. *Ibid.*, II, 132.
18. Fyfe, *History*, pp. 24–5.
19. Harry C. J. Luke, *A Bibliography of Sierra Leone* (Oxford: Clarendon Press, 1925), p. 8.
20. Crooks, *History*, p. 33.
21. Fyfe, *History*, pp. 32–3, 41–2. C. H. Fyfe, 'Thomas Peters: History and Legend', *Sierra Leone Studies*, new series (December 1953), number 1, pp. 4–13.
22. John Clarkson Diary, 2–4 August 1792, quoted in E. G. Ingham, *Sierra Leone after a Hundred Years* (London: Seeley and Company, 1894), pp. 102–4. Hereafter cited as: Clarkson Diary, Ingham, *Sierra Leone*.
23. *Ibid.*, 28 March 1792, pp. 30–1.
24. *Ibid.*, 29–30 March, 25 August 1792, pp. 31–3, 108–11. Crooks, *History*, p. 43.
25. Clarkson Diary, Ingham, *Sierra Leone*, 9–10 September, 6, 14, November 1792, pp. 115–17, 138–40, 142, 143.
26. Cox-George, 'Taxation', pp. 23, 28–9.
27. Fyfe, *History*, p. 51. Prince Hoare, *Memoirs of Granville Sharp, Esq. Composed from His Own Manuscripts, and Other Authentic Documents in the Possession of His Family and of the African Institution* (London: Henry Colburn and Company, 1820), 1st ed. pp. 285–6. Hoare, *Sharp*, 1st Ed.
28. Clarkson Diary, Ingham, *Sierra Leone*, 2 July 1792, pp. 92–4.
29. *Ibid.*, 183–7. Hoare, *Sharp*, 1st Ed., p. 293.
30. Cox-George, 'Taxation', p. 30.
31. PRO: CO267/91, Commission of Inquiry, 1827, *Report*, p. 10.
32. PRO: CO267/41, Thomas Clarkson to Lord Bathurst, 22 June 1815.
33. PRO: CO267/34, Zachary Macaulay to Robert Peel, 15 January 1812.
34. PRO: CO267/91, Commission of Inquiry, 1827, *Report*, p. 10.
35. T. N. Goddard, *Handbook of Sierra Leone* (London: Grant Richards, Limited, 1925), p. 26. Hereafter cited as: Goddard, *Handbook*. Hoare,

Sharp, 2nd Ed., II, 58. Sierra Leone Company, *Substance of the Report Delivered by the Court of Directors of the Sierra Leone Company to the General Court of Proprietors, on Thursday the 27th March, 1794* (London: James Phillips, 1794), p. 51. Hereafter cited as: S. L. Co., *Report*, 1794.

36. The Maroons, originally Koromanti from what is now Ghana, had been enslaved and sent to Jamaica where they successfully rebelled, freed themselves and established small communities in the Jamaican mountains. Eventually some fell foul of the British army and, as a result, were sent to Nova Scotia. Disliking their life there, they contracted with the Sierra Leone Company to be sent to Freetown.
37. Crooks, *History*, p. 55.
38. Fyfe, *History*, pp. 84–6.
39. Crooks, *History*, pp. 57–8.
40. PRO: WO1/352, Answer of Governor Dawes to queries of Commodore Hallowell, 12 January 1803, p. 137.
41. PRO: WO1/352, Answers of the Governor and Council to queries of Commodore Hallowell, 12 January 1803, p. 129.
42. *Ibid.*, pp. 131, 136, MMS: Sierra Leone, 1812–1834; 1812–1820, James Wise and others to Reverend James Wood, 14 April 1816. CMS: CA1/M3, Kissy Report, Reverend Nyländer, Kissy, 30 March 1825, p. 292.
43. PRO: WO1/352, Answers of the Governor and Council to queries of Commodore Hallowell, 12 January 1803, p. 133.
44. Fyfe, *History*, p. 71.
45. Crooks, *History*, pp. 60, 61, 65–6. Goddard, *Handbook*, p. 30.
46. A. F. Walls, 'The Nova Scotian Settlers and their Religion', *Sierra Leone Bulletin of Religion*, I (June 1959) 1, 22. Hereafter cited as: Walls, 'Nova Scotian Religion'.
47. Christopher Fyfe, 'The Baptist Churches in Sierra Leone', *Sierra Leone Bulletin of Religion*, V (December 1963) 2, 55–60.
48. Christopher Fyfe, 'The Countess of Huntingdon's Connexion in Nineteenth Century Sierra Leone', *Sierra Leone Bulletin of Religion*, IV (July, 1962) 2, 53–61.
49. Fyfe, *History*, pp. 32–3, 36, 63, 70, 73.
50. Walls, 'Nova Scotian Religion', pp. 23, 24, 29.
51. Fyfe, *History*, pp. 48, 56, 57, 63–4, 70, 73, 74, 76–7, 81–4.

Notes for Chapter 2

1. *Statutes of the United Kingdom and Ireland.* 47 Geo. III. 1807 Sessions 1 and 2 (London: His Majesty's Statute and Law Printers, 1807), pp. 143–4. *Journals of the House of Commons*, LXII (1806–1807), meeting of 10 February 1807, p. 115. 'A Bill intituled, An Act for the Abolition of the Slave

Trade', *British Sessional Papers*, 1806–1807, I, number 68, pp. 41–4. 'A Bill (As Ammended by the Committee) intituled, An Act for the Abolition of the Slave Trade', *British Sessional Papers*, 1806–1807, I, number 92, pp. 45–52.

2. SLA: Governor's Letter Book, 1808–1811, Ludlam to Hamilton, 10 May 1808, p. 28. Crooks, *History*, p. 75. PRO: CO267/24, Thompson to Castlereagh, 2 August 1808.

3. PRO: CO267/29, 'Sierra Leone', Report of the West African Commissioners, 1810, p. 167.

4. PRO: CO267/24, Thompson to Castlereagh, 8 August 1808, p. 4.

5. MMS: Sierra Leone (1812–1834; 1812–1820), J. Healey and T. Hirst to Dr. Coke, 24 April 1813. 'Sibthorpe's History of Sierra Leone', Volume II, *The Artisan*, II (29 April 1885) 1, 4. F. B. Spilsbury, *Account of a Voyage to the West Coast of Africa, Performed by H.M. Sloop* Favourite *in the Year 1805* (London: Richard Phillips, 1807), p. 38. Hereafter cited as: Spilsbury, *Voyage*.

6. MMS: Sierra Leone (1812–1834; 1812–1820), James Wise to MMS, 25 June 1819.

7. SLA: Governor's Letter Book, 1808–1811, Notice of Governor Ludlam, 6 February 1808, p. 15.

8. MMS: Sierra Leone (1812–1834; 1812–1820), J. Healey and T. Hirst to Dr. Coke, 24 April 1813.

9. SLA: G. Rickards to Anne DeWite, 6 February 1808, p. 14. Rickards was Governor Ludlam's secretary.

10. PRO: CO267/24, Thompson to Castlereagh, 2 November 1808.

11. A.B.C. Sibthorpe, *The History of Sierra Leone* (London: Elliot Stock, 1881), p. 21. Hereafter cited as: Sibthorpe, *History*.

12. Spilsbury, *Voyage*, pp. 38–9.

13. 'Governors of Sierra Leone', *Sierra Leone Weekly News*, XV (27 May 1899), 39, 4. PRO: CO267/25, Wilberforce to Castlereagh, 19 January 1808.

14. PRO: CO267/24, Thompson to Castlereagh, 27 July 1808. Crooks, *History*, p. 75.

15. PRO: CO267/25, *The Sierra Leone Gazette*, Number 19 (19 November 1808), p. 1.

16. *Ibid.* Crooks, *History*, p. 78. PRO: CO267/24, Ludlam to Z. Macaulay, 13 April 1808; 'Notice', *Sierra Leone Gazette*, Number 11 (3 September 1808), p. 33; Thompson to Castlereagh, 8 August 1808.

17. PRO: CO267/24, Thompson to Castlereagh, 2 November 1808. CO267/25, *The African Herald*, Numbers 1, 2, 6 (21 January, 25 February, 24 June 1809), pp. 1, 4, 17; Thompson to Castlereagh, 17 February 1809.

18. PRO: CO267/24, *The Sierra Leone Gazette*, Number 7 (1 August 1808), p. 25; Thompson to Castlereagh, 2 August 1808. SLA: Governor's Letter Book, 1808–1811, Rickards to Ludlam, 23 January 1809, p. 55; Rickards to Ludlam, 5 April 1809, p. 59.

19. PRO: CO267/24, Thompson to Castlereagh, 27 July 1808; 2 November

U

1808. CO267/25, Thompson to Castlereagh, 7 March 1809; 15 August 1809.
20. PRO: CO267/24, Thompson to Castlereagh, 2 November 1808.
21. PRO: CO267/25, Thompson to Castlereagh, 7 March 1809. CO267/27, Thompson to Castlereagh, 1 January 1810.
22. PRO: CO267/28, Representations transmitted to the Honorable Cecil Jenkinson by former Governor Thompson, London, 6 June 1810.
23. Thompson acknowledged the letter of recall of April, 1809 in PRO: CO267/25, Thompson to Castlereagh, 15 August 1809.
24. Captain Columbine, his successor, returned the name Freetown to official usage. PRO: CO267/27, Columbine to the Earl of Liverpool, 27 February 1810.
25. Crooks, *History*, p. 85. CMS: CA1/E2/29, Nyländer to Pratt, 2 March 1810. PRO: CO267/28, Columbine to Liverpool, 24 July 1810. CO267/29, Report of the West African Commissioners, 1810, Sierra Leone, p. 166.
26. SLA: Governor's Letter Book, 1808–1811, Four letters from the Secretary's Office to the heads of the Civil Establishment, G. Rickards to J. McGoane, T. Craig, Craig, Robertson, 8, 8, 11, 12 June 1810, pp. 108–9; General Orders, Secretary's Office, 8 May 1810, p. 108.
27. PRO: CO267/29 Report of the West African Commissioners, 1810, Sierra Leone, p. 175. SLA: Governor's Letter Book, 1808–1811, Samuel Curry to Officer Commanding the Royal Africa Corps, 9 April 1810, p. 102; Samuel Curry to Charles Hopkins, 3 March 1810, p. 97; Order from the Secretary's Office signed by Kenneth Macaulay, 4 June 1811; Proclamation of the Acting Governor, 15 June 1811.
28. PRO: CO267/28, Columbine to Liverpool, 10 December 1810. CO267/31, Curry to Liverpool, 12 July 1811.
29. PRO: CO267/30, Maxwell to Liverpool, 29 July 1811.
30. PRO: CO267/31, Ceddle to Maling, 3 September 1811. CO267/34, Maxwell to Liverpool, 7 May 1812.
31. PRO: CO267/31, James Willy to Lords of the Treasury, Bangor, North Wales, 30 September 1811.
32. PRO: CO267/30, Maxwell to Liverpool, Number 5, 10 December 1811. CO267/39, Frederick to Bathurst, 5 October 1914
33. PRO: CO267/30, Maxwell to Liverpool, 29 July 1811. CO267/34, Maxwell to Liverpool, 7 May 1812; Bathurst to Maxwell, 26 October 1812.
34. PRO: CO267/31, List of Captured Negroes on hand 31 December 1810, and those received, enlisted, apprenticed, etc. up to 31 December 1811.
35. PRO: CO267/35, Disposal of Captured Negroes received in the colony of Sierra Leone during the year 1812.
36. A Vice-Admiralty Court was established at Freetown in 1808. Its purposes were to try and adjudicate any captured slaves taken as prizes. All captured slaves as well as the vessels carrying them were sent before this court for trial. The officers of the naval vessels capturing the slave

ships were given certificates for the slaves which allowed them to claim a bounty for each slave. The Vice-Admiralty Court was empowered to handle British ships, and generally did. The majority of the slaves freed at Freetown were tried in the Mixed Commission Courts established by international treaties after the Napoleonic Wars. During its first fifty-four years, the Vice-Admiralty Court at Freetown tried cases involving 343 slave ships and approximately 25,000 slaves. Crooks, *History*, p. 71. Sibthorpe, *History*, p. 72. PRO: CO267/24, Letter from the Colonial Office accompanying the Order-in-Council to Governor Thompson, April 1808.

37. PRO: CO267/38, General Statement on the disposal of Captured Negroes at Sierra Leone up to 9 July 1814; Estimate of the population in Sierra Leone, Maxwell, 1814.

38. PRO: CO267/91, Abstract Statement of Expenditure in Sierra Leone, 1812–1825, in evidence presented with the *Report* of the Commission of Inquiry, 1827. CO267/27, Report of the Commissioners for Investigating the State of the Settlements and Government on the Coast of Africa Concerning the Contingent Civil Expenses of the Colony of Sierra Leone, 26 February 1810. CO267/40, Return of Captured Negroes at present maintained by His Majesty's Government in Sierra Leone, 23 March 1815; Statement of Necessaries and Implements required for use of Liberated Africans in Sierra Leone maintained by Government, 1815.

39. CMS: CA1/E2/42, Nyländer to Pratt, 7 December 1810.

40. Sibthorpe, *History*, pp. 19–20. PRO: CO267/40, Petition from the freeholders and principal inhabitants of Sierra Leone to Acting Governor Maling, 19 December 1814; Maxwell to Henry Goulburne, London [n.d., but in volume after letter of 30 June 1815].

41. The new act made slave trading a felony rather than a misdemeanour, and made it punishable by transportation. PRO: CO267/43, 51 Geo. III. Cap. 23, 14 May 1811, pp. 245–50.

42. Revd. Charles Marke, *The Origin of Wesleyan Methodism in Sierra Leone* (London: Charles H. Kelly, 1913), pp. 5, 11–14. Hereafter cited as: Marke, *Methodism*. MMS: Printed Reports, *Methodist Annual Report*, 1812, pp. 19–20.

43. Sibthorpe, *History*, p. 21. MMS: Sierra Leone (1812–1834; 1812–1820), William Davies to Buckley, 20 February 1815.

44. MMS: Sierra Leone (1859–1862), Mr. Blanshard on how the United Methodist Free Church came to Sierra Leone, 21 February 1861. (1812–1834; 1812–1820), Davies to Mr. and Mrs. Fleming, 1 January 1817.

45. MMS: Sierra Leone (1812–1834; 1812–1820), Davies to Buckley, 10 August 1815. (1834–1840; odd papers, 1837–1841), Memorial to Governor H. D. Campbell from the Wesleyan Missionary Society members at Congo Town, 19 September 1836. Marke, *Methodism*, p. 20.

46. Between 1811 and 1884 the Wesleyan Methodist Missionary Society lost nineteen missionaries out of a total of seventy through death in

Notes for Chapter 2

Sierra Leone. 'The Wesleyan Methodist Church and Missions in the Sierra Leone District', *Methodist Herald*, II (8 February 1884) 9, 2.

47. CMS: CA1/E1/82, Nyländer to Pratt, 28 October 1806.
48. SLA: Governor's Letter Book, 1808–1811, Rickards to Nyländer, 10 June 1809.
49. CMS: CA1/E1/113, Nyländer to Pratt, 19 May 1808. CA1/E2/31, Nyländer to Pratt, 11 April 1810. CA1/E2/32, Nyländer to Pratt, 25 July 1810. CA1/E2/30, Renner to Pratt, 13 March 1810.
50. CMS: CA1/E2/47, Nyländer to Pratt, 7 May 1811. CA1/E2/37, Pratt to Nyländer, 9 March 1811. CA1/E2/95, Pratt to Sierra Leone missionaries, 31 March 1811. CA1/E2/97, Nyländer to Pratt, 2 September 1811.
51. CMS: CA1/E3/4, Nyländer to Pratt, 21 April 1812.
52. CMS: CA1/E3/7, Nyländer to Pratt, 7 June 1812. CA1/E3/11, Nyländer to Pratt, 24 July 1812.
53. ——, *Register of Missionaries (Clerical, Lay and Female), and Native Clergy from 1804 to 1904* (London: Church Missionary Society, 1896), p. 2. Hereafter cited as: *CMS Register.* Stock, *CMS*, I, 81–83.
54. CMS: CA1/E3/22, Nyländer to Pratt, 30 October 1812.
55. CMS: CA1/E2/115, Journal of Revd. Wilhelm and Revd. Klein, 3 October 1811 to 12 January 1812, entry for 6 January 1812.
56. Thomas Fowell Buxton, *The African Slave Trade and Its Remedy* (London: John Murray, 1840), pp. 301–43. Hereafter cited as: Buxton, *Remedy.*
57. Stock, *CMS*, I, 159. *CMS Register*, p. 2.
58. MacCarthy had been appointed early in 1812 and had only recently arrived. PRO: CO267/34, Colonial Office to MacCarthy, 3 April 1812.
59. CMS: CA1/E3, MacCarthy to Butscher, 6 February 1813, enclosed in Butscher to Pratt, Goree, 14 November 1813.
60. CMS: CA1/E3, Butscher to Pratt, Goree, 27 February 1813; Pratt to Butscher, 16 August 1813. CA1/E4, MacCarthy to Pratt, 16 April 1814.
61. Stock, *CMS*, I, 107–9.
62. CMS: CA1/E3, Maxwell to Gambier, 17 March 1813; Renner to Pratt, 20 January 1813.
63. CMS: CA1/E3, Butscher to Pratt, 2 August 1813; Pratt to Butscher, 16 August 1813; Pratt to Butscher, 26 November 1813; Butscher to Pratt, 1 Februray 1814.
64. *Ibid.* CMS: CA1/E4, Butscher to Pratt, 4 October 1814.
65. CMS: CA1/E3, Pratt to Sierra Leone missionaries, 16 August 1813; Pratt to Butscher, 26 November 1813. CA1/E4, Pratt to Nyländer, 19 March 1814; Pratt to Butscher, 29 March 1814; Butscher to Pratt, 30 June 1814. Crooks, *History*, p. 113. Stock, *CMS*, I, 125–6.
66. CMS: CA1/E4, Pratt to Butscher, 21 November 1814.
67. The proposal was sent to the government late in 1814 with the support of Maxwell, and Pratt reported in May of the following year that the government had given their approval to the plan. CMS: CA1/E4, Pratt to Butscher, 1 December 1814; Pratt to Butscher, 16 May 1815. PRO: CO267/38, Maxwell to the Colonial Office, London, 23 December 1814.

68. PRO: CO267/40, Maxwell to Bathurst, London, 30 June 1815. CO267/42, MacCarthy to Bathurst, 1 January 1816.
69. CMS: CA1/E4, Butscher to Pratt, 25 May 1815. CA1/E5/32, MacCarthy to Pratt, 15 August 1815.
70. CMS: CA1/E4, Pratt to Renner, 25 November 1814.
71. CMS: CA1/E4, Pratt to Butscher, 21 November 1814.
72. CMS: CA1/E5/32, MacCarthy to Pratt, 15 August 1815.
73. CMS: CA1/E4, Butscher to Pratt, 14 December 1814; Pratt to Mac-Carthy, 16 June 1815. CA1/E5/20, Pratt to Renner, 9 August 1815. CA1/E5/69, Nyländer to Pratt, 23 January 1816.
74. CMS: CA1/E4, Butscher to Pratt, 25 May 1815. CA1/E5/20, Pratt to Renner, 9 August 1815. CA1/E5/34, Pratt to Butscher, 16 August 1815.
75. Revd. T. R. Birks, *The Memoir of the Reverend Edward Bickersteth* (London: Seeley, 1852), I, 4, 23, 28. Hereafter cited as: Birks, *Bickersteth*.
76. *Ibid.*, I, 207–11, 234–58, 90–1, 180–1. Stock, *CMS*, I, 159, 111–12. CMS: CA1/E5/48, Pratt to Butscher, 18 October 1815.
77. Birks, *Bickersteth*, I, 261–2, 278.
78. CMS: CA1/E5/87, Bickersteth to Pratt, 13 March 1816.
79. *Ibid.* CMS: CA1/E5/116, Bickersteth to Pratt, 20 April 1816. Birks, *Bickersteth*, I, 287–8.
80. *Ibid.*, I, 287–8, 301.
81. PRO: CO267/44, Pratt to Bathurst, 31 August 1816. Stock, *CMS*, I, 162–3. CMS: CA1/E5A/37, Garnon to Bickersteth, 7 February 1817. CA1/E5/151, Bickersteth to Butscher, London, 16 September 1816.
82. Stock, *CMS*, I, 162. PRO: CO267/44, Pratt to Bathurst, 31 August 1816.
83. PRO: CO267/42, MacCarthy to Bathurst, 31 May 1816. CMS: CA1/E5/130, MacCarthy to Pratt, 5 June 1816.
84. MacCarthy reported that 350 children were already under CMS training at Leicester Mountain. PRO: CO267/42, MacCarthy to Bathurst, 31 May 1816.
85. MacCarthy also included Nova Scotians not needed for trade in his plan.
86. The missionary's wife would be paid £50 per year to teach the Liberated African girls.

Notes for Chapter 3

1. PRO: CO267/47, Copy of MacCarthy pedigree signed by Sir William Belham, Deputy Ulster King of Arms and Principal Herald of Ireland, 6 August 1812; MacCarthy to Bathurst, 7 January 1818. CO267/34, Colonial Office to MacCarthy, 3 April 1812. CO267/42, MacCarthy to Bathurst, 1 January 1816. Fyfe, *History*, p. 124.
2. PRO: CO267/91, Commission of Inquiry, 1827, *Report*, Evidence,

Number 1A, Abstract of Statement of Expenditure in Sierra Leone, 1812–1825.

3. CMS: CA1/M2, Revd William A. B. Johnson to Revd Henry During, Regent, 18 June 1822, p. 66.

4. PRO: CO267/49, MacCarthy to Bathurst, 25 November 1819. CO267/45, MacCarthy to Bathurst, 6 February 1817. CO267/50, Report of Sir George Collier on Sierra Leone, 1819. Early in 1817 the foundation stones for St. George's Church, Freetown, and St. Patrick's Church, Kissy, were laid. CO267/46, Henry Chisholm to William Hill, Esq., Exchequer, London, 30 October 1817.

5. PRO: CO267/40, 42, 49, 51, 56, MacCarthy to Bathurst, 2 November 1815, 5 April 1816, 25 November 1819, 20 May 1820, 7 November 1822.

6. PRO: CO267/49, MacCarthy to Bathurst, 19 July 1819. Sibthorpe *History*, p. 24.

7. PRO: CO267/42, MacCarthy to Bathurst, 14 November 1816. Crooks, *History*, p. 92.

8. ASS: Mss.Brit.Emp.S22,G19, Sierra Leone, Ackim land dispute material, 1811–1878, No. 6, Minutes of Council, November, 1816, letter from Ackim to Council, March 1817.

9. *Ibid.*, Council Minutes, November, 1816. CMS: CA1/E3, Butscher to Pratt, 23 April 1813. CA1/E5/30, Butscher to Pratt, 12 August 1815. PRO: CO267/42, MacCarthy to Bathurst. 6 July 1816. CO267/86, *Royal Gazette and Sierra Leone Advertiser*, VIII (4 March 1826) 405, 660.

10. PRO: CO267/49, MacCarthy to Bathurst, 19 July 1819. Crooks, *History*, p. 96.

11. PRO: CO267/127, General Statement of the Population of the Villages, enclosed in Governor's Dispatch, 9 February 1833.

12. PRO: CO267/91, Commission of Inquiry, 1827, *Report*, p. 7.

13. ASS: Mss.Brit.Emp.S22.G122, Misc., James Hook to Lord Russell, Kensington, 25 July 1840.

14. CMS: CA1/E7A/1, *Royal Gazette and Sierra Leone Advertiser*, 1(3 April 1819)52, 185.

15. 'Sibthorpe's History of Sierra Leone', Volume II, Book VI, *The Artisan*, III(11 August 1888)9, 4.

16. MMS: West Africa (1858–1859), Samuel Brown to Wesleyan Methodist Missionary Society, King Tom's, 20 July 1858.

17. CMS: CA1/0126a, Johnson to Pratt and Bickersteth, 14 November 1822.

18. CMS: CA1/M1, E. Fitzgerald to Pratt, 8 June 1821, Confidential. CA1/E5A/98, Garnon to Pratt, 5 March 1817.

19. CMS: CA1/E6/113, *Royal Gazette and Sierra Leone Advertiser*, I(17 January 1818)14, 29; I(10 January 1818)13, 25.

20. PRO: CO267/47, MacCarthy to Bathurst, 21 July 1818. CO267/48, H. Hobhouse to Goulburn, Whitehall, 11 December 1818.

21. PRO: CO267/53, *Royal Gazette and Sierra Leone Advertiser*, I(20 March 1819)50, 177–178. SLA: LALB (1820–1826), [Reffell] to Von Sertemar,

20 July 1820. CMS: CA1/0126a, Johnson to Pratt and Bickersteth, Regent, 20 May 1820. Sibthorpe, *History*, pp. 24–5.

22. Sarah Biller (editor), *Memoir of the late Hannah Kilham; chiefly compiled from her Journal and edited by her daughter-in-law Sarah Biller of St. Petersburg* (London: Darton and Harvey, 1837), pp. 232–3. Hereafter cited as: Biller, *Kilham Memoir*. Mrs. Biller was, in fact, Mrs. Kilham's step-daughter. CMS: CA1/E7/63, Collier to Pratt, 9 November 1818.

23. CMS: CA1/0126a, Johnson to Pratt and Bickersteth, Regent, 3 June 1820.

24. CMS: CA1/E7/13, *Royal Gazette and Sierra Leone Advertiser*, I(9 May 1818)30, 96. SLA: Governor's Letter Book (1808–1811), Kenneth Macaulay to D. Edmonds, Jr., 30 May 1811; CSLB (1820–1834), J. O'Neil Walsh to the Mayor and Aldermen, 6 June 1820.

25. PRO: CO267/91, Commission of Inquiry, 1827, *Report*, p. 33.

26. PRO: CO267/45, Memorial to George, Prince Regent, from the people of Sierra Leone, 5 March 1817.

27. PRO: CO267/49, MacCarthy to Bathurst, 25 August 1819. CO267/40, MacCarthy to Bathurst, 22 July 1815; MacCarthy to Bathurst, 2 November 1815; CO267/42, MacCarthy to Bathurst, 15 February 1816; MacCarthy to Bathurst, 24 April 1816. CO267/47, MacCarthy to Bathurst, 11 May 1818, Insert No. 3. CO267/65, Hamilton to Bathurst, 31 January 1825, Insert No. 3, 'The Present State of the Liberated Africans in the Villages, 19 December 1823'.

28. PRO: CO267/40, Ordinance, Charles MacCarthy, Lieutenant Governor, Cap.III, 'An Act to prevent Persons from buying or receiving from Captured Negroes any Articles of Clothing or Provisions', 1 August 1815, p. 2.

29. CMS: CA1/E7/21, MacCarthy to Pratt, 19 June 1818. CA1/E5/81, Pratt to Butscher, 8 March 1816. CA1/E5/86, Pratt to Bickersteth, 9 March 1816. PRO: CO267/44, Pratt to Bathurst, 31 August 1816, note by Goulburn at end of letter.

30. ASS: Mss.Brit.Emp.S18, C107/150, Thomas Clarkson to John Wadkin, Bury, 10 February 1813.

31. CMS: CA1/E5/151, Bickersteth to Butscher, 16 September 1816. CA1/E5/162, Pratt to MacCarthy, 26 September 1816.

32. PRO: CO267/44, Treasury to Goulburn, 4 November 1816; CMS to Bathurst, 12 September 1816. CO267/46, Pratt to Goulburn, 5 November 1817. CO267/47, MacCarthy to Bathurst, 26 June 1818, Insert No. 1, Nine Parishes of the Sierra Leone Peninsula, 1818.

33. *Ibid.*, Insert numbers 1 and 2.

34. PRO: CO267/49, MacCarthy to Bathurst, 4 January 1819.

35. CMS: CA1/0126a, Johnson to Pratt, 25 March 1820. PRO: CO267/162, T. Cole to Russell, London, 11 August 1840, p. 145.

36. SLA: Local Letters Received (April–December 1869), Benjamin Tregaskis to Governor Kennedy, 23 April 1869. CMS: CA1/E7/33, Renner to Pratt, Leopold, 29 July 1818. CA1/E8/74, MacCarthy to Bickersteth and Pratt, 26 November 1819.

37. CMS: CA1/E7/61, Minutes of the half-yearly meeting at Freetown, 3 November 1818.

38. CMS: CA1/E7/21, MacCarthy to Pratt, 19 June 1818.

39. CMS: CA1/E5/134, Wenzel to Pratt, 21 June 1816. CA1/E5A/49, Wenzel to Pratt, Kissy, 5 February 1817.

40. The text was 1 Peter II, 6–8. *Ibid.*

41. CMS: CA1/E7/1, Wenzel to Pratt, Kissy, 11 March 1818. MMS: Sierra Leone (1812–1834; 1820–1822), Journal of George Lane, 15 November 1822.

42. CMS: CA1/E5/133, Butscher to Pratt, 19 June 1816. CA1/E5A/42, Butscher to Pratt, Leicester Mountain, 4 January 1817. CA1/E7A/39, During to Pratt and Bickersteth, Gloucester, 9 April 1819. *CMS Register*, p. 6.

43. CMS: CA1/E5A/51, During to Pratt, Gloucester, 5 February 1817. CA1/E6/106, Minutes of the half-yearly meeting, Freetown, 5 and 6 November 1817.

44. The street on which most communicants lived in Regent was called Christian Street. CMS: CA1/E7/66, Journal of W. A. B. Johnson, 27 March 1818, p. 54.

45. CMS: CA1/E6/106, Minutes of the half-yearly meeting, Freetown, 5 and 6 November 1817. PRO: CO267/91, Commission of Inquiry, 1827, *Report*, p. 34.

46. CMS: CA1/E7A/39, During to Pratt and Bickersteth, Gloucester, 9 April 1819.

47. William Singleton, *Report of the Committee on African Instruction* (London: Society of Friends, 1822), pp. 37–8, 55–6. Hereafter cited as: Singleton, *Report*, 1822.

48. Stock, *CMS*, I, 174. Sibthorpe, *History*, p. 25. Singleton, *Report*, 1822, p. 22.

49. PRO: CO267/57, Extracts from notes of Major Gray on Sierra Leone, 1817 and 1821. CMS: CA1/0126a, Johnson to Bickersteth and Pratt, Regent, 29 December 1821. CA1/M1, Tanney to Pratt and Bickersteth, London, 7 March 1822, pp. 528–30.

50. PRO: CO267/58, MacCarthy to Wilmot-Horton, Cape Coast Castle, 6 December 1823. Mrs. Johnson received a pension of £100 per annum until her death in 1837. CO267/68, Treasury to Colonial Office, 22 July 1825. *CMS Register*. p. 6.

51. Birks, *Bickersteth*, I, 290.

52. CMS: CA1/E7A/66, Journal of W. A. B. Johnson, Regent, 27 October 1817, p. 1. The journal begins with Johnson's arrival in London from Hanover in 1812. It was written, beginning on the above date, in Sierra Leone. It covers the first period of his superintendence, ending on 23 June 1819. The journal was published in an edited form as the *Memoir of W. A. B. Johnson* (London: Seeley, 1852), and in digested form by Dr. A. T. Pierson, *Seven Years in Sierra Leone* (New York, 1897).

53. *Ibid.*, 6 January 1818, p. 38.

54. *Ibid.*, 27 October 1817, pp. 1–8.

55. CMS: CA1/E5, Pratt to Butscher, 9 August 1815.

56. CMS: Johnson Journal, 27 October 1817, pp. 9–10.
57. *Ibid.*, pp. 11–13, 15.
58. *Ibid.*, pp. 15–16. CA1/E5/90, Johnson to Pratt, 29 May 1816.
59. CMS: CA1/E4, Butscher to Pratt, 7 May 1814. Hartwig had come to Freetown originally with Renner in 1804, but later had become a slave dealer and was dismissed. The CMS gave him a job as an interpreter in 1814 and hoped he would prove his repentance to the extent of eventually moving up to a higher position. His death in 1815 ended their hopes. *CMS Register*, p. 1.
60. CMS: CA1/E5/54, Butscher to Pratt, 9 November 1815. CA1/E5/46, K. Macaulay to Z. Macaulay, 25 September 1815. MMS: Sierra Leone (1812–1834; 1812–1820), Davies to Buckley, 27 May 1816.
61. PRO: CO267/42, MacCarthy to Bathurst, 31 May 1816. CO267/44, Pratt to Bathurst, 31 August 1816. Singleton, *Report*, 1822, p. 26.
62. PRO: CO267/43, Robert Hogan to Bathurst, 25 May 1816.
63. PRO: CO267/42, MacCarthy to Bathurst, 31 May 1816. CO267/43, Robert Hogan to Bathurst, 25 May 1816. CO267/44, Pratt to Bathurst, 31 August 1816.
64. CMS: CA1/E5/132, Johnson to Pratt, 18 June 1816. Johnson Journal, 27 October 1817, p. 17.
65. CMS: CA1/E7A/38, Jesty to Pratt, 7 April 1819. Johnson Journal, 27 October 1817, pp. 17–18, 20. CA1/E5/139, Journal of W. A. B. Johnson, Regent, 14 July 1816. CA1/E7/47, Journal of W. A. B. Johnson, Regent, 12 September 1818.
66. CMS: CA1/E6/83, Bickersteth to Johnson, 13 October 1817. Johnson Journal, 27 October 1817, pp. 23–4.
67. CMS: CA1/E7/23, Pratt to Johnson, 22 June 1818. CA1/E5A/30, Pratt to Johnson, 27 December 1816.
68. PRO: CO267/45, MacCarthy to Bathurst, 1 April 1817. CMS: CA1/E6/47, Johnson to Pratt, Regent, 13 May 1817.
69. CMS: CA1/E5/139, Journal of W. A. B. Johnson, Regent, 15 July 1816. CA1/E7/47, Journal of W. A. B. Johnson, Regent, 17 March 1818. CA1/0126a, Journal of W. A. B. Johnson, Regent, 8 February 1822.
70. CMS: CA1/M1, Report of the Second Anniversary of the Regent's Association, 25 February 1820, pp. 11–12. CA1/M2, Speech by Davd Noah at the Anniversary of the CMS Association at Kissy, n.d., pp. 462–4. Marked received at the CMS on 18 March 1824.
71. CMS: Johnson Journal, 8, 16 November 1817, 15 December 1817, pp. 24, 26, 33–4. CA1/M1, Minutes of the 3rd Anniversary of the CMS Association in Regent, 10 April 1821, p. 417; Report of G. S. Bull on Seminary at Regent, 30 June 1820, p. 114. CA1/M4, Reffell to Raban, 19 December 1826, p. 68.
72. CMS: CA1/0166, Norman to Pratt, Regent, 24 October 1822. CA1/E7A/35, Mrs. Jesty to Mrs. Bickersteth, 4 April 1819.
73. CMS: Johnson Journal, 27 October 1817, 13 May 1818, pp. 21–2, 60. CA1/E7/28, MacCarthy to Bickersteth, n.d. Probably written in the autumn of 1818.

74. CMS: Johnson Journal, 11 April 1819, p. 105. CA1/E7A/37, Report of Johnson to the Quarterly Meeting, 6 April 1819. CA1/0126b, Reports of Johnson, Regent, 27 December 1820, 26 June 1821, 25 November 1821, 25 March, 24 June, 24 September, 25 December 1822, 25 March 1823.

75. *Ibid.* CMS: CA1/0126a, Johnson to Pratt and Bickersteth, Regent, 12 February 1823.

76. CMS: CA1/0126b, Journal of W. A. B. Johnson, Regent, 21 February 1820, 11 April 1821.

77. *Ibid.*, 28 February 1820.

78. *Ibid.*, 5 August 1820, 21 April 1821, 5 February, 18 December 1822. CMS: Johnson Journal, 31 August 1818, pp. 75–6. CA1/E7A/38, Jesty to Pratt, 7 April 1819. CA1/0126a, Johnson to Pratt and Bickersteth, Regent, 29 November 1820.

79. CMS: Johnson Journal, 27 October 1817, 23 February, 11 July, 5 August 1818, pp. 23, 45–7, 66, 75. CA1/E7A/47, Journal of W. A. B. Johnson, Regent, 23 February 1818; CA1/0126b, Journal of W. A. B. Johnson, Regent, 4 June 1822.

80. CMS: CA1/E7A/38, Jesty to Pratt, 7 April 1819. CA1/0126b, Journal of W. A. B. Johnson, Regent, 20 May 19822.

81. CMS: CA1/E7A/12, MacCarthy to Pratt, 22 April 1819. CA1/E8/24, Pratt to MacCarthy, 14 July 1819.

82. CMS: CA1/0166, Norman to Pratt and Bickersteth, Regent, 21 April 1823; Journal of James Norman, 21 April to 24 April, 1823 pp. 47, 66.

83. In addition to the experience on board ship on Easter Sunday, 1816, Johnson's sermon in Freetown on Sunday, 2 August 1818, was laughed at by the European army officers. Johnson wrote in his journal that Cates, a CMS schoolteacher, 'thought that they would not ask me again'. Later in the same entry he noted, 'A little after 12 o'C I proceeded to Regent's Town; and I thought I came into another world'. CMS: Johnson Journal, 2 August 1818, p. 74.

84. *Ibid.*, 21 February, 22 February, 29 March 1819, pp. 41, 44, 55.

85. CMS: CA1/0126b, Report by Johnson on Regent, 24 June 1822.

86. MMS: Sierra Leone (1812–1834; 1823–1828), May to Methodist Missionary Society, 14 April 1828.

87. John Weeks, CMS Schoolmaster at Regent, reported in 1825 that only 230 attended Sunday services. Betts in 1826 said that not one-fifth of the population attended. When he wrote the CMS that Johnson had forced the people to come to church and that those who did not come were fined, Bickersteth replied, 'What shall we say to these things. Nature fails and the heart sinks—but the Divine Promise never fails—the Lord reigneth and you shall not fail to attain his favour and his recompense'. CMS: CA1/0129, Report by John Weeks on Regent, Quarter ending 25 September 1825. CA1/042, Report by Reverend W. K. Betts on Regent, Quarter ending 26 June 1826; Betts to D. Coates, Regent, 26 June 1826. CA1/L2, Bickersteth to Betts, 14 October 1826, p. 184.

88. CMS: CA1/E7A/40, Wilhelm to Pratt, Leicester Mountain, 13 April 1819.
89. CMS: CA1/0166, Report by James Norman on Regent, 24 June 1823. CA1/M2, Nyländer to Pratt, Kissy, 21 November 1823. CA1/0126a, Norman to Johnson, Regent, 2 May 1823.

Notes for Chapter 4

1. PRO: CO267/90, Rowan to Hay, Cape Coast Castle, 20 September 1826.
2. Crooks, *History*, p. 13. PRO: CO267/51, MacCarthy to Bathurst, 22 July 1820, number 260. CO267/54, Act of Parliament, 1 and 2 Geo. IV, Cap. 28, 7 May 1821, pp. 241–4. CO267/56, MacCarthy to Bathurst, 14 January 1822, number 265.
3. *Ibid.*
4. CMS: CA1/0126a, Johnson to Pratt and Bickersteth, Regent, 29 December 1821.
5. PRO: CO267/56, MacCarthy to Bathurst, 21 June 1822, number 284. CO267/58, MacCarthy to Bathurst, Bathurst, Gambia, 18 June 1823, number 320; MacCarthy to Bathurst, Cape Coast Castle, 16 May 1823, number 314. CO267/79, 'Remarks on Sierra Leone Communicated in January, 1824,' enclosed in Z. Macaulay to Hay, London, 8 July 1826.
6. PRO: CO267/58, Walsh to Wilmot, 1 May 1823. CO267/60, Reffell to Wilmot Horton, 12 February 1824.
7. PRO: CO267/79, Z. Macaulay to Hay, London, 8 July 1826.
8. PRO: CO267/63, '*Copie—Extrait d'une Lettre de Copenhague du 22 Mai, 1824*', enclosed in H.M. Ambassador at Paris to F.O., n.d.
9. PRO: CO267/47, MacCarthy to Bathurst, 1 September 1818, number 168. CO267/61, Chisholm to Horton, Cape Coast Castle, 3 February 1824. CO267/60, Hamilton to Bathurst, 27 April 1824, number 1; Hamilton to Bathurst, 30 April 1824, number 3.
10. CMS: CA1/E4, Pratt to MacCarthy, 16 June 1815. CA1/E5A/37, Garnon to Bickersteth, 7 February 1817.
11. CMS: CA1/E5A/64, Pratt to Garnon, 9 April 1817, marked 'Private'.
12. CMS: CA1/E6/102, MacCarthy to Pratt, 29 June 1817. CA1/E6/69, Bickersteth to MacCarthy, 8 October 1817.
13. CMS: CA1/E5/32, MacCarthy to Pratt, 15 August 1815. CA1/E5/46, Kenneth Macaulay to Zachary Macaulay, 25 September 1815. CA1/E5A/37, Garnon to Bickersteth, 7 February 1817. CA1/E6/91, Memorandum of Governor MacCarthy to Z. Macaulay in 1815, received at CMS in November, 1818.
14. CMS: CA1/E5A/3, Butscher to Pratt, Leicester Mountain, 9 September

Notes for Chapter 4

1816. Johnson Journal, 19 December 1818, pp. 96-7. Sibthorpe, *History*, p. 26.

15. CMS: CA1/0126a, Johnson to Bickersteth and Pratt, Regent, 29 April 1822.

16. CMS: CA1/0126b, Johnson to CMS, Regent, 24 June, 24 September, 25 December 1822.

17. Stock, *CMS*, I, 179. SLA: Governor's Letter Book, 1825-1827, Rishton to Haensel, 21 July 1827. CMS: CA1/E8/106, Report of J. G. Wilhelm on Regent, Quarterly meeting, 10 January 1820. CA1/M1, Report on Waterloo, 27 June 1820. CA1/E7/91, Minutes of the Special meeting, Freetown, 7 January 1819.

18. Stock, *CMS*, I, 91. PRO: CO267/44, Pratt to Bathurst, 31 August 1816.

19. CMS: CA1/E7A/72, MacCarthy to Pratt and Bickersteth, 8 June 1819.

20. CMS: Johnson Journal, 19 December 1818, pp. 96-7.

21. CMS: CA1/E8/51,MacCarthy to Bickersteth and Pratt, 21 August 1819. CA1/E7A/72, MacCarthy to Pratt and Bickersteth, 8 June 1819. CA1/E8/12, MacCarthy to Pratt and Bickersteth, July 1819. CA1/E8/2, Bickersteth and Pratt to Renner, 26 June 1819.

22. CMS: CA1/0108a/49, Haensel to Pearson, Fourah Bay, 24 November 1831.

23. CMS: CA1/E5/144, Wenzel to Pratt, 22 July 1816. CA1/E5A/6, Wenzel to Pratt, Kissy, 17 October 1816.

24. PRO: CO267/50, Pratt to Bathurst, 1 January 1819. CMS: CA1/E7/40, MacCarthy to Bathurst, 24 August 1818. CA1/M4, Notes on the late G. R. Nyländer by Rev. J. Raban, received at the CMS on 11 August 1827, pp. 323-4. CA1/E7/44, Nyländer to Pratt, Kissy, 22 September 1818.

25. CMS: CA1/M3, K. Macaulay (?) to Z. Macaulay, 27 May 1825, p. 254. Singleton, *Report*, 1822, p. 61.

26. Biller, *Kilham Memoir*, p. 208.

27. CMS: CA1/M3, Nyländer to Bickersteth, Kissy, 7 January 1825, pp. 181-2. CA1/M4, Notes on the late G. R. Nyländer by Rev. J. Raban, received at the CMS on 11 August 1827, p. 324.

28. CMS: CA1/M2, Nyländer to Pratt, Kissy, 1 May 1822, p. 41.

29. CMS: CA1/M4, Notes on the late G. R. Nyländer by Reverend J. Raban, received at the CMS on 11 August 1827, pp. 323-4.

30. CMS: CA1/E8/16, Nyländer's Report, Quarterly Meeting, 6 June 1819. CA1/E7A/30, Nyländer to Bickersteth, Kissy, 3 March 1819.

31. CMS: CA1/M1, Nyländer to Pratt, Kissy, 14 September 1821, pp. 494-5.

32. CMS: CA1/M1, Leopold Report, M. Renner, Quarterly Meeting, 26 December 1820, p. 292. CA1/E7/61, Minutes of the half-yearly meeting, 3 November 1818. CA1/0126a, Johnson to Bickersteth and Pratt, Regent, 29 December 1821. CA1/M2, Waterloo Reports, J. G. Wilhelm, 26 March, 24 September 1822, pp. 18, 97.

33. CMS: CA1/E6/60, Wenzel to Pratt, Kissy, 28 June 1817, marked 'Private'. Johnson Journal, 23 July 1818, pp. 70, 73. CA1/E6/77, Pratt to Garnon, 8 October 1817.

34. CMS: CA1/E7/11, Johnson to Pratt, Regent, 7 May 1818. CA1/0126a, Johnson to Pratt and Bickersteth, Regent, 29 December 1821.
35. CMS: CA1/E5/133, Butscher to Pratt, 19 June 1816. CA1/E5/146, Private Instructions to Edward Bickersteth, 1816, p. 2. CA1/E5A/8, Pratt to Butscher, 1 November 1816. Mrs. Johnson was able to sign her own name to the petition to Lord Bathurst requesting a pension in 1823. PRO: CO267/59, Memorial of Sarah Johnson to Lord Bathurst, n.d., received 5 August 1823.
36. CMS: CA1/E6/124, Horton to Sierra Leone missionaries, Leicester Mountain, 20 February 1818. CA1/M1, Reffell to Horton, 22 March 1821, p. 369. SLA: LALB, 1820–1826, Reffell to Horton, 22 March 1821.
37. CMS: CA1/E5/2, Butscher to Pratt, 24 June 1815. SLA: Local Letters Received, 1823–1829, T. Cole to H. D. Campbell, 20 August 1836, number 1126.
38. CMS: CA1/E5A/42, Butscher to Pratt, Leicester Mountain, 4 January 1817.
39. CMS: CA1/E6/62, Garnon to Pratt, 17 July 1817. CA1/E6/85, Bickersteth and Pratt to Garnon, 14 October 1817. CA1/E7/42, Wilhelm to Pratt, Leicester Mountain, 27 August 1818.
40. CMS: CA1/E7/63, Collier to Pratt, 9 November 1818. CA1/E8/18, J. G. Wilhelm's Report on Leicester Mountain, Quarterly meeting, 6 July 1819. CA1/E8/30, G. S. Bull to Pratt and Bickersteth, Leicester Mountain, 15 July 1819. CA1/M1, MacCarthy to Pratt and Bickersteth, 18 July 1820, p. 157.
41. CMS: CA1/E8/46, Morgan to Pratt and Bickersteth, Regent, 11 August 1819.
42. CMS: CA1/0166, Journal of James Norman, 1 February 1821, p. 18.
43. Biller, *Kilham Memoir*, pp. 306–7.
44. MMS: Sierra Leone and Gambia (1859–1862), T. W. Blanshard to Wesleyan Missionary Society, 21 January 1862. See above p. 66, n. 46, for slightly different figures on missionary deaths. Blanshard might have included deaths which occurred in the Gambia and which would explain the apparent discrepancy.
45. *CMS Atlas*, p. 14. Stock, *CMS*, I, 334–5.
46. PRO: CO267/40, MacCarthy to Bathurst, Fort St. Louis, Senegal, 13 March 1815; MacCarthy to Bathurst, Senegal, 5 May 1815, number 15.
47. P. Leonard, *Records of a Voyage to the West Coast of Africa in H.M.'s Ship Dryad, and of the Service of that Station for the Suppression of the Slave Trade* (Edinburgh, 1833), p. 100. Hereafter cited as: Leonard, *Voyage*. Stock, *CMS*, I, 171. PRO: CO267/58, MacCarthy to Bathurst, Gambia, 26 June 1823, number 322. CO267/59, G. Baillie to R. Wilmot Horton, London, 14 July 1823. CMS: CA1/M2, Nyländer to Pratt, Kissy, 13 May 1823, p. 255.
48. PRO: CO267/51, Nicol's Comments on List of Deaths Transmitted by Thomas Gregory, inserted in Nicol to MacCarthy, 24 January 1820.

CO267/58, William Barry, M.D., to MacCarthy, 10 August 1823, inserted in MacCarthy to Bathurst, 14 August 1823, number 327.

49. 'Dr. Lamprey's Article', *Sierra Leone Church Times*, II(16 December 1885)16, 3.

50. PRO: CO267/173, Madden Report on Climate, 1841, pp. 40–3.

51. CMS: CA1/E7A/66, Johnson Journal, 13 June 1818, p. 63. PRO: CO267/58, William Barry, M.D. to MacCarthy, 10 August 1823, inserted in MacCarthy to Bathurst, 14 August 1823, number 327.

52. SLA: Local Letters Received, 1829, Dr. Boyle's Medical Report sent to the Lieutenant Governor, 7 June 1829; Local Letters Received, 1823–1829, Dr. M. Sweeney to Major Ricketts, 6 June 1829.

53. Curtin, *Image*, pp. 74, 75, 76, 347.

54. Robert Clarke, *Sierra Leone: A Description of the Manners and Customs of the Liberated Africans; with Observations upon the Natural History of the Colony, and A Notice of the Native Tribes* (London: James Ridgeway, 1843), pp. 86–90. Hereafter cited as: Clarke, *Sierra Leone*.

55. CMS: CA1/0105, J. Grag to D. Coates, Fourah Bay, 13 January 1837. Clarke, *Sierra Leone*, p. 90. A note on the bottom of page 90, written in by Clarke after publication reads: 'The first favourable opportunity is always seized to administer Quinine.'

56. CMS: CA1/0105, Journal of J. Graf, 9 February to 25 June 1849, Hastings, entry of 31 March 1849, p. 5.

57. MMS: Sierra Leone (1845–1866; 1852–1853), James Edney to Wesleyan Missionary Society, 13 January 1852; (1854–1856), Robert Dillon to George Osborn, 22 June 1855; G. H. Decker to Wesleyan Missionary Society, Wellington, 15 October 1855; James Edney to E. Hoole, 8 April 1856.

58. SLA: Governor Hamilton's Letter Book, 1824–1825, Hamilton to Shower, 8 January 1825. Biller, *Kilham Memoir*, pp. 214, 216–19.

59. CMS: CA1/E8/51, MacCarthy to Bickersteth and Pratt, 21 August 1819.

60. PRO: CO267/66 Turner to Bathurst, 16 July 1825. FO84/21, *Royal Gazette and Sierra Leone Advertiser*, III(18 August 1821)168, 641. CMS: CA1/E5/30, Butscher to Pratt, 12 August 1815; Johnson Journal, 14 July 1818, p. 67. CA1/E8/65, Report of M. Renner to Quarterly Meeting, 5 October 1819. CA1/E7/39, Collier to Pratt, Regent, 22 August 1818.

61. CMS: CA1/E8/55, Dr. A. Nicol to Morgan, 3 September 1819.

62. PRO: CO267/63, Gambier to Bathurst, 12 April 1824.

63. PRO: CO267/90, Sir J. Cockburn to Hay, 23 July 1825; Wellington and Rowan to Hay, 28 January 1826. CO267/68, D. Coates to Hay, 14 December 1825. CO267/72, Macaulay to Bathurst, 24 April 1826. CO267/91, Commission of Inquiry, 1827, *Report*, p. 29.

64. PRO: CO267/63, Gambier to Bathurst, 12 April 1824.

65. PRO: CO267/68, Return of Clergymen and Teachers of the CMS at Sierra Leone, 6 July 1825, inserted in Coates to Hay, 14 December 1825. CO267/71, Turner to Bathurst, 25 January 1826, number 24. CO267/73, Return of Appointments in the Liberated African Department, in-

serted in Campbell to Bathurst, 8 September 1826. CMS: CA1/M4, Nyländer to Pratt, Kissy, n.d., marked received on 12 November 1826, p. 12. CA1/M3, Wilhelm to Bickersteth, Waterloo, 28 April 1825, p. 237; Wilhelm to Pratt, Waterloo, 8 March 1825, pp. 218–20. CMS: CA1/0128, James Johnston to Quarterly Meeting, Kent, 6 April 1826.

Notes for Chapter 5

1. Sibthorpe, *History*, p. 18.
2. William L. Mathieson, *Great Britain and the Slave Trade* (London, 1926), p. 29. Hereafter cited as: Mathieson, *Great Britain*.
3. SLA: LALB, 1820–1826, T. Cole to Village Superintendents, 22 October 1824.
4. PRO: CO267/66, Turner to Bathurst, 18 September 1825, number 57. Crooks, *History*, pp. 117–20.
5. Sibthorpe, *History*, pp. 29–30. SLA: LALB, 1820–1826, T. Cole to Village Superintendents, 16 December 1825; Liberated African Department, Letters and Papers (unbound), 1825–1826, Reffell to Campbell, 13 November 1826.
6. PRO: CO267/73, Campbell to Bathurst, 24 August 1826, number 3. CO267/83, *Royal Gazette and Sierra Leone Advertiser*, IX(18 August 1827)454, 857–8.
7. SLA: Liberated African Department, Letters and Papers (unbound), 1825–1826, Reffell to Village Superintendents, 16 September 1826.
8. The ration was reduced to 2d. per day in 1829, and to 1½d. per day in 1836. SLA: LALB, 1828–1830, T. Cole to J. R. Palin, 16 April 1829, p. 134; 1834–1837, C. B. Jones to Hamilton and others, 18 October 1836, p. 317. MMS: Sierra Leone (1834–1840; odd papers, 1837–1841), Reverend Maer to William Allen, 6 August 1836.
9. Crooks, *History*, pp. 130–2. Sibthorpe, *History*, pp. 32–4.
10. SLA: Governor's Letter Book, 1825–1827, Campbell to Denham, Kissy, 1 March 1827, pp. 60–3.
11. PRO: CO267/82, Campbell to Bathurst, At Sea between Sierra Leone and the Gambia, 22 April 1827, p. 6.
12. SLA: Governor's Letter Book, 1825–1827, Campbell to Denham, Isles de Los, 20 April 1827, pp. 77–9.
13. PRO: CO267/83, Denham to Hay, 4 July 1827; Denham to Hay, 25 April 1827, number 1; Denham to Hay, 27 August 1827. CO323/151, Denham to Hay, 10 May 1828, p. 147. SLA: LALB, 1827–1828, Denham to Hay, 27 August 1827.
14. PRO: CO267/83, Lumley to Goderich, 20 August 1827, number 1. CO323/151, Denham to Hay, 10 May 1828, p. 147. SLA: Dispatches from the Secretary of State, 1827–1828, Huskisson to Denham, London,

8 December 1827, number 1. Governor's Dispatches to the Secretary of State, 1828–1829, Medical Report on the Illness and Death of . . . Denham, 9 June 1828, enclosure number 1 in Lumley to Huskisson, 9 June 1828, number 1.

15. Quoted in Crooks, *History*, p. 149.
16. SLA: Local Letters Received, 1823–1829, J. W. Bannister to Hay, 20 June 1828. Dispatches from Baillie and Hay, 1828, Hay to Lumley, London, 8 August 1828.
17. PRO: CO267/91, Commission of Inquiry, 1827, *Report*, p. 25.
18. *Ibid.*, pp. 26, 59–60. PRO: CO267/92, Appendix C, number 20, 1827 Commissioners' *Report*, Joseph Reffell's replies, 2 May 1826.
19. SLA: LALB, 1828–1830, T. Cole to J. R. Palin, 28 August 1828, pp. 21–3.
20. CMS: CA1/0219, Weeks to D. Coates, Bathurst, 29 January 1829.
21. Governor Sir Neil Campbell had divided the rural areas of the colony into three districts. Each district was directed by a manager, and each village within a district was directed by a submanager.
22. SLA: LALB, 1830–1831, T. Cole to Managers, 10 March 1831, p. 260; 1837–1842, B. Stow to Reverend J. Weeks, 15 December 1840. Crooks, *History*, pp. 174–6.
23. The circular quite incidentally employed the use of the phrase Liberated African for the first time. Prior to this the department had been referred to simply as the Captured Negroes Office.
24. SLA: LALB, 1820–1826, Reffell to the Village Superintendents, 15 August 1822.
25. SLA: LALB, 1820–1826, Cole to Rowan and Wellington, 17 February 1826. PRO: CO267/73, Reffell to Campbell, 7 September 1826, enclosure number 5 in Campbell to Bathurst, At Sea, 17 September 1826, number 3, marked 'Confidential'.
26. PRO: CO267/83, Denham to Hay, 15 July 1827, marked 'Private'. SLA: LALB, 1827–1828, T. Cole to McFoy, 22 May 1828.
27. William Hamilton, 'Sierra Leone and the Liberated Africans', *The Colonial Magazine and Commercial-Maritime Journal*, VI (September–December, 1841), 466. Hereafter cited as: Hamilton, 'SL and LA', *Colonial Magazine*. PRO: CO267/91, Commission of Inquiry, 1827, *Report*, p. 28.
28. SLA: LALB, 1830–1831, Findlay to the Lords of the Treasury, 12 September 1830, p. 107.
29. SLA: LALB, 1820–1826, Cole to Reffell, 1 March 1825.
30. SLA: LALB, 1831–1834, F. Campbell to Findlay, 8 March 1832, pp. 48–9.
31. SLA: LALB, 1831–1834, Findlay to Goderich, 7 April 1832.
32. PRO: CO267/92, Appendix C, numbers 15 and 20, 1827 Commission *Report*, J. Reffell's replies, 2 May 1826; Raban to Wellington and Rowan, 28 April 1826.
33. *Ibid.*, number 22, John McCormack's replies, 1 May 1826, p. 7.
34. Hannah Kilham to William Allen, Gloucester, 8 March 1824, included

Notes for Chapter 5

in *Continuation of the Appendix to the Second Report of the Committee on African Instruction* (London: Harvey, Darton and Company, 1824), pp. 3–13. Hereafter cited as: *Continuation, Appendix, 2nd Report*.

35. PRO: CO267/90, Abstract of General Return of Slaves Received at Sierra Leone, 1808–1825, Enclosure number 4 in Wellington and Rowan to Hay, 28 January 1826. Hamilton, 'SL and LA', *Colonial Magazine*, VII, 220.

36. PRO: CO267/91, Appendix A, number 44, 1827 Commission *Report*, A List of Vessels Adjudicated in the Court of Vice Admiralty of Sierra Leone Showing the Number of Slaves Captured and Emancipated from 3 September 1809 to 31 December 1825.

37. PRO: CO267/76, J. T. Williams to Canning, 10 March 1826. CO267/91, Commission of Inquiry, 1827, *Report*, p. 22.

38. PRO: CO267/77, Wellington to Bathurst, London, 4 July 1826. ASS: Mss.Brit.Emp.S18, C-3/47, James Ogilvey to Robert Stokes, Edinburgh, 2 August 1837.

39. Hamilton, 'SL and LA', *Colonial Magazine*, VII, 220. PRO: CO267/44, James Lucas to John Wilson Croker, London, 7 November 1816.

40. Manuscript memoir of John Wright of Hastings. The memoir is in the possession of the Wright family of Hastings and was written by John Wright's fourth child, his first son, Theophilus, in a 'Royal Exercise Book'.

41. CMS: CA1/079/2, Samuel Crowther to Reverend William Jowett, Fourah Bay, 22 February 1837, pp. 1–9.

42. Biller, *Kilham Memoir*, p. 222.

43. PRO: FO84/3, Proceedings in the Case of John Discombe on an Indictment for Perjury at the General Quarter Sessions . . . December 1819, Thomas Gregory.

44. PRO: FO84/10, Extract of a letter dated Old Calabar River, August 8th 1821, addressed by Lt. Knight, Commanding H.M. Brig Snapper, to J. G. Altavilla, Esq., Portuguese Commissary Judge, Freetown. FO84/16, Examination of Tom, slave aboard the Spanish Schooner Rosalia, 16 March 1822.

45. K. O. Dike, *Trade and Politics in the Niger Delta* (Oxford: Clarendon Press, 1956), pp. 37–41.

46. Dr. Afzelius' account is at the library of the University of Upsala, Sweden: Upsala Univ. Bibliotek: Ms. X:406, b., Adam Afzelius Dagboksanteckingar under resan i Afrika, I., April 17–July 1795, Januari–Februari 1796. The account of the trial which he attended begins in the entry for 12 June 1795, p. 59. The quotation in the text is from Nyländer's account. CMS: CA1/E7A/30, Nyländer to Bickersteth, Kissy, 3 March 1819.

47. CMS: CA1/E7A/30, Nyländer to Bickersteth, Kissy, 3 March 1819.

48. SLA: Executive Council Minutes, 1870–1881, meeting of 14 November 1873, pp. 122–4.

49. MMS: Sierra Leone and Gambia (1859–1862), Charles Marke to Wesleyan Missionary Society, 21 June 1862. Sierra Leone (1841–1847;

Newspapers, 1843), Sierra Leone *Watchman*, II(12 August 1843)15, 8. CMS: CA1/o126b, Journal of W. A. B. Johnson, 4 March 1820; 11 March 1820. CA1/o126a, James Bell to Johnson, Regent, 29 April 1823. PRO: CO267/216, B. Campbell to Macdonald, Factory Island, Isles de Los, 31 August 1850, pp. 4–5, enclosed in Macdonald to Grey, 16 October 1850, number 130. FO84/4, Answers to Special Interrogation put to Popo, otherwise Will Carr, 25 February 1820. SLA: Governor's Letter Book, 1853–1854, Kennedy to King of Bullom, 3 June 1853, p. 42.

50. CMS: CA1/o79/2, Samuel Crowther to Reverend William Jowett, Fourah Bay, 22 February 1837, pp. 9–10.

51. PRO: CO267/91, Commission of Inquiry, 1827, *Report*, p. 23. FO84/15, List of Vessels Adjudged at Sierra Leone, June 1819 to 15 January 1822. FO84/11, Gregory and Fitzgerald to Castlereagh, 7 June 1821. Biller, *Kilham Memoir*, p. 209.

52. PRO: CO267/91, Commission of Inquiry, 1827, *Report*, pp. 23, 26. SLA: Governor's Letter Book, 1825–1827, K. Macaulay to W. H. Savage, 29 April 1826; 1846–1848, Macdonald to James Hook, 12 June 1847, pl. 133.

53. Leonard, *Voyage*, p. 106.

54. Before landing those who were obviously sick were taken by boat to Kissy Hospital, about five miles further up the estuary. SLA: LALB, 1842–1847, W. G. Terry to Macdonald, 14 August 1843.

55. SLA: LALB, 1827–1828, T. Cole to Reffell, 27 May 1828; 1834–1837, C. B. Jones to Melville, 26 October 1836, number 468, p. 319.

56. Hamilton, 'SL and LA', *Colonial Magazine*, VIII, 41.

57. Hamilton, 'SL and LA', *Colonial Magazine*, VI, 331–3, 463, 465.

58. SLA: LALB, 1827–1828, T. Cole to McFoy, 11 March 1827, p. 17.

59. SLA: LALB, 1842–1847, W. G. Terry to Macdonald, 14 August 1843.

60. Hamilton, 'SL and LA', *Colonial Magazine*, VI, 330.

61. SLA: LALB, 1831–1834, F. Campbell to Temple, 17 January 1834, number 28, p. 333; 1837–1842, C. B. Jones to Taylor, 31 July 1841, p. 392. CMS: CA1/o126b, Journal of W. A. B. Johnson, 31 July 1820. CA1/o79, Crowther to CMS (journal extracts), 25 June 1841.

Notes for Chapter 6

1. PRO: FO84/9, Gregory and Fitzgerald to Castlereagh, 6 June 1821. CMS: CA1/o126b, Journal of W. A. B. Johnson, Regent, entry for 21 May 1821.

2. CMS: CA1/o126b, Journal of W. A. B. Johnson, Regent, entry for 21 May 1821.

3. CMS: CA1/0126b, Johnson to CMS, Regent, 25 September 1821. CA1/0126a, Johnson to Pratt and Bickersteth, Regent, 10 October 1821.
4. CMS: CA1/M2, J. G. Wilhelm's Report on Waterloo, 25 June 1822, p. 135.
5. Hamilton, 'SL and LA', *Colonial Magazine*, VII, 30.
6. PRO: CO267/91, Commission of Inquiry, 1827, *Report*, pp. 28–9. CO267/172, Madden Report, 1841, III, 111. Hamilton, 'SL and LA', *Colonial Magazine*, VII, 293–5.
7. CMS: CA1/079/1, Samuel Crowther to Reverend William Jowett, Fourah Bay, 11 February 1837, p. 2. Biller, *Kilham Memoir*, pp. 372, 376.
8. CMS: CA1/079/1, S. Crowther to Jowett, Fourah Bay, 11 February 1837, pp. 1–2. CA1/M4, J. G. Wilhelm's Report on Waterloo, 25 September 1826, pp. 41–2.
9. PRO: CO267/73, Campbell to Bathurst, At Sea, 17 September 1826, number 3, marked 'Confidential', pp. 12–14.
10. PRO: CO267/82, Campbell to Bathurst, At Sea, 22 April 1827, number 51, pp. 15–16.
11. SLA: LALB, 1830–1831, T. Cole to Gerber, 1 September 1830, pp. 85–6. Governor's Letter Book, 1833–1837, Temple to Sessing, 16 May 1834, number 81, pp. 84–5.
12. Christopher Fyfe, *Sierra Leone Inheritance* (London: Oxford University Press, 1964), pp. 145–6. Hereafter cited as Fyfe, *Inheritance*.
13. Hamilton, 'SL and LA', *Colonial Magazine*, VII, 30.
14. Michael Banton, 'The Origins of Tribal Administration in Freetown', *Sierra Leone Studies*, new series (June, 1954) number 2, pp. 109–19. Michael Banton, *West African City: A Study of Tribal Life in Freetown* (London: Oxford University Press, 1957), pp. 11–17, 25–32, 142–61. Hereafter cited as: Banton, *City*.
15. MMS: Sierra Leone (1812–1834; 1812–1820), J. Baker to Secretaries of the MMS, 19 February 1819; (1828–1834), W. Peck and W. Munro to MMS, 2 March 1829.
16. CMS: CA1/E7A/34, Report on Wilberforce to the Quarterly Meeting, Reverend Decker, 6 April 1819.
17. CMS: CA1/E7A/22, Wilhelm to Bickersteth, Leicester Mountain, 25 January 1819.
18. Crooks, *History*, p. 136.
19. MMS: Sierra Leone (1834–1840; 1840), Edwards to Beecham, Hastings, 29 April 1840. SLA: LALB, 1828–1830, C. Cole to McFoy, 19 February 1830, pp. 242–3. CMS: CA1/046, S. Black to Secretaries, Kissy, 12 February 1859.
20. The five headmen were: Thomas Decker, Kosso; Jack Davison, Bassa; Luccas, Congo; Harry, Galla; and Peter Bandy, tribe not given.
21. CMS: CA1/M2, Contract between Reverend W. G. E. Metzger and the Headmen of Wilberforce, 1 September 1823, p. 406, enclosure number 1 in MacCarthy to Pratt, 17 September 1823, pp. 405–9.
22. CMS: CA1/M2, Nyländer to Pratt, Kissy, 21 November 1823, pp. 410–11.

23. PRO: CO267/128, Petition of Wilberforce headmen, inhabitants, and military pensioners, 8 April 1835, Petition of Waterloo military pensioners, inhabitants, and headmen, 16 April 1835, both enclosed in H. D. Campbell to Hay, 28 April 1835. CMS: CA1/025a, Bishop Vidal to CMS, Fourah Bay, 16 February 1853.

24. SLA: LALB, 1837–1842, W. G. Terry to G. Nicol, 27 August 1838, number 177.

25. S.L. Co., *Report*, 1794, pp. 80–1.

26. Sierra Leone Company, *Substance of the Report of the Court of Directors of the Sierra Leone Company, Delivered to the General Court of Proprietors, on Thursday the 26th February, 1795* (London: James Phillips, 1795), p. 8.

27. Fyfe, *History*, p. 136.

28. Tradition recorded at Hastings, January, 1960.

29. CMS: CA1/E7/47, Journal of W. A. B. Johnson, Regent, entry for 6 October 1818. CA1/E7A/66, Johnson Journal, 6 October 1818, p. 88.

30. PRO: CO267/81, Betts to Campbell, 1 December 1826, enclosure number 3 in Campbell to Bathurst, 18 January 1827, number 79.

31. SLA: LALB, 1820–1826, Reffell to Superintendents, March 1821; 1828–1830, T. Cole to Managers, 5 May 1829.

32. Biller, *Kilham Memoir*, p. 388.

33. SLA: Local Letters Received, 1823–1829, D. A. Coker to Ricketts, Waterloo, 12 August 1829. LALB, 1830–1831, T. Cole to C. Jones, 27 May 1830, p. 5; T. Cole to Gerber, 4 November 1830, p. 156.

34. Hamilton, 'SL and LA', *Colonial Magazine*, VII, 33.

35. PRO: CO267/91, Commission of Inquiry, 1827, *Report*, p. 39.

36. PRO: CO267/82, Declaration of Abraham Potts, enclosure number 2 in Campbell to Goderich. 30 July 1827, pp. 2–3, marked 'Confidential'.

37. PRO: CO267/82, Campbell to Goderich, 30 July 1827, p. 3, marked 'Confidential'.

38. PRO: CO267/82, Testimony of William Defou, attached to Declaration of Abraham Potts, enclosure number 2 in Campbell to Goderich, 30 July 1827, marked 'Confidential'.

39. PRO: CO267/82, Campbell to Goderich, 30 July 1827, p. 2, marked 'Confidential'. SLA: LALB, 1827–1828, C. Cole to Superintendents, 23 April 1827; Denham to Campbell, 6 July 1827.

40. SLA: Governor's Letter Book, 1825–1827, Campbell to Denham, 18 July 1827. LALB, 1820–1826, C. Cole to Managers, 12 August 1825. PRO: CO267/83, Denham to Hay, 25 April 1827, number 1.

41. Aku was used in nineteenth-century Sierra Leone to refer to a Yoruba. The name Aku came from the form of greeting used by the Yoruba, 'Akuseio'. The linguist Koelle used Aku rather than Yoruba in his *Polyglotta Africana* which also includes a long argument against the use of the word Yoruba. S. W. Koelle, *Polyglotta Africana* (London: Church Missionary Society, 1854), p. 5. The tendency of recent authors such as Michael Banton has been to use Aku to refer exclusively to Muslim Yoruba in Sierra Leone. I have chosen not to follow this procedure, however, since I found during field work in Freetown in 1959 and 1960

that Sierra Leoneans still referred to Muslim Aku and Christian Aku. I have used Aku and Yoruba interchangeably here and have indicated when a religious difference is important by the adjectives, Christian or Muslim.

42. Hamilton, 'SL and LA', *Colonial Magazine*, VII, 34.
43. CMS: CA1/M4, Report on Waterloo, Wilhelm, Christmas, 1826, pp. 91–2.
44. PRO: CO267/81, Extract of Mr. Cole's letter dated Waterloo, 8 December 1826, enclosure number 1 in Campbell to Bathurst, 20 January 1827, number 81.
45. CMS: CA1/M2, Report on Waterloo, Wilhelm, 25 June 1822, p. 135. CA1/M3, Report on Waterloo, Wilhelm, 29 September 1824, pp. 190–3; Wilhelm to Bickersteth, Waterloo, 4 June 1825, p. 315. CA1/M4, Minutes of Special Meeting, Freetown, 20 December 1826, pp. 59–60; W. K. Betts to Bickersteth, 22 December 1826, pp. 55–6. PRO: CO267/81, Campbell to Bathurst, 20 January 1827, number 81. SLA: Local Letters Received, 1823–1829, Raban to Reffell, 20 December 1826.
46. SLA: Governor's Letter Book, 1825–1827, Rishton to Haensell, 21 July 1827. It was not until 1844 that someone questioned the wisdom of Campbell's decision to remove Wilhelm from Waterloo nearly twenty years earlier. Chief administrator, Lieutenant Governor William Fergusson, suggested in 1844 that the removal had been 'capricious, and uncalled for by any obvious or pressing emergency'. Moreover, it had caused Wilhelm 'a very great grievance'. Fergusson, in 1826, was surgeon to the Royal African Corps in Freetown. Wilhelm, meanwhile, went on serving the CMS as a missionary at various stations in Freetown and the colony until his death in April, 1834. PRO: CO267/184, Fergusson to Stanley, 8 July 1844, number 18. CO267/72, Proceedings of a Board of Medical Officers, enclosure number 1 in Macaulay to Bathurst, 24 March 1826, number 1. CMS: CA1/M6, Minutes of a Special Meeting at Fourah Bay, 30 April to 1 May 1834, p. 584.
47. CMS: CA1/M4, Pierce to Betts, Charlotte, 3 February 1827, pp. 119–20.
48. SLA: LALB, 1830–1831, T. Cole to Gerber, 4 September 1830, p. 87. Sibthorpe, *History*, pp. 38–9. Crooks, *History*, pp. 158–9.
49. As Findlay himself later wrote, the number was considerably closer to 100 than the estimated 1,000. SLA: LALB, 1831–1834, Findlay to Goderich, 15 May 1833, p. 205; Jones to Dougherty, 12 November 1832, pp. 116–17; Jones to Sessing, 16 November 1832, p. 119. Governor's Letter Book, 1827–1832, Findlay to Lieutenant Crawford, 17 November 1832.
50. SLA: LALB, 1831–1834, F. Campbell to Caulker, 21 October 1832, p. 107. PRO: CO267/118, Findlay to Goderich, 23 January 1833.
51. SLA: LALB, 1831–1834, Findlay to Goderich, 15 May 1833, p. 205; 1830–1831, F. Campbell to Thorpe, 1 August 1831, p. 381. PRO: CO267/119, Findlay to Hay, 2 March 1833.
52. PRO: CO267/118, Findlay to Hay, 19 January 1833. CO267/119,

Acting King's Advocate Opinion in Cobolo murder case, enclosure number 1 in Findlay to Hay, 15 April 1833.

53. PRO: CO323/151, Savage to Hay, 11 July 1828, p. 253. CO267/113, Savage to Goderich, 22 June 1831.

54. PRO: CO267/92, Appendix C, number 26, 1827 Commission *Report*, replies of S. Gabbidon and H. Savage, 10 May 1826. MMS: Sierra Leone (1834–1840; odd papers, 1837–1841), Memorial of W. H. Savage before Walter Robertson, J.P., enclosure number 3 in Reverend Maer's Memorial to Glenelg, 14 July 1836.

55. PRO: CO267/91, Appendix A, numbers 15 and 28, 1827 Commission *Report*, Abstract of all Contracts which have been entered into for the Supply of Liberated Africans, Customs House Return for Exports from 1816 to 1824; Commission of Inquiry, 1827, Report, pp. 56, 95. CO267/119, Findlay to Hay, 8 May 1833. CO267/139, Colonial Office to Campbell, 25 October 1836, number 92; Savage to Campbell, 23 July 1836, enclosure number 3 in Campbell to Glenelg, 26 July 1836. SLA: Local Letters Received, 1823–1829, Merchant's Powder Magazine Company to Reffell, 6 February 1827; T. Cole to K. Macaulay, 29 April 1826; Savage to K. Macaulay, 29 April 1826.

56. MMS: Sierra Leone (1812–1834; 1820–1822), Huddleston to MMS, 19 April 1821; (1823–1828), S. Dawson to MMS, 21 September 1826. PRO: CO267/139, Sworn Affidavit of W. H. Savage before W. Robertson, J.P., enclosure number 3 in Maer to Glenelg, 14 July 1836, enclosure number 1 in Campbell to Glenelg, 26 July 1836. CO267/111, 1831 Freetown Census Return.

57. ——, 'Fourah Bay Mohammedan Case', *Sierra Leone Weekly News*, XV (1 April 1899)31, 2. Hereafter cited as: 'Fourah Bay Case', *SLWN*.

58. PRO: CO806/129, Huggins to Sir Michael Hicks-Beach, London, 19 April 1879, pp. 182, 185, number 131.

59. 'Fourah Bay Case', *SLWN*, p. 3.

60. Tradition recorded at Fourah Bay, January 1960.

61. CMS: CA1/079/12, Journal Extracts, Quarter ending 25 June 1844, S. Crowther, p. 2.

62. 'Death of Mohammed Shitta Bey', *Sierra Leone Weekly News*, XI(6 July 1895) 45, 5.

63. Sibthorpe, *History*, p. 43. Colony of Sierra Leone, *Blue Book, 1861* (Freetown: Government Printer, 1862), p. 162. SLA: Governor's Letter Book, 1853–1854, Browning to J. Macaulay, 10 September 1853, pp. 78–9.

64. 'A President Elected for the 17 Nations', *Sierra Leone Weekly News*, III (25 December 1886)17, 3.

65. *Ibid.*

66. CMS: CA1/0105, Journal of Reverend Graf, Hastings, entry for 13 January 1851, p. 8; entry for 22 January 1851, pp. 8–9.

67. PRO: CO267/204, Pine to Grey, 16 June 1848, number 58.

68. PRO: CO267/207, Pine to Grey, 2 January 1849, number 3. CO267/210, Pine to Grey, 10 February 1849, number 16.

69. PRO: CO267/234, Kennedy to Newcastle, 15 October 1853, number 188.

70. PRO: CO267/214, Macdonald to Grey, 22 April 1850, number 53, pp. 74–9.

71. PRO: CO267/214, Colonial Office to Macdonald, London, 20 June 1850, pp. 9–10, number 339.

72. Fyfe, *History*, p. 233.

73. 'Inaugural Address on the Installation of Mr. G. M. Macaulay,' *Sierra Leone Weekly News*, VII (18 April 1891)38, 3. Hereafter cited as: 'Inaugural Address', *SLWN*.

74. CMS: CA1/0123, Report on Pademba Road District, J. Johnson, March 1863.

75. CMS: CA1/0123, Report on Pademba Road District, J. Johnson, April 1868. 'Inaugural Address', *SLWN*, p. 3.

76. *Ibid.* PRO: CO267/82, Enclosure number 1 in Campbell to Goderich, 30 July 1827, marked 'Confidential'.

77. PRO: CO267/234, Kennedy to Newcastle, 15 October 1853, number 188.

78. Colony of Sierra Leone, *Blue Book, 1853* (Freetown: Government Printer, 1854), p. 127. SLA: Governor's Letter Book, 1853–1854, E. A. Macartney to J. Macaulay and J. George, 9 June 1854, pp. 169–70; 1854–1859, Hill to B. Campbell, 21 August 1857, p. 221, number 55.

79. 'The Crown Lands in Sierra Leone', *The Watchman and West African Record*, V(23 February 1880)4, 3.

80. 'Our Visit to the 2nd Eastern District', *The Watchman and West African Record*, VII(30 April 1881)8, 3.

81. MMS: West Africa, Sierra Leone (1868–1873; 1872–1873), Dannatt to MMS, Wilberforce, 26 December 1872. 'The Rural District', *The Artisan*, II(27 May 1885)2, 2.

82. SLA: Governor's Letter Book, 1859–1862, Short to Ormsby, 6 August 1860, p. 187, number 146.

83. MMS: Sierra Leone (1868–1873; 1868–1869), May to Boyce, York, 23 December 1868.

84. MMS: Sierra Leone (1868–1873; 1868–1869), May to Boyce, York, 28 November 1868.

85. SLA: Governor's Letter Book, 1881–1884, Lascombe to the Manager of the Western District, 8 November 1882, p. 241, number 412.

86. PRO: CO267/147, Doherty to Glenelg, 24 September 1838, p. 12, number 66; Doherty to Glenelg, 23 September 1838, pp. 3–5, number 65. PRO: CO267/191, Macdonald to Gladstone, 3 April 1846, number 68. CO267/233, Kennedy to Newcastle, 1 August 1853, pp. 19–20, marked 'Confidential'. SLA: Governor's Letter Book, 1878–1880, Rowe to Adolphus, 11 March 1879, p. 109, number 102; 1880–1881, Jackson to Adolphus, 24 August 1881, p. 338, number 363.

87. SLA: Governor's Letter Book, 1868–1875, Rowe to Elliott, 29 September 1875, p. 433, number 108; 1876–1878, Rowe to Elliott, 20 April 1876, pp. 39–40, number 66; 1880–1881, Jackson to Elliott, 9 November

1881, p. 396, number 472; 1881–1884, Pinkett to Colonial Secretary, 11 June 1883, p. 410, number 257. Executive Council Minutes, 1881–1890, minutes of 19 April 1882, 29 January, 7 September 1883, 23 October 1884, pp. 12, 139, 370, 425–6.

Notes for Chapter 7

1. Arthur T. Porter, 'Religious Affiliation in Freetown, Sierra Leone', *Africa*, XVII(1953), pp. 3–14.
2. CMS: CA1/M1, Fitzgerald to Pratt, 3 May 1821, pp. 437–52.
3. PRO: CO267/47, MacCarthy to Bathurst, 21 June 1818, number 152. CMS: CA1/M1, Fitzgerald to Pratt, 3 May 1821, pp. 437, 441.
4. MMS: Sierra Leone (1845–1866; 1848), Reply to Statements in the *Blue Book* by Acting Governor Pine, T. Rashton, September 1850.
5. MMS: Sierra Leone (1845–1866; 1849), T. Rashton to MMS, 30 July 1849. Sierra Leone and Gambia (1859–1862), Blanshard on how the UMFC came to Sierra Leone, 21 February 1861, enclosed in Blanshard to Osborne, 21 February 1861. Sierra Leone (1841–1847; 1846) Badger to MMS, 12 March 1846. Christopher Fyfe, 'The West African Methodists in the Nineteenth Century', *Sierra Leone Bulletin of Religion*, III(June 1961)1, 22–8.
6. CMS: CA1/0108a/34, Haensell to CMS, 5 June 1829. SLA: LALB, 1830–1831, Findlay to Hay, 30 November 1830, pp. 172–3.
7. MMS: Sierra Leone (1834–1840; 1834–1836), Maer and others to MMS, 2 March 1836. Sierra Leone (1862–1867; 1866–1867), Marke to MMS, Hastings, 20 April 1866.
8. MMS: Sierra Leone (1845–1866; 1854–1856), Teal to MMS, 24 March 1854; Edney to MMS, 31 March 1854; Weatherston to Hoole, 19 December 1856; Ezzidio to Hoole, 20 October 1856; (1857–1858), Hill to Weatherston, 11 February 1857. Sierra Leone and Gambia (1859–1862), Ezzidio to MMS, 19 October 1860; (1862–1867; 1862–1865), Marke to MMS, 21 August 1862. West Africa (1858–1859), Proceedings at the laying the foundation stone of Wesley Chapel, Oxford Street, Freetown, Weatherston, n.d., received August 1858. SLA: Governor's Letter Book, 1859–1862, Hill to Knight, 19 September 1861, number 49; 1862–1863, Blackall to Commissary, 19 November 1862.
9. CMS: CA1/0195, Journal of J. F. Schön, Bathurst, 17 September 1836. CA1/0105, Journal of Graf, Hastings, 5 July 1844, pp. 2–3. CA1/M3, Waterloo Report, Wilhelm, 30 March 1825, p. 298; Pierce to Pratt, Waterloo, 25 May 1825, pp. 253–4.
10. 'Greegreeolatory', *Sierra Leone Weekly News*, II(19 June 1886)42, 2.
11. CMS: CA1/0195, Journal and Report of J. F. Schön, Gloucester, 2 July 1846.

12. MMS: West Africa, Sierra Leone (1868–1873; 1868–1869), Waite to MMS, 11 August 1868.
13. CMS: CA1/0195, Journal and Report of J. F. Schön, Hastings, 8 June 1837.
14. MMS: Sierra Leone and Gambia (1859–1862), Berry to MMS, 21 June 1860. Sierra Leone (1868–1873; 1868–1869), Fletcher to Boyce, Wilberforce, 13 December 1867.
15. MMS: West Africa, Sierra Leone (1868–1873; 1870–1871), Marke to Boyce, Wellington, 14 December 1870.
16. James A. Fitz-John, 'Our Native Manners and Customs', *Independent* IV(28 September 1876)78, 1.
17. CMS: CA1/M4, Freetown Report, Wilhelm, 25 June 1828, p. 612.
18. Arthur T. Porter, *Creoledom: A Study of the Development of Creole Society* (London: Oxford University Press, 1963), pp. 12–13. Banton, *City*, p. 7.
19. 'The Mohammedan Burial Ground', *Sierra Leone Church Times*, II(16 September 1885)10, 4. 'Our Native Manners and Customs', *Methodist Herald*, II(8 February 1884)9, 2. CMS: CA1/M6, Gibraltar Chapel Report, Wilhelm, 25 December 1833, p. 509.
20. PRO: CO267/382, *Criticisms on the Sierra Leone Draft Municipal Ordinance, 1889* (Freetown: T. J. Sawyerr, 1890), p. 32, enclosed in Hay to Knutsford, 31 May 1890, marked 'Secret'. CMS: CA1/079/12, Journal Extracts, Quarter ending 25 June 1844, Crowther, pp. 1–2.
21. *A Statement by Alhaj Mubashir Lascandri, Justice of the Peace and Vice-President of the National Congress of British West Africa* (Freetown, n.d.), p. 3. PRO: CO267/154, Petition of Fourah Bay Muslims, 21 June 1839, enclosed in Doherty to Russell, 4 December 1839, number 77.
22. PRO: CO267/193, Macdonald to Gladstone, 13 July 1846, number 119; Diary of Thomas George Lawson, 13 July 1846, enclosure number 25 in same dispatch. CO267/209, Macdonald to Grey, London, 10 July 1849, p. 11.
23. PRO: CO267/204, Report on the 1847 *Blue Book*, enclosed in Pine to Grey, 27 October 1848, number 88.
24. Mandinka Tradition recorded in Freetown, February 1960.
25. PRO: CO267/91, Commission of Inquiry, 1827, *Report*, p. 18. CO267/92, Appendix C, numbers 22 and 25, 1827 Commission *Report*, replies of John MacCormack and Robert Clouston, 1 May 1826.
26. CMS: CA1/047, Blyden to Venn, 6 September 1871.
27. SLA: LALB, 1830–1831, T. Cole to Gerber, 11 September 1830, pp. 93–4. CMS: CA1/047, Blyden to Venn, 6 September 1871. *West African Reporter*, IV(10 January 1877)2, 4. 'An Address to His Excellency', *West African Reporter*, VII(30 July 1881)186, 3. 'Mohammedan Election', *Sierra Leone Weekly News*, IV(24 September 1887)4, 2–3. 'Addresses of Welcome to Sir Francis Fleming', *Sierra Leone Weekly News*, VIII(2 July 1892)44, 8.
28. Tradition recorded at Fourah Bay and Foulah Town, December 1959. 'Mohammed Langley alias Ghewa (Appellant) versus Yekinny Renner, Amadu Williams, Tyjan Renner and Tiru Renner (Respondent),'

Sierra Leone Government, *Law Reports, Being a Selection from the Cases Decided in the Full Court of the Colony of Sierra Leone in the Years 1912 to 1924* (London: Waterlow and Sons, 1925), pp. 126–32.

29. Horatio Bridge, *Journal of an African Cruiser* (New York, 1852), edited by Nathaniel Hawthorne, pp. 183–4.

30. Tradition recorded in Magazine Cut (Mandinka community), Freetown, February 1960. CMS: Ca1/0182, Reichardt to Venn, Fourah Bay, 15 November 1856. 'Fourah Bay Mohammedan Case', *SLWN*, p. 3.

31. Typescript Document, 'The Division at Fourah Bay', pp. 1–3. The document was among the papers of the late Suli D. Gabisi, Acting Imam of the Fourah Bay mosque in 1959 and 1960. He was its author. SLA: Council Papers, 1855–1884, Montague to Kennedy, 17 July 1869, and enclosure by the Bishop of Sirera Leone.

32. CMS: CA1/047, Blyden to Venn, 6 September 1871. CA1/0182, Reichardt to Venn, Fourah Bay, 21 March 1862; Reichardt to Venn, Regent, 21 August 1862.

33. The Reverend M. Sunter, Inspector of Schools for the West African colonies, estimated that there were 500 students in about 20 Muslim schools in Sierra Leone in 1891. SLA: Secretary of State's Dispatches to Governor, 1891, Knutsford to Administrator, London, 26 September 1891. PRO: CO267/385, Hay to Knutsford, 4 October 1890, p. 2, number 403.

34. 'Muslim Education in Freetown', *Sierra Leone Weekly News*, XI(26 January 1895)22, 5. 'Opening of Muslim Elementary School', *Sierra Leone Times*, X(12 August 1899)2, 3. 'Dr. Blyden's Turkish Decoration', *Sierra Leone Weekly News*, XXII(9 September 1905)2, 2–3.

35. SLA: Local Letters Received, 1872, J. Harding and others to Pope-Hennessy, 29 August 1872. Governor's Letter Book, 1881–1884, Havelock to Alimamy Amarah and others, 16 May 1882, p. 100, number 160. 'The Ramadhan', *Sierra Leone Weekly News*, I(27 June 1885)41, 2. 'Fourah Bay College', *West African Reporter*, III(26 September 1876)44, 2–3.

36. 'A Novel Gathering', *Sierra Leone Weekly News*, V(9 January 1889)19, 5. 'A New Feature', *Sierra Leone Weekly News*, V(12 January 1889)20, 4.

37. 'Birth—Macaulay', *Independent*, III(14 October 1875)55, 2. *Watchman and Sierra Leone Record*, VI(27 October 1879)18, 2. SLA: Executive Council Minutes, 1881–1890, meeting of 25 January 1883, p. 108. 'Local—Native Church', *Sierra Leone Times*, III(5 November 1892)15, 3. 'Death of Prince Macaulay', *Sierra Leone Weekly News*, XVI(28 October 1899)9, 5, 8.

38. 'Inaugural Address on the Installation of Mr. G. M. Macaulay', *Sierra Leone Weekly News*, VII(18 April 1891)38, 3.

39. 'Installation of Mr. George M. Macaulay', *Sierra Leone Weekly News*, VII(11 April 1891)32, 4.

40. 'Trade Topics', *The Trader*, I(30 April 1891)4, 2–3.

41. Ahmed Alhadi, *The Re-Emancipation of the Colony of Sierra Leone* (Free-town, 1956), pp. 6–8.
42. CMS: CA1/079/11, Journal Extracts, Quarter ending 25 March 1844, Crowther, p. 4. MMS: West Africa (1858–1859), Dillon to Hoole and Osborn, Wilberforce, 20 June 1858. Sierra Leone and Gambia (1859–1862), Joseph May to MMS, Wellington, 25 March 1861.
43. CMS: CA1/0219, Hastings Report, Quarter ending 25 September 1831, Weeks, CA1/0105, Journal of J. U. Graf, Hastings, 1 October 1844, p. 1. MMS: West Africa (1858–1859), Marke to MMS, 19 March 1859.
44. MMS: Sierra Leone (1845–1866; 1852–1853), G. H. Decker to MMS, 6 August 1852.
45. MMS: Sierra Leone (1845–1866; 1852–1853), Fletcher to MMS, 27 December 1852.
46. MMS: Sierra Leone (1845–1866; 1857–1858), Dillon to Hoole and Osborn, Wilberforce, 18 August 1857. CMS: CA1/0195, Kissy Report, J. F. Schon, Quarter ending 25 March 1833.
47. CMS: CA1/0219, Hastings Report, Weeks, Quarter ending 25 September 1831. MMS: Sierra Leone (1834–1840; 1839), Edwards to MMS, 23 October 1839.
48. CMS: CA1/0219, Hastings Report, Weeks, Quarter ending 25 September 1831. CA1/0195, Kissy Report, Schon, Quarter ending 25 March 1833.
49. CMS: CA1/079/11, Journal Extracts, Crowther, Quarter ending 25 March 1844, p. 3.
50. CMS: CA1/079/12, Journal Extracts, Crowther, Quarter ending 25 June 1844, p. 9.
51. *Ibid.*, pp. 7–8.
52. CMS: CA1/079/11, Journal Extracts, Crowther, Quarter ending 25 March 1844, pp. 4–7.
53. CMS: CA1/0123, Pademba Road District Report, J. Johnson, October 1867.
54. CMS: CA1/0123, Pademba Road District Report, J. Johnson, March 1866.
55. CMS: CA1/0123, Pademba Road District Report, J. Johnson, September 1863. CA1/042, Journal of W. K. Betts, Regent, 22 August 1826.
56. Hamilton, 'SL and LA', *Colonial Magazine*, VI, 327–8, 464. PRO: CO267/90, Wellington and Rowan to Hay, 28 January 1826. CO267/162, T. Cole to Russell, London, 11 August 1840, pp. 143–4.
57. PRO: CO267/92, 1827 Commission of Inquiry, Appendix C, number 4, replies of William Fergusson, 24 April 1826. SLA: LALB, 1827–1828, Denham to Lumley, 28 September 1827. 1830–1831, T. Cole to Weeks and T. Cole to Jones and McFoy, 25 August 1830, pp. 82–4. 1834–1837, Pratt to Boyle, 6 May 1834, p. 38, number 440. 1837–1842, Jones to Cummings, 10 October 1838, number 242.
58. MMS: Sierra Leone and Gambia (1859–1862), May to MMS, Welling-ton, 19 August 1859; May to Osborn, Wellington, 18 November 1859. CMS: CA1/E6/4, Butscher to Pratt, Leicester Mountain, 14 May 1817. CA1/0219, Regent School Report, Weeks, Quarter ending 25 June

1830. CA1/046, Kissy Report, Samuel Black, 9 April 1859. PRO: CO267/45, MacCarthy to Bathurst, 1 April 1817, number 104. CO267/47, MacCarthy to Bathurst, 10 May 1818, number 145. CO267/56, MacCarthy to Bathurst, 3 August 1822, number 289. SLA: LALB, 1828–1830, T. Cole to Weeks and Davey, 8 April 1830, p. 297. 1830–1831, T. Cole to Gerber, 24 July 1830, pp. 61–2. 1834–1837, C. B. Jones to C. Jones, 3 June 1836, p. 250, number 290. Governor's Letter Book, 1833–1837, Campbell to Rendall, 13 May 1836, p. 208. 1853–1854, Searle to Marchant, 21 March 1853, p. 20. 1864–1867, Thomas to Pike, 28 July 1866, p. 165. Local Letters Received, January to August 1868, Quashie to Elliott, Waterloo, 12 February 1868.

59. PRO: CO267/175, Yearly Return of Cases Treated at Kissy Hospital, 31 December 1840 to 31 December 1841, enclosed in Macdonald to Stanley, 20 June 1842, number 31.

60. PRO: CO267/186, Return of Cases treated at Kissy Hospital, 1 April to 30 September 1842, enclosed in Gordon to Hope, 26 April 1844.

61. SLA: Governor's Letter Book, 1853–1854, Kennedy to Graf, 30 December 1853, p. 116.

62. Clarke, *Sierra Leone*, p. 72.

63. Hamilton, 'SL and LA', *Colonial Magazine*, VIII, 41.

64. SLA: LALB, 1830–1831, T. Cole to Findlay, 24 May 1830, pp. 11–16. Local Letters Received, 1868–1869, Patman to Kennedy, December 1868.

65. CMS: CA1/0195, Kissy Report, Schon, Quarter ending 25 March 1833, Quarter ending 25 September 1833. CA1/0123, Pademba Road District Report, J. Johnson, 31 March 1865.

66. 'Our Native Manners and Customs', *Methodist Herald*, II(14 December 1883), 2. CMS: CA1/0105, Journal of Reverend Graf, Hastings, 19 October 1850, p. 2.

67. PRO: CO267/172, Madden Report, III, 12.

68. 'Correspondence—Native Manners and Customs', *Methodist Herald*, II(13 June 1884)17, 3. CMS: CA1/0219, Journal of Reverend Weeks, Regent, 17 November 1837.

69. CMS: CA1/0195, Journal of Reverend Schön, Bathurst, 10 September 1836. CA1/0105, Journal of Reverend Graf, Hastings, 23 August 1844, pp. 4–5.

70. CMS: CA1/E6/106, Minutes of half-yearly meeting, Freetown, 5–6 November 1817.

71. CMS: CA1/E8/117, Johnson to Pratt and Bickersteth, Regent, 7 February 1820.

72. CMS: CA1/042, Mountain District Report, Betts, Quarter ending 25 September 1832. CA1/0195, Mountain District Report, Schön, Quarter ending 25 December 1834. CA1/0219, Journal of Reverend Weeks, Regent, 10 November 1836.

73. CMS: CA1/0219, Journal of Reverend Weeks, Regent, 16 August, 2 September 1842.

74. CMS: CA1/0105, Journal of Reverend Graf, 6 October to 25 December 1849, Hastings. CA1/0123, J. Johnson to CMS, 15 April 1869.

75. Hamilton, 'SL and LA', *Colonial Magazine*, VII, 34–36.
76. CMS: CA1/0219, Journal of Reverend Weeks, Regent, 1 October to 25 December 1843, pp. 3–6. CA1/0105, Journal of Reverend Graf, Hastings, 22 January 1851, p. 9.
77. CMS: CA1/079/12, Journal Extracts, Crowther, Quarter ending 25 June 1844, pp. 3–5.
78. *Ibid.*, pp. 5–7.
79. *Hastings Descendant's Association, Part I. Centenary Celebration Committee, 1915–1922; Part II, Descendants Association—1915, Re-organised 1933. Responsible for completion and opening of the Centenary Hall . . . on Boxing Day, December 26, 1952* . . . (Freetown: New Era Press, 1952), p. 6. Hereafter cited as: *Hastings Centenary, 1919.*
80. CMS: CA1/0105, Journal of Reverend Graf, Hastings, 28 June 1849, p. 1.
81. *Hastings Centenary, 1919*, p. 6.
82. MMS: Sierra Leone (1845–1866; 1852–1853), Fletcher to MMS, 27 December 1852. Sierra Leone and Gambia (1859–1862), Thorpe to MMS, Hastings, 16 May 1869.
83. Tradition recorded at Fourah Bay, January 1960. 'Fourah Bay Mohammedan Case', *SLWN*, p. 3. SLA: Local Letters Received, 1863, Muslim petition to Governor Blackall, 8 January 1863.
84. CMS: CA1/079/12, Journal Extracts, Crowther, Quarter ending 25 June 1844, p. 3.
85. MMS: West Africa (1858–1859), May to MMS, Wellington, 18 November 1858.
86. 'Our Native Manners and Customs', *Methodist Herald*, II(23 November 1883)4, 2.
87. Hamilton, 'SL and LA', *Colonial Magazine*, VII, 406. Ms. Memoir of U. W. Coker, in the possession of Dr. S. George-Coker, Freetown.
88. PRO: CO267/167, Lewis to Palmerston, 9 November 1840, enclosed in Backhouse to Stephen, Foreign Office, 22 January 1841. Buxton, *Remedy*, p. 371. Sibthorpe, *History*, p. 47.
89. PRO: CO267/160, Doherty to Russell, 3 October 1840, number 48.
90. PRO: CO267/60, Hamilton to Bathurst, 21 April 1824, number 6.
91. SLA: Colonial Secretary's Letters Received, 1850–1869, Traders at Kambia to Governor Hill, 27 December 1855; Governor's Letter Book, 1854–1859, Hill to The Alikarlie, 20 March 1857, p. 204, number 28; 1868–1875, Kennedy to Pa Nekneh, Bei Cobbolo, and Pa Suba, 17 March 1869, pp. 125–6, number 201.
92. Robert Campbell, *A Pilgrimage to My Motherland* (New York: T. Hamilton, 1861), p. 72. 'Subscription Bond or Asusu', *The Artisan*, II(27 May 1885)2, 1.
93. CMS: CA1/0126a, Johnson to Pratt and Bickersteth, Regent, 12 February 1823.
94. Buxton, *Remedy*, p. 371.
95. PRO: CO267/162, T. Cole to Russell, London, 11 August 1840, p. 167.
96. SLA: Local Letters Received to 1862, Misc. to 1871, 1850–1862, Jolly to Hill, 11 November 1857.

97. Hamilton, 'SL and LA', *Colonial Magazine*, VII, 405. Biller, *Kilham Memoir*, p. 212. PRO: CO267/65, Return of Produce Purchased at the Villages between 1 April and 30 September 1824, enclosure number 5 in Hamilton to Bathurst, 31 January 1825, number 36. CO267/91, 1827 Commission *Report*, Appendix A, number 27, Amount of produce which appears from the Accounts of the Liberated African Department to have been purchased by the Department in the several villages between 1819 and 1824. CO267/204, Report on the 1847 *Blue Book*, enclosed in Pine to Grey, 27 October 1848, number 88. SLA: LALB, 1831–1834, Findlay to Goderich, 15 May 1833, pp. 203–4.

98. PRO: CO267/146, Record of Quarter Sessions, 19 December 1837, enclosed in Rankin to Doherty, 3 January 1838 which in turn was enclosed in Doherty to Glenelg, 19 January 1838.

99. MMS: Sierra Leone (1868–1873; 1868–1869), Marke to Boyce Wellington, 26 October 1869. CMS: CA1/0219, Bathurst Report, Weeks, Quarter ending 25 September 1833. SLA: LALB, 1842–1847, Terry to Vincent, 25 May 1843.

100. CO267/82, Denham to Bathurst, 21 May 1827, enclosure number 1 in Campbell to Goderich, 14 July 1827.

101. CMS: CA1/0165, Noah to CMS, Kissy, 6 Jay 1826. CA1/042, Journal of Reverend Betts, 29 January 1827. Hamilton, 'SL and LA', *Colonial Magazine*, VII, 406–8.

102. MMS: Sierra Leone (1868–1873; 1868–1869), May to Boyce, York, 28 November 1868. CO267/147, Doherty to Glenelg, 23 September 1838, pp. 12–13, 15, number 65.

103. Fyfe, *History*, p. 354.

104. PRO: CO267/204, Report on the 1847 *Blue Book*, enclosed in Pine to Grey, 27 October 1848, number 88.

105. PRO: CO267/82, Campbell to Bathurst, 8 April 1827, pp. 1–4, marked 'Confidential'. CO267/87, Affidavit of Wm. McAulay before Grand Jury, 30 March 1827, enclosed in Barber and others to Hay, 14 April 1827. CO323/148, Statement of W. B. Pratt, Acting Registrar of Grants, 15 March 1827, enclosure number 2 in Campbell to Hay, 14 April 1827, marked 'Confidential'.

106. CMS: CA1/079/2g, Crowther to Kissling, Fourah Bay, 13 August 1838. SLA: LALB, 1828–1830, Cleugh to Haensell, 28 January 1829, p. 90.

107. Ms. Family Papers of U. W. Coker and J. G. Wright, Freetown.

Notes for Chapter 8

1. CMS: CA1/0123, J. Johnson to CMS, 15 April 1869. 'Sibthorpe's History of Sierra Leone', Volume II, Book 7, in *The Artisan*, III(8 September 1888)11, 4.

2. Buxton, *Remedy*, pp. 370–2. Sibthorpe, *History*, pp. 46–50.
3. MMS: Sierra Leone and Gambia (1859–1862), Address to Mr. Fletcher from recent converts at Sierra Leone, n.d., follows letter, Berry to Osborn, 21 July 1860.
4. 'Is the Sierra Leone Vernacular a Language, and Is It Likely to become Obsolete?' *Sawyerr's* . . . *Circular*, I(19 December 1885)4, 7–8.
5. E. D. Jones, 'Some Aspects of the Sierra Leone Patois or Krio', *Sierra Leone Studies*, new series (June 1956) number 6, p. 98.
6. 'Prize Essay on Foofoo', *The Artisan*, III(22 September 1888)12, 3. 'Sibthorpe's Essay on Foofoo', *The Artisan*, IV(24 December 1888)1, 4.
7. 'Death of Imam Amara of Foulah Town', *Sierra Leone Weekly News*. XIV (16 July 1898) 46, 6.
8. MMS: West African, Sierra Leone (1868–1873; 1870–1871), Thorpe to Boyce, Hastings, 22 November 1870; Thorpe to MMS, Hastings, 28 February 1871, pp. 8–10. Ms. memoir of John Wright, Hastings.
9. Christopher Fyfe, 'The Life and Times of John Ezzidio', *Sierra Leone Studies*, new series, number 4 (June 1955), pp. 213–23. Marke, *Methodism*, pp. 58–9.
10. Ms. Diary of Joseph G. Wright, Freetown.
11. 'Mr. C. E. Wright, B.A., B.C.L.', *Sierra Leone Weekly News*, VIII(10 October 1891)6, 5.
12. 'Nuptial Ceremony Between C. E. Wright, B.L., and Miss Laura Davies', *Sierra Leone Times*, V(1 December 1894)18, 3. 'Marriage of Mr. C. E. Wright, B.A., B.C.L., and Miss Laura Davies', *Sierra Leone Weekly News*, XI(1 December 1894)14, 4–5.
13. 'Death of J. G. Wright, Esq.', *Sierra Leone Weekly News*, XXIV(11 January 1908)19, 5.
14. 'The Social and Political Relations of Sierra Leone Natives to the English People', *Sierra Leone Weekly News*, IX(15 April 1893)33, 5. 16 and 17 Vic., Cap. 16, An Act to remove doubts as to the rights of the Liberated Africans in Sierra Leone, 20 August 1853.

Bibliography

The major sources used in this study comprise unpublished letters, papers, and reports of individuals living in or having contact with Sierra Leone during the nineteenth century. These sources include both government and non-government materials. In addition, during a nine month period in Sierra Leone during 1959 and 1960, the author collected and recorded data on individual families and separate communities in Freetown and the Western Province. Special attention was paid to the history of the Muslim Creole community. Some of the data was in the form of unpublished diaries and memoirs, some in the form of letters and papers, and the remainder was oral information which was recorded on tapes which are in the possession of the author. Oral information was collected in Freetown at Fourah Bay, Foulah Town, and Magazine Cut, and in the villages of Regent, Hastings, and Murraytown. This material is composed of family histories and lists of headmen. The oral information in most cases was confirmed by published sources. For example, lists of headmen gathered from non-literate informants were confirmed by later study of the Sierra Leone press for the period. A description of the sources follows:

I. Unpublished Sources

A. *Public Record Office, London*

FO84—Foreign Office letters and reports concerning the Slave Trade. Letters from the Judges and Registrars of the Courts of Mixed Commission, Freetown. Registers of Slaves landed by ship.

FO315—Slave Trade: Sierra Leone; Correspondence, Minute Books, Registers of slaves emancipated, papers of ships tried.

CO267—Correspondence from Sierra Leone to the Secretary of State in London. Mainly letters and reports of the Sierra Leone governors. Volumes 21 through 309 cover the years between 1785 and 1870. The series includes the Parliamentary Reports and the Reports of the Commissions of Inquiry with evidence for 1810, 1827, 1842, and 1865.

CO268—Letters, warrants, entry books for Commissions, Instructions and Charters for the years between 1771 and 1872.

CO323—Undersecretary of State R. W. Hay's private correspondence. Of special relevance was Volumes 148, 151, 159, and 161 which contain Chief Superintendent Dixon Denham's private correspondence with the Undersecretary.

CO324/69—Précis of Correspondence from Senegal, Sierra Leone, and Goree.

Bibliography

CO325/37—Colonial Office Memoranda on the Slave Trade, 1826–1840.
CO269/1—Acts of the Sierra Leone Government, 1801–1823; –/2, 1859–1871.
CO383/1—Register of Acts, Sierra Leone Government, 1868–1875.
CO270/10–27—Sessional Papers, Sierra Leone, 1801–1880.
CO271/1–2—Sierra Leone Government *Gazettes*, 1817–1825; –/3, 1870–1882.
CO272/1–48—*Blue Books*, Sierra Leone Government statistics, 1819–1871.
CO714/143–147—Chronological and Alphabetical Index to Correspondence, 1815–1866.
WO1—War Office material in the form of letters and reports on Sierra Leone, 1800–1808.
T1—Treasury material on Sierra Leone expedition of 1787.

B. Church Missionary Society Archives, London
CA1/E1–E9—Letters and reports from the Sierra Leone missionaries sent to the London headquarters of the Society. These volumes cover the period between the opening of the mission in 1804 to 1820, and are organized chronologically by date of sending. After 1820, the letters and reports are organized by missionary. For example, the letters of the Reverend W. A. B. Johnson are to be found under the following citation: CA1/0126a, and his reports, CA1/0126b. Not all of the missionaries are included in this different system after 1820.
CA1/M1–M4—Missionaries such as Nyländer and Wilhelm who are not included above have their letters and reports for the period after 1820 recorded in these CMS copybooks which were prepared for the CMS London committee. As with the letters and reports before 1820, these are organized chronologically.

C. Methodist Missionary Society Archives, London
Material in boxes marked: Sierra Leone, Sierra Leone and Gambia, and West Africa. Records comprise letters and reports from the Sierra Leone missionaries to the parent committee in London between 1812 and 1870. Each box is dated and contains letters and reports in folders which are also dated.

D. Rhodes House Library, Oxford
MSS British Empire, S22—Papers of the Anti-Slavery Society and of the Aborigines Rights Protection Society. Located in the Territorial Section, 19th and 20th Century, Africa. Volume marked G19 contains letters, records and reports from and on Sierra Leone. Although the bulk of the material on Sierra Leone is not large, it reveals that the interests of the British abolitionists had moved away from the idea of resettlement by the 1820's.

E. Private Papers of Thomas Hodgkin, M.D.
Located at Crab Mill; Ilmington, Shipston-on-Stour; Warwickshire, these papers comprise Dr. Hodgkin's correspondence with numerous people

337

Y

such as William Allen, Thomas Clarkson, Luke Howard, and Hannah Kilham. Each was interested in or actually in Sierra Leone in the nineteenth century. Dr. Hodgkin was the secretary-treasurer of the Aborigines Rights Protection Society.

F. Sierra Leone Archives, Fourah Bay College, Freetown

Governor's Letter Books—These cover the period between 1808 and 1870, and contain in addition to the dispatches to the Secretary of State local letters which the governor sent to his administrators in Freetown and the rural areas.

Local Letters Received—Covers the period after 1820. In the 1830's, 1840's, and 1850's these volumes proved particularly valuable as they revealed the movement of Liberated Africans into the interior. The volumes contain numerous petitions and letters from traders and residents of the colony.

Liberated African Letter Book—Copybook of letters sent and received from the Liberated African Department. Includes instructions for village superintendents and managers as well as registers of the villages and the hospitals. Includes also a volume of letters and papers and the Department's slave register.

Colonial Secretary's Letter Book.

Dispatches from the Secretary of State to the Governor.

Early Records of Fourah Bay College.

Executive Council Minutes.

Legislative Council Minutes.

Note: Christopher Fyfe who organized the archives has prepared a mimeographed catalogue which is available in Sierra Leone, at the Colonial Office Library, London, and at the library of the School of Oriental and African Studies, London. *Catalogue of Archives the Property of Sierra Leone Deposited at Fourah Bay College, Sierra Leone, West Africa.* Freetown, 1953. 33pp.

G. Family Papers, Sierra Leone

Ms. Diary of Joseph G. Wright, 1850–1908, Freetown.

Ms. Memoir of John Wright, 1820?–1870, Hastings. Includes data at the back on medicines used by the Liberated Africans at Hastings in the nineteenth century, and also a description of a village wedding.

Papers of U. W. Coker, Freetown—Contained mainly the original manuscript of an article written by Mr. Coker on life in Hastings and the Hunters Society.

Papers of Ahmed Alhadi—personal letters and papers of a highly respected member of the Foulah Town community until his death in 1959. I owe a particular debt of gratitude to his son and his brother from allowing me access to the papers so close to the time of Mr. Alhadi's death. Mr. Alhadi had done considerable research of his own on the history of Islam in Sierra Leone, and most of this was preserved in his notes. His papers also contained important numbers of the nineteenth century

Bibliography

newspaper, *The Artisan*, which were not to be found in the excellent collection of the British Museum, London. These papers have subsequently become the property of the Fourah Bay College library.

H. Oral Sources, Freetown and the villages, 1959–1960
Histories of Foulah Town, Fourah Bay, Hastings, Regent, and Murraytown, as well as of the Mandinka community of Magazine Cut, Freetown.

I. Typescript Documents, Fourah Bay, Freetown, 1960
'History of Fourah Bay'. 'Division at Fourah Bay'.

II. Published Sources

A. Government Documents

Great Britain. Colonial Office. *Colonial Laws Re Slaves . . . Copies of Laws . . . Relative to the Importation of Slaves . . . since the Year 1788.* London, 1816–1817. 55pp.

——. *Copies of all papers Relating Further Progress of Emigration from Africa to the West Indies.* London, 1847. 13pp.

——. *Copies of Any Correspondence with the Secr. of State for the Colonies Regarding Emigration of Labourers from Sierra Leone and St. Helena to the West Indies.* London, 1850. 407pp.

——. Foreign Office. *Correspondence with Foreign Courts Regarding Execution of Treaties Contracted . . . for the Prevention of Illicit Traffic in Slaves.* London, 1821. 110pp.

——. *Convention between His Britannic Majesty and His Most Faithful Majesty, signed at London, the 28th of July, 1817.* London, 1818. 31pp.

——. Sierra Leone, Survey and Lands Department. *Atlas of Sierra Leone.* London: E. Stanford, 1953. 16pp.

——. Sierra Leone. *Bluebook, 1837–1870.* Freetown: Government Printer, 1838–1871.

B. Non-government Printed Sources

——. *Addresses, Petitions, etc., from the Kings and Chiefs of Sudan and the Inhabitants of Sierra Leone to . . . King William the 4th, and His Excellency H. D. Campbell.* London: Private Printer, 1838. 59pp.

——. *An Account of the Colony of Sierra Leone from its First Establishment in 1793.* London: James Philips, 1795.

The Annual Report of the State of the Missions which are Carried On Both at Home and Abroad by the Society Late in Connexion with the Reverend John Wesley. London: Thomas Cordean, 1812. 56pp.

Banbury, G. A. L. *Sierra Leone or the White Man's Grave.* London: S. Sonnenschein, 1888. 296pp.

Banton, Michael. *West African City: A Study of Tribal Life in Freetown.* London: Oxford University Press, 1957. 228pp.

Beaver, Philip. *African Memoranda . . . 1792.* London: R. and C. Baldwin, 1805. 500pp.

*Y

Bibliography

Biller, Sarah, editor. *Memoir of the late Hannah Kilham; Chiefly Compiled from Her Journal and Edited by Her Daughter-in-Law Sarah Biller at St. Petersburg.* London: Darton and Harvey, 1837. 506pp.

Birks, T. R. *Memoir of the Reverend Edward Bickersteth.* London: Seeley, 1852. 2 vols.

Blyden, Edward W. *Christianity, Islam and the Negro Race.* London: W. B. Whittingham and Company, 1888. 432pp.

Bowen, John. *Memorials of John Bowen, L.L.D., late Bishop of Sierra Leone; Compiled from His Letters and Journals by His Sister.* London: John Nisbet and Company, 1862.

Bridge, Horatio. *Journal of an African Cruiser*, edited by Nathaniel Hawthorne. New York, 1852. 194pp.

Burford, Robert and Henry C. Sclons. *Descriptions of a View of Sierra Leone including the city of Freetown and the Adjacent Country.* London: W. G. Goldburn, 1857.

Burton, Sir Richard. *Wanderings in West Africa from Liverpool to Fernando Po.* London: Tinsley Brothers, 1863. 2 vols.

Buxton, Sir Thomas Fowell. *The African Slave Trade and Its Remedy.* London: John Murray, 1840.

Caillie, René. *Travels through Central Africa to Timbuctoo and across the Great Desert to Morocco, 1824–1828.* London, 1830. 2 vols.

Campbell, Robert. *A Pilgrimage to My Motherland; An Account of a Journey among the Egbas and Yorubas of Central Africa in 1859 and 1860.* New York: T. Hamilton, 1861. 145pp.

Carter, Charles W. *A Half Century of American Wesleyan Missions in West Africa.* Syracuse: Wesleyan Methodist Publishing Association, 1940. 278pp.

The Church Missionary Society Atlas. London: Church Missionary Society, 1873. 58pp.

Church Missionary Society. *Register of Missionaries (Clerical, Lay and Female), and Native Clergy from 1804 to 1904.* London: Printed for Private Circulation, 1896. 513pp.

Clarke, George H. and Mary Lane. *American Wesleyan Methodist Missions of Sierra Leone, West Africa.* Syracuse: Wesleyan Methodist Publishing Association, n.d. 250pp.

Clarke, Robert. *Sierra Leone.* London: J. Ridgeway, 1843. 178pp.

Clarkson, Thomas. *An Essay on the Impolicy of the African Slave Trade.* London: J. Philips, 1788. 134pp.

——. *An Essay on Slavery and the Commerce of the Human Species particularly the African.* London: J. Philips, 1788.

——. *The History of the Rise, Progress, and Accomplishment of the Abolition of the African Slave Trade by the British Parliament.* London: Longman, Hurst, Nees, and Orme, 1808. 2 vols.

Coupland R. *Wilberforce: A Narrative.* Oxford: Clarendon Press, 1923. 528pp.

——. *The British Anti-Slavery Movement.* London: Thornton Butterworth, Limited, 1933.

Bibliography

Crooks, J.J. *A History of the Colony of Sierra Leone, Western Africa.* Dublin: Browne and Nolan, 1903. 375pp.

Curtin, Philip D. *The Image of Africa: British Ideas and Action, 1780–1850.* London: Macmillan, 1965. 526pp.

Dallas, R. C. *History of the Maroons.* London, 1803. 2 vols.

Falconbridge, Anna Marie. *Narrative of Two Voyages to the River Sierra Leone, during the Years 1791, 1792, 1793.* London: B. White and Son, 1793. 381pp.

Findlay, G. G., and W. W. Holdsworth. *The History of the Wesleyan Missionary Society.* London: The Epworth Press, 1921–1924. 5 vols.

Fyfe, Christopher. *A History of Sierra Leone.* London: Oxford University Press, 1962. 773pp.

——. *Sierra Leone Inheritance.* London: Oxford University Press, 1964. 352pp.

George Claud. *Rise of British West Africa.* London: Houlston and Sons, 1902. 468pp.

Goddard, T. N. *Handbook of Sierra Leone.* London: Grant Richards, 1925. 331pp.

Gray, John. *Letter to Sir Joseph Banks on the Subject of the Slave Trade.* Freetown, 1794.

Hall, A. W. *Three Hundred Miles in a Hammock, or Six Weeks in Africa.* Houghton, New York: Wesleyan Methodist Publishing Association, 1889. 165pp.

Hargreaves, J. D. *A Life of Sir Samuel Lewis.* London: Oxford University Press, 1958. 112pp.

Harris, John M. *Annexations to Sierra Leone, and their Influence on British Trade with West Africa.* London: George Berridge and Company, 1883. 66pp.

Hastings Descendant's Association, Part I. Centenary Celebration Committee, 1915–1922. Part II, Descendants Association—1915. Re-organized 1933. Responsible for Completion and Opening of the Centenary Hall, on Boxing Day, December 26, 1952, Sponsored by the Hastings Village Area Committee. Freetown: New Era Press, 1952. 20pp.

Hill, William. *An Alphabetical Arrangement of all the Wesleyan Methodist Ministers. . . .* London: Wesleyan Conference Office, 1874. 221pp.

Hoare, Prince. *Memoirs of Granville Sharp, Esq. Composed from His Own Manuscripts, and Other Authentic Documents in the Possession of His Family and of the African Institution.* London: Henry Coulburn and Company, 1820. 1st edition, 524pp. 2nd edition, 1828, 2 vols.

Horton, J. A. B. *Physical and Medical Climate and Meteorology of the West Coast of Africa.* London: Churchill and Sons, 1867.

——. *West African Countries and Peoples.* London: W. F. Johnson, 1868.

Ingham, E. G. *Sierra Leone after a Hundred Years.* London: Seeley, 1894. 368pp.

Johnson, Samuel. *History of the Yorubas.* London: G. Routledge and Sons, 1921. 684pp.

Johnson, Thomas S. C. *The Story of a Mission: the Sierra Leone Church.* London: S.P.C.K., 1953. 148pp.

341

Johnson, W. A. B. *Memoir of the Reverend W. A. B. Johnson.* London: Church Missionary Society, 1852.

Kennan, R. H. *Freetown, 1800–1870, from a Sanitarian Point of View.* Dublin: John Falconer, 1910. 45pp.

Kilham, Hannah. *Specimens of African Languages Spoken in the Colony of Sierra Leone.* London: Committee of the Society of Friends for Promoting African Instruction, 1828. 3 parts.

Kuczynsky, R. R. *Demographic Survey of the British Colonial Empire.* London: Oxford University Press, 1948. 2 vols.

Koelle, S. W. *Polyglotta Africana.* London: Church Missionary Society, 1854. 188pp.

Knutsford, Viscountess. *Life and Letters of Zachary Macaulay.* London, 1900.

Knight, William. *Memoirs of Henry Venn, D.D.* London: Seeley, Jackson and Halliday, 1882.

Laing, A. G. *Travels in Timanee, Kooranko, and Soolima countries in Western Africa.* London: John Murray, 1825. 464pp.

Lardner, H. H. *The Agricultural Question: A Letter to His Excellency Samuel Rowe, M.B., C.M.G., Governor in Chief.* . . . London: Hamilton, Adams and Company; Freetown; T. J. Sawyerr, 1880. 39pp.

Lascelles, E. C. P. *Granville Sharp and the Freedom of Slaves in England.* London: Oxford University Press, 1928. 151pp.

Lemberg, P. *The Commerce of Sierra Leone: A Lecture.* Freetown: T. J. Sawyerr, 1885. 23pp.

Leonard, Peter. *Records of a Voyage to the West Coast of Africa, . . . 1830–1832.* Edinburgh: William Tait, 1883. 267pp.

Life of William Allen with Selections from His Correspondence. Philadelphia: Henry Longstreth, 1847. 2 vols.

Little, Kenneth. *The Mende of Sierra Leone: A West African People in Transition.* London: Routledge and Kegan Paul, 1951. 307pp.

Luke, Harry C. J. *A Bibliography of Sierra Leone.* Oxford: Clarendon Press, 1925. 250pp.

Marke, Charles. *Origin of Wesleyan Methodism in Sierra Leone.* London: C. H. Kelly, 1913. 240pp.

Martin, E. C. *British West African Settlements, 1750–1821; a Study in Local Administration.* London: Royal Colonial Institute, 1927. 186pp.

Mathews, John. *A Voyage to the River Sierra Leone.* London: B. White and Son, 1791. 183pp.

Mathieson, William L. *British Slavery and Its Abolition, 1823–1838.* London: Longmans, Green, 1926. 318pp.

——. *Great Britain and the Slave Trade, 1839–1865.* London: Longmans, Green, 1929. 203pp.

Melville, Elizabeth. *A Residence at Sierra Leone.* London: John Murray, 1849. 335pp.

Memoir of Captain Paul Cuffee. York: C. Peacock, 1811. 32pp.

Moister, William. *Missionary Worthies.* London: T. Woolmer, 1885. 438pp.

Montagu, Algernon. *Ordinances of the Colony of Sierra Leone.* London: Her Majesty's Stationery Office, 1857–1881. 6 vols.

Bibliography

Pierson, A. T. *Seven Years in Sierra Leone: the Story of the Work of William A. B. Johnson.* . . . New York: Fleming H. Revell Company, 1897. 252pp.

Porter, Arthur T. *Creoledom.* London: Oxford University Press, 1963. 151pp.

Rankin, F. Harrison. *White Man's Grave; a Visit to Sierra Leone in 1834.* London: R. Bentley, 1836. 2 vols.

Second Report of the Committee Managing a Fund Raised for the Purpose of promoting African Instruction. London: Harvey Darton and Company, 1824. 48pp.

Sharp, Granville. *An Appendix to the Representation (Printed in the Year 1769) of the Injustice and Dangerous Tendency of Tolerating Slavery, or of Admitting the least Claim of Private Property in the Persons of Men in England.* London: Benjamin White and Robert Horsefield, 1772. 28pp.

——. *A General Plan for Laying Out Towns and Townships on the New-Acquired Lands in the East Indies, America, or Elsewhere.* London, 1794. 24pp.

——. *The Just Limitation of Slavery in the Laws of God, Compared with the Unbounded Claims of the African Traders and British American Slaveholders.* London: B. White and E. and C. Dilly, 1776. 67pp.

——. *The Law of Liberty, or, Royal Law, by which All Mankind Will Certainly Be Judged!* London: B. White and E. and C. Dilly, 1776. 55pp.

——. *The Law of Passive Obedience or Christian Submission to Personal Injuries.* London: B. White, 1776. 102pp.

——. *Serious Reflections on the Slave Trade and Slavery. Wrote in March, 1797.* London: W. Calvert, 1805. 46pp.

——. *A Short Sketch of Temporary Regulations (Until Better Shall be Proposed) for the Intended Settlement on the Grain Coast of Africa near Sierra Leone.* London: H. Baldwin, 1786. 88pp.

——. *The System of Colonial Law Compared with the Eternal Laws of God; and with the Indispensable Principles of the English Constitution.* London: Richard Edwards, 1807. 20pp.

——. *A Tract on Duelling.* London: B. White and Son, and C. Dilly, 1790. 2nd edition. 75pp.

——. *A Tract on the Law of Nature and Principles of Action in Man.* London: W. Calvert, 1809. 2nd edition. 467pp.

Sierra Leone Association. *Paper by Samuel Lewis.* Freetown: T. J. Sawyerr, 1885. 37pp.

Sierra Leone Company. *Substance of the Report Delivered by the Court of Directors of the Sierra Leone Company to the General Court of Proprietors, on Thursday the 27th March, 1794.* London: James Phillips, 1794. 175pp.

——. *Substance of the Report of the Court of Directors of the Sierra Leone Company, Delivered to the General Court of Proprietors, on Thursday the 26th February, 1795.* London: James Phillips, 1795. 23pp.

Sibthorpe, A. B. C. *The History of Sierra Leone.* London: Elliot Stock, 1881. 86pp.

Singleton, William. *Report of the Committee Managing a Fund . . . for the Purpose of Promoting African Instruction.* London: Harvey Darton and Company, 1822. 71pp.

Spilsbury, F. B. *Account of a Voyage to the West Coast of Africa . . . 1805.* London: Richard Phillips, 1807. 43pp.

Bibliography

Stock, Eugene. *History of the Church Missionary Society; Its Environment, Its Men, and Its Work.* London: Church Missionary Society, 1899. 3 vols.

Walker, Samuel A. *The Church of England Mission in Sierra Leone.* London: Seeley, Burnside, and Seeley, 1847.

Wadstrom, Carl B. *Essay on Colonization.* London: Darton and Harvey, 1794. 363pp.

Whitehouse, John C. *London Missionary Society; A Register of Missionaries, 1796–1896.* London: London Missionary Society, 1896. 392pp.

C. Articles

Banton, Michael, 'The Origins of Tribal Administration in Freetown', *Sierra Leone Studies*, new series (June 1953), number 2, pp. 109–19.

Blyden, E. W., 'Islam in the Western Sudan', *African Society*, II(1902), 11–37.

Buxton, Sir Thomas F. V., 'Creole in West Africa', *African Society*, XII (1913), 384–94.

Cox-George, N. A., 'Direct Taxation in the Early History of Sierra Leone', *Sierra Leone Studies*, new series (December 1955), number 5, pp. 20–35.

——, 'The Economic Significance of Grants-in-Aid of Sierra Leone in the 19th Century', *Sierra Leone Studies*, new series (June 1957), number 8, pp. 237–44.

DeHart, J., editor, 'The Caulker Manuscript', *Sierra Leone Studies*, old series (1920, 1922, 1925), numbers 4, 6, 7, pp. 17–48, 1–30, 1–18.

Easmon, M. C. F., 'Sierra Leone Doctors', *Sierra Leone Studies*, new series (June 1956), number 6, pp. 81–96.

Fiddes, Edward, 'Lord Mansfield and the Sommersett Case', *The Law Quarterly Review*, number CC(October 1934), pp. 499–511.

Fyfe, Christopher, 'The Baptist Churches in Sierra Leone', *Sierra Leone Bulletin of Religion*, V(December 1963)2, 55–60.

——, 'The Countess of Huntingdon's Connexion in Nineteenth Century Sierra Leone', *Sierra Leone Bulletin of Religion*, IV(July 1962)2, 53–61.

——, 'European and Creole Influences in the Hinterland of Sierra Leone before 1896', *Sierra Leone Studies*, new series (June 1956), number 6, pp. 113–23.

——, 'Four Sierra Leone Recaptives', *Journal of African History*, II(1961)1, 77–85.

——, 'The Life and Times of John Ezzidio', *Sierra Leone Studies*, new series (June 1955), number 4, pp. 223–312.

——, 'Thomas Peters: History and Legend', *Sierra Leone Studies*, new series (December 1953), number 1, pp. 4–13.

——, 'The West African Methodists in the Nineteenth Century', *Sierra Leone Bulletin of Religion*, III(June 1961)1, 22–8.

——, 'The Sierra Leone Press in the Nineteenth Century', *Sierra Leone Studies*, new series (June 1957), number 8, pp. 226–36.

Ghazali, Abdul Karim, 'Sierra Leone Muslims and Sacrificial Rituals', *Sierra Leone Bulletin of Religion*, II(June 1960)1, 27–32.

Bibliography

Hair, P. E. H., 'An Analysis of the Register of Fourah Bay College, 1827–1950', *Sierra Leone Studies*, new series (December 1956), number 7, pp. 155–60.

Hamilton, William, 'Sierra Leone and the Liberated Africans', *The Colonial Magazine and Commercial-Maritime Journal*, VI–VIII (September 1841–June 1842), 327–34, 463–9, 29–43, 214–25, 286–96, 404–12, 37–44, 220–3.

Jones, E. D., 'Some Aspects of the Sierra Leone Patois or Krio', *Sierra Leone Studies*, new series (June 1956), number 6, pp. 97–109.

Lynch, Hollis R., 'The Native Pastorate Controversy and Cultural Ethno-Centrism', *Journal of African History*, V(1964)3, 395–413.

Porter, Arthur T., 'Religious Affiliation in Freetown, Sierra Leone', *Africa*, XXIII(1953), 3–14.

Sawyerr, Harry, 'Sacrificial Rituals in Sierra Leone', *Sierra Leone Bulletin of Religion*, I(June 1959)1, 1–9.

Walls, A. F., 'The Nova Scotian Settlers and their Religion', *Sierra Leone Bulletin of Religion*, I(June 1959)1, 19–31.

D. Newspapers—all published in Freetown in the nineteenth century
African Interpreter and Advocate
African Times
The Agency and Mercantile, Shipping, Agricultural, Advertising and General Register
The Artisan
Commonwealth
Freetown Express and Christian Observer
Independent
Methodist Herald
Sawyerr's Trade Circular
Sierra Leone Church Times
Sierra Leone Farm and Trade Report
Sierra Leone Ram
Sierra Leone Times
Sierra Leone Watchman
Sierra Leone Weekly News
Trader
The Warder
West African Herald
West African Record

Index